The new international politics
of South Asia

MANCHESTER
UNIVERSITY PRESS

Regional International Politics series

The new international politics of South Asia

Vernon Hewitt

Manchester University Press
Manchester and New York
distributed exclusively in the USA by St. Martin's Press

Published by Manchester University Press,
Oxford Road, Manchester M13 9NR, UK
and Room 400, 175 Fifth Avenue, New York, NY 10010, USA

Distributed exclusively in the USA by
St. Martin's Press, Inc., 175 Fifth Avenue, New York, NY 10010, USA

Distrbuted exclusively in Canada by
UBC Press, University of British Columbia, 6344 Memorial Road,
Vancouver, BC, Canada V6T 1Z2

British Library Cataloguing-in-Publication Data
A catalogue record for this book is available from the British Library

Library of Congress Cataloging-in-Publication Data
Hewitt, Vernon.
    New international politics of South Asia / Vernon Hewitt
        p.   cm.—(Regional international politics)
    ISBN 0–7190–5121–5 (hb). — ISBN 0–7190–5122–3 (pb)
    1. South Asia—Politics and government.   2. South Asia—Foreign
relations.   I. Title.   II. Series.
    DS431.H49   1997
    327'0959—dc21
                                                                    97–5367

ISBN 0 7190 5121 5 *hardback*
     0 7190 5122 3 *paperback*

First published 1997

01 00 99 98 97   10 9 8 7 6 5 4 3 2 1

Typeset in Great Britain
by Northern Phototypesetting Co Ltd, Bolton
Printed in Great Britain
by Bell & Bain Ltd, Glasgow

Contents

*To Neville, Lilian, Matthew,
Ben and Daniel.
For their many kindnesses
and hot dinners.*

Acknowledgements

Many people helped me in revising my thoughts on the international politics of South Asia. Doctors Wickham-Jones and Rengger have been *definitively* loyal, to me if not to each other, implacable in their condemnation of my desire to become a lighthouse keeper or a herbalist, and available twenty-four hours a day despite the fact that they have both recently become fathers.

Subrata Mitra, despite the difficulties of learning German and settling in Heidelberg, has found time to console and to advise me, and Gurhapal Singh of De Montford (who secretly shares my cravings to be a lighthouse keeper, or at least a businessman) has been solid in his support and assistance. He has also forgiven me for my continual failure to attend as many conferences as I ought to.

Throughout 1995 I was especially appreciative of long-standing friends and allies who rallied at need. I would like, in particular, to mention Tracy Parr, Nick Adams, Gary Warsop, Tamsen Thomas, Peter Philips (alias 'Dodger') and Simon Leadbeater. Matthew Waites continued his role as *agent provocateur* and critic, covering many a manuscript with precise, candid observations. I am especially grateful for the amount of time he spent looking at the Introduction and Chapter 3. I continue to find his Vulcan-like dedication to clarity pleasantly alarming.

Finally, there are my students, past and present, who have stayed in touch and write and ring me up on various things South Asian. In an era that might forget the intimacies of teaching *and* research, their interests and enthusiasms have been invaluable. I would like to thank Gareth Price and Andrew Wyatt in particular for hearing my views on India frequently and at length without any lasting damage to their social skills.

Maps

Abbreviations

ASEAN	Association of South East Asian Nations
BD	basic democracy
BDFC	Bhutanese Development Financial Corporation
BJP	Bharatiya Janata Party
BNP	Bangladesh National Party
BSF	Border Security Force
CAP	Common Action Programme
CAR	Central Asian Republic
CENTO	Central Treaty Organisation
CIS	Confederation of Independent States
CPI	Communist Party of India
CPM	Communist Party – Marxist
EPRLF	Eelam Popular Revolutionary Liberation Front
EROS	Eelam Revolutionary Organisation of Students
FAO	Food and Agriculture Organisation
GATT	General Agreement on Tariffs and Trade
GDP	gross domestic product
IAEA	International Atomic Energy Association
IBRD	International Bank for Reconstruction and Development
ILO	International Labour Organisation
IMF	International Monetary Fund
INF	Intermediate Nuclear Force
IPKF	Indian Peace-Keeping Force
IRBM	intermediate-range ballistic missile
ISI	Inter-Services Intelligence Unit
JI	Jamaat-i-Islami
JMC	Joint Military Commission

JRC	Joint Rivers Commission
JUI	Jamait-ul-Ulema-Islam
JUP	Jamait-ul-Ulema-Pakistan
JVP	Jathika Vimukthi Peramuna
LCA	light combat aircraft
LDC	less developed country
LOC	line of control
LOF	Legal Order Framework
LTTE	Liberation Tigers of Tamil Eelam
MFA	Multi-Fibre Agreement
MOU	Moratorium of Understanding
MQM	Mohajir Qaumi Movement
MTCR	Missile Technology Control Regime
NAFTA	North American Free Trade Association
NAM	Non-Aligned Movement
NFZ	nuclear free zone
NGO	non-governmental organisation
NIC	newly industrialising country
NIEO	New International Economic Order
NPT	Nuclear Non-Proliferation Treaty
NTB	non-tariff barrier
NWFP	North-West Frontier Province
OECD	Organisation for Economic Co-operation and Development
OIC	Organisation of Islam Conferences
OPEC	Organisation of Petroleum Exporting Countries
PLO	Palestine Liberation Organisation
PNA	Pakistan National Alliance
PPP	Pakistan's People's Party
PRC	People's Republic of China
RIA	regionally integrated area
RSS	Rashtriya Swayamsevak Sangh
SAARC	South Asian Association of Regional Co-operation
SDRs	special drawing rights
SEATO	South East Asia Treaty Organisation
SLFP	Sri Lankan Freedom Party
SRBM	short-range ballistic missile
TULF	Tamil United Liberation Front
UN	United Nations

UNCTAD	United Nations Conference on Trade and Development
UNEP	United Nations Environmental Programme
UNOGIP	United Nations Observers' Group for India and Pakistan
UNP	United National Party
VHP	Vishwa Hindu Parishad
WTO	World Trade Organisation
ZOP	zone of peace

Preface to the new edition

The first edition of *The International Politics of South Asia*, published in 1992, was generally well received. Although many reviewers noted the usefulness of the book, others, especially Islamic scholars, felt that Pakistan had been cast in a rather unfavourable light, and that this represented a fundamental prejudice (or ignorance) on behalf of the writer. Raju Thomas, reviewing the book in *The Pacific Review*, praised the extent and breadth of the empirical detail, but made the telling remark that there appeared to be no overall argument or set of arguments for the student to follow or engage with. A second edition is always an excellent opportunity to update a text, but in my case it is also a chance to significantly revise a work in the light of informed criticism as well as rapidly changing events. Comprehensiveness is no excuse for a lack of clarity, or indeed precision, and I hope that the faults and failures of the first edition have been dealt with below in what is, to all intents and purposes, a new book.

When I first started on this project in 1991, it was partly in response to the scarcity of single-authored, comparative texts written on the countries of South Asia. In contrast with other regions, notably Tropical Africa and Latin America, South Asia seemed to be poorly served. Some books did exist (such as Farmer's *An Introduction to South Asia*, and Hugh Tinker's *South Asia: A Short History*) and some of the edited books were of excellent quality – I pointed to the works of Alavi and Harriss, Wilson and Dalton, and Baxter *et al.*, – as notable examples. Indeed, a new edition of Baxter, and a planned new edition of Dalton (co-authored this time by David Taylor) show that edited texts continue to find a ready market, but such undertakings have obvious drawbacks.

It is still my conviction that, although useful, edited books suffer from differences in style and approach, which mitigate against their obvious clarity, however bold or forthright the editor. Different scholars have slightly differing preoccupations, differing ways of identifying and 'processing' their research agendas, thus making the process of intellectual convergence difficult and uneven. Moreover – and this observation is not intended to be invidious – edited books are increasingly the product of uneven conferences, the result of pressures to satisfy departmental research assessment exercises, or used as rapid fuel for specific career trajectories. Yet as several attempts have recently confirmed (my own included), there are great setbacks for the lone author in taking on the whole of South Asia and attempting to write about the entire 'sub-continent' as if its component parts and sub-categories can in fact be compared at all, or usefully summarised. It is not just a question of scale or even of priority, it is a serious question of generality and – I would like to suggest – of representation. There are, to my mind at least, two sets of problems which beset comparative politics generally, and although it is my belief that they can be overcome, they should none the less be set out in detail.

Problem one: issues of methodology

The first problem is the somewhat obvious one of methodology. To some extent, it is shared with well-edited, well-collated anthologies. Comparing and contrasting sociological, economic or political data involves the prior act of deduction over what is similar and what is different. More critically, and a point to which I shall return below, it is necessary to bear in mind that the conception of difference – what makes X different from Y in a specific case – is often a function of their wider *similarities*. In Indian literature for example, it is because caste has, in certain instances, similar socio-economic properties to class, that a comparison can be made: but it does not follow from this that caste is the same as class. In specific cases it is radically different. There is a further problem of methodology here, extreme in the case of caste, but not uncommon elsewhere throughout the social sciences. Many academics working on caste have noted the sheer complexity of reconciling a rationalised, somewhat abstract concept of the caste system, with its application to everyday life. The subject's perception of caste will be different to the observer, and the observer's findings introduce a dichotomy which may well be false or misleading.

This particular problem – the problem of comparison – can be easily overcome. It is merely necessary for the act of comparison to be made intellectually explicit, and to recognise along the way (generously, if possible) the areas of controversy over identification. Yet this methodological issue is compounded by the second and perhaps more serious problem – the problem of attribution – which draws attention not merely to the difficulties of comparing like with like, but to the thorny question of whether anyone can adequately comprehend and compare meanings derived from differing cultural contexts.

Problem two: conceptualising difference

In the first edition, I used my obvious commitment to comparative politics as an excuse to wax enthusiastically about Barrington Moore's magisterial *Social Origins of Dictatorship and Democracy*, in which the advantages of comparative sociological history are set out for all to see. With Moore, the commitment to the act of comparison 'constitutes a single intellectual process' however bold or arrogant the resulting canvas. I am now aware that, many years after first encountering *Social Origins*, the scholarly landscape has changed dramatically. My enthusiasm – thrown back at me by second-year students from the bear pits of the Bristol University lecture theatres – falls now on cynical ears.

Many students would not touch Moore's apparent 'empiricism' with a barge-pole, because they assess Moore's narrative from the perspective of *exclusion*, from what it has unconsciously left out or ignored. Young scholars are circumspect, indeed cynical, of Moore's methodology and of the intellectual categories he deploys. The age after Foucault can be, paradoxically perhaps, stridently judgemental. In Moore's chapter on India's gradual revolution, for example, students would be anxious to clarify what sources Moore has used, how he is defining caste, which 'Indians' he is referring to, or – to lay claim to that most damning blunderbuss – whether he has read anything in the vernacular. These are all valid points – it would be futile, even reactionary, to pretend otherwise. Yet if overdone, these observations jeopardise not just the undertaking of comparisons, they also undermine the ability to know or comprehend anything beyond immediate experience. It is no longer a question of refining the context in which X is compared to Y, because there is no universal framework or chart in which to compare them. Thus the act of comparison is specious, hierarchical, entirely subjective.

The problem of 'knowing' about South Asian society raises problems for Western scholars in particular, because of the legacies of Empire. It should be clear why Said's famous text entitled *Orientalism* should have struck such a note of chill in the hearts of – to use a disagreeable Americanism – the area specialist. Any British academic working on South Asia does so still within a specific historical context of British imperialism and involvement in South Asia generally. Within the imperial embrace, the links between 'academic' knowledge and power were pervasive, especially in areas such as anthropology or linguistics, which claimed to be objective and free of political consideration. Fifty years after independence, colonially derived generalisations or categories remain to snare the unwary and uninformed.

Lord Curzon's aside that ethnography was part of 'the furniture of the imperial mind', and that cataloguing and investigating divergent Indian social customs were necessary in order to control them, has been elevated by Said into a formidable critique against a type of comparative politics, but not against comparison itself. Much of Said's anger is directed at Western Islamic scholars working either directly with, or under the influence of, Western governments, and he is contemptuous of any scholars who seek to arrogate to themselves the right to categorically assert truth and fact about someone else's culture and lifestyle. Such a process of assertion denies the investigated object of all agency. Such scholarship asserts an essentialist, 'pure' culture, in this specific case Islam, which ignores the numerous interpretations – and struggles – of Islam within the Muslim world itself. Comparisons with Islam and Christianity, or within Islamic institutions and so-called secular ones, can still be made: but they must be made in a context free of categorical or fundamental assertion. Categories used must by definition be tentative, with the recognition that they are subject to constant change and political reinterpretation. Again, the academic wrests with the subjectivity of the categories in use and the fluidity in the way they are used.

To return to the example of caste, or indeed recent scholarship on Hinduism, much work is shot through with assumptions established by colonial scholarship or, more vaguely, the prejudicial habits of the Western mind, over the links between caste and land ownership, social power, religion and culture. Any understanding of caste must be informed by the experiences and vantage points of those who live within a caste system. If Hindus experience any division between religion and culture as something artificial, something alien to their everyday experiences of being Hindu, scholars cannot ignore this fact, however difficult it makes the job of comparison. As a well-known Indian ethnographer has recently argued:

> The distinction between the religious and the secular, which is funda-mental in western thought, is not easily made [in India]. Such a dif-ferentiation and further elaborations of it ... are a characteristic of the outsider's efforts to understand Indian society ... The autonomy of the domain of religion in Hindu society is postulated from outside: it represents at best legitimate anthropological procedure, but if one is not careful, may result in a thoughtless and injurious fragmentation of the integrity of actual experience.[1]

Comprehending and comparing the role of religion and culture within South Asian politics is notoriously difficult. For example, the partition of British India was carried out in a context in which nationalist discourse had become shot through with religious ideas and symbols. This discourse, far from stressing the similarities between Hinduism and Islam, stressed their differences. The cat-egories of Hindu and Muslim were made into monoliths, exclusive of differing regional and sectarian interpretations of the same reli-gious traditions, such as Sufic Islam, Brahmanical Hinduism, and the complex associations between Jainism, Sikhism, Buddhism and the various Hindu devotional cults. Such traditions were also mat-ters of what ought, rightly, to be called culture and the interplay of cultural similarities, regardless of the differences in religion.

This emphasis on absolute religious difference, and the links between differences and political rights, was a direct legacy of British imperialism. The British believed that the key political unit in India was the community, not necessarily the individual, and that the defining characteristic of a community was its religious identity. From the 1870s onwards, the British had sought to categorise and then politicise 'sets' of social relations by confessional affinity, ignoring cross-linkages in terms of shared social practices such as language, diet, customs, or shared myths and stories. In her excellent investigation into the rebuilding of colonial Lucknow after the 'mutiny' in 1857, Oldenburg noted how principles of colonial administration helped create the very sets of social relations they believed were essential to Indian society:

> The British ignored the complex affinities that cut across religious and cultural lines. They chose to see ... society ... as simple aggregations of Hindus and Muslims, and accorded representation on official bodies likewise. In time, when local representatives began to understand the implications of a religious and vertical division of the polity, this straight forward division of the polity ... generat[ed] communal constituencies.[2]

The creation of communal constituencies in turn acted to 'prove' the official British conviction that Indian society was indeed made up of religious differences, and had always been so. To ignore this 'self-evident' truth was to court turmoil and invite disaster. The logic of this strategy proved decisive in the subsequent division of South Asia into India and Pakistan, although it did not make this end-game inevitable. Of direct relevance to the post-independence period, these categories did not disappear when the British departed. They remained *in situ*, taken up by a new elite, and articulated in such a manner as to include and exclude specific interest's access to power. Such categories – created in the context of colonialism – remained to provide the 'rules' of the political game.

Any attempt to understand South Asian politics – be it either domestically or regionally – which ignores the context in which religious identity had, by the nineteenth century, become politicised, would be poor scholarship indeed. It would also be poor comparative politics, in that it would underplay the similarities between contemporary Indian and Pakistani politics. Both India and Pakistan have, since the mid-1980s, engaged themselves in a complex, intraelite debate about the 'proper' or 'acceptable' links between religion, culture, politics and images and symbolisms of the nation. This debate has taken place within a context still dominated by the legacies of the colonial state, complicated in some cases by an electoral input which, in theory at least, empowers the poor because of their sheer numbers.

It seems to me that, while an appreciation of the subjectivity of categories makes the job of comparison more difficult, Said is absolutely right to expect scholars to consciously and rigorously investigate the terms they use and the generalisations they make. Said's advice is surely to be sensitive over the act of interpretation, careful over the act of attribution; it is not against comparison and interpretation themselves. Furthermore, it strikes me that this is a different type of exercise than merely defining your terms in order to prime the basis for a comparison to take place: the consequences can be much more radical and useful. If cautious of the degree of generalisation, and aware of the source of information, the role of comparative politics becomes infinitely enriched and profoundly more purposeful in critically engaging the links between secularism and cultural Hinduism in India, democracy and Islam in Pakistan, economic growth and national security within the region, and a whole host of other issues from federalism to ideas on human rights. 'Area specialists' have much to gain from reading Said, and far less to fear, than our initial hostility implied.

Just a brief overview of the changes within European historiography on South Asia between the 1970s and the early 1990s reveals the extent to which our understanding of Indian society has been furthered by the 'reclaiming' or 'empowerment' of subaltern, previously excluded, experiences and perspectives of the colonised themselves, and the deployment of these experiences to correct the systematic bias of colonially derived categories and generalised studies. Recently Ayesha Jalal has undertaken a bold and imaginative attempt to write a text on comparative politics, entitled *Democracy and Authoritarianism in South Asia*.

Jalal consciously stresses the similarities of state formation in India, Pakistan, Sri Lanka and Bangladesh, by stressing their colonial origins, and their subsequent artificiality from domestic society as a whole. Jalal is critical of the academic tendency to study India and Pakistan as if they had always consisted of 'separate constructs', the one democratic and secular, the other confessional and authoritarian. In her work Jalal establishes a clear historical framework in which all the states of South Asia exhibit both authoritarian and democratic characteristics because of their shared colonial legacy, and because of the commitment, by their respective elites, to the Western paradigm of state- and nation-building. These organising principles were, Jalal argues, absent from South Asia prior to the coming of the Europeans, and in some critical sense have remained unsuitable for the task of creating a just, political order for the people of the sub-continent.

Following independence, Jalal points to the inherent tension between the centralised state, attempting to assert a monolithic national identity, and the degree of social and cultural pluralism in South Asia as a whole. Such dynamic pluralism, rooted in the history of the sub-continent, has confounded the state at every turn, contested its legitimacy, and has led to a crisis of domestic and regional control. Moreover – and here the input of post-modernist writings will start to become clearer – given the hybridity of South Asian 'little' traditions, and the resilience of such complex cultural forms to enforced homogenisation – these hybrid identities persist and reproduce themselves over time. One very important consequence follows from these observations: the 'crisis' of the Indian state, or the crisis of the 'Pakistani' state, is not episodic, it is not solvable in the way that many people (scholars and state leaders) believed in the 1950s or 1960s, when they assumed that through broad processes of socio-economic change national identities would emerge and legitimate the territorial configurations of the new states and give them legitimacy. Even though society has continued to change and to challenge the state at every turn the way in which we have come to think about *politics*, with reference to institutional and constitutional formats, is inappropriately static, comprehending and comparing the interface between state and society is made even more difficult.

On 'soft' and 'hard' sceptics: a cautionary tale

However, before I safely assert that area specialists can negotiate themselves over the epistemological rapids of the Saidian Injunction, there are some set-backs, if not with Said himself then with his associations with post-modernism generally. In an *Afterword* to the 1995 reprint, Said takes note of *Orientalism*'s intellectual trajectory after its first publication in 1978, and makes reference to broader changes within academic scholarship, especially within the humanities. The Afterword serves to show the commonalties between Said and the post-modernists, as well as the differences. Said consciously followed Foucault in utilising the term 'discourse' as a means of understanding knowledge and information as power. Said also shared the anti-essentialist credentials of later post-modernist writers who also wished to contest categories, to overcome simplistic dichotomies, and to undermine monolithic identities. To some extent at least, Said is also critical of prioritising – 'privileging' – academic work through the claim that it lays hold of a 'higher truth' to everyday experience, although there is some ambiguity here. Said does not go as far as to dismember the distinction between observer and the observed, between the subject and the object, which takes us towards the Lyotardian realm in which *narrative* is truth, and in which the subject daily invents itself.

Where Said arguably parts company with some later post-modernist writings is in his commitment to the idea and indeed necessity of social (as opposed to simply individual or subjective) emancipation, a notion that reveals quite how old-fashioned he can be. Post-modernists, notably Lyotard, not only dispense with 'the grand narratives' but they also note the inability of emancipatory ideologies to address people's needs and aspirations. In coming to terms with, and contesting, the sheer scale of modernism and globalisation, post-modernists have sought to undermine universalistic rational thought, and while the resulting onslaught has generated some brilliantly imaginative work on sexuality, identity, culture and politics, it has created problems of relativism, as well as a peculiar form of cynical, anti-intellectual, nihilism. Some post-modernists, while seeking to avoid the failures of modernist 'meta-narratives', encounter the familiar problems of either being structural determinists or indeed voluntarists *par excellence*. More tellingly perhaps, post-modernism has emerged in the context of the advanced capitalist economies, and has rarely addressed – or acknowledged – the issues of social and economic development so prevalent within many existing post-colonial societies, in which issues of absolute poverty and death are more pressing than the 'surface' of mass consumerism and the liberating potential of the Internet.

In a recent edited volume entitled *Principled Positions: Postmodernism and the Rediscovery of Values* Judith Squires divides postmodern ideas and methods into 'soft' and 'hard' sceptics, arguing that soft sceptics can be anti-foundational while still believing in ethics, and in the *necessity* of making informed judgements both within and between cultural systems. It seems to me that the distinction Squires makes is an important one, allowing for a selective use of post-modernist methodology without taking on the absurdities and intellectual contortions of the hard sceptics.

Many traditions define values which, although 'invented', and thus anti-foundational, provide valid guidelines for living out ethical lives, and many traditions coexist side by side, through either a shared concept of tolerance, or a shared civilised dialogue of respect. More profoundly, the rejection of 'hard' scepticism is a recognition that differences and similarities can coexist and be in part a function of each other: in terms of conscious political and social action for example, there will always be much that people have in common which can provide the basis for building up larger and more inclusive communities. Again, comparative politics must have as its premise a shared concept of what is desirable, or at least avoidable.

Space precludes a fuller discussion of this position however, and the difficulties that can be associated with soft scepticism. There are problems with the mere 'toleration' of difference, which although liberal in origin, falls far short of the enrichment and respect some theorists, such as Bauman believes 'civilised' cultures can or ought to engage in.[3] Indian Muslims do not want to be tolerated: they want to be respected, even honoured as part of India's diversity. More seriously, what if traditions contest values in the same space, the same territory, within the state itself? What if traditions become fundamental? Many post-modernist writers, despite their attempts to invent a new intellectual vocabulary for describing positive social action, have difficulties condemning specific cultural practices as wrong, and this is arguably true of 'soft' scepticism as well.

Whatever its drawbacks, or however voluminous the literature, it is necessary to engage with the 'soft' post-modernist agenda because it is no longer possible to write seriously on the politics of South Asia without acknowledging its relevance. As I hope to show, the most immediate overlap here concerns works on culture and, above all, the 'politics' of ethnicity and ethnic identity. The problem of ethnic 'revivalism', or more pointedly, ethnic imaginings and inventions, is, to my mind, *the* problem of South Asian politics, and this can be informed by a direct cross-fertilisation with post-modernist literature, and work carried on within cultural studies.

There is space here for only one example. In an extremely lucid chapter in the Squires volume, Jeffrey Weeks cites as an example of 'category politics' the activities of the Greater London Council in the mid-1980s. Weeks cites Kobena Mercer's observations that: 'expectations about equal participation and representation in decision making were converted into sectional demands and competing claims about the legitimation of differing needs. The possibility of coalitions was pre-empted by the competing dynamic of who would have priority access to resources'.[4] The relevance of this quote to an understanding of socio-economic policy in South Asia is immediate. Both India and Pakistan have attempted to empower political and/or ethnic communities through some type of privileged access to state resources. Reservation policies and commitments to affirmative action, involving definitions of 'backward' or economically disadvantaged groups, have created 'essentialised' categories for the purposes of social improvement which are in reality fluid and contested. Understanding the rise of such competing communities, which often involves incredibly high levels of social violence, takes us to the heart of the concerns of the post-moderns: how should we live amid cultural and social diversity, in which social values are contested or controversial? Is the community more important than the individual? and (note here, the colonial echo of the same debate), how should the state judge between competing claims for scarce resources from differing communities? How can we create a just political order?

It is on this point that I come to the case of Kashmir. Since the writing of the first edition of *International Politics*, my interest in this particular 'problem area' has increased dramatically. In 1994 I was invited to write a book on the subject and to offer some suggestions as to how the political impasse between the Kashmiris and New Delhi, and by implication, between New Delhi and Islamabad, could be resolved. For someone with a background in Indian constitutionalism and federal politics, my starting point seemed self-evident.

The Indian constitution, if properly implemented, ought to be able to provide a viable political settlement in which the *legitimate* aspirations of the Kashmiri people could be realised. Such a mantra, typical I now realise of a generation of Indianists who over-praised the flexibility of the Indian polity, and to some extent reified the political process to the constitution itself, is no longer good enough. There is little comfort in the old dispensations. In conducting fieldwork, in 1994 and 1995, I suddenly appreciated how flexible and contradictory the various concepts of being a Kashmiri were. Such an appreciation opened up the issues of representation – who are the Kashmiris? – into deep and uncharted waters, as exciting as they were unnerving. As events since 1988 have shown, to codify and sanction a political order on the premise that ethnicity is primordial, and that with 'proper management', primordial, fixed identities can be accommodated within a large, homogeneous structure, is a recipe for disaster, for the continuation of social violence and the overloading of the state itself

Rethinking the concept of international relations

It follows from what has been said so far, that the more traditional conceptions of the state and nation associated with international relations are too static to deal with the complexities and interactions of the modern, even the post-modern, world. This is a subject to which I shall return, all that need be said here is that in as much as writings on South Asian politics and social history have been influenced by the so-called post-modern turn, mainstream IR too has been influenced, and not always for the good, by advances within critical theory. In attempting to come to terms with, and assess, the changes to the international system since the collapse of the Soviet Union, many theorists have raised questions about the viability of certain categories used to explain change within the international system. Such theorists question the viability of the state as an adequate unit of analysis, raising similar issues to those of Jalal's, or seek to link issues of security with new political movements such as environmentalism or civil liberties, which move international relations beyond neat territoriality and issues of sovereignty. Other writers point to changes in the *meanings* of categories, and how these changes are linked to recent transformations within the international political and economic system.

Much of the rethink is encouraging, not just in breaking down the distinctions between academic boundaries, but in recognising the importance of domestic and regional factors as well. The search for domestic order within the states of South Asia is being carried out in a radically changing international system, in which cultural and economic forces are all-pervasive, and in which issues such as human rights and representation are set up as preconditions for economic aid and development. In order to realistically comprehend the international politics of South Asia, the distinctions between domestic and international politics cannot be hard and fast, for the state – besieged and beleaguered, authoritarian and democratic –

provides the link between these differing levels of analysis. Now is a good time to be in favour of comparative politics within IR.

Summary

To return to Raju Thomas's nagging question, what do I think about these issues, what are my arguments here, what is this book offering? Because of the nature of this book, it would be impossible to present one clear argument throughout. What I have to offer is a series of arguments that help explain the political and regional configurations of the states within South Asia.

Chapter 1 begins by looking at the current interests and concerns of the states of South Asia. The chapter stresses the centrality of Indo-Pak relations, and touches upon India's wider concerns with China. The Non-Aligned Movement and the Commonwealth are also touched upon. Chapter 2 looks at how the states of South Asia have related historically to the superpowers, the Islamic world, the newly emergent states of Central Asia, and the collapse of the Soviet Union. The chapter also examines how the states of South Asia have responded to international institutions such as the United Nations. Chapter 3 lies very much at the heart of this study. It examines the problems caused by rapid social change and political instability, both in terms of ethnic identity and the fears of political disintegration. The importance of this chapter reflects my belief that domestic politics, and the perceptions and priorities of domestic elites, are a vital starting point to conceptualising – and allying – regional insecurities. Chapter 4 examines the links between South Asia and the international economic system. Finally, chapter 5 looks at the future of South Asia in an era of growing multipolarity and the current thinking on the so-called New World Order. The chapter examines the likelihood of India's endorsement of the NPT treaty

I have endeavoured to derive a broad definition of what the international politics of South Asia means, and to discuss the problems this region faces within a changing global order. Such an undertaking involves a historical approach to South Asia, a critical investigation into the origins and processes of state and domestic social and economic policies, as well as an understanding of cultural phenomena such as ethnic identity and social hybridity. At a more general level, it is my intention to convey my own fascination with South

Asia, to introduce to others something that has given me much pleasure and intellectual satisfaction. More specifically, in attempting to
identify and discuss problems germane to South Asia, I have tried to
indicate how the dynamics of differing social, economic and cultural processes interact. Here I convey my own hopes and fears for
the region as a whole.

My fears – put bluntly – are that the interactions are potentially
catastrophic. Part of me believes that they pull in differing directions: economic policies conflict with issues of democracy, democracy complicates issues of equality, communitarian rights
exaggerate cultural differences, inter-state rivalries shore up
anachronistic state structures and prevent political elites asking
awkward and difficult questions about their own motives and the
basis of their own political legitimacy. The circle cannot be squared
without encouraging either social disintegration, massive economic
disparities, or massive state coercion. My hope is in the tenacity of
the political process itself, in the determination of South Asia's
political elite to respond to democratic pressure, and to recognise
their contribution to world politics as part of a wider community of
nations and peoples who share surprisingly similar hopes and aspirations. The restoration of democracy in Pakistan, although only
partial, was a huge victory for the peoples of that troubled state,
even if it has not yet delivered them into their promised land.
Finally, if the interrelatedness of the region's problems are grasped,
we can begin to rethink some of the old solutions, discard or
redefine some of our old academic habits, and arrive at a clearer
conception of what is necessary, or even desirable.

Notes

1   T. N. Madan, *Non-Renunciation: Themes and Interpretions of
      Hindu Culture*, New Delhi, Oxford University Press, 1987, p. 144.

2   Veena Oldenberg, *The Making of Colonial Lucknow*, Princeton,
      Guildford, 1984, p. 81.

3   See Zygmunt Bauman's fascinating *Postmodern Ethics*, Oxford,
      Blackwell, 1993.

4   Jeffrey Weeks, 'Rediscovering Values' in J. Squires (ed.), *Principled
      Positions: Postmodernism and the Rediscovery of Value*, London,
      Lawrence and Wishart, 1993, pp. 189–209.

Introduction

It is useful to begin with some definitions. Many a prejudice is disguised by a title and a cover design. The eager student may well feel that the expression 'international politics' has a rather dated feel about it. It appears to lack, for example, both the analytical rigour of the term 'international political economy', as well as the *immediacy* of the fashionable words 'international relations'. The reader may suspect that the author is being self-consciously quaint, or worse still, conservative. In spite of such potential misunderstandings I have good reasons for retaining the use of this term.

For the purpose of this book 'international relations' is too narrow to yield significant domestic and regional insights because of its association with realism, and an overtly systemic approach that concentrates on states as the component parts of an anarchic international environment. Any study of the international relations of South Asia that treats these states as 'black boxes' (billiard balls), and isolates the interaction between the states from the complex processes taking place within them, would be useless for the purposes of this book.

Even if packaged by the so-called area specialist (or worse still, reduced to a series of charts and over-head projections by the dreaded 'strategic' analyst), the approaches and methodologies associated with main-stream international relations have an odd effect upon the size and importance of South Asia, similar to that caused by looking at a large object through the wrong end of a telescope. What is by itself impressive, worthy of study in and for its own right, becomes small and marginal, uninteresting, and often premised on someone else's interests, usually 'Washington's' or even (still, perhaps) the view from Moscow.[1] A systemic approach to regional politics has historically exaggerated the importance of superpower involvement, and failed to realise that the prime dynamic behind a great deal of foreign policy arises within a domestic context of pressing economic and political instability, increasing environmental degradation,[2] and the complex problems associated with ethnic formation and regionalism.

Having dismissed the term international relations, what of the newer and more comparative label of international political economy (IPE)? On first sight, this term is much more attractive. As an emerging field of study, it has done much to correct the systemic bias within IR, and to draw attention to the interconnectedness of domestic, regional and international politics.[3] It draws much needed attention to the links between political elites and resource allocation, critically examines the role of the state and reassesses the importance of non-state actors. More usefully, IPE broadens the concepts of power and 'influence', away from an obsession with military capabilities and projection, towards ideas linked to production and consumption. While it fails to account for the cultural arena in which power is coded and acted out, it certainly helps us move away from an unwholesome obsession with bombs and bullets. In his book *The Political Economy of International Relations* (a good read in desperate need of a re-edition), Robert Gilpin concentrates on the dynamics between international market forces (that in principle have no bounds and seek continuously to increase their domain), and the nation-state, which is inclusive and territorial. For Gilpin the key questions raised by an international political economy perspective are: 'how the state and its associate political processes affect the production and distribution of wealth and, in particular, how political decisions and interests influence the location of economic activity'.[4]

There have been many significant works on particular countries within the South Asia region which have consciously used Gilpin's approach, but none have moved to incorporate – through linking up issues of economic growth with foreign policy – a perspective that deals with both regional and international linkages, or seeks to locate the states of South Asia within a broad historical, and above all, cultural context.[5]

Moreover, like the systemic literature of the realists, most of the writings on political economy are biased – for obvious reasons – towards the 'core' economies of the United States and the Pacific, and not the more peripheral areas of the world with their specific (and pressing) search for economic and political viability. It is my conviction that a broad concept of international politics enables us to comprehend this multi-dimensionality without replacing it with abstract theory, or without fragmenting the empirical and intellectual links between these various issues and problems. The strength of 'international politics' can be gauged by looking back at what the late Hedley Bull referred to as the 'world politics' paradigm, a paradigm that transcends 'the distinction between the study of international relations and the study of domestic politics by focusing upon the global political system of which the states system and the national political systems are both part'.[6] As will become clear, this degree of 'linkage' is crucial for an understanding of South Asia.

Other terms need clarification. The use of categories such as Less Developed, or Third World, or even the South, to identify a distinct sub-set of states within the international system is now increasingly problematic. However, like several other recent commentators, I have good reasons to retain the usage of an aggregate, my preferred one being that of less developed. Yet the status, and to an extent, the self-identification of the South Asian states as 'developing states' is central to an understanding of their domestic, regional and foreign policy, and still serves (especially in the case of India) as a self-conscious reference point through which to carve out a particular global identity.

Without exception, the governments of South Asia are seeking to sustain and deepen a process of industrialisation, which involves the integration of their respective economies into a global market system. Along with other states elsewhere, these strategies create a certain commonality of foreign policy. While the ideologies of capitalism, and more specifically, liberalism are still challenged domestically as foreign and 'irrelevant', as a type of *economic* management they rule supreme. Competing perspectives, involving wide-spread nationalisation, or the curtailment of foreign investment, are now economically redundant. At best, anti-market sentiment survives to pressure governments to provide short-term palliatives to deal with, or regulate, the social costs of economic adjustments, but they do not seek to curtail market activity.

At the same time, however, the political and cultural critics of globalisation have gained in power, be it under the guise of Hindu revivalism, Islamic fundamentalism, the rights of the 'indigenous'

Bhutanese Lepcha, or the rights of the Bodos of Assam. Pressures initiated by the integration of the states of South Asia into a market system still largely perceived to be 'Western' have generated cultural and political movements aimed at 'protecting' indigenous identities, or preserving cultural uniqueness, while at the same time seeking to maintain the dynamics and material gains of the market system itself. This disjuncture between economic and socio-cultural agendas is most noticeable in India, although it is present in Pakistan, Bangladesh and the Himalayan kingdoms. The resulting paradoxes and contradictions caused by materially defined and consumerist elites none the less afraid of cultural emasculation, or worse still, cultural challenges from below, are central to understanding both the aspirations and the policies of the states of South Asia.

Defining the region

For the main purposes of this study the region of South Asia contains the states of India, Pakistan, Bangladesh, Sri Lanka, Nepal, Bhutan and the Maldives. Sikkim will be dealt with as an integral part of India (to which it ceded in 1975). Tibet will be referred to briefly although since the 1950s it has, for good or ill, fallen into the domain of the Sinologist. I will discuss the Indian Ocean with reference to the Indian Union Territories of the Andaman and Nicobar Islands, Daman and Diu and the Lakshadweep archipelago.

The sovereign states of India, Pakistan, Bangladesh, Nepal and Bhutan constitute an area situated between the Himalayan mountain ranges to the north and the Indian Ocean littoral to the south. The region is bordered to the west by the Kithar Mountains of Baluchistan, the Hindu Kush, the Karakarams, the high plateau of Tibet; and to the east the foothills of Bhutan, and the Chittagong, Mizo, Chin, Naga and Patkai hills on the Bangladesh–Burmese border. The Republic of the Maldives is situated just over 500 km to the south-west of Sri Lanka, and the Indian island dependencies of Lakshadweep, Daman, Diu and the Andaman and Nicobar Islands.

The interactions of domestic and international state systems can be most clearly conceived with reference to what Buzan and Rizvi called a 'security complex'. While the security complex is above all a regional configuration, it is perceived in the context of both the international and domestic political system. A security complex is a sub-system of the international community of states that for reasons of geography, history and culture are intimately related to each other. This concept allows an understanding of the states of South Asia from a genuinely regional perspective and not as a mere extension of the international security environment as perceived by the dominant actors situated within the international system generally.

More usefully still, a security complex is not static: it can be changed by the deliberate policy of a state and the changing perceptions of an elite; it can be 'overlaid' by wider complexes through invasion or internal collapse, as with the case of the Soviet–East European complex focused upon a divided Germany. Following the collapse of the USSR, Central Asia was no longer compelled to act within a regional and global framework determined by Moscow.

Regionally, the states of South Asia share a common history of British colonial rule and common constitutional habits derived from the British period. For much of the nineteenth century, the entire area existed either under the British colonial administration of the *Raj* or, as in the case of Nepal and Bhutan, as sovereign or notionally separate states under varying degrees of British paramountcy. All of the states with the exception of Bhutan and Nepal are currently members of the British Commonwealth of Nations, with Pakistan rejoining in 1989.

As with all regional concepts, the territorial dimensions of South Asia are rather fluid and open to some criticism. In its annual reports the World Bank classifies Pakistan as part of Europe, Middle East and North Africa, a notion that ignores the basic cultural and linguistic ties which make Pakistan a fundamental part of the South Asian region, but one which stresses the religious affinities between Pakistan and the Arab world. One of the reasons why India has never appreciated Pakistan's suggestions for a South Asian nuclear-free zone is that Pakistan's definition of South Asia excludes China, while India's does not. Since China is already a nuclear power (and, following its acceptance of the Nuclear Non-Proliferation Treaty in May 1995, has no stated intention of renouncing the use of nuclear weapons) this distinction is a rather crucial one to make.

Furthermore, although China is not a superpower in an economic sense, India's elite have been conscious of the degree of Western comparisons made between 'Communist China' and 'Free India', especially with regard to levels of economic growth, political stability and social well-being. Blunted by the extent of China's hesitant pro-market reforms since 1978, the implied bias in favour of China has frequently irritated New Delhi, and made India a rival for US (and to a limited extent Japanese and Association of South East Asian Nations (ASEAN)) affections, high-profile foreign visits and, more recently, private foreign investments. It is often argued that the real challenger to Indian claims and ambitions comes from Beijing, and not from Islamabad, and that only China can checkmate any global ambitions by New Delhi.

For a regional study centred upon India and Pakistan, China presents something of problem. In order to simplify matters I have treated China as both a regional and an extra-regional power, because although it clearly lies outside of South Asia, it impinges directly on India's perception of wider Asian and international interests, and since the mid-1960s has been involved in Pakistan's calculations of regional security.

My definition largely ignores the relations between Pakistan and the Islamic world of the Middle East, excludes Afghanistan with its ethnic and cultural links across the Pakistan border into Baluchistan and North West Frontier Province. It also ignores India's associations with the states of east and central Asia, especially Burma (which was administered as part of British India until the mid-1930s). Of more immediate concern, this somewhat traditional view of South Asia ignores the emergence since 1990–91 of the Central Asian Republics (CARs) of Tajikistan, Turkmenistan, Uzbekistan, Kazakhstan and Kyrgystan.

At the moment, it seems clear to continue to treat these states as external players. Despite potential cultural overlays with the northwestern territories of Pakistan in particular, and the presence within the CARs of an apparent Islamic/secular divide similar in outline to that within Pakistan itself, the CARs are seen by South Asia as regionally distinct, as possible conduits for wider international influence (especially to the Islamic world), and possible trading partners. Moreover, the CARs provide another arena, rather like the Middle East, in which India and Pakistan compete politically and economically, along side such states as Iran, Turkey and Saudi Arabia.

The dramatic changes and restructuring within the CARs, especially with reference to their religious and ideological orientations, could have direct repercussions for Pakistan's foreign and domestic politics. My approach does not rule out the possibility that, at some future date, the CARs may wish to join up with South Asian regional bodies, such as the South Asian Council for Regional Co-operation (SAARC). Nor does it rule out a more dramatic redefinition of the South Asian security complex, with Pakistan seeking to associate itself with Central Asia in order to turn its back upon Indian competition and rivalry in South Asia. While such a move would be an admission of failure by Islamabad, it would be in keeping with clear trends within Pakistan's foreign policy established in the early 1970s when, with the loss of East Pakistan, a new regime turned towards the Islamic world in general, and the Middle East in particular. However, for the immediate future, Pakistani links are likely to be mediated through the multilateral institutions of the Islamic world, or on a bilateral basis, rather than through a new regional configuration.

Finally, as well as the neat geographical and historical packaging of the region, there is also the remarkable degree of shared socioeconomic and political experience. Domestically, the politics of South Asia are dominated by either the decay of established political institutions (as in India and Sri Lanka) or the difficulties that arise when trying to create and sustain new ones (as in Bangladesh, Pakistan and, to a lesser extent, Nepal). All the states are beset by a growing assertion of regionalism and ethnicity, problems of political legitimacy, and the stresses caused by volatile political participation. In 1995, all the states faced ethnic challenges and were engaged to a greater or lesser extent in asserting the primacy of a specific territorial configuration in the face of regional challenges. Throughout the region, these challenges range from demands for greater decentralisation to outright separation.

A brief profile of the states of South Asia

The size and population of the states of South Asia differ enormously: from the micro-state of Bhutan with a population of just over 1.4 million living within an area of 47 thousand square kilometres, to the Republic of India with a population in excess of 800 million and a territorial area of 3,288 thousand square kilometres. The states of South Asia have notably differing capacities to rule and administer their complex societies. Pakistan was one of the few post-colonial states to actually disintegrate.

By the mid-1990s, the population of South Asia accounted for just over one-fifth of the total global population. Each month, the regional population increases by just under one million individuals, a demographic trend that maintains continual pressure upon the resources and productive capacities of the respective states. Moreover, the population is extraordinarily young. In the mid-1980s 40 per cent of India's population was below the age of eighteen.

The quality of life varies between states and most significantly within each state. The average life expectancy in India, for both men and women, was sixty years of age, although landless labourers in the states of Bihar and Orissa are much less likely to achieve this.[7] In the kingdom of Bhutan, men are expected to live until about forty-eight, with women more likely to make it into their fifties. In Sri Lanka, life expectancy is seventy-one years, a figure that compares favourably with Britain's figure of seventy-eight, and Japan's of eighty-one. In Pakistan, life expectancy for men and women is fifty-eight years, with Bangladesh on fifty-seven.

Levels of literacy vary between the states and within the states. In the 1991 census, India's literacy rate was 52 per cent, 64 per cent for men and just under 40 per cent for women. Bhutan is worse than India, with barely 35 per cent of the country literate, while Sri Lanka boasts the highest mean average of adult literacy. Within India, the southern state of Kerala has an adult literacy rate of over 70 per cent, while the east state of Orissa has a rate under 30 per cent. Pakistan has a surprisingly low literacy rate of 34 per cent, with women worse off than men. Nepal is, on average, the most illiterate state in South Asia, with just over a third of the population able to read and write. In Sri Lanka, 88 per cent of the country are literate.

As would be expected, the economic powers of these states reflects their size. In 1988–89 India's gross domestic product (GDP) was approximately US$ 270.64 billion, making it approximately the tenth largest economy in the world. For the same period, Pakistan's GDP was calculated at US $ 39.07 billion. By contrast Nepal's productive capacity was just over US $ 3 billion. Close by, the state of Bangladesh – the erstwhile 'East Wing' of Old Pakistan – has a GDP of US$19.01 billion. Most of the economies of the South Asia region are mixed economies, containing various mixes of public and private enterprises and, until very recently, *dirigiste* styles of economic planning aimed at achieving industrialisation.

Gross national production (GNP) divided by population, generates a series of per capita figures that, although highly aggregate, none the less give some indications of the potential resources at the command of each state. In 1992, the GNP per capita of the United States of America was $23,120. In the same year, India's GNP per capita was US$320, Sri Lanka's was US$540, Nepal's was US$170, Pakistan's was US$410, Bhutan's was US$180, while Bangladesh was US$220. Obviously, the distribution of national wealth and income is unevenly distributed in each country, both in terms of socio-economic backgrounds and in terms of regions. Aggregate figures for India disguise a huge and growing degree of regional differentiation between poor states such as Orissa, Bihar and, arguably, West Bengal, and the more prosperous states of Kerala, Gujarat, Punjab and Maharashtra. Recent evidence suggests that such differentiation has increased as the Indian economy has liberalised.

Although each state of South Asia has followed a slightly different set of development strategies since independence, recently there has been a significant degree of convergence. India has moved from being the most inward orientated of the regional economies, to one committed to selling off state-owned assets, liberalising trade policies to encourage direct foreign investment, and committed to winning new export markets in an increasing range of services and value added goods. Pakistan, although historically more open than its large neighbour, has sought to further similar reforms.

Nepal has, following the constitutional changes of the early 1990s, and arguably unavoidably influenced by India, switched to a liberation pro-market strategy. Sri Lanka continues to attract foreign investment (notably from South Korea and Malaysia) despite serious internal unrest. The Bangladesh economy remains hostage to rapid population growth and extreme variations in the climate which inhibit much needed improvements in agricultural output. None the less, a key theme in the economic rethink of the Begum Zia regime (1991–96) concerned itself with economic reform and liberalisation to ensure viable and sustained economic development.

The states of South Asia are interlinked by a whole series of economic and trade agreements, most notably the conditions set by World Bank loans for development projects, and the conditionality agreements negotiated with the International Monetary Fund (IMF) as part of various structural adjustment programmes. All the South Asian states, regardless of their respective strengths, rely upon concessional borrowing and grants from multilateral institutions such as the World Bank, the IMF, the Colombo Plan, European-based aid consortiums, and bilateral assistance from the US, Europe, and increasingly Japan. The fact that the states of South Asia face similar economic problems, and are all attempting to diversify their economic activity with an eye to foreign capital and possible market shares, paradoxically discourages co-operation and limits the effects of intra-regional trading agreements.

While India remains a net receiver of aid, it provides financial contributions to the states of Nepal and Bhutan, and has since the mid-1980s extended credits to Sri Lanka, as well as a whole series of soft loans and trade deals. This is in addition to various aid and trade schemes aimed at Africa and the Far East both in the fields of financial and technical assistance, and in addition to contributions to the Colombo plan and the Asian Development Bank.[8] Compared to the economic position of Sub-Saharan and Latin American countries, the prospects for South Asian development look promising.

The 1994 Annual Report of the International Monetary Fund noted that India, Pakistan and Bangladesh had succeeded in increasing foreign exports, direct foreign investments, fiscal and monetary reform and deregulation of the existing state sector. The 1995/96 GDP growth rate of 5.7 per cent was robust by Indian standards, slightly higher than Pakistan, and up from the infamous 'Hindu' rate of growth in the 1970s. The 1994 World Bank report noted that the 'poverty' level in India and Pakistan continued to fall, from 55 per cent to 39 per cent in the case of India (1975–89), and from 35 per cent to 25 per cent in Pakistan (1975–91). However, the general World Bank view that 'it is now universally recognised that high and sustained economic growth is necessary for reducing levels of poverty' still draws a large number of critics. Even by its own figures, Bangladesh remains one of the poorest countries in the world.

Social pluralism

The region contains a huge and complex mix of socio-cultural identities, dominated by the primacy of language and religion. Within India itself, the social diversities are notorious: 19 national languages, over 250 primary dialects, and 6 major religions. This is to say nothing of the diversities and complexities of a caste-based society, in which ritualised, religious concepts of pollution interact, and to an extent restructure, economic activities and access to political power. Despite its smaller size, Pakistan boasts as many differences: tribal and Pashto speakers in the north, Sindi and Punjabi speakers to the south-west, and a minority of Urdu speakers closest (still, despite a powerful Pathani element) to the institutions of national power.

India is a secular republic, despite the fact that over 80 per cent of the population are Hindus, and despite the fact that in 1996 the Bharatiya Janata Party (BJP) emerged as a serious contender for national power, winning over 180 seats. Since the mid-1980s, there has been a growing debate in India over the links between Hinduism as a culture and Hinduism as a religious practice. Many Hindus now question the appropriateness of a secular state and wish to either redefine secularism or indeed to replace it with a confessional state. However, interestingly enough, the Indian National Congress Party remained the single largest party in parliament (despite sufferings its worst ever defeat). In the 1996 elections, it secured 28 per cent of the national vote, as opposed to the BJP's 23.9 per cent. Yet as India faces a period of political instability, it is clear that the issue of Hinduism will remain on the political agenda.

Pakistan, Bangladesh and the Maldives are all Islamic republics of the Sunni sect. Pakistan has a small but articulate minority of Shiites, and various tribal and animist societies situated in Baluchistan and North-West Frontier Province. The association between religious and political authority remains ambiguous in Pakistan and Bangladesh. While both states specify Islam within their constitutions, political leaders in both states have sought to direct and control religious forces, but remain vulnerable to ex-parliamentary pressures linked to Islamic issues. Both Benazir Bhutto and Begum Zia remained politically hostage to Islamic parties and heightened sentiments over issues of blasphemy and the extent to which Islamic law should dominate over secular laws inherited from the British period.[9]

Sri Lanka's second republican constitution, promulgated in 1978, underlines the supremacy of Buddhism as the official religion, while recognising the rights of its Christian, Muslim and Hindu minorities to practice their own religions unmolested. Nepal is a monarchical Hindu state, while the Bhutanese monarchy – the *Shabdrung* – is heavily influenced by Tibetan Lamaist Buddhism, despite the large presence of Nepalese immigrants speaking Nepali and Hindi dialects. Since 1989, Bhutanese policies aimed at removing Nepalese 'foreigners', and preserving the linguistic purity of the tribal groups, has created tensions with Nepal and, because of Bhutan's curious relationship with India, between Kathmandu and New Delhi. Accusations about human rights violations have been made by various Nepalese officials in several international forums.

The kingdom of Sikkim – formally a part of the Indian federal system since 1975 – is inhabited by the large tribal group known as the Lepcha, although as with Bhutan, the area is again dominated by a number of Nepalese Hindu immigrants, creating ethnic tensions and allegations of differential birth rates and/or immigration. The monarchical tradition of the *Chogyal* drew from both the Buddhist and Hindu traditions of royalty before being formally abolished by indigenous political parties calling for greater democracy, and closer association with India. The social and cultural costs of such an association are still creating tensions.

While many of these societies are very old – India can (and does) boast one of the oldest cultures in the world dating back to *c.* 2500 BC – the present territorial boundaries are new. None of the states of South Asia are nation-states in the classic sense of the term; they are rather juridical and territorial, although supported by the precedents and requirements of international law; they lack, to varying degrees, established national identities and even, in some cases, the ability to secure democratic procedures and legitimate governments.[10] The sovereign state of Pakistan only came into existence in 1947 when it was carved out of the north-western (West Pakistan) and the north-eastern (the erstwhile East Pakistan) wings of British India on the basis of a homeland for the Muslims of South Asian, outlined in the Lahore declaration of 1940.

Linkages between domestic and regional politics

No writing on the international politics of South Asia would make any sense without an understanding of the legacies of partition and the origins and forms of Indian and Pakistani nationalism. The boundaries drawn up in the closing weeks of British rule crossed areas of linguistic and cultural affinity and divided them into two ethnically diverse states. One of the most enduring legacies of the colonial period for South Asia remains that of unresolved boundaries and unspecified borders, and the fact that India and Pakistan continue to share extraordinary degrees of commonality, in terms of popular and political culture and indeed religion. These legacies have been a cause of considerable regional friction and stress, frequently blurring the distinction between 'internal' and 'external' threat perceptions, and complicating the need to devolve power to local and regional elites. Pakistan's consistent failure to establish a federal constitution is to a large extent explained in the context of provincial animosity to a centralist state structure after partition, and the continuous failure of the centre to accommodate the political, cultural and economic aspirations of the provinces.

The extraordinary high degree of ethnic, cultural and linguistic overlap in South Asia, both within and between states, gives rise to the fear of 'balkanisation': a process wherein parts of a territorially defined state attempt to cede on the grounds of ethno-linguistic self-determination – often with overt or covert support from a rival state – or to join another state altogether. India has frequently accused the Pakistani state of assisting and arming Kashmiri and Sikh militants, while the Pakistanis argue that they have convincing evidence that the Indians have helped stir up ethnic troubles in Sind and Baluchistan. In March 1993, 250 people were killed in Bombay by a series of car bombs. Within hours, the Indian Home Minister, S. B. Chavan, stated that such explosions were part of a foreign conspiracy, while the leader of the BJP, A. K. Advani, publicly mentioned Pakistani involvement. A bomb explosion in Lahore in early 1996 led to Pakistani allegations of Indian involvement.

Such accusations have become part of both Indian and Pakistani attempts to 'de-legitimate' various ethnic groups, or to reduce complex issues of poor social, political and economic management to matters of 'foreign intervention'. Since 1989, India has refused to deal with the Kashmir crisis as a crisis of political legitimacy and representation within the Indian Union, choosing to deal with it instead as a crisis of foreign intervention or, even more obscurely, an issue of Islamic fundamentalism. While both these elements are present, they are not the cause. As will be explored more fully below, ethnic strife in South Asia is part of the dynamic of the state–society relationship itself, and not some extraneous process projected on to South Asia from 'outside' the region.

Moreover, secessionist demands are not confined to the larger states of the region. The most tragic example of secession based upon a sub-nationalist movement comes from Sri Lanka, where since 1983 the Sri Lankan Tamil minority have been at war with the Sinhalese majority. Various attempts at finding a political solution, usually through the adoption of some form of political devolution or federalism, have come to nothing.

Following the withdrawal of Indian troops from Sri Lanka in March 1990, and the collapse of the Indian sponsored constitutional settlement, the Sri Lankan government resorted to large scale military operations against the Tamil bases in and around the Jaffna peninsula. Again in 1995, following the breakdown of a truce brokered by a newly elected government of national reconciliation, the Tamil stronghold of Jaffna came once more under siege. The social, cultural and economic cost of this violence is extraordinary. As early as 1990, a European Parliamentary Report stated that since 1987 over 60,000 people have been killed in ethnic violence throughout the island. Bangladesh too – perhaps the most homogeneous state of the region – has had difficulties with a Hindu minority and with tribal groups in the Chittagong Hill Tracts crossing into the states of North-East India. Bilateral negotiations with India over the return of Chakma refugees to the Chittagong Hill tracts stalled in 1993 over the instance by the separatist group, the *Shanti Banhini*, that Chakma refugees will only return if they are assured greater regional autonomy within Bangladesh.

Since 1989, India has witnessed instances of Hindu–Muslim violence on a scale not seen since partition. The killing of Indian Muslims by Hindu militants has direct and immediate repercussions on Indo-Pak relations. As the demolition of the Ayodhya Mosque in 1992 showed, Bangladesh and Pakistan protested that Delhi was incapable of defending her religious minorities, and atrocities against Indian Muslims led to violence against non-Muslims in the Pakistani province of Sind, and throughout several western districts of Bangladesh. In India, violence between indigenous Bodo peoples in Assam and Muslim refugees from Bangladesh has led to sporadic violence throughout the early 1990s, and has also involved the displacement of up to 10,000 people.

Political violence, authoritarianism and democratisation

The primacy of ethnic challenges to the state, and the difficulties of politically uniting divergent (and diverging) ethnies, go to make the states of South Asia amongst the most violent in the world. In the first seven months of 1990 alone, 1,159 people were killed in Jammu and Kashmir, while 2,420 died in the Punjab. In 1995, it was reported by the US-based organisation *Human Rights Watch* that, since 1993, an estimated 1,000 people have been killed in and around Nagaland and India's troubled north-east.

In Pakistan, serious ethnic violence in and around the city of Karachi continued to claim innocent lives and became part of the general domestic crisis that led to the dismissal of the Benazir Bhutto government in August 1990, while widespread domestic violence in Sind led to the dismissal of the Sharif government in 1993. Karachi continues to be one of the most violent cities in the world, with over 1,500 ethnic killings in 1994 alone.

Towards the end of 1989, the Ershad regime of Bangladesh was swept out of power by a student-based movement that seemed to be quite independent of the (many) established political parties, and although subsequent elections restored the principle of civilian government, certain activities of Begum Zia's regime have been highhanded and arbitrary, especially with reference to opposition parties. The 1996 election campaign was boycotted by the opposition parties, the results being that the re-election of the Bangladesh National Party was not recognised. In an admission of their lack of legitimacy, Begum Zia's government resigned in the spring of 1996 and conceded the need for fresh elections under a caretaker government. Following the election of Sheikh Hasina to power in June 1996, it remained unclear whether the Bangladesh National Party (BNP) would recognise the election of the Awami League government.

In the Himalayan kingdom of Nepal, a pro-democracy movement – influenced by events in Eastern Europe – led to the scrapping of a partyless political system after a ban that had been in force since 1962. In November 1990, Nepal proclaimed itself to be a constitutional monarchy, with a popularly elected lower house (of 205 members) and an indirectly elected upper chamber. Throughout the 1990s, this new political system led to a series of coalition governments and a level of political instability quite new to Nepal. Pro-Nepalese agitation in India and Bhutan – in India to establish a

Nepali-speaking Gorkha state *within* India, and in Bhutan, to protest at the displacement of so-called Nepalse immigrants – affected India, Nepal, Bhutan and even China.

In all the states of South Asia, political leaders have been assassinated predominantly for alleged crimes of ethnic favouritism or 'ethnic' betrayal. In 1948, Mahatma Gandhi was killed by a young Brahmin, outraged that Gandhi had condoned the partition of Mother India. In 1951, for somewhat obscure reasons, the Pakistani Prime Minister Liquat Ali Khan was shot dead on an electoral rally in Punjab. In 1959, Mr Bandaranaike of Ceylon was shot on his veranda by a Buddhist clergy outraged that the pro-Sinhalese prime minister had struck a deal with the Tamil speakers. Mrs Gandhi was killed by her Sikh body guards in 1984 in a revenge attack for her storming of the Golden Temple in Amritsa, the Sikhs holiest shrine.

Her son, Rajiv Gandhi, was killed in 1992, ironically by a Tamil in revenge for India's mishandling of Tamil aspirations in Sri Lanka. The Liberation Tigers of Tamil Eelan (LTTE) then went on to assassinate both Premadasa and Wijetunga in 1993. In 1988 President Zia of Pakistan was blown up, along with the American Ambassador, after attending a military inspection. It is still the case today that Zia's death produced one of the longest list of suspects in South Asian history. If ethnicity has not provided the basis for execution or murder, ideology has: in both Pakistan and Bangladesh, leaders have been removed from office. Somewhat akin to the Rome of the Julian-Claudian Emperors, few South Asian leaders have died peacefully in their sleep. The cost of political failure within South Asia is likely to be paid for in blood, and not just in electoral defeat and public criticism.

While such degrees of domestic instability cannot be ignored in both the regional and international context, to concentrate solely on political violence would none the less distort the regional picture and caricature the political process. Amid various political crises, almost all of the states in question were engaged in some form of 'normal' political process such as elections and referenda, and many of the ethnic groups and movements involved in direct action used elections – or the call for referendums – as part of their overall campaign to establish their right to exist. India, with the notable exception of 1975–77, has held elections at various levels throughout the federal system. Despite accusations (and in some cases, hard evidence) of electoral rigging and malpractice, India's statutory Electoral Commission had ensured that, on the whole, democratic procedures and norms are followed. In 1995, despite considerable political pressure, the Electoral Commission twice over-ruled the national governments attempts to hold state elections in Jammu and Kashmir, noting that conditions in the state were far from normal, that the electoral register was outdated, and that a 'free and fair' election result could not be ensured.

Somewhat surprisingly, much of the continuing violence in Bangladesh throughout the 1990s concerns the exact timing of elections, and particular types of political practice which, having been forged in the context of unrepresentative, military regimes, are ill-suited to civilian parliamentary government. As Ayesha Jalal has recently stated, the belief that the states of South Asia can be ranked upon a simple continuum of military and civilian, authoritarian and democratic, is absurd: at various times and in various contexts, these states exhibit contradictory tendencies, each sharing in what is above all a historical and regional legacy. These contradictions are also part of the dynamic of nation-building. When examining the domestic politics of South Asia it is extremely useful to make a distinction between procedural and substantive definitions of democracy, and to avoid the rather bland dichotomy of democratic state A versus authoritarian state B.

Notes

1   There are some notable exceptions however. See B. Buzan and G. Rizvi, *South Asian Insecurity and the Great Powers*, Macmillan, Basingstoke, 1985. For further discussion of the concept of a 'security complex' see B. Buzan's book, *People, States and Fear*, Harvester, London, 1991. Many writers have made contributions to works on the foreign policy of India generally, or a specific bilateral relationship. R. W. Bradnock's *Indian Foreign Policy Since 1971*, Pinter, London, 1990, is timely but brief. P. Duncan's book, *The Soviet Union and India*, Routledge, London, 1985 is also very good.

2   See the introduction to the second edition of Buzan's book, *People, States, Fear*.

3   See, for example, R. Stubbs and G. Underhill, *Political Economy and the Changing Global Order*, Macmillan, Basingstoke, 1994.

4   R. Gilpin, *The Political Economy of International Relations*, Princeton University Press, Princeton, 1987, p. 9

5   There has been a tendency to extend the concept of security to deal with issues of economic stability and development. See C. Thomas *In Search of Security*, Wheatsheaf, Brighton, 1987, and also P. Saravanamuttu and C. Thomas, *Conflict and Consensus in South–North Security*, Pinter, London, 1989.

6   Hedley Bull *The Anarchical Society: A Study of Order in World Politics*, Macmillan, London, 1977, p. 297

7   This information comes from the 1991 census by the Government of India (GOI) unless otherwise stated.

8   The 1989–90 *Ministry of External Affairs*, New Delhi. The report listed twenty-four countries as in receipt of Indian aid, p. 4

9   For a fuller discussion on the matter of law, see Rubya Mehdi's *The Islamization of the Law in Pakistan*, Curzon Press, London, 1994.

10   See R. H. Jackson, *Quasi-States: Sovereignty, International Relations, and the Third World*, Cambridge University Press, Cambridge, 1990, especially chapter four.

1

The states of South Asia (I): bilateral relations

The territorial state of India dominates the political geography of South Asia. Even a cursory view over the region reveals the extent of India's centrality. It is the only state that shares borders and cultural affinities with all the other states. India has 72 per cent of the territorial area, 77 per cent of its population and approximately 78 per cent of the region's natural resources. It has recently been noted, by observers within India and especially within the region, that it is India's long-term goal to translate this physical domination into a political and economic one. This is certainly the perception of India's neighbours, especially Pakistan, who from the moment of its separation from British India feared apparent Indian designs. Other states have also raised concerns about the motives of Indian actions. One Bangladeshi analyst noted recently that 'the international role of a state is essentially a function of its power capabilities and an elite's perception of their role ... India has all the nascent tendencies for great power ability.'[1] A recent book on the Indo-Sri Lankan Accord records these same views from the perspective of Colombo.[2] The term 'great power', used frequently by Indian commentators, and commentaries on Indian foreign policy generally, denotes global as well as regional ambitions. This chapter will review the regional aspirations of India, Pakistan, Bangladesh, Sri Lanka and the Himalayan kingdoms of Bhutan and Sikkim. The global implications of Indian power will be discussed later in chapter 5. The main focus of this chapter is the nature and extent of Indo-Pak rivlary. Despite its size, Pakistan has refused to concede to India the role of regional hegemony, and has made it clear that it must be judged as India's equal by the smaller states of South Asia and by the wider international community.

India: the emerging military giant?

Until the collapse of the Soviet Union, and the resulting realignment of global politics in the early 1990s, India's foreign policy had been traditionally shaped around the principles of non-alignment, both regionally, with reference to Pakistan and to China, and then with reference to the international system as a whole.[3] In 1957 Nehru had noted that

> the cold war is based not only upon hatred and violence, but also upon a continuous denunciation, on picking out the faults of others. I tried [in a recent visit to the Far East] to reverse this process, even when I differed radically from those that I addressed.[4]

Internationally, non-alignment meant keeping out of Cold War 'denunciation', and forgoing Western offers to join in defensive alliances against the Soviet Union and vice-versa. It was New Delhi's express hope that their immediate neighbours would follow India's lead and deny foreign countries the use of military bases and facilities, in the interests of both regional and global stability. For India, the main issues confronting the newly independent states were issues of socio-economic development and growth.

Yet regional stability appeared difficult to maintain in the bloody aftermath of partition. By October 1947 a state of war existed between India and Pakistan over the princely state of Kashmir. Other conflicts between India and Pakistan were to take place in 1965 and 1971, and between China and India in 1962. These conflicts forced India to reassess its regional policy, and to change its mind on the need for military as opposed to moral strength. In the wake of China's attack especially, India's foreign policy became somewhat Janus-faced. Within the region it attempted to provide the state with a coherent defence doctrine committed to the use of force to uphold clearly defined Indian interests, while internationally Indian foreign policy has stressed non-interference and dialogue. Such a stance has allowed a relatively poor country room to manoeuvre within the emerging post-colonial world and indeed to claim that it was its leader.

Thus, after 1962 and the shock of the China attack,

> an involution of preoccupations took place. India became less concerned about having a high international profile in various fora, and more concerned about strengthening the components of its national

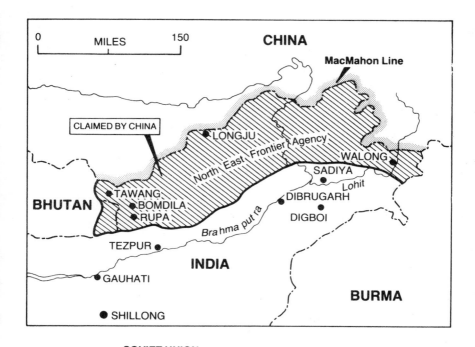

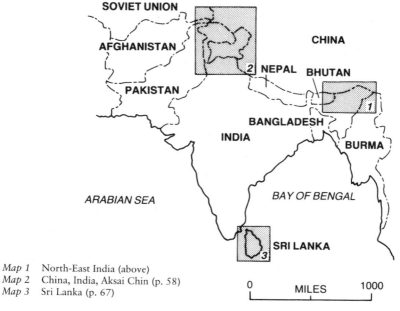

Map 1   North-East India (above)
Map 2   China, India, Aksai Chin (p. 58)
Map 3   Sri Lanka (p. 67)

power. Non-alignment became, more or less, a loose synonym for a tradition *realpolitik* approach.[5]

In the early 1980s the clearest indication of an Indian 'Monroe' doctrine for the region was given by Sen Gupta, a foreign policy analyst working then at the Centre for Policy Studies in New Delhi: 'No South Asian government must ask for extensive military assistance with an anti-Indian bias. If a South Asian country genuinely needs to deal with a serious internal conflict it should ask for help from neighbouring countries, including India.'[6] The rationale of this position was to become abundantly clear in 1987 when India claimed the right, as the regional 'policeman', to assist Sri Lanka in place of other 'non-regional' powers. Yet such a claim rested upon an exaggerated claim of Indian power projection.

The initial expansion of India's military potential relied upon US and British help in the wake of the Chinese border incident. From the late 1960s onwards, India increasingly turned towards the Soviet Union for both weapon imports and technological assistance to create an indigenous arms industry aimed primarily at China, and then increasingly at Pakistan. In 1953 Indian army personnel numbered between 325,000 and 355,000 men. Since 1991, India has diversified its weapons procurement to European and American arms manufacturers, although unlike the old Soviet Union, Western powers still ensure that specific types of technologies are not freely available to New Delhi. As will be discussed below, this has been a point of some contention between India and the USA in particular, and has often involved Washington pressurising third parties (namely France, and recently, the Russian Federation) to ban specific sales to India.

In 1994 India had one of the largest standing armies in the world. Excluding a large pool of reserves, the Indian army numbered over one million men. While the army continues to take the lion's share of the Indian defence budget, both the airforce and the navy have been considerably expanded since the mid-1970s.[7] In 1994–95, the Indian airforce consisted of 844 combat aircraft, an impressive assortment of various MiGs, including the latest MiG-27, and a recently purchased squadron of Mirage jets. Throughout the 1980s India has pressed ahead with an ambitious naval modernisation programme. By 1994, the Indian navy numbered 47,000 men (excluding 5,000 manned airforce wing and 1,000 marines). The fleet consisted of over twenty-five principal surface vessels, including two aircraft carriers, five destroyers and twenty-one frigates. It also has fifteen operational submarines. In 1989 it was announced that India plans to construct her own nuclear submarine, following on from the success of its indigenously produced frigates. In 1993 it was announced that India intends to build its own aircraft carriers.

Soviet assistance in the 1980s had given the Indians access to the MiG-29s (Flogger), which continue to be produced in India under a turnkey arrangement, and access to the then latest Soviet-designed battle tanks.[8] By 1986 however, India was attempting to gain access to Western technology through various licensing agreements with French, German and American companies, and had already purchased a squadron of Mirage 2000 jet fighters. The Soviets continued to provide between 60 and 70 per cent of Indian arms imports, and although India is now self-sufficient in a whole range of ordinance productions, the escalation in the cost of importing Soviet (now Russian) equipment, and the increasing unreliability of delivery, have seriously affected India's various modernisation programmes.

In 1989 it was announced that the Indian government would be setting up a special trading committee to encourage the export of arms to raise much needed foreign capital to be ploughed back into weapons modernisation and the development of indigenous technologies. Unlike the states of Brazil (or China) India has not actively sought to export arms in the past, one reason being India's historic association with the principles of non-violence, the belief – however erroneous – that Hindus are largely passive and peace-loving, and India's own past record in condeming the international arms industry.[9]

Following the establishment of the Integrated Missile Programme in 1983, India has also been able to research and develop an indigenous missile system made up of a mobile short range missile, and an intermediate range missile, known as the *Prithvi* and the *Agni* respectively. The Agni missiles are still being tested, but the Indian government was committed to the deployment of the first batch of Prithvi missiles by 1994. By late 1995 there was still some confusion as to whether Prithvi had been deployed, or whether it had even gone into serial production. There can be little doubt, however, that it will soon be in service, implicit US pressure notwithstanding. American pressure continues, however, to try and get the Indians to stop development of the Agni intermediate missile. Since the early 1970s India has also undertaken independent satellite production which has involved extensive collaboration with the Soviet Union, and to a lesser extent the European Space Agency and NASA. By 1995, the Integrated Missile Programme had developed and started to test up to five different missile systems.[10]

India draws upon the third largest pool of qualified technicians and engineers throughout the world, and these have been deployed not just within space and ballistics research, but also in a civilian nuclear power programme. India is self-reliant throughout the nuclear fuel cycle, using natural uranium for the CADMUS-type reactors and for an ageing generation of R-5 reactors. Supplies of enriched uranium for the Tarapur station came firstly from the USA, then from France, and from 1993–94, from the Chinese. India is still committed to an ambitious extension of its civilian power programme, and supplies many Third World states with nuclear expertise. It was one of the first states to be committed to the peaceful use of nuclear energy, and set up its first research institute in 1947.[11] All of these technological achievements, a satellite and missile programme, and a general consensus on the need for civilian nuclear power have implied to many observers that India has also been working upon a nuclear weapons programme. Indeed in the mid-1970s the evidence seemed overwhelming, following India's detonation of a so-called 'peaceful' nuclear device in 1974.

The test profoundly alarmed Pakistan and led, in the context of the collapse of a united Pakistan, to sustained attempts by Islamabad to develop a device of their own. As in so many other things, Indian accusations against Pakistan duplicated Pakistani allegations against India. Talk of the infamous Islamic bomb was started in Pakistan in the mid-1960s, and appeared to gain momentum during the 1970s – mainly through the enthusiasm of Pakistan's civilian president, Zulfikar Bhutto, who had earlier been the cabinet minister for energy. In the early 1990s Pakistan was convinced that India was working on a highly sophisticated process of inertial confinement fusion to produce a hydrogen bomb without risk of international detection. In turn Pakistan has accused the Indians of secretly developing or even stockpiling nuclear weapons.

The Indians have accused the Chinese of testing a nuclear device on behalf of the Pakistanis, or at the very least, of sharing the results and observations of their own tests. In August 1994, Nawaz Sharif, the ex-prime minister, revealed at a political rally that Pakistan did indeed have the bomb and that it ought to press ahead with weapons production. Pakistan was further implicated as the potential buyer of smuggled weapons-grade plutonium, intercepted on the black market in Russia. By early 1996, there was general speculation that both India and Pakistan were preparing to carry out nuclear tests, although both states denied this.

Commenting on the scope and nature of India's military developments since the mid-1970s, a Pakistani observer stated that 'it requires no great insight to divine what India envisions for herself – the status of the 3rd or 4th great world power by the end of the century'.[12] That this status involves a known nuclear capability apparently goes without saying. Since the 1974 test, India and Pakistan have stood on the brink of escalating a conventional arms race into a nuclear one, remaining both 'threshold states' and non-signatories of the Nuclear Non-Proliferation Treaty (NPT). This was in spite of the fact that the NPT was extended 'indefinitely' by an informal vote at the New York review conference in 1995.

Such technical developments give contemporary India an oxymoronic image of a Third World superpower. This long list of Indian achievements clashes with strongly held concepts and images of mass poverty, political corruption and the vagaries of a caste-based society. Both these images are subject to exaggeration. There has been a tendency to overstate India's indigenous technological capability, both in the field of weapons production, and in the wider field of industrial research and development. This exaggeration is particularly prevalent in the Pakistani literature on India and upon Indian intentions. Yet it also follows that the classic 'Third World' sterotypical image of poverty and squalor – held still by many Westerners – is also highly misleading.

The limitations on Indian military power

Even in those areas where India has adapted foreign technological designs to suit its particular needs in both the military and industrial spheres, the finished products have often been unsatisfactory and have ended up containing a large proportion of imported components. Even when licensing agreements have explicitly handed over patents to Indian developers from foreign companies there have been difficulties in continuing production once all foreign collaboration has ended. Examples of such difficulties can be found in the development of an indigenous light combat aircraft (LCA).

The design for the LCA encorporated the General Electric's F-404 engine produced in America, since the Indian-produced engines could not meet the Indian airforce specifications. The plane included imported radar and missile guidance systems. Although not typical of all joint ventures, the apparent fate of the LCA is none the less illustrative of wider drawbacks. Production costs for the LCA escalated because of a reduction in the number ordered by the airforce, especially following the MiG-29 deal, and it has been calculated that by the time the LCA was deployed by the Indian airforce it already contained redundant technology.

Defence analyst Raju Thomas has remarked that when the project was completed 'the only thing Indian on the LCA will be the coconut which, in accordance with Indian traditions is broken over the prototype'.[13] There are similar problems with the Indian-produced battle tank, whose home-produced engine has so far proved inadequate for the army. In a more substantive work entitled *India's Ad Hoc Arsenal*, analyst Chris Smith discusses the relative failure of Indian attempts to push ahead with indigenous technologies, to deploy them on time, and to adequately integrate them into standing battle orders and tactical strategies. In conclusion, Smith notes:

> India's defence posture is as unstructured and anarchic as it is profligate. Arguably, India commands much less defence capability than might have been expected following the massive investment programme of the 1980s. The available evidence of logistical shortcomings may tell only a fraction of the story. Weaponry has been imported and produced under license from a considerable array of suppliers. This in itself would provide a logistical nightmare, in terms of spare parts, maintenance and training.[14]

Although these findings have been disputed, they stand as a corrective to the assertion that India has become a formidable power. Moreover, the probable weaknesses highlighted by Smith are also to found throughout India's wider industrial and corporate sector as well, despite recent successes in economic and financial restructuring.

The electronic and computer software industries, areas of strength within the Indian economy and encouraged to export in the mid-1980s, were intially unable to compete abroad since their designs were quickly superseded by Western or Japanese patents. Again joint ventures – often successful in opening up new areas for software production and marketing production – often fail to innovate on acquired information. Moreover, the formerly lucrative markets such as Russia and Eastern Europe are in a state of turmoil and adjustment, and have increasingly turned towards the American and European markets. It remains to be seen whether India will be able to compensate for the losses of these markets by gaining economic access to the newly created states of Central Asia, or the more competitive homemarkets of USA, European and East Asian producers.

While probable structural and tactical weaknesses do not detract from the sheer size of India's military machine, it raises questions about its credibility and its effectiveness in any future conflict. Without doubt, it is by far the largest within the South Asia region. In 1994 India spent US$ 8.1 bn on its armed forces, compared to Pakistan's expenditure of US$ 2.63 bn.[15] Of this, about US$ 4 bn goes to the army. As a proportion of gross domestic product (GDP), Pakistan's expenditure on the military is about three times that of India's. Despite budget cuts in 1989 by the Gandhi government, the defence estimates were increased by 8.9 per cent by the V. P. Singh government in 1990 because of increased tension along the Kashmir border with Pakistan.

Despite increased austerity measures, both India and Pakistan increased their defence budgets by 6–7 per cent in real terms in 1994–95. Outside the region India's military modernisation programme has caused some anxiety in Australia and Indonesia, where it is believed that the extent of its rearmament and weapons modernisation is unnecessary for any 'legitimate' defence. Mohammad Ayoob noted that:

> Indonesian concerns about Indian intentions have been recently heightened by India's attempts to augment her naval power and acquire a power projection capability in the vicinity of the sub-continent[16]

and especially by Indian naval developments in and around the Port Blair base on the Andaman and Nicobar islands. Within the region, Pakistan has consistently denounced India's defence spending, and the evolution of Indian military doctrine, as part of a plan to undermine Pakistan's sovereignty and undo partition. These denunciations have continued despite international assurance and (until recently) the supply of advanced US weapons, and despite Indian claims that it is merely trying to match the developments of Pakistan, and more distantly, China.

Pakistan and the search for parity

The great difficulty for Indo-Pak relations is that India's perceptions of the Pakistani conspiracy are mirrored almost exactly by the Pakistani view of the 'Indian grand design', a design within which Pakistan has at best a secondary, decorative role, or at worst, no role at all. From the Indian position, Pakistan was (until very recently) a military-led, authoritarian government – the 'Sparta of Asia' – whose regional policy often appeared aggressive and dishonest, premised upon the eventual collapse of India. Paradoxically, since 1988 and the partial restoration of a civilian government in Islamabad, Indo-Pak relations have deteriorated to an all time low. Brassey's definitive text, *The Strategic Survey* noted that, 'in 1994, India and Pakistan effectively stopped talking to each other'. Respective consulates in Bombay and Karachi were closed, and it appeared that neither state was capable, or willing, to stop the rapid collapse in bilateral relations.

Increases in trade, commerce and intra-regional tourism remained marginal. At an international conference in Wilton Park, England, convened in July 1995, former senior Indian and Pakistani diplomats lamented the breakdown in communications and warned of its seriousness. In 1996, a Rand publication stressed the need for India and Pakistan to come to some form of arms control agreement in order to stabilise the situation and prevent an escalating – and destabilising – arms race.

An implicit arms race started almost before the process of partition was complete, and by the autumn of 1947 (barely three months after independence) the two dominions were informally at war over Kashmir. The Pakistani government turned first to the British, then to the Americans and then to the Chinese. The success of this extra-regional search for support is plain to see within contemporary Pakistan. By 1994 Pakistan had assembled a powerful and well-integrated army of approximately 520,000 personnel (excluding reserves), and an airforce made up of at least 430 combat aircraft. In contrast to India, most of these are Western (American, British and French) and have been imported into Pakistan under various international security arrangements aimed (or so they believed) at the Soviets.

The Pakistan navy, partially to offset Indian developments, has increased quite dramatically in the last decade. In 1994 it consisted of eleven principal surface combatants and nine submarines, a small reduction on previous years. Over the last year purchases and lease-back arrangements with the United States and Britain have doubled the tonnage of the Pakistan fleet. In 1994, the Pakistanis signed a deal with France for the purchase of four Agnosta-class diesel sub-marines. Pakistan insisted that the deal ought also to include a clause forbidding the French to sell the same class of submarine to the Indians. In 1995, the Chinese agreed to a credit deal which allowed Islamabad to buy Chinese weapons at concessional rates.

Until very recently the security environment of Pakistan was com-parable to that of Israel during the 1960s and 1970s. To the north and east lay the mass of India with its apparently implacable hatreds, while to the west lay Afghanistan and Iran. After 1979, and the Soviet invasion of Afghanistan, over three million Muslim refugees crossed into the North-west Frontier Province and the Baluchistani province of Pakistan. Such circumstances – coupled with the apparent threat of further Soviet attacks against Pakistan itself because of Islamabad's support for the rebels – appeared to justify a dramatic increase in weapons procurement and a demand for sophisticated weapon technologies from the United States.

These weapons, such as advanced F-16s, were eventually pro-vided by the Reagan Administration in the face of vigorous Indian protests that, far from being deployed against the Soviets (or the Soviet-backed Afghan government), they would end up being deployed against India. The settlement of the Afghanistan situation at Geneva in 1988 eased the refugee situation somewhat, although the level of instability within Afghanistan and the fate of the Muja-hadeen resistance are still a matter of concern for Islamabad, as was the outbreak of civil fighting in Tajikistan. Throughout the early 1990s, various factional governments came and went in Kabul. In 1994, the emergence of a radical Islamic student group known as *Talibar* held out the prospects of reconciliation, but subsequent fighting once more polarised the country along ethnic and regional lines, with domestic implications for Pakistani politics.

During 1990 and 1995, disagreements between the United States and Pakistan over Islamabad's nuclear capabilities and nuclear research programme led to a cut-back in both military and economic aid. From 1991 onwards, the USA actually refused to deliver F-16s (a majority of which had already been paid for) because Pakistan would not allow access to some of its nuclear facilities, or cooperate with USA sponsored policies on non-proliferation, control on the transfer of missile technology, or attempts to eliminate stocks of fissile materials. Such a deterioration in US–Pakistan relations was brought about primarily by the collapse of the Soviet Union, which removed Pakistan's option of playing the 'Cold War' card over Afghanistan and appealing to America's strategic interest generally. Following consultations in 1995, however, the US relaxed its attitude, and reconvened the Joint Military Commission (JMC).

Pakistan remains highly sensitive to US pressure. Cut off from extra-regional support, Pakistan entered the 1990s acutely aware of India's indigenous military power. In 1989 one Indian analyst noted (somewhat too emphatically, perhaps) that 'India's military power greatly exceeds that of Pakistan's ... and the weight that Bangladesh and Sri Lanka are able to bring to bear is minimal. The problems for Pakistan are accentuated by the relative decline in Pakistan's defensive capability.'[17] Recent weapons deals with China, including the apparent deployment of the surface-to-surface M11 missile, are a deliberate attempt by Islamabad to match India's deployment of *Prithvi*.[18] Pakistan's size relative to India raises acute problems of defence. Flat open borders in the Punjab and Sind area favour armoured infantry and tank warfare. What is referred to as 'in depth defence' – the ability of a state to absorb an initial attack and over-extend an enemy's supply lines – is made particularly difficult for Pakistan because of its territorial 'narrowness' *vis-à-vis* India. Most of its rail and road networks travel on a south-west/north-east axis and would quickly fall to an advancing Indian army if the forward defences fell or pulled back, and would remain vulnerable to Indian air strikes.

In 1965, for example, the Indian army crossed the international border in the Punjab/Sind areas and directly threatened Lahore and Rawalpindi, despite the Pakistani calculation that Indian counter-offensives against *Operation Gibraltar* would be confined to the Kashmir area.[19] It is not surprising therefore that Indian demands in the 1980s for 'deep strike' aircraft – leading to the purchase of Jaguar and Mirage – caused particular concern in Islamabad, even if India argued that the purchase of deep strike fighters was merely a response to the Pakistani purchasing of F-16s from the USA.

Because of India's industrial and economic size relative to Pakistan, it is likely that the longer any potential hostilities continue, the more likely it is that India will win. Given the physical inability of Pakistan to resist a determined Indian land attack, several Western analysts have suggested that Pakistan's official defence doctrine has become overtly and understandably *offensive*. In times of regional tension and crisis the Pakistan military are inclined to pre-empt any potential Indian attack and launch their own offensive against India's forward positions, especially against forward airfields in north-west India.

As will be discussed, both the 1965 and the 1971 conflicts show some aspects of this strategy, since in both conflicts Pakistan calculated that its best option was to strike against India first. In 1991, Sumit Ganguly cited Stephen Cohen's remarks that since the mid-1980s, both India and Pakistan have moved to 'offensive defence' strategies. If Cohen's observations are correct, in such circumstances incidents of misperception, misinformation or error, could well accidentally precipitate a war. This is a serious situation to exist between two states, both armed with sophisticated weapons systems. It is even more serious if both states have relatively quick access to (or already possess) nuclear technology.

Whether or not Pakistan can maintain military parity with India is a difficult question to assess. Pakistan has attempted to match India not through sheer numbers (an impossible task given the differences of size in their respective economies) but through more sophisticated technologies. A sheer listing of numbers of planes, ships and men does not give much insight into how successful they will be in wartime. Different weapons systems have different strengths and weaknesses, as do the command structures and strategic flexibility of the respective armies, and the viability of particular battle orders.

It is now widely accepted that, on the whole, the Pakistani airforce out-performed its Indian counterpart in 1965, despite a numerical inferiority. Various defence analysts have noted that Indian defence doctrines – especially with regard to its navy and the ideas of 'floating sea control' and carrier-battle groups[20] – are antediluvian, expensive to maintain and vulnerable to air and submarine attack. Moreover, since the Gulf crisis over Kuwait, analysts have noted the poor performance of much Soviet hardware against so-called Western 'smart' weapons.

Because of its size, and in part because of differences in nationalist ideology, Pakistan has followed a different course to India in terms of military developments. Its reliance upon foreign weapons imports is much greater than India's since no real attempt has been made to develop an indigenous arms industry. Islamabad's technological sophistication is none the less impressive, although it lacks India's economic and industrial depth. In 1989 Pakistan tested its own surface-to-surface missile, although as noted earlier, this does not seem to have affected the decision to purchase Chinese equipment. Such reliance on foreign imports means that Pakistan has been far more vulnerable to arms embargoes than India, a fact that merely acts to increase its insecurity further. Pakistan's military strength is clearly a force to be reckoned with, even if Indian critics imply that it has been bought at the price of national dependence upon the USA. Pakistan's forces are especially impressive when it is recalled how the origins of the state were so shaky. In 1947 few believed that Pakistan would survive at all.

If Indo-Pak relations have been characterised by wars and profound mistrust, what are the chances for a peaceful settlement and a normalisation of relations in the immediate future? A considerable part of the problem behind Indo-Pak relations is that what India considers to be its legitimate defence requirements appear to deny the legitimate defence requirements of others, especially Pakistan: India's insistence that Pakistan should not go to the USA for arms, or that New Delhi should vet what arms Pakistan can buy, remains unacceptable to Pakistan. Yet Pakistan's continued refusal to acknowledge the 'realities of regional power' (a euphemism for Indian predominance) is a source of continued irritation to New Delhi. The overall situation is further complicated by the interaction between Indian and Pakistani domestic politics, and the accusations (often, and perhaps significantly, made during electoral campaigns) of mutual interference. In 1995, it was noted that:

> many take the view that extremist politicians are dominating foreign policy-making, and that this has led to the recent increase in tension and mutual suspicion. Groups within the government and state

bureaucracies appear to be deliberately confrontational, and they argue that their publics support this policy.[21]

The evolution of Indo-Pak relations

Since 1962 successive Indian governments have justified their military modernisation programmes in terms of regional threats from both China and Pakistan. India's perceptions of the Pakistani threat remain despite the disintegration of the eastern wing in 1971, as do the concerns about a nuclear China and the still outstanding (and, indeed, ongoing) issue of border demarcation. The mutual mistrust that lies at the heart of the South Asian security complex has been historically and politically constructed in the minds of specific elites, and although they have been modified since independence, they remain profoundly linked to the colonial period. What are the reasons for this degree of profound hostility, and how can we explain its continuation over the years since independence?

Indo-Pak relations can, in outline, be traced to the nature of communal-based politics within British India. A great deal of writing and research has discussed the crisis that followed the bifurcation of the British Raj along so-called Hindu–Muslim lines, much of it unfortunately beyond the scope of this book.[22] It is necessary, however, to note at the outset three fallacies that have long dogged historical and political writings on South Asia.

There has been a tendency to imply that, somehow or other, the partitioning of British India was inevitable, a natural outcome of real differences within the social fabric of India itself. As discussed in the preface, such essentialism is entirely misplaced. It could be argued that partition was the outcome of a specific international context (the British urgency to disengage from South Asia) more than it was a result of genuine concerns over representation.[23] Related to this point, it is often argued that Jinnah and the Muslim League, having turned their back on co-operation with the Indian National Congress Party by the mid-1930s, were determined to have a separate state and would have settled for nothing less. There is a great deal of evidence to suggest that Jinnah attempted, unsuccessfully, to use the threat of partition to negotiate for a weak all-Indian federal structure and the guarantee that, at the national level, the Muslim League would be granted parity with the Congress.[24]

Such a strategy foundered on Congress tenacity and the differing and divergent demands of the Muslim majority provinces. A 'two-winged' nation, or, more emotively, Jinnah's moth-eaten state, was the last thing that the League had wanted. Finally, there has been the tendency to begin the post-colonial history of India and Pakistan as if they have always constituted two separate states. In part this is a reflection of deliberate state policy, but to take such a policy at face value detracts from the considerable similarity between India and Pakistan which is part of the problem of Indo-Pak relations itself, and the fact that each country's perception of the other differs between specific ethnic groups.

Pakistan was created, intentionally or otherwise, as a consequence of the 'two-nation theory' advanced by the Muslim League, a nationalist political party, which stated that the Hindu and Muslim communities within the Raj constituted two separate *cultures*. In 1940, the League had issued the infamous Lahore declaration which stated that: 'those areas in which the Muslims are in a numerical majority, as in the north-west and the north-eastern zones, should be grouped to constitute independent states in which the constituent units shall be autonomous and sovereign.' This argument was resisted by the Indian National Congress Party, the main source of nationalist opposition to the British. Under the leadership of a Westernised, secular middle class, the Congress claimed to represent all Indians regardless of their religion, language or race, evolving a Westernised ideal of 'the nation' and an associated Western, democratic and secular state. Despite initial resistance to the idea, articulated most notably by Viceroy Wavell, who wished to 'expose the absurdity of Jinnah's Pakistan' through a Royal Commission of Enquiry, the British conceded just a few weeks before leaving the sub-continent. Just prior to the British departure, the Radcliffe Boundary Commission of 1947 created a 'moth-eaten Pakistan state' consisting of a two-winged nation, one in the north-west, the other in the north-east. Between them lay over 1,000 miles of Indian territory.

The geographical randomness of the subsequent boundary award, and the speed with which the international borders were demarcated, were a direct consequence of a British-derived concept of partition, issued by fiat without consultation of the parties. Of the five provinces that went into forming Pakistan, two were to be physically divided. No referenda were held in Punjab and Bengal to clarify the decision of their respective (and indirectly elected) assemblies, despite the complex inter- and intra-ethnic politics of each state, and the popular confusion over what, in reality, Jinnah's Pakistani state entailed.

Jinnah's call of 'Islam in danger' created within the Muslim minority provinces of British India the sincere belief that Congress' talk of secularism would not be enough to protect Muslim rights after 1947. Yet – and this is the most astounding irony of partition – the territorial domain of the Pakistani state would be situated in Muslim majority areas in which the Muslim League was not well represented or, in some cases, not even present at all.

The first and foremost problem that the British and the League faced was how to create a sovereign state in two separate parts of the Raj that were culturally and linguistically diverse, with no previous experience of working together. Moreover, the territories that went into Pakistan had very few natural resources, little urbanisation, no significant industrial development and virtually no infrastructure. All they had in common was the fact that they were populated by Muslims. Following the breakdown of the interim Indian government set up in early 1947 before the British had accepted the 'inevitability' of Pakistan, the Viceroy divided the executive council into two sub-committees, one for the eventual state of Pakistan and one for the India dominion. Until the territorial boundaries of Pakistan were released, which they were the day after the British left India, the Pakistani sub-committee was

a cabinet claiming to be a government, but as yet without any ground under its feet or a roof over its head. Mountbatten showed his contempt when he let slip that the government of Pakistan would have to make do with a tent in the initial years of independence.[26]

While it is not necessary to go into the details of the process of state formation in Pakistan, the legacy of partition is vital. Partition left a serious psychological and emotional cloud over the future of Indo-Pak relations. Over two million people are said to have died following independence, as Muslims left for Pakistan, and Hindus left for India. The spectre of social and territorial disintegration has remained within both India and Pakistan to this day despite the change in generations.[27]

The demarcation of the international border left many serious anomalies, in and around the Chittagong Hill tracks of East Bengal, the Kutch of Rann area in the west, parts of the Punjab and, most seriously, in the then princely state of Jammu and Kashmir. Partition created a state with a 1,400-mile border with India to the west, and a 13,000-mile border with Afghanistan. In 1947 the Afghan government argued that, with the ending of British India, the Afghan–Indian border (the so-called Durand Line) was invalid and that significant parts of the new state ought by right to be within Afghanistan.[28] The situation of East Pakistan created a logistical nightmare for Pakistan's defence requirements. The Radcliffe award had also failed to clarify the border between East Pakistan and Burma in the area of the Naaf river.[29]

Once the territorial dimensions of partition had been accepted, controversy continued as to how the physical assets of the Raj were to be divided between the two dominions. As Jalal notes:

> The Partition machinery set up to determine Pakistan's share of the assets of undivided India had seventy-two days in which to dismantle a government structure it had taken the British over a hundred years to construct. Settling who was to get what … took place against a backdrop of an unprecedented communal carnage.[30]

Every financial asset was fought over, including postal services, civil servants, sterling balances and, most significantly of all, the armed forces. The resulting breakdown was far from favourable for the Pakistanis. After partition for example, all of the ordnance factories were situated within India and there were serious disagreements over the allocation of surplus stores for the armies. After protracted negotiations, Pakistan was given 17.5 per cent of the financial assets of the Raj, most of which was held up within India until 1948/49. Pakistan was never to receive the full settlement. Rs 750 million should have been repaid to Karachi, yet India suspended payments after Rs 200 million, following the outbreak of violence in Kashmir. Pakistan's share of the undivided British Indian army came to just over 30 per cent (140, 000 out of 410, 000), 40 per cent of the navy and 20 per cent of the airforce, although much of the airforce remained on Indian territory.

In such circumstances, it was appreciated that from the outset of its existence, and for some time to come, Pakistan's defence potential would be poor: of sixty-seven battalions with British India, only thirty-five went to Pakistan and even these were stripped of their Hindu and Sikh companies. Once the prospects of war over Kashmir appeared, India refused to allow any military stores or hardware to reach the hands of the Pakistani army. Jinnah accused the Indian National Congress of attempting to 'strangle Pakistan at birth'.

The security environment within South Asia was thus deeply hostile to Pakistan's existence.[31] The first priority – even above that of setting up district and provincial governments – was to defend itself against India's perceived determination to reintegrate the Muslim majority areas under the control of New Delhi. The first part of Pakistan's strategy was to construct a highly centralised state with a powerful military establishment that would prevent India utilising internal instability in the first turbulent years to undermine Pakistan's sovereignty and its attempts to nation-build. The political consequences of such centralisation for a democratic, pluralist and federal Pakistan were to be catastrophic. Moreover, the only way this military establishment could be built with any speed was to turn to foreign, extra-regional help.

The open invitation by Pakistan to 'foreign powers' in the early 1950s led to an Indian condemnation that has never really stopped. Yet Pakistan has argued that India's subsequent policy of non-alignment, and the need for Cold War rivalry to be kept out of the South Asia region, was a rather purple Indian version of simple power politics, a cunning disguise of Indian expansionist interests dressed up in the language of moral virtues. This belief is still held to this day. A recent Pakistani commentator has pointed out that 'It is significant that many Indians, when they speak of the Indian land mass cannot refrain from making it clear that what they are really talking about is the entire South Asian region.'[32] For reasons of size and weakness Pakistan still has no option but to seek multilateral agreements to regional problems, either through the United States, the Middle East, or China to checkmate India's obvious advantage. Such a policy is diametrically opposed to India's continual stress upon bilateralism and regional primacy.

There is little danger in exaggerating Pakistani paranoia over India: India remains the prime focus of Pakistan's foreign policy, and the degree of this obsession distorts much of its thinking on India and Indian politics. Waseem has astutely noted that:

> Ever since the emergence of Pakistan, India has been our greatest preoccupation in the context of international relations ... and yet what is

most often dished up to us as so-called scholarly analysis on India's internal and external policies are all highly subjective ... even inaccurate.[33]

Such analysis often stresses the centrality of Hinduism and dismisses India's claims to secularism as mere propaganda. Much can be said, in response, of India's preoccupations with the 'Muslim mind' in which prejudice is dressed up as scholarship, and more recently, images and sterotypes of Islamic fundamentalism and 'terrorism'. In the preface to a book entitled (tellingly) *Understanding the Muslim Mind*, Rajmohan Gandhi, the grandson of Mahatma Gandhi, noted stoically 'Any nuclear clash between India and Pakistan (may God forbid it) would, in part, be due to history. Though living side by side for centuries, Hindus and Muslims have never adequately understood or trusted one another.'[34] Whether true or not, there is a certain irony here however, in that recent changes within India, associated with the rise of the BJP and talk of cultural Hinduism, have come close to confirming much of Pakistan's earlier scepticism of the realities of Indian nationalism. The BJP's 1996 election campaign was hawkish on defence, on the role of Kashmir within India, and the need to press ahead with the development of nuclear weapons.

The Kashmir issue

As the domestic situation within the Indian state of Jammu and Kashmir deteriorated from 1987 onwards, it looked to many that India and Pakistan stood on the brink of a fourth war. Pakistan revived old hopes that the disputed territory might well one day wrest itself from the Indian Union. In 1987 there was a serious escalation of tension in the Kashmir area, with both sides exchanging heavy artillery fire over the so-called line of control (LOC). The situation was diffused when President Zia and Prime Minister Rajiv Gandhi met at Jaipur, ostensibly to watch a cricket match. In August 1990, further fighting took place in the Siachen glacier area, where a large number of casualties were caused by frostbite.

The 1990 crisis – the worst for some time – followed in the wake of a serious political breakdown within Kashmir over the nature of political representation and the degree of autonomy desired by Srinagar. The marginalisation of established political parties (especially the National Conference, a Kashmiri party linked to Sheikh Abdulla, the initial architect of the Indian political settlement) led to a rise in militancy against the Indian 'occupation'.

The Indian central government responded by deploying a large number of troops to isolate the various (and multiplying) groups working for an independent Islamic Kashmir, an Islamic Kashmir within Pakistan, or an independent secular Kashmir. Each group sought to define its respective state along the territorial lines of the former Dogra Kingdom.[35] It has been estimated that since the crisis developed in 1989, between 7,000 and 10,000 people have been killed, 10,000 have been placed in detention, and well over $2 billion dollars' worth of damage has been caused to homes and to infrastructure. Unofficial figures put the number of dead since 1990 much higher, as high as 20,000. Most deaths involve innocent civilians killed in shoot-outs between militants and the Border Security Force (BSF), so-called custodial killings, bomb blasts and grenade attacks.

Despite claims by New Delhi that the situation was largely under control, to all intents and purposes, Srinagar and the nearby settlements such as Gulmarg, Baramula, Anantnag, and Sonamarg have remained tense throughout the 1990s, with the rural areas under constant monitoring by the Indian security forces. While the BSF seem able to contain the situation in the urban areas, militant violence had, by late 1994, shifted to the country, and to the southern districts such as Doda. All the roads frequently have sandbagged border positions, and following the issuing of identity cards to every Indian citizen in the state of Jammu and Kashmir in 1990, it is common for people to be stopped on journeys and asked to report their name and destination. Two attempts in 1995 to restart the political process, and to hold state elections within the Indian constitution, were subsequently abandoned. The Indian government, as well as the various militant groups involved within the area, are all accused of human rights violations.

As in other areas of 'insurgency', the Indians have experienced great difficulties in separating militants from the local population, using such techniques as 'crack-downs' and house-to-house searches, leading to serious over-reactions by the army and the BSF, and in some cases to the use of excessive force, resulting in inexcusable attrocities, such as an incident in Malangam in April 1991, where the BSF killed seven members of a family believed to be holding militants.

Although New Delhi has been internationally embarrassed by certain activities of the BSF, and the sheer unpopularity of the Indian miltary presence in the valley, many militant groups have themselves become extremely unpopular, linked to petty crime, illegal fund-raising activities and drugs. In September of 1994, the first incident was reported of Kashmiri villagers turning on and killing several militants. Numerous strikes and protests, bomb threats and warnings, add up to an atmosphere of mistrust and mutual suspicion in which many Kashmiris, whatever their specific (and real) grievances against New Delhi, none the less feel trapped and encircled in a worsening situation they no longer control.

If partition itself has been the subject of much anguished and rhetorical writings, so too has the drama of the Kashmiri Maharaja's indecision whether to join the Dominion of India, become an independent Kashmiri state, or become part of Muslim Pakistan. Being a Hindu leader over a Muslim majority state, Pakistan's claims to the kingdom seemed to be justified on the basis of the two-nation theory, although as all subsequent Indian arguments have made clear, the principles of the two-nation theory only applied to British India, and not to so-called 'princely' India.

Although the British ruled India for over 200 years, large areas of the sub-continent were administered indirectly through so-called native rulers. In 1947, two-fifths of the Indian sub-continent was administered through native rulers, constituting over 600 individual states and principalities, tied to the British Crown through a series of treaty rights and obligations which recognised the British Raj as the paramount power in India. The principle of paramountcy, an ill-defined and somewhat flexible constitutional concept, regulated the activities between British and princely India. Of the 600 or so states that went into making up princely India, only twenty-eight had populations of over 500,000 people, and of these, two were particularly dominant: the Dogra State of Jammu and Kashmir, and the Kingdom of Hyderabad. Some were minute, one being as small as three-tenths of a square mile, and were tied not just to the British through separate treaty obligations, but to other princely states through vassal status which predated the British presence. Of greater significance for the future, given the evolution of princely India, and the nature of the cultural and religious interaction within the sub-continent, it was not uncommon for a Hindu ruler to preside over a predominantly Muslim population (as was to be the case in Kashmir), or for a Muslim Nizam to preside over a predominantly Hindu one (as was the case in Hyderabad).

To a large extent, princely India was relatively immune from the processes of socio-economic and political reform which characterised British India after 1919. Although in Kashmir political parties and forums were beginning to organise by the time of the early 1930s, nationalist politics, as dominated by the League and the Congress, were largely absent. As the British began to prepare for independence, and to deal with the intractable difficulties of the so-called Hindu–Muslim question, they were slow to appreciate the constitutional – and indeed territorial – issues presented to them by princely India. In *theory* at least, the concept of paramountcy held out to the leaders of the states the possibility that, as the British prepared to hand over independence, the states would lapse back into sovereign powers, as they were before the East India Company's sepoys forced them to concede to British suzerainty. By 1937 such ideas were complete anathema to the emerging political forces of the Indian National Congress and the Muslim League.

Yet there were several princely states to whom the concept of independence was both attractive and plausible. As late as 1942, the princes were assured that they had three alternatives before them: to join some future Indian federation[36] (as indeed had been held out to them within the provisions of the 1935 Act); to retain some relationship with the British Crown (such as crown colony status or a protectorate); or to become a fully sovereign state.[37] The latter alternative opened the prospect of the complete balkanisation of India, which Congress was adamant to avoid, and after heavy lobbying in 1946 the British ruled out the last two interpretations completely. Yet even as late as July 1947, with the general issue complicated by the acceptance by the British of the principles of partition, V. P. Menon, the Congress man in charge of the States Department (the new name for the old political department), felt it necessary to impress the British with the need to stick to their *agreed procedures* towards the princes: 'Even an inkling that HMG would accord independent recognition [to the states] would make infinitely difficult all attempts to bring the states and the New Dominions together.'[38] What these 'agreed procedures' were had been outlined in the statement of May 12 1946, which had been circulated to all

the residents. The Memorandum on States' Treaties and Paramountcy noted that:

> when a new fully self-governing or independent government or gov-
> ernments come into being in British India, HMG's influence with
> these governments will not be such as to enable them to carry out the
> obligations of paramountcy ... Paramountcy will cease to exist. This
> means that the rights of the states which flow from their relationship
> with the crown will no longer exist.[39]

As such, the princely states would have to join either India or Pakistan. To this end, the States Department drew up two documents:
the Stand-by Agreement and the Instrument of Accession. A Standstill Agreement was an interim measure whereby a princely state,
indecisive about the exact conditions of its membership with India
or Pakistan, could provide for the continuation of essential services
despite the collapse of the constitutional foundation of paramountcy. The Instrument of Accession, however, was a permanent
agreement wherein the state would join the state of India or Pakistan and immediately concede external affairs, defence, finance and
communications to the new central government. By 2 August blank
forms were being distributed to the British residents for due
princely consideration.

The decision to join India or Pakistan was to be decided by the
prince alone. Only where consultative procedures were already part
of princely government was there any reason to seek wider agreement. There was no compulsion by the British for the prince to consult the population at large, or to ratify his decision through a
referendum. The Dogra Kingdom of Jammu and Kashmir, along
with several other states, including Hyderabad, delayed signing the
Instrument of Accession, although the Maharaja signed Standstill
Agreements with both New Delhi and Karachi. By 15 August 1947,
it was clear that the Maharaja was thinking seriously of independence, although some, such as the newly appointed prime minister,
favoured merging with India. Others were in favour of joining Pakistan.

The Maharaja's indecision led to pressure from both Karachi and
New Delhi. There appears to be a considerable body of evidence to
suggest that, in spite of having signed the Standstill Agreement, the
Pakistanis were holding up supplies going into the valley. Later, by
October, the valley was invaded from the Pakistani side by so-called

tribals, Pathanis from North-west Frontier Province, and Kashmiri Muslims from the districts of Poonch. Following implicit Pakistani support for a tribal invasion into the valley to help their fellow Muslims, the Maharaja signed up to secede to India some time around 26 October 1947, opening the way to immediate military help from India. This led to outrage in Karachi and, by May 1948, open conflict between the two dominions.[40]

While timely Indian moves prevented the 'tribals' from taking the capital Srinagar, the Indians did not succeed in totally removing the Pakistani army, leaving Pakistan in control of an area of approximately 30,503 square kilometres referred to as 'Azad' (free) Kashmir, and a separate area, including Gilgit and Hunza, known as the Northern Territories. Both states continue to claim the state in its entirety. One commentator noted that India's 'arguments for holding on to Kashmir are hollow, fallacious, shifting and confused'.[41] Indian academics often reiterate the same accusation in reverse, maintaining that the legality of the signature on the Instrument of Accession is proof enough of India's legitimacy. Both states have pressed on with the integration of their respective portions of Kashmir into their wider political frameworks, and both states remain committed to 'restoring' Kashmir to their respective political federations. Gradually, however, there has grown up a significant minority who wish for the former Dogra Kingdom to be an independent state, along the lines implied in pre-1946 British thinking on paramountcy.

Nehru referred the matter to the United Nations Security Council in 1947, allegedly following the suggestion of the then Governor-General, Mountbatten. In a letter sent in November 1947 to his Pakistani counterpart – Liquat Ali Khan – Nehru also held out the prospects for settling the issue through a plebiscite, a matter that had already been discussed earlier between Jinnah and Mountbatten. The subsequent role of the UN in the Kashmir problem profoundly shocked Nehru, since Pakistan was not only able to canvass international support, it was also able to elicit sympathy on a whole series of issues that were, from the Indian point of view, matters for bilateral negotiation only. Initially supportive of the presence of the United Nations Observers' Group for India and Pakistan (UNOGIP) and a UN regulated ceasefire line, India gradually came to see the observation group as unwarranted interference. In 1948 Nehru noted bitterly:

> I must confess that the attitude of the great powers [on the question
> of Kashmir] has been astonishing. Our experience of international
> politics and the ways things are done in the higher regions of the UN
> has been disappointing to the extreme – no doubt all this will affect
> our conduct of international relations in the future.[42]

The handling of the Kashmir issue by the international community goes a long way to explaining India's antipathy to the role of
'external' mediation in regional affairs. This aversion would, over
time, become directed not just against third power mediation, but
also against most forms of multilateral negotiation within the region
itself. Following the United Nations fiasco, India was determined to
solve the Kashmir crisis on the basis of bilateral relations with Pakistan. It was, however, to accept brief Soviet mediation after the
1965 war with Pakistan.

The 1947–48 conflict was halted through a combination of
Indian diplomatic naïvity, the weakness of the respective armies,
and the curious fact that a British Commander-in-Chief (Field Mar-
shal Sir Claude Auchinleck) was in command of both Indian and
Pakistani forces, and that a large percentage of the office corps on
both sides were also British.[43]

Yet India's perceptions of a pernicious, calculating Pakistan, were
set firmly in their mould. Matters were made worse when in 1958
the civilian government in Pakistan was removed by a military coup.
The dispute between Indian and Pakistani nationalism was now
heightened through the conflict of a democracy against a military
oligarchy, led by General Ayub Khan. Extreme and mutual threat
perceptions stalled attempted political dialogue, with India turning
down a Pakistan offer of a mutual defence pact in the late 1950s.
Ayub Khan, in his autobiography *Friends, Not Masters* believed that
the future for Indo-Pak relations was bleak because of Indian arro-
gance, a point reiterated many years later by another Pakistani military leader, Zia-ul-Haq.

Indian mistrust was further reinforced in 1965, following a
second clash with Pakistan, with Kashmir once more at the centre
of the dispute. India's military humiliation over the 1962 border
clash with China (discussed below) had revealed serious weaknesses
in India's military capability. In early April 1965 the Pakistan army
carried out a careful probe of India's defences in the Rann of Kutch
area, adjacent to the Indian state of Gujarat and Rajasthan. Satisfied

that Indian morale was low, Ayub Khan launched the infamous *Operation Gibraltar* to take Kashmir by force. The result of the conflict was another draw that failed to alter the already existing UN ceasefire line. To Pakistan's surprise, India launched an attack across the international Punjabi border, and the key Pakistani assumption – that Muslim Kashmiris would welcome the Pakistanis as liberators – badly misfired. The stalemate was made official through the Tashkent Declaration of January 1966 signed in Soviet Central Asia, which reinstated the *status quo ante*.

The period between 1965 and 1971 saw little improvement between the two states over Kashmir. The restoration of democracy in Pakistan in 1971 (a fact welcomed by India as a precondition for the normalisation of Indo-Pak relations), and the current civilian regime of Nawaz Sharif (who is himself a Punjabi of Kashmiri descent) has not provided the kind of political breakthrough desired. Since 1972, Indo-Pak relations have oscillated between open hostility to suggested reconciliation. In December 1985, Prime Minister Rajiv Gandhi and President Zia-ul-Haq signed an agreement not to attack each other's nuclear installations, an agreement that was reiterated in 1988 by the then Pakistan Prime Minister Benazir Bhutto. Pakistan has offered various solutions to the standoff between them, from a joint non-nuclear agreement, to a 'no first strike' agreement, but the Indian response has always been mistrustful of Pakistan's real intentions, and guarded about its own.

The present and continuing impasse over Kashmir remains the most likely cause for any further scrap between India and Pakistan. Only when this issue is resolved, peacefully, and in line with the concepts of representation and accountability, will Indo-Pak relations improve. Yet, ironically, the peaceful resolution of the Kashmiri issue requires Indo-Pak co-operation. Despite Nehru's promise of a plebiscite, the Indians will not hold one. The Pakistanis are committed to holding a plebiscite premised on two questions: do the Kashmiris wish to stay with India or to join with Pakistan? Many Kashmiris want a third question: do you wish to be a separate, sovereign state?

The Pakistan civil war 1970–1971

Pakistan's fear of Indian expansionism was dramatically substantiated with the loss of East Pakistan, during a civil war in which the predominantly West Pakistani government (made up disproportionately of Punjabis and *Mohajirs*) refused to concede to Bengali demands for greater autonomy. This was in spite of the fact that Bengalis made up 54 per cent of the Pakistani population. What made matters so critical, is that Bengal's success in breaking away rested on Indian involvement. Very few colonial states have disintegrated since independence, and although the geographical separation of east from west made Pakistan's case rather unusual, the fact that 1971 happened at all (with the loss of 32 per cent of its territory) terrified future Pakistani governments that, with future Indian help, Pakistan would disintegrate further. Sajjad Hyder, who was Pakistan's High Commissioner in New Delhi on the run-up to the Bangladesh crisis noted in a recent book:

> Our perceptions of India are that, beneath a thin veneer, the Indian leadership and a sizeable segment of Indian opinion continue to regard the formation of Pakistan as an historical error and that given the opportunity they would wish in some way to redress the situation.[44]

The degree and extent of Indian involvement in the civil war has been well documented, and the war has produced several studies from both the Indian and the Pakistani side.[45] While India acted to make the most out of Pakistani difficulties, New Delhi was provoked into action through the fear that an influx of Bengali refugees would complicate matters in India's already troubled north-east. By August 1971, up to ten million Bengalis had crossed into West Bengal and Assam to escape the fighting. Moreover, unsure of the ideological views of many of the refugees India feared that they would add to its problems with left-wing groups already active in West Bengal against a Congress administration.

During the late 1960s West Bengal was the scene of intra-communist violence, and fighting between the left and the Congress Party in power at the centre. The prospect of the 'two Bengals' falling to the left raised the spectre of a united Bengali nation under its own state, and a Marxist one to boot, and gave rise to concern within India over the prospects of her territorial disintegration. India watched throughout the summer of 1971 as the Pakistan military abandoned any real search for a political solution with Mujib Rehman, the leader of the Bengal nationalist party, the Awami

League. His arrest – and incarceration in West Pakistan – marked the beginning of a 'military solution'. By early September, it was clear that India was in favour of intervening directly, having stepped up its covert support for the Bengali rebels. In December 1971, with Indian military forces grouped in the eastern sector ready to 'liberate' East Pakistan, the Pakistan leadership in the west wing launched a pre-emptive air strike in the western sector against Indian airfields, following in outline the earlier strategies of the 1965 campaign.

The resurrection of the Kashmir issue by the Pakistan leadership failed either to distract the Indians from their primary objective of liberating Bengal, or to rally round the Bengalis to an issue that had never really concerned them in the first place. Fighting in the western sector was not as dramatic as that in the eastern sector, although it involved some incursions across the ceasefire line. India's declaration of a unilateral ceasefire in the west on 17 December following the fall of Dhaka (now the capital of Bangladesh) followed some Indian gains across the international border with Pakistan in the west, in the provinces of Sind and Punjab.

Unlike the previous wars, the 1971 conflict fundamentally altered the balance of power within the region. The eastern wing was now an independent state, and erstwhile West Pakistan was in turmoil. The break-up of Pakistan confirmed India's long-held prejudices that religion could not provide the basis for enduring nationalism (and that Congress' political objection to the 'two-nation' theory was largely correct). 1971 confirmed India, in her own eyes at least, as the dominant regional power. The Simla Accord of 1972 (signed in the old summer capital of the British Raj) was the first significant bilateral agreement between India and Pakistan in which New Delhi attempted to get Pakistan to accept the 'realities of power within the sub-continent'. At first it seemed that Pakistan could do little to prevent the Indians from renegotiating events, especially with reference to Kashmir, in their favour.

India was able to bargain territorial gains made in Punjab and Sind for a readjustment of the old UN ceasefire line towards a new LOC in Kashmir which improved India's forward positions. The Simla Accord also opened the way for the eventual recognition of Bangladesh by Pakistan (extended in 1974), and the return of PoWs held in the east. The 1973 repatriation agreement between India and Pakistan was complicated by Pakistan's initial reluctance to deal with Bangladesh, and Bangladeshi determination to place several prominent PoWs on trial in Dhaka. On 9 April 1974 India held a trilateral conference with Pakistan and Bangladesh, which further underscored its new-found influence within the sub-continent.

A great many myths have grown up around the so-called 'spirit of Simla' over the degree of its durability, and the degree of its success for India. Various studies on Indian foreign policy still hail the declaration as India's 'Congress of Vienna', the onset of India's key role as regional manager and regime builder, and the end to Pakistani hopes to be treated as an equal, or to use international pressure to help resolve the Kashmir issue to its liking.[46] While there can be no doubt that India's intention was to try and use the 1971 victory to set the regional agenda in its favour, and to provide the framework within which Indo-Pak relations would evolve, it is questionable whether such an approach succeeded, especially in reference to the Kashmir issue.

Even by 1976, there existed doubt as to how committed Islamabad was to the spirit of Simla. On a visit to Beijing, Bhutto appeared to question Pakistan's acceptance of the principles of bilateralism. In the joint communiqué there appeared the telling lines that while all was well in South Asia 'only the Jammu and Kashmir dispute remains to be resolved peacefully in accordance with the right of self-determination recognised in the United Nations Resolutions and accepted by both India and Pakistan.'[47] The belief that the Simla agreement is still valid in the mid-1990s, when Pakistan has to all intents and purposes reneged on its commitment to bilateralism, is very questionable indeed.

There are several explanations for Pakistan's apparent duplicity over Simla and its post-1972 relationship with India. Pakistan's new civilian leader – Zulfikar Ali Bhutto – was anxious to settle with India on terms that would not discredit him domestically; he was himself atop a fragile and divided state, traumatised by war and the collapse of the east. Initially the mood was one of realism. After the war the *Pakistan Times* noted bleakly: 'we on our part have to rid ourselves of the fiction of equality of status with India. If India plays fair by us, if she does not seek to weaken or isolate us, we should advance rather than checkmate her legitimate regional interests.'[48] But this view did not last, if for the simple reason that India did not appear to play 'fair' with Pakistan's security interests. The Simla negotiations were only concluded after protracted wrangling (and were settled late into the night, since neither side could afford to draw a political blank). The Indian prime minister faced accusations of a 'sell out' since it seemed to several right-wing parties that Pakistan ought perhaps to have been finally dismembered, or certainly taught the lesson it deserved. By the late 1970s, Pakistan had recovered its prestige, even though the civilian government of Zulfikar Bhutto did not long survive. Rizvi has noted that: 'Pakistan has refused to acknowledge [her] inferior status ... despite being truncated in 1971 ... Pakistan remains determined to hold the balance of power in South Asia.'[49]

Although Pakistan's pursuit of military parity against India was severely weakened, it was able to turn more to external help from China and the USA. China was particularly useful to Pakistan during the period of isolation experienced under the Bhutto government, especially between Islamabad and Washington, and could well remain an important source of support during the current disagreements between the USA and its most 'allied ally'.

Bangladesh: the reaction against Indian dominance

A few weeks before his removal from power in November 1989, President Ershad of Bangladesh accused India of engineering popular unrest and assisting – as he put it somewhat obscurely – 'the octopus of destructive politics'. Since the death of Mujib Rehman in 1975, Dhaka has been in the habit of accusing India of 'anti-national designs' either over the suggestion to construct a link canal between the Brahmaputra and the Ganges river systems, or over the construction of the Indian Farakka barrage, across the Ganges itself, and just fifteen kilometres from the Bangladesh border. For two states united by war against Pakistan, the cause of such hostility seems, at first sight, difficult to comprehend. Did not Mujib Rehman fly back to a liberated Bengal via New Delhi, cheered on by a mass crowd of Indians during his stop-over at New Delhi? Did he not, on behalf of the Bengali peoples, swear eternal gratitude to India for coming at their hour of need?

Having grasped the bull by the horns in 1971, India was determined to shape the political future of the new state both in keeping with its wider security interests in the north-east and as an insurance policy against China. This twin approach – a new departure for Indian foreign policy in the region – continued until the basis of a secular Bengali nationalism collapsed, and the language of gratitude turned into charges of political domination.

Between 1971 and 1975 Bangladesh was tied to India through a whole series of bilateral treaties and agreements, and had become by 1975 the largest recipient of Indian aid. Having acted as the 'midwife' of the newest independent state in South Asia, it seemed a natural continuation of a close and intimate relationship. In 1975 Indian aid was in the region of Rs 299.88 crore, almost 60 per cent of India's total foreign outlay. India's total aid since the early 1950s to the Himalayan kingdoms of Nepal and Bhutan came to only Rs 305.32 crore. Even after the sundering of the New Delhi–Dhaka axis, aid programmes continued. By 1979 India's commitment to Bangladesh was Rs 335.27 crore.[50]

Immediately after the 1971 ceasefire had been declared, India granted Bangladesh Rs 25 crore for immediate relief, as well as over £5 million sterling in foreign exchange to help stimulate reconstruction and trade. A majority of the aid programmes between 1971 and 1973 involved foodgrains and edible oils, although by 1974 Indian assistance had broadened out to deal with joint economic ventures in which Indian capital imports would help Bangladesh reconstruct its roads and railways. A 1974 agreement also covered co-operation in the fields of nuclear power and nuclear research, seeking to assist Bangladesh while at the same time to further India's own nuclear expertise.

By 1974 India had also concluded various border demarcations that had been outstanding at the time of East Pakistan's demise in and around the Indian territories of Assam and Tripura. Other agreements involved the incorporation of various Muslim Bengali enclaves into Bangladesh without compensation, although it was only in 1982 that India finally agreed to lease 'in perpetuity' the so-called Tin Bigha corridors that connected Bangladesh with four Muslim enclaves in the Indian state of West Bengal, and even to this day the agreement has not been fully implemented.

The keystone of Indian policy towards Bangladesh – and a vital input into the Bangladeshi perception of Indian intent – was the Twenty-Five Years of Friendship and Co-operation treaty signed in Dhaka on 19 May 1972. This treaty had been consciously modelled on an earlier Indo-Soviet treaty, discussed in chapter 2. The co-operation referred to was as much strategic as it was economic. The treaty spelled out at some length that neither country would participate in any military alliance directed against the other, both would refrain from aggression against each other, neither would give any assistance to a third party involved in an armed conflict against the other, and, in the event of an attack against either, the parties would immediately enter into consultations in order to take measures to eliminate the threat.[51]

In retrospect, given Bangladesh's size relative to India, such a candid assertion of bilateralism could only give rise to mistrust and suspicion. Bangladesh is surrounded by India on all sides, the cultural affinities between the two – refracted by fourteen years within a united Pakistan – could be both supportive and suffocating. To make matters worse, India was quick to send in constitutional advisers, the result being that the 1972 prime ministerial constitution of Bangladesh was a virtual replica of the Indian constitution of 1950, ignoring the presidential forms experienced under Pakistan. Moreover, the 1972 document made no reference to federalism, although district administration was revised and given, in principle, greater scope for revenue collection and development outlays.

By the early 1975 period – when the domestic support for the Mujib regime was melting away in the face of anti-Indian propaganda and accusations of domestic corruption – the left wing of Bangladeshi politics argued that a glorious free Bengal had been reduced to a mere satellite, 'another Himalayan kingdom' within an extended Indian economic zone run by Indian traders and smugglers. To the political right – and in spite of previous charges of collaboration with Pakistan during the civil war – the Muslim fundamentalists charged that Bangladesh had escaped from the Punjabi embrace of West Pakistan only to fall under the Hindu juggernaut.

The domestic events of August 1975 – the killing of a large part of the Rehman family by the military – ended India's hopes of a lasting friendship with Bangladesh, and indeed the hope that Bangladesh would remain democratic. When news reached New Delhi about the murder of Mujib, Indira Gandhi noted in response that 'we feel that there is an effort to disturb stability in the region … we cannot help expressing our deep concern over these events'. Pakistan, afraid that such a statement was the first tentative move for another 'liberation war' (to remove the military and restore a democracy, a move that could have been legally bolstered by the 1972 Friendship Treaty), warned of the serious consequences that would follow from any further Indian intervention.[52]

Bangladesh–Indian relations deteriorated rapidly after August 1975. Most of the Awami League fled to India, while several former guerrillas took to the Myminsingh area of north-eastern Bangladesh to fight against an Islamic restoration under the title of the *Shanti Bahini*, where they remain operative to this day. Although it has been denied on numerous occasions, it is frequently asserted by the Bangladesh authorities that India is supporting the rebels. Over the years successive Indian governments have accused Bangladesh of supporting its own rebellious tribals in the troubled north-eastern states, who are attempting to gain independence from New Delhi. Certainly, illegal Muslim immigrants from Bangladesh have continued to complicate an already delicate ethnic balance.

In 1981 the Indian navy laid claim to Purbasha, an island that had been emerging in the mouth of the Hariya Bhanga river – one of the numerous rivers of the Ganges delta – since the 1970s. Indian attempts in 1984 to position fencing along the West Bengal/Bangladesh border led to incidents between India's BSF and the Bangladeshi Rifles. Following the demolition of the Ayodhya Mosque, Bangladesh formally protested to the Indian government that it was incapable of defending its Muslim citizens, a peculiar echo of the original sentiments of the Lahore declaration.

Pakistani attempts to normalise relations with Bangladesh were complicated by India's role in the liberation of Bangladesh and Islamabad's relationship with the Mujib Rehman regime. Prime Minister Mujib Rehman, the leader of the Bengali Awami League, was determined that before any negotiations could be made to release PoWs, Pakistan must acknowledge Bangladesh as a sovereign nation. This was a bitter pill to swallow, since Pakistan perceived it as a demand conveyed on the back of the Indian army. By 1972 Bhutto had already come to see the Mujib regime as a set of Indian stooges imposed and maintained by New Delhi, and it was this prejudice, along with the problems of domestic reaction to the Simla Agreement, that delayed Pakistani recognition of Bangladesh until 1974. Moreover, Bhutto argued that since a Pakistani army had surrendered to an Indian army, there was no need to bring in any Bengali representatives at all. Relying upon Chinese support, Pakistan also blocked various attempts by India and the Non-Aligned Movement to introduce Bangladesh to a seat in the United Nations.

There were limits to how long the 'new' Pakistan could afford to sulk over the issue of Bangladesh, however. The longer it ignored the proclaimed secular state of Bangladesh, the more deeply entrenched Indian vested interests would become. Yet even after recognition was extended, Pakistan remained aloof from serious involvement until after 1975, and the demise of the pro-Indian government of Mujib Rehman through a military coup. Ironically, it was only when President Bhutto himself had been removed in Pakistan by the army, that Pakistan–Bangladesh relations improved dramatically. China did not recognise Bangladesh until the establishment of the Ziaul–Reham military regime in November 1975. The subsequent restoration of Islam in Bangladesh as the official state religion brought it back into closer relations with Pakistan.

Throughout the 1980s both Pakistan and Bangladesh were committed to creating Islamic republics under the auspices of the military, a common task that created obvious affinities between their foreign policies with respect to secular India and to the Middle East. By 1988 and the death of President Zia, Pakistan returned to a quasi-form of civilian government and in late 1990 Bangladesh had momentarily rid itself of the army and was preparing itself for party-based, parliamentary elections. In what is perhaps a rather curious testimony to the 'two-nation' theory, events within Pakistan and Bangladesh have remained closely associated long after the two wings had appeared to go their separate ways.

Developing close relations with Pakistan was vital for the Bangladeshi policy of escaping Indian dominance, and pressurising the Indians into making some concessions on the pressing issue of shared water resources.

The construction of the Farakka Barrage started in India in 1962. The aim of the project was to occasionally divert water from the Ganges into the Hooghly to prevent the Calcutta–Howrah port complex from silting up, especially during the pre-monsoon period when the flow of the north Indian river systems are dramatically reduced. The barrage would also provide irrigation facilities for India. The then province of East Pakistan objected that the resulting 'theft' of water seriously affected its own irrigation projects, and threatened fresh water supplies further down in the delta by lowering the water table, and increased the risks of contaminating fresh water supplies with sea water.

Extensive consultations between India and Pakistan proved incapable of resolving the issue along the lines of the Indus River Treaty, and the matter was inherited by the Awami League government in 1971. Part of the problem – and a serious one with reference to international law – was India's insistence that the Farakka Barrage was a barrage and Pakistan's insistence that it was in fact a dam. Pakistan referred the matter to the World Bank and to the UN.

In 1972 India and Bangladesh decided to create a permanent Joint Rivers Commission (JRC) to attempt to agree on guidelines for shared usage of the Ganges. Yet by 1975 the talks were stalling amid Bangladeshi accusations of unilateral Indian action just before the onset of the July monsoons. In 1975 Bangladesh accused India of so reducing the water level in the Ganges that the Bangladesh Water Board pumping station at Hardinge Bridge was in danger of stopping, thus jeopardising extensive irrigation works. By 1980 a decision was taken to wind up the JRC and move to a series of interim settlements to share the water on a yearly basis, but none of these have been to the lasting satisfaction of Dhaka.

Furthermore India believes that the problems of shared water resources can be solved by joining the two major river systems in the north-east – the Brahmaputra and the Ganges – by a link canal. This would enable greater control over the flow of the rivers and would help share scarce water resources by transferring water across the watersheds and drainage basins of the two systems if and when it was required. Such a scheme, India believes, would also help trade and commerce throughout the South Asia region. The canal would start and end in Indian territory but would almost be entirely located within Bangladesh, cross-cutting the Barind Upland and separating the extreme north of the country from the delta area. Bangladeshi objections are based on ecological, technical as well as strategic grounds.

Bangladesh has suggested an alternative scheme, which involves the construction of storage reservoirs and canal complexes in Nepal and India away to the north-east of the sub-continent. Such a scheme has the apparent advantages of providing Nepal with a riverine outlet through Bangladesh (made possible by canal links across five rivers), as well as giving Nepal and north-west India access to hydro-electric power stations. Despite Nepalese agreement, India objects on the grounds that this scheme is too expensive, that it would involve too many other states, and it would flood valuable (and scarce) land in the Hindi-speaking states of northern India. In turn various Bangladeshi governments have pointed out that even the Brahmaputra–Ganges canal could not be a solely bilateral affair, since it would have to involve China as a 'watershed' state. This in turn would raise a hornets' nest of legal claims and counter-claims in a part of the world already thick in territorial disputes, especially between India and China.

Since 1975 Bangladesh has returned to the former Pakistan practice of internationalising the Farakka Barrage by referring it to the UN at the opening of the 31st session of the General Assembly (where both India and the Soviet Union protested), the Islamic Conference of Foreign Ministers, and to India's particular irritation, the summit of the Non-Aligned Movement in Colombo 1976. India has consistently refused to have any outside mediation in the affair, despite several precedents set in both the developed and developing world, and despite the involvement of the International Bank for Reconstruction and Development (IBRD) in the Indus Water Treaty.

In recent years – based upon the creation of the South Asian Association of Regional Co-operation (SAARC) in 1985 – Bangladesh has tried to further involve the other regional states, especially Nepal, in a comprehensive settlement. Yet India's mistrust of multilateralism remains. On 2 June 1985, Rajiv Gandhi and President Ershad signed a Moratorium of Understanding (MOU) and decided to reconvene a Joint Committee of Experts which, like the JRC before it, has so far failed to come to any acceptable agreements. It is not known what policies Begum Zia's government will adopt. Her husband Zial-Reham was the architect of a Bangladesh foreign policy that sought to distance the state from Indian dominance. The opposition to the canal scheme remains.

Finally, and unlike any other state in South Asia with the possible exception of Nepal, Bangladesh's regional policy is totally determined by its general poverty, and the degree to which its sovereignty can be compromised through environmental disasters. Bangladesh is not a powerful state in military terms. In 1989–90 its army numbered some 90,000 personnel, its navy was made up of three ex-British frigates, and its airforce consisted of 64 combat aircraft.[54] In the late 1980s most of these units were busy dealing with domestic security matters as President Ershad attempted to address his country's economic ills, and shore up his own political future. In 1990, with an estimated GDP of US$ 19.01 billion, the World Bank listed Bangladesh as the fifth poorest country in the world.

The explanations for this continuing poverty are complex. In part they are linked with political incompetence and war, in part still the misfortune of partition and the consequences of the 1971 civil war. In a short but precise lecture to the British Royal Asian Society in 1988, Hugh Evans noted simply that 'Bangladesh is just over 16 years old ... For a people to have to build a new state from scratch is unfortunate. To have to do so twice in 25 years seems almost extravagant'.[55] Bangladeshi priorities are first and foremost the need for economic and industrial development, and since 1971 these goals require greater – not less – regional co-operation.

Between 1980 and 1988 Bangladesh witnessed two devastating monsoons, two droughts, one typhoon and one earthquake. The floods of 1988 alone resulted in over US$ 2 billion of damage. There now exists overwhelming evidence that increased run-off in the northern Himalayas, caused by deforestation in Nepal and north-west India, has contributed to the ferocity of the floods and to the high degree of sedimentation. In 1988 a Bangladesh English-language paper noted that 'the dimensions of this year's floods should make it clear to all that the complete destruction of Bangladesh is now a distinct possibility'.[56]

In April 1991, coastal Bangladesh was hit by a typhoon which claimed over 200,000 lives. Bangladesh's recognition that only regional co-operation can bring any lasting relief explains why Bangladesh took the initiative to create the SAARC in the early 1980s, but it has been difficult to prove to India that a forum for regional co-operation is anything other than an attempt by the other states to gang up against it. Yet any analysis of Bangladesh's foreign policy must stress the importance of environmental degradation. Policy formulation must be premised on the fact that 'the whole notion of security as traditionally understood in terms of political and military threats must be expanded to include the growing impact of environmental disaster'.[57]

Sino-Indian relations

What makes Pakistan's intransigence so irritating to enthusiastic students of India's strategic interests is that it detracts attention away from what some analysts believe is New Delhi's 'real' rival, the People's Republic of China (PRC).[58] Much has been made about the asymmetry of Sino-Indian relations, with China's cultural and political heartlands far off on the Pacific coast, while in contrast, the remote Tibetan plateau looks down on to the Hindi heartlands of the Gangetic plains. Far from facing each other (as with India and Pakistan), India and China sit back to back, their elites facing in differing directions. This asymmetry is given particular relevance since, as a nuclear power, China can potentially strike at India's main population centres while India cannot yet hit at China's, although recent missile tests have underlined India's clear potential in intermediate range missiles. India remains concerned about China's nuclear capabilities and the current nuclear modernisation programme. Because of technical bilateral agreements with Pakistan, the Chinese bomb is part of the general Indian anxiety over the 'Islamic bomb'. Ashok Kapor has noted that 'the Indian perception of its role in Asia needs to be viewed in conjunction with the Chinese world view' because India has long recognised that, unlike Pakistan, China is both an ideological and a cultural force to compete with throughout the Third World and throughout international politics generally.[59]

While formally outside the region, China is linked to India's immediate security environment because of unresolved border disputes with India to the north-east (including claims on Bhutan and Sikkim, and the present Indian states of Arunchal Pradesh and Assam) and to the north-west area of Aksai Chin, adjacent to Ladakh.

Although India has never claimed Tibet, it has implicitly supported Tibetan claims for greater autonomy from China both in the late 1950s, and during subsequent periods of political instability. India provides the exiled Dalai Lama (the spiritual leader of the Tibetan Buddhists) a home in Dharamsala, in the Indian state of Himachal Pradesh. Interestingly enough, India has not granted the Dalai Lama the status of a government in exile, and the Indian government remained suprisingly reticent in 1987 over China's suppression of Tibetan Buddhist agitations in and around Lhasa.

Even during the heyday of Sino-Indian co-operation, from 1949 until 1959, China did not drop its claims to substantially large areas of Indian territory. In 1950 and 1959, the communists moved to substantiate claims to Tibet despite Indian protests. The 1954

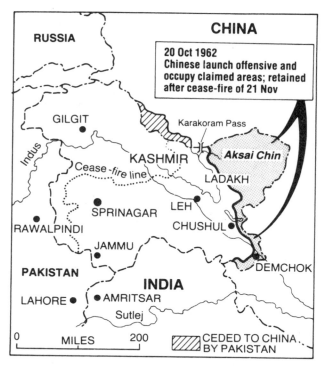

Map 2 China, India, Aksai Chin

Agreement on Tibet (that recognised Tibet as an 'autonomous' region of China) established the importance of the 'five principles' of *Panscheel* which were: mutual respect for each other's territorial integrity, mutual non-aggression, mutual non-interference, equality and mutual benefit, and peaceful coexistence. Praised as 'bold, wholesome principles' they did not survive the border crisis of 1962 (although, as shall be discussed, they remain as the basis of the Non-Aligned Movement).

Since 1962 the implied Chinese negotiating position has been a trade-off between disputed territories over the MacMahon Line in the north-east for recognised Chinese sovereignty over Aksai Chin in the north-west. Zhou En Lai's 1960 statement referred to 'recipricol abandonment of conflicting aims in the eastern and the western sectors' but India has refused to budge from what it considers its rightful inheritance.[60]

The Sino-Indian borders remained unresolved throughout the British period and were not, like the Kashmir crisis, a product of British disengagement. Settlements between the Raj and Manchu China at Simla in 1914 made vague references to watersheds and 'natural boundaries' without verification, and with reference to remote areas that were either poorly mapped, or largely remained unexplored. Anxious to avoid great power rivalry with the Russian Empire, the British – masters of practicality – had prefered the notion of 'buffers' and 'spheres of influence' to actually demarcated borders. To the players of the Great Game, China had not been a serious concern at all, and prior to the successful conclusion of the Communist Revolution in 1949, no government in Beijing was in a position to reclaim so-called lost territory.

In 1949, Mao Tse Tung denounced the 1914 Simla treaty as one of a whole series of unequal agreements forced on China by the European powers, and one that would be renegotiated. India's subsequent inflexibility, and its refusal to depart from a previous British discourse of demarcation, frustrated China and finally precipitated an act of Chinese aggression. While Indian intransigence does not excuse the use of force, it illustrates that Sino-Indian negotiations approach the matter from quite different premises. In 1987 Raju Thomas noted that: 'the border issue is not a difficult one *provided that the Chinese accept* the Himalayan Crest and the Indus river watershed as the legitimate and logical borders between the [two] countries'.[61] The problem arises from the Chinese refusal to recognise the 'legitimate' and 'logical' borders provided by geographical concepts such as 'crests' and watersheds. More recently Ramesh Thakur has stated that 'the Indian position on the border dispute appears to be inflexible even to sympathetic observers because it is based upon a legalistic framework of questionable authenticity with no scope for political manoeuvring'.[62]

In turn India denounces Chinese assumptions of pre-1949 borders as arrogant and unrealistic. It is within this impasse, and in spite of several political initiatives from both sides, that the border issue has come to rest. India reinstated ambassadorial links with Beijing in 1976, despite earlier Chinese complaints over the merger of Sikkim with India in 1975, Chinese support for tribal rebels situated in the north-east, and rhetorical support for the various Marxist (so-called Naxalite) violence against New Delhi since the mid-1960s. In 1978, the Indian Foreign Minister A. B. Vaypayee went on a goodwill tour, and in 1981 the Chinese Foreign Minister Huang Hua visited New Delhi. During the ASIAD Games in New Delhi, in 1982, China complained over the presence of an Arunachal Pradesh dancing troupe in the opening festival. The Rajiv Gandhi visit of 1988 – the first visit of an Indian prime minister since Nehru's – did not visibly improve the pace of border negotiations.

In 1988–89, the Indian Defence Ministry's annual report still played the 'China card' as part of the justification to maintain Indian defence expenditure. Yet, since the 1962 war, and apart from the odd border panics such as those that occurred in 1987 along the Bhutanese/Arunachal Pradesh sector of the MacMahon Line (and earlier around the Sumdurong Chu district), Sino-Indian relations have been significantly less tense than Indo-Pak relations. The two sets of equations cannot be separated because of the degree of Sino-Pakistan co-operation that began in the mid-1960s.

If historical and cultural misperceptions lie at the root of the Sino-Indian stand-off, they are further complicated by the fact that China's claims in the north-western sector impinged upon parts of Azad Kashmir and Indian-controlled Ladakh. Parts of Azad Kashmir, having been under effective Pakistani administration since 1948, were given to China through the Sino-Pakistan border agreement of 1964 despite the fact that the area was in effect claimed by India.[63] Indian protests were ignored. Thus shared perceptions of India provided the cement between Pakistan and China, in spite of Ayub Khan's keenly felt anti-communism, and the antipathy of the Americans to China prior to the 1972 breakthrough. After the 1965 war (when the Americans had temporarily withdrawn military assistance from Pakistan) China stepped into the breach as a major arms supplier to Pakistan and as a significant giver of aid. Throughout the 1970s, China provided Pakistan with about US$ 2.6 billion of weapons, and various soft loans and grants.

Because of this *entente cordiale*, India sees Pakistan and China as part of the same security dilemma. In the middle of the August war in 1965, China demanded that India should withdraw various observation posts from Sikkim that were apparently violating the border, thus raising the possibility of a two-front war. The fear that China would come to Pakistan's aid during a war with India has had a profound influence upon India's perception of its own legitimate defence requirements. The construction of the strategically significant Karakoram Pass highway (that opened in 1978) further raised the possibility of Chinese forces being deployed to reinforce Pakistan in any future Kashmiri conflict. Yet China's failure to come to Pakistan's help in 1971 following India's invasion of East Pakistan was seen as a telling failure. Another important obstacle to Sino-Indian relations has been the degree of co-operation between the Soviet Union and India after the onset of the Sino-Soviet split, although with the collapse of bipolarity, this particular threat perception has been substantially moderated.

The Himalayan kingdoms of Nepal and Bhutan

In 1989, P. N. Haksar, a retired senior civil servant in the Ministry of Foreign Affairs, and an influential principal private secretary to Indira Gandhi, noted that 'India should not be concerned about Nepal. If they want to play their China card let them, it is of no consequence.'[64] Since 1988 various Nepali communiqués stated that in retaliation for an independent foreign policy (allegedly involving an arms deal with China signed in 1988), India had closed down all but two of the fifteen trade crossings into India which were vital for its survival. In 1989 India refused to renew the separate Trade and Transfer Agreements, arguing that it was New Delhi's wish for them to be negotiated separately. By late 1989 the economic effects of the alleged 'embargo' were serious enough for the IMF to announce approved special drawing rights (SDRs) of up to US\$ 9,500,000 for immediate economic relief. World Bank estimates in late 1990 calculated that India's unilateral action had seriously reduced Nepal's economic prospects and was responsible for a virtual zero growth rate in the financial year 1989–90.[65] India initially denied that this unilateral action was in retaliation for the purchase of Chinese arms, and cited the Nepalese refusal in 1988 to grant work permits to Indian residents, or deal with the problems of smuggling and re-exporting Indian produce across the Indo-Nepalese border without due payment of sales taxes and customs.

India's policy towards Nepal gave rise to strong anti-Indian sentiments within the Nepalese court because it coincided with renewed Indian support for a widespread popular movement to reinstate a multiparty democracy after a long period of partyless, *panchayat* government. In a recent article, Leo Rose has speculated that the possible explanations for India's attitude towards Nepal are linked to several factors. One factor concerns the Nepali government awarding a building contract to a Chinese construction company, despite the closeness of the Indian border and the risks of spying. Another factor certainly seems to involve the selling of arms, but most critically, the recent argument seems to have been started by 'a secret agreement between China and Nepal, apparently concluded in the late fall of 1988, providing for the exchange of intelligence'.[66] Even if such claims can be substantiated, can India's actions be justified, or are its actions towards Nepal merely the result of paranoia?

Nepal's perception of India is a stereotypical case of the 'small state' complex, in which it has attempted to play off Indian dominance by making diplomatic overtures towards China. This is also true of Bhutan, since both states exist in the cultural–political 'grey area' where Indian and Chinese cultural traditions mix. In 1768 Prithvinarayan Shah, the Raja of Gorkha announced to his court that Nepal was like a 'yam between two boulders' and that their policies to British India and Manchu China should, while attempting to play them off for mutual benefit, provoke neither. Such a sound recommendation is still valid, although the logical consequences of such an understanding significantly constrain Nepal (and Bhutan's) independence. Moreover, the geographical asymmetry between India and China means that Nepal is in greater need of Indian co-operation than it is of Chinese, a reality not lost on Nepal's political leadership.

Ramesh Thapur has noted generally that: 'India views China as an intruder within the region, while China believes that her participation within South Asia is legitimate [and] other states welcome the Chinese counterweight to Indian pretensions to regional hegemony.'[67] This is particularly the case with Nepal and Bhutan. These kingdoms occupy the strategic 'commanding heights' of the Himalayan watershed – the so-called 'logical' border between India and China. These states were directly involved in the Sino-Indian Cold War that started after the assertion of Chinese control over Tibet in 1959. Nepal had established diplomatic relations with China in 1955, and following India's lead on the 1954 agreement over 'the autonomous region of Tibet' has used the five principles of *Panscheel* to govern bilateral relations with Beijing. Over the years, and especially after the 1962 border war, the degree of flexibility in Nepali–Indian and Bhutan–Indian relations has thus varied considerably under the influence of Sino-Indian relations. Periods of high tension between Beijing and New Delhi have increased the flexibility of these kingdoms although it has never weakened the Indian resolve to retain them as, to all intents and purposes, buffer states.

In 1988, Nepal finally concluded a border settlement with China, based upon the principle that a border inspection will verify the situation on the ground every five years, a telling diplomatic victory that further isolated India as one of the only remaining states yet to settle its borders with China. Since the 1980s Nepal has benefited from a significant amount of Chinese aid. In 1986 it was estimated that China contributed about US$ 5. 9 million to Nepal (twice as much as the 1979 figure, although less than half of the Indian figure) and that Chinese experts were working on about twenty projects. As already noted, Chinese co-operation on various road-building projects has, however, touched upon Indian security concerns, especially in the sensitive Xianping district which in turn borders on 'Azad Kashmir'.[68]

This said, however, Bhutan and Nepal have broadly accepted their so-called 'special relationship with India'. Their socio-cultural links with India are obvious enough – Nepal is closely associated to India through Hinduism[69] – while Nepal and Bhutan are interlinked in terms of ethnicity and language, especially with spoken Nepali.[70] For reasons of size, Bhutan's relationship with Delhi is more direct. In 1950, India and Nepal signed a treaty of 'everlasting peace and friendship', while in 1954 an *aide memoire* issued in New Delhi suggested closer association between India and Nepal on matters of foreign policy, especially in relation to China and Tibet.[71] In 1965 New Delhi and Kathmandu signed an 'arms assistance agreement' which recognised the rights of Nepal to arm itself from anyone, except China, and only when India could not itself provide the weapons. It was this agreement that Nepal had appeared to violate in 1988.

The intimacy of these complex socio-economic and cultural links – as is so often the case within the region – is as much a source of tension within bilateral relations as they are a source of agreement. Moreover, such links tend to extend domestic political traumas in one state into the domestic political arena of another. In 1989 the Nepali community within Bhutan set up the Nepal Forum for Human Rights to defend their culture and political rights against the 1988 'code of conduct' which aimed to discourage the use of Nepali, and to defend the land rights of the indigenous Bhutanese. Such a proclamation is indicative of the ethnic animosity between the Nepali immigrants and Hinduism and the 'indigenous' *Drukpa* tribes who are Buddhist. Recent attempts to control immigration, and strip descendants of Nepali immigrants of Bhutanese citizenship have led to moments of tension between Nepal and Bhutan, and to political violence within Bhutan against the monarchy.[72]

The origins of the 'special relationships' between these states and India originated under the British. In 1941 King Jigme Wangchuk of Bhutan extended a previous treaty signed with the British allowing India to 'guide and direct' its foreign policy. Following the agreement between Bhutan and British India in 1911, the Bhutanese Maharaja came under pressure from the Chinese for signing an agreement with the British without first referring it to the Emperor. The British agent protested against this 'Chinese habit of tentative aggression, which if unchecked is simply escalated'. Since its gradual emergence as a state after 1947, Bhutan has been sure to avoid excessive complications with China, and its implicit use of China to concentrate the mind of the Indian External Affairs ministry has not been as forthright as Nepal's. Following the 1962 war, India and Bhutan undertook to clarify their defence positions over Chinese aggression, tentative or otherwise. Unlike Nepal, Bhutan – probably for reasons of size – is more willing to accept Indian hegemony and the benefits of Indian protection, in a way reminiscent of Paramountcy.

While Bangladesh has the advantages of independent access to the region (and the wider international community) through the Bay of Bengal, Nepal, Bhutan (and until 1975, the Kingdom of Sikkim) are landlocked political entities that rely almost exclusively upon Indian co-operation for their economic well-being. Apart from a small trade relationship with Tibet virtually all of Nepal's imports and exports must be transported through India, and India provides by far the largest market for Nepalese goods. In 1989 Nepal imported US$ 199.20 million worth of goods from India (the next largest market being Singapore at US$ 66.89 million), while India dominated Nepalese exports. In 1989 the Indian market absorbed US$ 55.4 million. Nepal and Bhutan have also received large amounts of Indian aid in terms of both loans and grants. Between 1954 and 1973 India provided Nepal with Rs 11,049 lakhs, over 80 per cent of total Nepali aid, although this figure decline after 1971 when Nepal turned increasingly to multilateral sources from the IBRD and the UN.

With India's economic dominance has also come the charge of political interference within the internal affairs of the kingdoms. That this interference has taken place is impossible to deny, but India claims moral and ideological justifications behind its invitations to support nascent democratic forces. There are obvious parallels here with the Bangladesh situation, although unlike Bangladesh, in both Nepal and Bhutan authoritarian forces as such are associated not with the military, but with courtly faction and established aristocratic families. In 1950–51, India intervened within the domestic politics of Nepal to rally the pro-democracy movement under the leadership of the monarch against the powerful Rana family, and has since then been closely associated with political developments.

In 1961 India implicitly condemned King Mahendra's decision to ban political parties by offering support to the outlawed Nepalese Congress, and a well-organised communist party. As in Bangladesh and Pakistan, India has supported calls for a democratic government, although following the Sino-Indian border clash of 1962 India reconciled its differences with the Nepalese court by curtailing support for the pro-democracy forces from inside India. Just before the border clash King Mahendra had visited Beijing and had been able to persuade the Chinese to implicitly condemn Indian interference, a move calculated to irritate New Delhi.

India resumed the rights of the paramount power over Sikkim after 1947, along with the other kingdoms, although an actual agreement was not signed until 1950. Indian involvement within an internal dispute between a popular-based political movement and the *Chogyal* (monarchy) over the degree of democratic involvement, resulted in Sikkim's eventual incorporation into India.

The Sikkim Agreement of 8 May 1973 ended a period of internal instability in which both the *Chogyal* and the Indian government 'recognised the need to establish responsible government'. Under the auspices of the Indian Electoral Commission, and a nominated Indian chief executive to advise the monarch, Sikkim entered into a new and more turbulent phase of political development, in which the Sikkim National Congress, and some other small parties, pressed for parliamentary government. In 1974, the *Chogyal* was converted into a constitutional monarch presiding over an elected cabinet and was then eventually 'deposed' in 1975. Preparations were then made for popular elections within the framework of the Indian Union.[73]

The integration (or, from an alternative perspective, the annexation) of Sikkim furthered the anxiety in Nepal and especially Bhutan that India's ultimate policy was to absorb them within the Indian political system. It is also possible that the culmination of India's policy towards Bhutan will end up in its 'integration' into the Indian Union, since the parallels with Sikkim are much more relevant for India than for Nepal. Since 1975, not long after the coronation of King Birendra in 1972, Nepal has redoubled its attempts to differentiate its foreign policy from India by calling for an internationally recognised Himalayan peace zone, recognised by the UN, thus ignoring India's stress upon its regional primacy and in apparent disregard for India's strategic obsessions with the Himalayan crests.

The 'yam between two boulders' metaphor is also useful, if less accurate, for an understanding of the Himalayan kingdoms' approach to Pakistan, although Islamabad is much more removed both physically and culturally. Since the late 1980s – with the intensification of regional co-operation – Nepal and Bhutan have been brought closer to Pakistan, Sri Lanka and Bangladesh. Nepal supports Bangladesh objections to the link canal proposal, while Bangladesh and Pakistan support Nepal's calls for a Himalayan peace zone. Nepali–Pakistan relations have flourished 'at arm's length', with Pakistan encouraging Nepal to be independent from India's foreign policy. In 1984 Nepal signed a joint trade agreement with Pakistan in an attempt to diversify its trade relations throughout the region. In 1989 the Pakistani minister for finance promised to step in to the Nepali–Indian breach with credits worth US$ 1 million.

Sri Lanka

Critics of India's regional policy usually cite the example of Indo-Bangladesh relations, or recently Nepal, as an example of how *not* to win favours with small, relatively defenceless states. By the late 1980s some critics were using the experience of Sri Lanka to argue

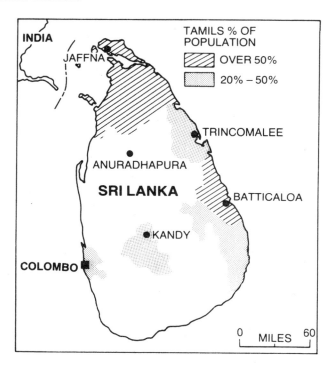

TAMILS % OF POPULATION

OVER 50%

20% – 50%

INDIA

JAFFNA

TRINCOMALEE

ANURADHAPURA

SRI LANKA

BATTICALOA

KANDY

COLOMBO

0 MILES 60

Map 3 Sri Lanka

that, far from constructing some durable system based upon Indian hegemony, New Delhi's regional designs merely fuelled anti-Indian sentiment, and further eroded the possibility of long-term regional stability.

In 1987 it was announced that India and Sri Lanka had signed a dramatic accord wherein India would deploy an Indian Peace-Keeping Force (IPKF) to assist the Sri Lankan government in solving the 'Tamil problem'. The Indian government felt it necessary to intervene because the Sri Lankan Tamils no longer trusted the Sri Lankan government (made up predominantly of Sinhalese) and because New Delhi was afraid that Tamils living in India were offering support to the rebels without official sanction. Having convened various meetings between the Tamil militants, (primarily the Tamil Tigers of Eelam), the parliamentary-orientated Tamil United Liberation Front (TULF) and the Sri Lankan government throughout the

1985–86 period, the Rajiv Gandhi government decided that the time had come for direct Indian intervention.

The so-called IPKF was a veritable failure. In 1989, following increased demands from the Sri Lankan President R. Premadasa that Indian troops must withdraw from Sri Lanka by 31 December 1990, India's attempts to give Sri Lanka's Tamil minority greater constitutional protection had failed. On the date of their eventual withdrawal on 24 March 1990, after almost three years in action and three months after the deadline set by the Sri Lankan government, the Indian army had lost 1,100 men, and had failed to assist the government of Sri Lanka to find a political settlement of the Tamil problem.

While both India and Sri Lanka wish to replace the accord with some form of friendship treaty, they disagree profoundly over its contents. India is anxious to retain the recognition of Indian primacy contained within the accord, while Sri Lanka is determined to enshrine the principle of mutual consultation and joint 'co-operation' only. Unlike the case of Bangladesh, that of Sri Lanka is even more damning since Indo-Sri Lankan relations have traditionally been friendly, based upon a shared commitment to non-alignment and free from the legacies of either partition or secession. Yet like the other small states in the South Asian region, Sri Lanka's geographical location is of strategic importance to India and the Indian Ocean, and has since the time of the British been incorporated within Indian defence policies.

K. M. Panikkar, in his influential book *India and the Indian Ocean*, noted that Sri Lanka was intimately linked to India's security, although he refrained from spelling out the consequences of this. This geographical proximity is underscored by the clear ethnic–linguistic relationship between the Tamil majority province of India (Tamil Nadu) and the Sri Lankan Tamils. Sri Lankan Tamils make up approximately 18 per cent of the island population, a minority within a predominantly Sinhalese society.

Other minorities include 'Moors' and Eurasians. These ethno-linguistic identities cut across religious identities. Tamils are predominantly Hindu, but some are Muslim. Sinhalese speakers are predominantly Buddhists but some are Protestant and Catholic Christians. Again, despite its size, Sri Lanka duplicates the socio-ethnic complexities found throughout the South Asian region. The deterioration in Tamil–Sinhalese relations on the island was one of the main incentives for Indian intervention, as well as rumours of extra-regional help.

Sri Lanka is fifty times smaller than India, and is at one stage separated by a mere twenty miles of water. At the time of independence Sri Lanka had no defined maritime border with India through the Palk Straits and had inherited the problem of stateless Indian Tamils, brought over from Tamil Nadu in the nineteenth century to work the plantations. These were in need of repatriation or settlement. While all the above factors did not amount to a very high or imminent 'threat perception' from India, they have encouraged a certain degree of anxiety which noticeably increased during the 1980s.

Sri Lanka's response to India's physical domination of the region has been to evolve a careful balance of intra-regional relations (with India, Pakistan and China) with wider international links, initially through the Commonwealth. As early as 1947 the Sri Lankan delegation to the South-East Asian Prime Minister's Conference of New Delhi, referred to the dangers of the smaller states falling under the domination 'emanating' from either China or India and stressed the need for multilateralism.[74] Again, as in all the other smaller states, this commitment contrasted with India's growing determination to deal with each state bilaterally.

Indo-Sri Lankan relations were complicated by Sri Lanka's close links with the Commonwealth under its first United National Party (UNP) governments between 1947 and 1952, and 1952 and 1956, which opened up the possibility of Sri Lanka offering military bases to Western powers. Moreover, Prime Minister Sir John Kotelawala was virulently anti-communist and caused various 'scenes' at the Bandung Afro-Asian conference of 1955 by denoucing communism. Although they endeared him to the Pakistanis (and the Americans), such incidents only served to embarrass and irritate Nehru, who was still convinced that close Sino-Indian relations could develop, in spite of the outstanding territorial disagreement, and that communism ought to be seen as a legitimate alternative to capitalism.[75]

Although Kotelawala made several accusations against both China and the USSR for offering material assistance to communist groups in Sri Lanka, such statements did not rule out a realistic appraisal of China's uses. Sri Lanka recognised China in 1950 (following the British decision) and signed a rubber–rice barter agreement with China in 1952 which enabled Sri Lanka to import cheap rice and bolster up demand from its rubber plantations. Following a change in government after 1956 and the election of a socialist-orientated United Front, Sri Lanka pursued various diplomatic links with the communist powers and established cordial relations with China and the Soviet Union. Typical of Sri Lankan flexibility, following the Sino-Soviet split, Colombo attempted to balance its relations with the two communist giants.

The 1956–60 socialist government brought India and Sri Lanka to closer co-operation and facilitated agreements over various foreign and domestic issues. The so-called Shastri–Sirima agreement signed in 1964, and the later 1974 agreement between Mrs Gandhi and Mrs Bandaranaike solved the Indian Tamil problem, although it understated the probable number of forced repatriations resulting from the difficulties of illiterate and poor Tamils 'proving' citizenship through documentation and family records.[76] 1974 also saw the demarcation of the maritime border in the Palk straits and some settlement of the wider matter of territorial waters, an issue that had been aggravated by India's unilateral extension of its territorial waters in 1956 and 1957. The matter of extended 'zones' eventually involved a trilateral agreement between India, Sri Lanka and the Maldives that has yet to be concluded, but which is now on the agenda of SAARC. India claims an extended economic zone across the Indian Ocean of 715,000 square miles, and 'primary access' to a further six million square miles, and implicit dominance of Sri Lanka's own maritime interests.

Regardless of the vagaries of party politics – and there have been more frequent changes of elected government in Sri Lanka than in any other state of South Asia – the one theme that emerges is the theme of balance. At critical moments, when the regional framework has been disturbed by war Sri Lanka has found itself in a delicate position. A policy of strict neutrality throughout all three Indo-Pak wars has led in some cases to charges of being anti-Indian. During the Indo-China war of 1962 Sri Lanka convened a meeting of the so-called Colombo powers to try and bring China and India to the negotiating table. This was in spite of the fact that earlier the Chinese repression of Tibetan autonomy and the flight of the Dalai Lama had adversely affected Buddhist sentiments on the island, and caused the government to call for a peaceful solution based upon the 'five principles' of *Panscheel*.

During the Indo-Pak war of 1971 Sri Lanka would not yield to Indian requests to ban the use of airport facilities by Pakistan, although Colombo insisted that flights were being inspected to ensure that no military supplies or personnel were finding their way into 'East Pakistan'. Sri Lanka was also extremely late in recognising the independent status of Bangladesh for fear of offending either Pakistan or China. It was only after fifty countries had extended diplomatic recognition to Bangladesh, that Sri Lanka agreed to do the same, on 5 April 1971 (over four months after India). Even then there was some ambivalence as to how it was to conduct relations with Dhaka until the wider regional patterns had established themselves. Sri Lanka took several more years to establish a residential High Commissioner in Dhaka.

Sri Lanka's relations with India and China have also to an extent been characterised by economic considerations, especially aid. Under the anti-communist proclivities of governments formed by the United National Party, most of Sri Lanka's foreign aid came from multilateral sources such as the Colombo Plan, or direct from Western countries. After 1956 Sri Lanka began to receive various economic resources from Eastern bloc countries, and by 1964–65, China was supplying Rs 18.4 million, compared to Rs 2.4 million from the United Kingdom.[77] Between 1970 and 1976, the socialist government of Mrs Bandaranaike received Rs 421.9 million in interest-free loans from China.

Apart from Indian financial resources sent to Sri Lanka via the Colombo Plan, bilateral Indian aid has been until recently in the form of technical assistance under a Joint Commission. Since the early 1980s Indian loans and assistance – tied in part to the issues of the Tamil problem – have increased dramatically. Part of the Indo-Sri Lankan accord dealt with financial and technical assistance schemes. Yet, as with the economic dimensions of the pre-1975 Indo-Bangladesh agreements the extent of these economic and trading incentives has quickly furthered anti-Indian sentiments, especially amongst the violently inclined Sinhalese nationalist party, the JVP. Unlike the Bangladeshi example however, the Sri Lankan economy is far more viable and the basic human indices of development much higher.

The Sri Lankan Tamil demand for Eelam – the creation of a separate Tamil state that would involve the partitioning of the island – has dominated Indo-Sri Lankan relations since the early 1980s. Sri

Lankan attempts to deal decisively with Tamil militants through the large-scale deployment of its security forces in the north and around Jaffna led to protests from Tamil Nadu, and accusations within the Indian parliament that Sri Lanka was killing innocent Tamil civilians. Such remarks led to vigorous protests from Sri Lanka. On 22 March 1984 *India Today*, a pretigious Indian news magazine, published a report that revealed 'terrorist' training camps in Tamil Nadu, revelations that were subsequently denied by New Delhi.

Outraged, the Sri Lankan government purchased vast numbers of the magazine and sent them out to the international community as proof that India was interfering in the internal affairs of the country. Concerns about Indian 'designs' – a curious echo of the Pakistani and Bangladeshi fears – led to the same demands that Sri Lanka must seek external, extra-regional help. This predominantly Sinhalese perception of Indian intentions was again based upon a reading of Indian actions in 1971, and Indian assistance (at first covertly) for the Bengali rebels. How could the island best defend itself against its giant neighbour? Some even pointed to a previous defence agreement signed with the British in 1947 which had never been invoked. Siri Perera QC, and former High Commissioner to Britain, hinted that Sri Lanka ought to forge an alliance with its ancient Buddhist associate, China.

Such implied extra-regionalism – leading to the involvement of Israeli and Pakistani intelligence sources – merely compounded the domestic pressure from Tamil Nadu and forced New Delhi to 'act decisively'. Rajiv Gandhi escalated Indian involvement prior to the actual signing of the accord by sanctioning a small-scale naval relief operation – and when this failed – authorising an airdrop of food over Jaffna in blatant violation of Sri Lankan airspace, with a provocative and gratuitous display of newly purchased Mirage 2000 jets.

It was in such circumstances that Jayewardene and the UNP probably decided to invite the Indians in, rather than resist unwarranted interference. It is most likely that the 'invitation' – sanctioned by the cordial exchange of letters – was exacted under some pressure. It is not known with any certainty which of the two pressures – fear of domestic entanglements or foreign complications – set New Delhi on the course of mediation. In one of the annexes of the Indo-Sri Lankan Accord, Rajiv Gandhi noted in a letter to the then President of the Sri Lankan Republic:

Conscious of the friendship between our two countries stretching over two millennia ... your excellency and myself will reach an early understanding about the relevance and employment of foreign military and intelligence personnel with a view to ensuring that such presences will not prejudice Indo-Sri Lankan relations.[78]

The accord also attempted to ensure that India had a prominent role in the future training of Sri Lanka's security and intelligence forces and attempted to ensure that Sri Lanka would purchase Indian arms and weapons, along lines similar to the Indian–Nepal treaty.

Far from conveying the impression of a benign, non-aligned state, India's action towards Sri Lanka gave the overwhelming impression that India was bullying its neighbours into submission, a situation subsequently supported by the Indian–Nepal crisis. Both Pakistan and Bangladesh supported the subsequent calls by the Sri Lankan government for India to withdraw. The Indian presence on the island became a key part of the 1988 Sri Lankan presidential election campaign. India's apparent refusal to leave, despite continual pressure from the Sri Lankan government – brought Indo-Sri Lankan relations to an all-time low, and isolated India further within the region. Since March 1990, when India finally completed its withdrawal, the Sri Lankan government has resumed massive military operations against the Tamil rebels. In late January 1991, New Delhi dismissed the state government of Tamil Nadu for, amongst other things, close links with Tamil rebels in the north-eastern state. The Sri Lankan Tamil crisis remains. By 1995, despite a ceasefire agreed by a newly elected government in Colombo and the Tamil Tigers in August 1994, the fighting was continuing with renewed vigour. India's official position under the Rao government had been to remain aloof, although there is clear evidence that implies covert Indian naval support to the Sri Lankan navy in stopping smuggled supplies reaching the Tamil provinces across the Palk straits.

Summary

In 1988 – while engaged in Sri Lanka – India also went to the assistance of the Gayoom government in the Maldives following an attempted coup by Tamil militants from Sri Lanka who had put ashore on inflatables. These remote islands – consisting of over 2,500 low-lying coral atolls, of which only 200 are inhabited – were declared a republic in 1967 following the overthrow of the Sultan.

Predominantly Muslim, the political system is presidential, with a cabinet (the *Mahjlis*) constituted at the president's pleasure. The citizens of the atolls elect a lower chamber, while legislation conforms to the concepts of Islamic law laid down in the Shariat. As an Islamic republican state without political parties, the Maldives are closer to Pakistan's political traditions, although few cultural links exist between them. Most of the trade links (and most of the wealth is based upon tourism and fish) are closer to Sri Lanka and Japan than India. In 1977 Indian Airlines undertook a joint venture to help the Maldivian airport company. India has also made a gift of a tuna-canning factory, and other minor technical help has been forthcoming.

Although remote from its troubled neighbours, even the Maldives have felt the pull of India. Throughout the 1988 trial of those Sri Lankans involved in the coup attempt, Indian paratroopers remained on the island, and although Gayoom and Rajiv Gandhi held several meetings to assess Maldivian security interests, Gayoom was anxious to secure the return of Indian troops. Thus the Maldives conform to the patterns of trust/mistrust that characterise most of India's relations with its neighbours, and underscore the apparent failure of India in being accepted as the legitimate regional peace-keeper.

There are very few official statements made concerning India's strategic doctrine. Unlike Western Europe at the height of the Cold War, there is little public discussion, and India has no policy of disclosure or any freedom of information acts that release such documents for public and academic scrutiny. Yet much evidence exists to imply that, under the so-called 'Indira Gandhi' doctrine, as defined by the Bangladesh campaign in 1971, India supports and has encouraged regional democracy (as pro-Indian governments) and that it has increasingly sought to tie up its regional primacy through a series of regional, bilateral accords covering defence trade and technical co-operation. These policies have caused concern within the region, and disagreements where earlier there was understanding and concord. A good illustration of how, since the 1970s, the smaller states of South Asia have been growing uneasy about Indian intentions, concerns the Indian Ocean Zone of Peace Initiative.

Following the British withdrawal in the late 1960s and early 1970s, India expressed concern that increased US naval activity, and especially the presence of the American base at Diego Garcia, would lead to increased Soviet activity and pull the area into the Cold War. India was able to find broad agreement with Sri Lanka, and both states called for a 'zone of peace' (ZOP). Both states also favoured declaring the Indian Ocean a nuclear free zone (NFZ).

These initiatives, discussed frequently at the UN (and presided over by a Commission under UN auspices) were rejected by both superpowers on the grounds that such a zone would interfere with international trade and the laws of the sea. After 1985, however, following changes in Soviet thinking, the USSR came around to agreeing with the NFZ proposal, only to find that New Delhi was backtracking. The reasons behind this change of policy were not hard to find.

The rationale behind India's previous support for the ZOP and NFZ was that they would exclude foreign powers (primarily the superpowers) from the Indian Ocean, but not its own (growing) navy. Since the late 1980s this navy came to contain nuclear-powered submarines. Pakistan and to an extent Sri Lanka, quick to spot the sleight of hand, continued to expressed their support for a NFZ, and the ZOP, on the condition that it includes all naval and military deployments, including the regional states. One Pakistani analyst had noted that 'India's advocacy of the demilitarisation of the Indian Ocean by the superpowers is an essential element of her goal to establish naval supremacy'[79] and to convert the Indian Ocean into an Indian lake. The remarks of one recent Bangladeshi commentator sum up the attitude of all the small states of South Asia, and even the views of Pakistan:

> Bangladesh realistically perceived that a security system that sought to remove the extra-regional military presences, but left the questions relating to security threats emanating from within the region would not be workable or acceptable.[80]

The difficulties that emerge from coming to an understanding with India confront even the casual observer of sub-continental affairs. The causes of these perceptions are internal to the region and are intimately tied up with how India has come increasingly to perceive itself. As we shall see, while this does not exclude wider international events from opening up possible channels of mediation and compromise within the region, it rules out the possibility of any externally imposed security arrangement, or, with an eye to Kashmir, imposed solutions.

The divisions and mistrust that dominate the South Asia region are historically and *regionally* based. The South Asian security complex has not been imposed from outside and, as will be discussed in the next chapter, although it has been supported and greatly exaggerated by US and Soviet help, future settlements must come – ultimately – from some form of political dialogue within the region. The roots of this animosity are perhaps paradoxical. Given the proximity of India to Pakistan, S. Gangal noted sadly that 'India and Pakistan have more in common, river systems, climates, languages, cultures and religion than perhaps any two nations anywhere else'.[81] This is true of all the states of South Asia, even the land of the Thunder Dragon (Bhutan) and the remote Maldives. It is *because* of this commonality that the region is so insecure. One of the many consequences of partition has been a conventional arms race. Another has been the lack of economic trade and co-operation between India and Pakistan, and between the region as a whole. The odd cricket match apart, surprisingly little takes place to bring these states together.

The British placed the Bengali jute fields in East Pakistan while they gave the jute processing plants (situated in and around Calcutta), to India. For a time there was some doubt in the minds of the boundary commission whether to give Lahore to India or to Pakistan. The animosity of those early years (amplified by China and then other 'external powers') closed off various avenues of development. These avenues remain closed to this day.

Notes

1   M. G. Kabir and S. Hassan, *Issues and Challenges Facing Bangladesh Foreign Policy*, People's Press, Dhaka, 1983, p. xi.

2   See ch. 2 of K. M. de Silva, *Regional Powers and Small State Security*, Johns Hopkins University Press, London, 1995.

3   See V. P. Dutt, *India's Foreign Policy*, Sangam Books, New Delhi, 1984 for a basic introduction to the literature. See P. Singh, *India and the Future of Asia*, Progress Publishers, New Delhi, 1966, and O. Marwah and J. Pollack, *Asia's Major Powers*, Westview Press,

Boulder, 1978.

4   J. Nehru, *Letters to the Chief Ministers*, 5 vols, Oxford University Press, New Delhi, 1988, III, 25.10.57.

5   A. Vanaik and P. Bidwai, 'India and Pakistan', in R. C. Karp (ed.), *Security Without Nuclear Weapons? Differing Perspectives on Nonnuclear Security*, Oxford University Press/SIPRI, London, 1992, p. 263.

6   Kabir and Hassan, *Issues and Challenges*, p. 23.

7   The defence breakdown is usually in the order of 70/20/10 for the army, airforce and navy respectively. The navy has always been the most junior of the services. See R. Thomas, *The Defence of India: A Budgetary Perspective of Strategy and Politics*, Lexington, 1978, and R. Thomas 'The Armed Services and India's Defence Budget', *Asian Survey*, 20, 1980, pp. 280–97.

8   See P. Duncan, *The Soviet Union and India*, Routledge, London, 1989.

9   In the mid-1980s India declined from selling Zimbabwe MiG-21s produced by Hindustan Aeronautics for the fear of offending international opinion. See Amit Gupta, 'The Indian Arms Industry', *Asian Survey*, 29, 1989, pp. 846–61.

10 H. Kapur, *India's Foreign Policy: 1947–92: Shadows and Substance*, Sage Publications, New Delhi, 1994. p. 40.

11 For a revealing insight into the connection between nuclear power, the ideology of modernisation, and the views and aspirations of India's elite after independence see Peter Lavoy, *India as a Great Power: Assimilating the Pressures of Political Culture and International Competition*, ISA paper, April 1996.

12 A. Shahi, *Pakistan's Security and Foreign Policy*, Minotaur Press, Lahore, 1988

13 Raju Thomas, 'U.S. Transfers of Dual-Use Technologies', *Asian Survey*, 30, 1990, pp. 825–45.

14 Chris Smith, *India's Ad Hoc Arsenal*, Oxford University Press/SIPRI, London, 1994, p. 223.

15 *The Military Balance 1989–90*, IISS, London, 1990. Put another way, however, India still spends less on defence as a percentage of her GNP (about 4 per cent) than Pakistan's estimated 7 per cent. There are difficulties in calculating or estimating China's defence expenditure and quotes vary from 4 to 8 per cent. See *Brassey's Asian Security*, RIPS, London, 1989, p. 43.

16 M. Ayoob, *India and South East Asia: Indian Perceptions and Policies*, Routledge, London, 1990, p. 42.

17 I. Husain, *The Strategic Dimensions of Pakistan's Foreign Policy*, Vanguard Books, Lahore, 1989. Little or no argument is advanced to

support many of the extraordinary statements in this book.

18   Again confusion abounds as to whether delivery, let alone deployment, of the M-11 has taken place. Brassey's *The Strategic Survey*, IISS, Oxford, 1994–95 noted that they believe some have arrived at Lahore, but both China and Pakistan deny this.

19   See S. Cohen *The Pakistan Army*, University of California Press, Berkeley, 1984, and the second edition of S. Ganguly, *The Origins of War in South Asia*, Westview Press, Boulder, 1994.

20   Carrier battle groups involve a main aircraft carrier with an air wing and a series of support ships which are capable of sustaining themselves in a combat area relatively autonomously. For an Indian perspective on this see the *Indian Defence Review, 1990*, New Delhi, 1989.

21   Richard Latter, *Strengthening Security in South Asia*, Wilton Park Paper 108, HMSO, London, 1995, p. 4.

22   For a good oversight see H. V. Hobson, *The Great Divide: Great Britain, India and Pakistan*, Oxford University Press, Karachi, 1985.

23   For an elaboration of this argument see my essay entitled 'Provincial Indentity in Baluchistan' in Subrata Mitra (ed.), *Sub-Nationalism in South Asia*, Westview Press, Boulder. 1996.

24   The two main 'revisionist' texts that I have come across on the exact view the Muslim League took over the issue of Pakistan are A. Jalal, *Jinnah: The Muslim League and the Demand for Pakistan*, Cambridge University Press, Cambridge, 1985 and Yunus Samad, *A Nation in Turmoil: Nationalism and Ethnicity in Pakistan 1937–1958*, Sage, London, 1995.

25   A forthcoming book by Sayed Ali Shah entitled *Ethnicity and Foreign Policy of Pakistan 1971–1994*, makes the fascinating observation that Baluchi and Sindi views of India are far less hawkish than Punjabi or Mohajir. Likewise in India, Kashmiri views are more ambivalent in their views on Pakistan than northern Hindi speakers. I am indebted to Lester Crook of Tauris Books for allowing me to see this manuscript.

26   A. Jalal, *The State of Martial Rule*, Cambridge University Press, Cambridge, 1992, p. 29.

27   For a fascinating study of the problems faced by the boundary commission see R. J. Moore, *Making the New Commonwealth*, Clarendon Press, Oxford, 1987. Moore notes that 'the essential conditions of [Radcliffe's] brief [from the government] which he took up on 8 July was that he must excercise independent judgement to bring down the awards by 15 August' (p. 25). It is not surprising that later 'he could never relive the experience by rereading the evidence of which he took account'.

28 The Afghan claims on Pakistan primarily involved the province of Baluchistan. As late as 1969 the Afghan government issued a postage stamp that showed the borders of Afghanistan as incorporating Baluchistan and parts of the Pakistan tribal belt. See M. Z. Ispanhani, *Roads and Rivals: The Politics of Access in the Borderlands of Asia*, Tauris Books, London, 1991.

29 Interestingly enough, this issue was settled in 1985 when Bangladesh settled the border with Burma on the basis of an earlier agreement in 1979 to 'prepare a joint survey' of the Nagar hill tracts.

30 Jalal, *The State of Martial Rule*, p. 25.

31 In 1965 India extended diplomatic support to Afghanistan and called for the upholding of the legitimate rights of the Pashto people to be given due recognition by the Pakistan government. See Ispanhani, *Roads and Rivals*.

32 Z. A. Khan, *Pakistan's Security*, People's Publishing House, Lahore, 1990.

33 M. Waseem, *Pakistan Under Martial Law 1977–1985*, People's Publishing House, Lahore, 1987, p. 222.

34 R. Gandhi, *Understanding the Muslim Mind*, Penguin, Harmondsworth, 1987, p. 2.

35 For a detailed discussion of these events see my book *Reclaiming the Past? The Search for Political and Cultural Unity in Contemporary Jammu and Kashmir*, Portland Books, London, 1995. See also Alastair Lamb, *Kashmir: A Disputed Legacy, 1846–1990*, Roxford Press, Herefordshire, 1991. See also Victoria Schofield, *Kashmir: In the Crossfire*, Tauris Books, London, 1996.

36 In 1942, of course, the concept of Pakistan was not considered to be a serious possibility, and the Cripp's Mission still held on to the concept that independence meant self-government or dominion status within the British Empire.

37 Only one state appears to have been encouraged to stake a claim for full sovereign independence, the small princely state of Kalat in Baluchistan, which was nominally independent for over 200 days until finally annexed by the Pakistan army.

38 Telegram from V. P. Menon to Sir P. Patrick, 8 July 1947, in Sir Panderel Moon (ed.), *Transfer of Power*, HMSO, London, 1983, vol. XII, p. 1.

39 Statement of 12 May 1946 in *Transfer of Power*, vol. VII, p. 595.

40 On 26 October 1947 the Maharaja of Kashmir joined India and signed an agreement with New Delhi. Indian troops were dispatched on 27 October. One of the most extraordinary aspects of the conflict was that both the Indian and Pakistan armies were under British commanders and during the initial outbreak of hostilities under a British

commander-in-chief.

41 G. Rizvi, 'Arms Control in South Asia', in G. Segal (ed.), *Arms Control in Asia*, Macmillan, Basingstoke, 1987, p. 121.

42 Nehru, *Letters to the Chief Ministers*, I, letter dated 5.2.48, p. 61.

43 For a discussion of this peculiar involvement of the British army, see Moore, *New Commonwealth*.

44 Sajjad Hyder, *Reflections of an Ambassador*, Vanguard, Lahore, 1988, p. 75

45 See, for example, Rashiduzzaman 'East–West Conflict in Pakistan: Bengali Regionalism', in D. Dalton and A. J. Wilson (eds), *The States of South Asia: The Problems of Natural Integration*, C. Hurst, London, 1982; L. Lifschutz *Bangladesh: The Unfinished Revolution*, Zed Books, London, 1979. The most recent account of the event, from both the Pakistan and the Indian side, is L. Rose and R. Sisson, *War and Secession: India, Pakistan and the Creation of Bangladesh*, Princeton University Press, Princeton, 1990.

46 See P. N. Haksar, *India's Foreign Policies and Its Problems*, Orient Longman, New Delhi, 1989. Haksar was a key advisor to Indira Gandhi on the Simla Accord.

47 Text of communiqué printed in *Keesing Contemporary Archive*, Longman, London, 1976, p. 27846.

48 Editorial 30 July 1972, cited in M. Ayoob, *India, Pakistan and Banglandesh*, Sangam Books, New Delhi, 1975, p. 37.

49 Rizvi, 'Arms Control', p. 116.

50 For details see D. C. Vohra, *India's Aid Diplomacy and the Third World*, Zed Books, London, 1980.

51 N. J. Rengger, (ed.), *Treaties and Alliances of the World*, 5th edition, Cartermill, London, 1990, p. 385.

52 *Keesing's Archives, 1976*, p. 27523.

53 Under international laws that deal with trans-boundary flows, it is illegal for a country to dam the flow of a shared river resource and prevent a downriver state from a fair share of water. A barrage – defined as a temporary structure that does not obstruct the flow of water – is apparently exempt.

54 IISA, *The Military Balance*, IISS, London, 1989–90. It is noted in the report that spare parts are in short supply and that the serviceability of the airforce and the navy is questionable.

55 Hugh Evens, 'Bangladesh: South Asia's Unknown Quantity', *Asian Affairs*, 75, 1988, pp. 306–16.

56 Cited in E. Ahamed, *The Foreign Policy of Bangladesh: Imperatives of a Small State*, People's Press, Dhaka, 1984, p. 130.

57 Caroline Thomas, 'New Directions in Thinking About Security in the Third World', in K. Booth (ed.) *New Thinking About Strategy and*

International Security, Harper Collins, London, 1991, pp. 267–86.

58   See Jasjit Singh 'Indian Security: A Framework for National Strategy', *Stategic Analysis*, 11, 1987, pp. 898–917.

59   Ashok Kapur, 'India's Foreign Policy: Perspectives and Present Predicaments', *Round Table*, 295, 1985, pp. 230–9.

60   N. Maxwell, *India's China War*, Penguin, Harmondsworth, 1962. See also A. Ramakant, *Nepal, China and Indian Relations*, Vikas, New Delhi, 1976; and B. Sen Gupta, *The Fulcrum of Asia: Relations Amongst China, India, Pakistan and the USSR*, Vikas, New Delhi, 1970. Kuldip Nayar's *Distant Neighbours*, Vikas, New Delhi, 1972 remains a very readable book on India's early regional policy. See also S. P. Varma and K. P. Misra, *The Foreign Policy of South Asia*, Orient Longman, New Delhi, 1969.

61   R. Thomas, *India's Security Policy*, Princeton University Press, Princeton, 1986, p. 59, emphasis added.

62   Ramesh Thakur, 'Normalising Sino-Indian Relations', *Pacific Review*, 4, 1991, p. 9.

63   B. N. Goswami, *Pakistan and China: A Study in Their Relations*, Progess Publishers, New Delhi, 1971.

64   Haksar, *India's Foreign Policy*, p. 56

65   *World Bank Annual Report*, Washington, 1990.

66   L. Rose 'India's Foreign Relations: Reassessing Basic Policies', in M. Bouton and P. Oldenburg (eds), *India Briefing 1990*, Westview Press, Boulder, 1990, p. 63.

67   Thakur, 'Normalising Sino-Indian Relations', p. 15.

68   See Wang Hong Wei 'Sino-Nepali Relations in the 1980s', *Asian Survey*, 25, 1985, pp. 512–34.

69   The Hindu credentials of the monarchy are visible in the fact that the Nepalese king is the only individual – apart from the high priest – who can enter the inner sanctum of the Jagarnath temple in Puri, Orissa. Priests for the temple of Pashupati Nath, the presiding deity of Nepal, are chosen from Southern India and retain close links with their districts. See M. D. Dharamdasari, *India's Diplomacy in Nepal*, Keynotes, Jaipur, 1976.

70   See L. Rose and J. Scholz, *Nepal: Profile of a Himalayan Kingdom*, Westview Press, Boulder, 1980, and R. Shaha, *Nepali Politics*, Sangam Books, New Delhi, 1978.

71   Throughout the colonial period the British recognised Nepal as an 'independent' kingdom, on the condition that it would continue its 'natural policy of isolation' and remain on good terms with the British. In 1923 the British signed a treaty of friendship and co-operation with the King of Nepal. In 1890 the government of India deprived Sikkim's *Chogyal* of all powers and appointed a political

officer, although in 1918 the *Chogyal* was restored and Sikkim granted full autonomy as a associated member of British India. Bhutan first encountered the British in the form of Ashley Eden's mission in 1864 which, in retaliation for 'a poor reception and ill mannered porters' annexed some rather crucial border areas which are now compensated for by an annual grant from India. In 1911 Bhutan concluded a paramountcy agreement with British India.

72   See 'Violence Comes to Shangri-La', *The Economist*, London, 6–12 October 1990, p. 84.

73   India's Sikkim policy has been controversial within India as well as within China. See Datta Ray, *Smash and Grab: The Annexation of Sikkim*, Vikas, New Delhi, 1984, and R. Rao, *Sikkim: The Story of its Integration with India*, Chanakya, New Delhi, 1978.

74   S. U. Kodikara *The Foreign Policy of Sri Lanka: A Third World Perspective*, Chanakya, New Delhi, 1982, see ch. 7, *Sri Lanka and Asian Regionalism*.

75   Sir John wanted to condemn Soviet imperialism in Eastern Europe in the final communiqué of the Afro-Asian summit. He also called for the disbanding of Comiform and accused Cho En Lai of funding Marxist movements within Sri Lanka. See H. S. S. Nissanka, *Sri Lanka's Foreign Policy: A Study in Non-Alignment*, Vikas, New Delhi, 1984.

76   The Sirima–Shastri agreement meant that India would give Indian citizenship to 525,000 Tamils of Indian origin, and that Sri Lanka would give citizenship to 300,000. The agreement was not without problems, and there were various delays that compelled a further settlement. Following the 1974 agreement India and Sri Lanka decided to halve the remaining community – 75,000 to be expatriated to India, 75,000 settled in Sri Lanka.

77   Nissanka, *Foreign Policy of Sri Lanka*, p. 255.

78   Reproduced in Shankar Bhaduri and Afsir Karim, *The Sri Lankan Crisis*, Popular Press, New Delhi, 1989.

79   Cited in Duncan, *The Soviet Union and India*, p. 60.

80   Ahamed, *The Foreign Policy of Bangladesh*, p. 85.

81   S. C. Gangal, *India and the Commonwealth*, Vikas, New Delhi, 1970, p. 63.

2

The states of South Asia (II): the international setting

By 1992, the Soviet Union had disintegrated, leaving in its wake a series of republics, a majority of which purported to be federal and a majority of which remained loosely associated under the aegis of the Confederation of Independent States (CIS). In the wake of the Moscow coup of 1991 and the disintegration of communist regimes in Eastern Europe, the sudden end of the Cold War took many in India by surprise. Yet as early as 1989, one British analyst had noted triumphantly that 'the Cold War is over, and we have won it. The West is secure, and its societies enjoy considerable material comfort'.[1] Yet in South Asia the end of bipolarity opened up, as well as closed off, certain foreign policy strategies that had to an extent characterised the region since independence.

Seemingly overnight, the centrality of non-alignment to India's foreign policy seemed irrelevant, and its reliance on a failed superpower was a cause of heated domestic argument. The end of the Soviet Union left India exposed in the Security Council of the UN (wherein it had relied heavily on the Soviet veto), and exposed to a possible *rapprochement* between China and the new Russian Federation, a process already in place by the late 1980s. India's apparent confusion over events in the East was evident from New Delhi's non-committal statement over the Moscow coup. It was one of only a handful of countries (including Cuba and China) which failed to condemn the overthrow of Gorbachev and to denounce the attempted restoration of Communist control.

For Pakistan, the collapse of the Soviet Union significantly reduced its strategic significance to the United States, and weakened its security environment further as Washington sought further guarantees over Pakistan's non-nuclear status. Although relations were partially restored in 1995, the old alacrity has gone, probably for good. As recently as 1993, the United States was involved in an internal debate over whether Pakistan ought to be named as a 'terrorist' state, an event that would have been unimaginable to an earlier generation of analysts. Frozen out of the American embrace, Pakistan was anxious to avoid any possible *rapprochement* between Washington and New Delhi. The end of the Cold War also paid some dividends: it opened up, for Pakistan and India alike, a large part of Central Asia to diplomatic and economic initiatives.

The apparent breakdown of bipolarity, in which the old landmarks of superpower influence were eroded, raised the question of a New World Order and the interests such an order would represent. On the face of it, it appeared to be a global order dominated by the principles of democracy and democratic representation and the logic of an international capitalist market. In the aftermath of the Iraqi invasion of Kuwait in 1991, the Bush administration took the lead in trying to shape the forces that could emerge in the 1990s and beyond, in active co-operation with a truncated Russian Federation, and wider elements of a so-called international community working actively with the UN. Less dramatically, in South Asia (and a greater part of the Third World) there was some scepticism about any so-called New World Order, and what it would actually entail for non-OECD countries.[2]

As the initial euphoria declined, many less developed countries (LDCs) felt excluded from various international institutions and regimes. The activities of the World Bank and the International Monetary Fund (IMF) were unchecked by any ideological counterbalance advocating statism or socialism, and the role of specific UN operations concerned with humanitarian aid raised questions of sovereignty for many LDC states, linked to US global hegemony. For the Muslim world in particular, however divided by sectarian and cultural differences, the indecision of the UN in Bosnia, and the evident failures of UN initiatives, reflected the agenda of a predominantly Western world, one apparently indifferent, or openly hostile, to Islam.

Of most immediate interest following the collapse of the Soviet Union was the prospect that India would have to come to some form of new understanding with the United States however difficult or intellectually impalpable, based upon the 'realities' of global power and economic necessity. Traditionally, the profile that India commanded in America was minute. In the mid-1970s Mellor noted that: 'The US state department included India in its Near East/South West Asia Desk, which [was] under an assistant secretary of state, who [was] almost totally preoccupied with Israel'.[3] Added to this rather curious act of institutional marginalisation, was the somewhat more intangible 'image' problem that India suffered from in the minds of the American public. To an extent this was mirrored by various well-established stereotypes of Americans held by the Indian elite itself. It has recently been suggested that the Indians inherited from the British a general belief that Americans were vulgar and unsophisticated, and the state of America was somewhat akin to a strapping adolescent with an inclination to bully.[4] For the Americans, the belief that India was a weak nation characterised by appalling levels of poverty was combined with a dislike of its native intelligentsia's commitment to socialism, forged as it had been in the crucible of colonialism and British rule.

Rhetoric and style aside, Nihal Singh noted that by the 1980s what has continually bedevilled US–Indian relations, Pakistan notwithstanding, is 'India's putative if not actual power status and the American refusal to acknowledge it'.[5] Since India considers itself a powerful state with regional (and potentially global) interests and responsibilities, it is essential that India somehow acquires a higher profile within American thinking, despite New Delhi's mistrust of Washington's supremacy. In the 1990s, India has much to fear from a invigorated United States, especially one that 'thumps any country that gets out of line, shakes down its rich friends to pay for the mugging, gets a meek go ahead from the cops in the UN and tells the Soviet Union [Russia] to butt out'.[6] It has almost as much to fear from an America reluctant to involve itself in extra-regional affairs, especially in the face of continuing Japanese (and German) reluctance to assume wider international responsibilities towards regime management. Sisir Gupta commented perceptively that 'new nations have more reason to be afraid of international anarchy than powerful states … For one thing, instability may aggravate their domestic problems of nation building'[7]

Five years after the collapse of the Soviet Union, there is still a pressing need for India to rethink its foreign policy, and indeed for the United States to reassess India's wider utility to American foreign policy generally. Despite the momentous events of the early 1990s, one is struck by the continuities within Indo-US relations, and not any radical breaks or departures. There has, to be sure, been a change in the tone within bilateral relations, including previously unheard joint naval exercises in the Indian Ocean in 1993, but nothing indicative of a radical restructuring. While various overtures have been made to America, for example, in 1985 by Rajiv Gandhi (with his themes of 'shared democratic values and democratic experiences'), the visit in 1995 by Narashima Rao, and a tentative defence agreement signed in January 1995, there remain serious obstacles in the way of any sustained, and strategically significant, Indo-American *rapprochement*.

India's continual refusal to sign up to the NPT, reiterated again in New York in May 1995, and New Delhi's condemnation of American attempts to control the spread of missile technology through the Missile Technology Control Regime (MTCR) are continual irritants to Washington. Despite considerable US pressure, including a whole series of US-sponsored security talks in India in 1994, India will not budge on its traditional image of the NPT and its rights to develop and deploy nuclear weapons. Other obstacles involve potentially hostile US views on Kashmir and India's human rights record. In 1993, a statement by the foreign spokesperson Robin Raphael noted that, with regard to the Instrument of Accession document, the United States did not necessarily regard Jammu and Kashmir as part of the Indian Union for all time. The resulting outcry from India led to some improvised clarifications, but the statement alerted India to some of the possible implications of US hegemony for Indian domestic policies.

There remains also the case of Pakistan, and the continuing failure of the Indians to persuade Washington that Pakistan constitutes a major threat to regional peace. The final decision in 1993 not to declare Pakistan a terrorist state was met with criticism and resentment in India, which believed that the decision was neither 'objective' nor fair. The resumption of arms supplies to Pakistan, made possible by the restoration of the Joint Military Commission, has also led to complaints and indignation in New Delhi. Other matters that still prevent any real convergence of interests between these two large democratic states are differences on such matters as environmental pollution, technology transfers and trading policies (discussed below). In 1993, the United States once more threatened to take punitive action against India for its failure to enforce intellectual property rights and copyright regulations on entertainments and services.

If a gradual *rapprochement* with the United States has been problematic, Indian attempts to come to terms with the demise of the Soviet Union have been painfully slow. One commentator suggested that, by 1993, the Indians had buried their heads in the sand and were continuing with the fiction that the Soviet Union still existed, albeit in the guise of the Confederation of Independent States, and the Republics of Russia, Ukraine and Georgia in particular. Certainly India remains committed to the Russian Republic as the legatee and indeed surrogate of the Soviet Union, although recent state visits have lacked the old pomp and circumstance, and much was made of the fact that Prime Minister Rao's first foreign visit in 1991 was to Germany, and not the usual friendly stop-over in Moscow.

The disintegration of the Soviet Union, as much as the previous disturbances within Eastern Europe, profoundly disrupted established diplomatic and trade links. In 1980 India had signed a US$ 1.6 billion arms deal with the Soviets and in 1989 India signed another trade protocol worth Rs 70,000 million, principally to import weaponry. The sudden increase in imports from the Russian Federation, as both the rupee and the rouble began the painful transition to hard currencies, increased the costs of Indian procurement, while chaos within the former Soviet Union affected delivery dates, threatened maintenance agreements because of shortages and lack of spare parts, or worst still, raised questions about the viability of such weapon systems in the face of so-called 'smart' Western weapons.[8]

None the less, both Indian and Russian leaders have pressed ahead with the maintenance of close bilateral ties and at least the fiction that little has changed between them. In 1993, Boris Yelstin and Prime Minister Rao announced a 'new era' in Indo-Russian affairs, revealing a new military accord between the two states, a fresh rouble–rupee exchange agreement, and a rescheduling of India's debt over a period of forty-five years. However, there are problems for this alliance. One is the growing Russian pressure, in concert with the United States to get the Indians to agree with both the NPT and MTCR. In 1993 the Russians appeared to cancel a deal to sell cryogenic rockets to the Indians under American pressure.[9] Moreover, as early as 1991, the Indian external affairs minister expressed 'disappointment' over Russian support, at the UN, for a Pakistani and Bangladeshi sponsored resolution calling for a nuclear-free South Asia. This change of attitude was a significant one.

Georgia and the Ukraine have also, to some extent, continued to follow a reasonably robust bilateral relation with New Delhi. Both states were quick to open up diplomatic offices in India, sign trade protocols dealing with manufacturing and services, and to facilitate the exchange (not trade) of spare parts for India's MiGs and other Soviet hardware suffering from the collapse of support and servicing arrangements contained in the original contracts.

Unfortunately for the Pakistanis, a certain cruel irony has prevented them from making the most of Indian difficulties *vis-à-vis* the Soviet Union. Despite having backed the right side, the 1990s started with Indo-Pak relations at an all-time low, the air thick with recrimination and charges of betrayal. On 1 October 1990 the Bush administration cut off a five-year aid package signed in 1987 worth between US$ 564 and 578 million for 1991 alone, in response to reports that Pakistan was still constructing a nuclear bomb. Early in 1987 the House Appropriations Committee held up an aid package worth US$ 4.02 billion following Pakistan's refusal to open up some of its nuclear installations to international inspection.

In 1990 a remark by US senator Stephen Solarz about future American aid being conditional on a 'free and fair' election following the dismissal of the Benazir Bhutto government, led to the accusation that Washington was interfering in the internal affairs of a 'friendly yet independent' state. During the Kuwait crisis, General Beig, the most senior officer in the Pakistan army, issued a statement in 1992 regretting US-led actions against Iraq and referring to Saddam Hussein as an important leader in the Islamic world, distancing himself (and by implication, the army) from the foreign policy of the civilian government headed by Sharif.

Once more in opposition, following his dismissal in 1993, Sharif's throw-away interview about the bomb in 1994 led to further American pressure, with the Clinton administration threatening to widen the accusations against Pakistan to include international Islamic terrorism and drug dealing. In 1995, the murder of two US embassy employees in Karachi raised concerns that Pakistan was not a safe place to work in, and that the state could not maintain essential levels of law and order.

The United States and South Asia: an overview

It has always been something of a mystery (even to some an embarrassment) that the United States of America should have found itself, on the whole, on more intimate terms with Pakistan (and invariably Pakistani generals) than with democratically elected Indian leaders.[10]

As the basis of its foreign policy, non-alignment has been invariably too clever for the Americans by half, who perceived it as a piece of muddled logic, or worse an act of calculated duplicity, allowing India to condemn 'power block' rivalries and military alliances, while gaining tangible benefits from a close association with the Soviets.

Krishna Menon, India's first High Commissioner to London, and by 1952, India's representative at the UN, became a particular irritant to the Americans, symbolic of Indian bad habits. His sentiments towards non-alignment and Third World solidarity were closely related to Nehru's own thinking on the matter, and his speeches in the UN were often interpreted as close to those of the Indian Prime Minister and a large faction of the ruling Congress Party. He shared Nehru's strengths as well as his weaknesses, a commitment to internationalism combined with a failure to understand the logic of crude power politics, a flair for detail that often bordered on irrelevancy. He personified the image that Indians were arrogant, sanctimonious and moralistic, frequently preachy, while at the same time being devious and equivocal on practical matters of concern to India's immediate national interest.

In a speech to the General Assembly dealing with 'The World in the Tenth Year of the United Nations', Menon noted: 'the present does not really exist, because the moment one has spoken about the present – or is even aware of it – it has already become the past', going on later to conclude that, with regard to China's seat at the UN: 'It is not a question of the admission of China to the United Nations ... it is merely a question of who represents China ... this is a straightforward question ... and it surprises and amazes me how this straightforward question has been twisted round about and made the cause of infinite troubles'. One wonders what was going through the minds of various Western delegates during the one and a half hours it took Menon to deliver this keynote address, especially the Americans, whose continual failure to recognise the

People's Republic of China to which Menon was referring.

Menon, typical of a generation of statesmen and diplomats, combined the high moral cant and pedantic warm-up to form what the Americans would come to see by the 1960s as a peculiar variant of the Indian rope trick: an ability to use the same intellectual premise to defend and advance a bewildering variety of nationalist inspired policies, a majority of which were anti-Western and anti-American. At the same time, the Indians expected to gain the support of America in undertaking its own economic and social revolution.

India's stand on issues such as the Dutch–Indonesian war (1948–50), the Korean war (1950–51), and the Soviet invasion of Hungary (1956) alarmed American sensibilities further. India's decision to abstain from the UN vote condemning the Soviet invasion of Hungary and Czechoslovakia was met with consternation: did not the act contradict India's professed support for the rules of international law and political independence? How could India condemn Anglo-French actions against the Egyptians at Suez, and yet ignore Soviet actions in Eastern Europe?

For Foster Dulles and his generation of American strategic thinkers, this refusal to uphold the principles of a 'free world' through an active commitment to the United States, in favour of seeking reconciliation through negotiation, was simply so much hot air, or at least a stark display of international naiveté. The talk of Afro-Asian solidarity and 'global peace' was even pernicious since it detracted attention away from the real threat to global security and led to the 'fraternisation' with revisionist states such as the Soviet Union and the People's Republic of China.

To the Americans at least, the Sino-Indian war of 1962 was a welcome development: it appeared to snap Nehru out of his obsession with 'peaceful coexistence' and force him to think seriously about defence and the realities of world politics. New Delhi's rush for Anglo-American aid – to the tune of US$ 70 million by 1965 – was further seen by Chester Bowles, then the US ambassador to Washington, as opening up the possibility for greater US–Indian co-operation against a common Chinese foe, even if India continued to receive financial support from the Soviets. The emerging realities of the Sino-Soviet split, and the potential *rapprochement* between Beijing and Washington, soon put an end to this emerging strategy.[11]

Under the Kennedy regime, American goodwill was extended with significant aid and trade agreements, but usually with disdain or active American cynicism. Chester Bowles, US ambassador to India at the beginning of the Johnston era, criticised the US State Department's habit of treating India as a 'beggar' state, and urged America to indulge, not condemn, Indian foreign policy aspirations. The scale of American aid and assistance to India was belied by its mean-spiritedness. India was already receiving a significant amount of food under the 1954 Agricultural Trade and Development Act, and would continue to receive large amounts of cheap American grains throughout the 1960s. Between 1946 and 1966 India received US\$ 6,810.2 million from the United States in aid, compared to Pakistan's US\$ 3,095 million. Yet such associations did not contribute to any positive or warm breakthrough in US–Indian relations.

India's mistrust of the United States, as a military power, remains, at least at the popular level. New Delhi's role in the Kuwait crisis was marginal compared to that of Pakistan, or even Bangladesh. Throughout 1991–92, New Delhi was determined to follow its own diplomacy through the Non-Aligned Movement (NAM). Yet the decision to send ex-prime minister Rajiv Gandhi on a fact-finding mission to Iraq, followed by a visit from the Indian Foreign Minister (I. K. Gujral), seemed poorly thought through and failed to create any real momentum of their own. The decision by the Chandra Senkhar government in 1991 to allow American planes to refuel at Bombay during the Kuwait crisis, for example, created an open rift in the cabinet and had to be withdrawn. Popular demonstrations against India's ratification of the GATT Uruguay Round was, in large part, because of the popular perception that Indian economic sovereignty had been sold under American pressure.

Compared to this historical indifference, US economic, military and technological relations with Islamabad appear well-established and genuinely friendly, despite two arms embargoes (1965 and 1971) and doses of pro-Indian sentiment. Throughout the 1950s the United States provided Pakistan with US\$ 1.3 billion for 'infrastructural support' as well as US\$ 700 million worth of Patton tanks.[13] Between 1954 and 1965 US weapons to Pakistan came to US\$ 1.5 billion. Unlike US–Indian relations, the explanation for the success of US–Pakistan relations is that they have come to share a particular geo-strategic view of the world. The fact that Pakistan found the Americans so accommodating was largely coincidental, it could well have been the Soviet Union or even the Commonwealth, since Pakistan approached each one in turn to help it fend off Indian aggression after partition.[14]

Although the Indians believed that the British were pro-Muslim, the British government had indicated its unwillingness to release foreign exchange to Pakistan for the purpose of buying arms. A memo from the then Secretary for Commonwealth Relations regarding Anglo-US differences over Pakistan stated: 'Let's talk with the Americans, but for heaven's sake don't let's be rushed into some paper guarantees [to Pakistan's territorial integrity] ... India's friendship is very important and must not be jeopardised.'[15]

The Western bias within the Pakistani military elite made thoughts of close links with the Soviets difficult but not impossible to contemplate. In the wake of partition, the Muslim states of the Middle East were too weak and divided to offer much assistance. In 1956 H. S. Suhrawardy, a notable Pakistani leader and statesman, remarked sarcastically that the power of the Arab world could be summarised as 'zero plus zero'.

From 1952 onwards, and in particular after General Ayub Khan came to power in the 1958 coup, the Pakistan elite played consciously on their anti-communist credentials, and skilfully combined Pakistan's strategic position (next to the Gulf and part of the Indian Ocean littoral) with notions of Islam's natural abhorrence to a godless Soviet regime.[16] Yet had the Soviet Union actively courted Pakistan after 1947, the relationship could well have been otherwise.

From the 1950s then, the Americans were keen to enlist Pakistan's active involvement in any joint Western defence plan for the Middle East, although the British were afraid of India's 'adverse reactions to Pakistan's membership in a Middle East Defence Command and Pakistan receiving additional arms'.[17] Such British sensitivities, made largely irrelevant by British decline after the war, encouraged the Americans to make direct approaches to Pakistan itself. Thus if India had no place in Foster Dulles' 'northern tier' against the Soviet Union, Pakistan certainly did.

In 1954, Pakistan signed an agreement with the United States and with Turkey and in 1955 it became a member of the Central Treaty Organisation (CENTO). In 1964 Pakistan signed up as a member of the Regional Co-operation for Development with Turkey and Iran, a broadly pro-Western association of states that further integrated Pakistan into the strategic land bridge that linked Europe to Asia and encircled Soviet Central Asia. The curious location of 'East Pakistan' also invited ideas that would eventually lead to Pakistan's membership of the South East Asian Treaty Organisation (SEATO) and direct association with US strategic thinking on the Indian Ocean–Pacific area. By the mid-1960s Pakistan was emerging as America's most 'allied ally'. Each move in this process was accompanied by Indian complaints against US designs and intransigence.

The risk that such blatant association with the United States would alienate Pakistan within emerging Third World forums was considered by the Ayub Khan regime as a risk worth taking as long as the United States committed itself to defend Pakistan's territorial integrity. Such a commitment was spelled out in the Mutual Defence Pact of 1954, amid some American reluctance,[18] and was reiterated again in 1959 when the United States committed itself to defending Pakistan 'through force if necessary'.[19]

The logic that bound US and Pakistan relations together was mutually beneficial, and while the Cold War lasted, pretty consistent. Pakistan's association with other states, in the Middle and Far East, Western Europe and to an extent Latin America, mirrored American ties, with the initial exception of China.

American ties to Pakistan threatened the basis of Pakistan's emerging *entente cordiale* with Beijing after China's 1962 clash with India. Although his anti-communism was very real, Ayub Khan quickly appreciated China's utility as a second front against India, and was anxious not to allow American mistrust of Beijing to spoil his scheme, particularly when the United States seemed willing to offer assistance to India against China in 1962. In his autobiography the general noted that Pakistan's foreign policy must be guided by 'two sets of bilateral equations, one between Pakistan and the United States, and one between Pakistan and China, which must in turn now be allowed to constrain US–Pak relations'.[20] There was little indication then that these two equations would come together into a veritable triple entente. The Nixon visit to China in 1972, made possible through the good offices of Pakistan, was a day of particular celebration in Islamabad.

The Pakistani price for the use of their good offices was for the Americans to pressurise (and indeed, intimidate) New Delhi as they prepared to intervene within the Pakistani civil war on the side of the Bengalis, and to prevent any initial internationalisation of the issue by vetoing Indian initiatives at the UN. By mid-1971, American indifference, and indeed hostility to Indira Gandhi's depiction of the plight of refugees escaping from the civil war prompted the Indians into speeding up the preparations for the signing of the friendship treaty with Moscow.

American analyst Van Hollen has argued convincingly that 'the Nixon–Kissenger geo-political approach to South Asia was flawed both in conception and implementation'.[21] American policy during the 1971 civil war was aimed at preventing Indo-Soviet designs against Pakistan complicating US policy towards China. To India, the US attitude towards South Asia implied that since India did not fit into Washington's policies, it was expendable, as was the future of an independent Bangladesh. Such an attitude was out of keeping with popular US sentiments in favour of the Bengalis, and against advice being received from US officials in Dhaka.[22]

America's approach to the crisis is an extraordinary testimony to the extent to which the 'view from Washington' and the 'view from New Delhi' not only diverged but actually conflicted. In the various meetings of the Security Council's senior review group Nixon found Mrs Gandhi (referred to by the president starkly – and frequently – as 'that bitch') uncompromising and dishonest, and Indian policies incomprehensible. In a subsequent examination of the crisis, Rose and Sisson also highlight the degree to which American calculations over Soviet intentions were widely inaccurate. The belief that the Soviets were pushing India into a war were simply incorrect. Throughout the August–November period, the Soviets were attempting to constrain India and even seeking to open diplomatic channels to Pakistan. In his biography of Kissinger, Isaacson notes that the State Department's analysis of the South Asian crisis was

> incorrect. India would claim throughout the crisis that it had no designs on Pakistani territory, and it ended up acting accordingly. The Soviets would claim they were counselling restraint, and they acted accordingly. The Chinese never offered to come to Pakistan's aid, and it would be Pakistan, not India, that launched the first full scale attack.[23]

Raju Thomas notes that the 'basic problem of Indo-American relations [has been] their divergent security interests and the fact that Indo-Pak rivalry has complicated US global strategy'.[24] Such complications have compelled the United States to contain India's regional ambitions in order to achieve its own global agenda. Nowhere is this more clearly illustrated than in the events of 1971. The decision to deploy the US nuclear aircraft carrier, *The Enterprise*, into the Bay of Bengal was interpreted by New Delhi as a blatant attempt by Washington to intimidate India and constrain its policy towards Pakistan. It was an act that was (and still is) deeply resented by India's political elite.

If, however, Washington and India seem rarely to see and talk about the same international system, the basis of US–Pakistan understanding was also circumstantial. Based upon differing premises – on the one hand Pakistan's pro-Western leanings and its role within the wider American interests of CENTO, and on the other, the vital need of American aid against India – the security arrangement was fragile, and in the late 1980s it slowly unwound. That the United States proved ultimately unwilling to intervene within the Bangladesh crisis impressed itself profoundly into the thinking of Prime Minister Bhutto, Pakistan's first civilian leader since 1958. So too did the subsequent US arms and aid embargo which was not lifted until 1975. It was quickly reimposed by President Carter over issues such as the Islamic bomb and human rights. Although aid and trade restrictions were once more removed by Reagan, in the context of the Soviet invasion of Afghanistan, they were once more reimposed by the Bush Administration, and continued in force under Clinton until 1995. Even now, Pakistan must be seen to consult the United States on a whole series of issues in order to retain its support and interest, and to convince Washington that Pakistan is complying with US interests.

Zulfikar Bhutto had come to power on an electoral programme which involved a commitment to Islamic socialism, and more critically, further links with the Arab Muslim world and with China. One of Bhutto's first acts following the secession of Bangladesh was to visit leading states within the Islamic world. Ziring notes in a history of Pakistani foreign policy that Bhutto

> envisaged a foreign policy that liberated Pakistan from American independence. Pakistan was, Bhutto declared, a Middle East Country, a nation which drew its purpose and identity from the sands of the Arabian peninsula, not from the steaming jungles of the sub-continent.[25]

Zulfikar Bhutto, and senior members of the Pakistani armed forces, constructed a powerful myth of US betrayal. One consequence of this apparent betrayal – Bhutto's relentless quest to construct a Pakistani nuclear device – has only led to further American pressure.

The degree of mistrust between Islamabad and Washington deepened following the military coup of 1977 that brought the military back to power. The successful implementation of *Operation Fair Play* – the code name for General Zia–el Haq's seizure of power – coincided with the Carter Administration's stress upon human rights and democracy, and a fresh round of openings to India. Had not the decrepit Brezhnev come to the rescue by invading Afghanistan, the US–Pakistan security arrangement might well have come undone a decade earlier.[26]

The tragedy of Afghanistan, which has been the subject of several informative studies[27] is a crucial reminder of how external factors can often come to the rescue of a state's foreign policy and even how it can sustain a particular political regime. Not only did the Soviet action put Pakistan back into the centre of the US global perspective, and convert General (by 1985, President) Zia from being a dictator into the defender of democracy, it transformed an illegal regime into a loyal friend of the West, a front-line state standing alone in the way of the inexorable Soviet march to the Gulf.

The entire tenor of US–Pakistan relations was transformed overnight, much to the misgivings of India, and once more contributed its fair share to closing off any possibility of sustained improvements between India and the United States The election of the Reagan Administration in 1984 saw a further hardening of American attitudes towards supporting strident anti-communist regimes, regardless of their particular human rights records.

By 1983 the Americans had waived the Symington Amendment to the US Trades Act that outlawed US aid to 'threshold nuclear states'.[28] After a token gesture of aid, the Americans agreed to give Pakistan a US$ 3.2 billion aid package, half of which was made up of sophisticated weapons such as the F-16. Further aid packages were announced in 1987 to the sum of US$ 4.7 billion. Indian denunciations of the United States were once again strident. New Delhi accused the Americans of assisting the Pakistan nuclear weapons programme by exempting it from anti-proliferation legislation, and providing Pakistan with weapons far in excess of its legitimate defence requirements.

While Carter had at least tried to square the circle of pleasing both Islamabad and New Delhi, the attitude of the Reagan Administration towards India was blunt, made worse by India's apparent condoning of Soviet action, its own long-standing links with Afghanistan, and its support for the Soviet-backed Afghanistan government. For the duration of the Afghanistan crisis, mutual US–Indian suspicion returned to the forefront of their relationship.

Having been revived by an escalation in East–West tensions, it follows that the Soviet withdrawal from Afghanistan, and the much more dramatic global disengagement of the superpowers that has been taking place since the break-up of the Soviet Union itself, once more marginalised Pakistan. Yet even during the Afghanistan crisis, there were differences between US and Pakistani objectives, especially over which faction of the Afghan resistance – the *Mujahadeen* – should be promoted to oust the Soviet-backed regime. Zia was keen to support the Islamic fundamentalist faction led by Gulbadeen Hekbatyar, while Washington – and some domestic critics of the Zia regime – favoured support for the moderates.

America's attitude to any future Indo-Pak war would, in all probability, be more like its 1965 response: joint embargoes and pressures on both sides to negotiate. In a recent article, Sumit Ganguly has noted that 'at a time of declining world tensions ... a war on the sub-continent would divert US attention from on-going attempts to shape the new world order',[29] but it is increasingly clear that India cannot tolerate being seen by Washington as a diversion. It still remains unclear how India (or even Pakistan) fits into these wider American schemes. If Washington was to accept India as the regional peace-keeper, committed to upholding security within the region as a whole, it would open the way for sustained Indian–US co-operation but would terrify Pakistan. In 1987, the Bush Administration welcomed the deployment of Indian troops to Sri Lanka as an act of 'regional responsibility'. Even if Washington was willing to recognise India as a 'rising great power', it is not clear to what extent India would concur with US hegemony.

While Indian attitudes towards the global economy (as clarified at the end of the Uruguay Round) appear to concur with US interests, there remains the distinct possibility that the 'new world order' will be as divergent from New Delhi's ideas and instincts as Foster Dulles' northern tier was. India's foreign policy approach to the Gulf crisis of 1991 underscored the very fundamental differences about the concept of sovereignty, and was characterised by ex-colonial sentiments and anxieties about neo-imperialism. Having been seen to prevaricate over Iraq's invasion of Kuwait, India remained ambivalent towards the so-called 'coalition' because of US involvement. Suspicious of American designs on the Arabs, Indian sensitivities are fuelled by its dependency on oil, its own not inconsiderable Muslim population, and the ideology of non-alignment. As American interests in Pakistan decline, and if interest in India does not improve, the importance of South Asia as a whole could well diminish, especially if India holds out against American attempts to prevent the proliferation of missile technology, or goes slow on eliminating – as opposed to restricting – nuclear weapons generally.

What of US relations with the other South Asian states? Sri Lanka, pro-Western under the UNP governments and pro-Eastern under the Sri Lankan Freedom Party (SLFP) and SLFP-coalition governments, had some strategic weight in the 1960s, offering the United States prospects of base facilities in the Indian Ocean. The Americans were permitted to use Sri Lanka to refuel planes on their way to the Korean war, and Sri Lanka has frequently voted with the United States within the UN. Yet Sri Lanka's somewhat more categorical commitment to non-alignment after 1956, combined with an appreciation of India's security interests, ended all such arrangements, and ended the prospects of extra-regional forces being provided port facilities in Trincomlee. Given the base facilities available on the island of Diego Garcia however, the strategic relevance of Sri Lanka has declined.

India has always been suspicious of close US–Sri Lankan co-operation. The Indian government believed that J. R. Jayawardene's visit to Washington in 1984 involved a request for military help in the event of an Indian invasion of the island, and as the Indo-Sri Lankan Accord reveals, India remains highly sensitive to potential US designs on Trincomlee, a splendid deep-water harbour on the eastern coast. The disagreement apart, since 1977 and the election of the Premadasa presidency in 1988, US–Sri Lankan relations have been particularly cordial, supported by trade and Sri Lankan hopes for further US investment.

Sri Lanka has also been prominent in the move aimed to make the Indian Ocean a 'zone of peace', both during the UN General Assembly in December 1971, and again in 1973 at the summit of the non-aligned states. Sri Lanka has also supported similar recommendations for the South Pacific and has supported Nepal's call for a Himalayan peace zone.

The US approach to Bangladesh – remarkably good considering the circumstances of its birth – and US foreign policy approaches to the Himalayan kingdoms generally, have been dominated by aid and economic assistance. The reasoning behind such aid has been to encourage 'Third World' enthusiasm for the United States, and to encourage where possible the adoption of capitalist and world market orientated activities, such as the opening out of domestic economies for US investment. Much of the US aid to Bangladesh has been of a multilateral and humanitarian kind. Importantly, Nepali, Bhutanese and Bangladeshi support for American interests and actions within the South Asia region followed the same compulsions that have figured so prominently in US-Pak relations: the need to head off Indian dominance, and to act as an irritant to New Delhi. This is especially true of Bangladesh after 1975. By 1988 the Americans had endorsed King Birendra's plans for a Himalayan 'zone of peace' proposal. China had supported it, while India and the Soviet Union rejected it as 'impractical'. As already noted, however, the Russian Republic's views on South Asian nuclear free zones have changed.

The Soviet Union and South Asia

To a large extent, Americans have consistently misunderstood the nature of Indo-Soviet relations. For example, in 1984 it was seriously suggested by one analyst that the Soviet invasion of Afghanistan might well encourage India to 'annex territory' with implicit Soviet support, the suggestion being that the USSR had informed India about Afghanistan and offered it some share in the action.[30] As with the Nixon–Kissenger view of the 1970s, such a belief can only rest on a complete misreading of events in the 1980s.[31] The first and most important explanation as to why the Indian–Soviet bilateral relationship has been so successful is that Moscow has given to New Delhi the sort of categorical regional and international recognition that it has never been able to secure from Washington. As Duncan notes, like US–Pakistan relations 'the key to the success of the Soviet–Indian relationship was geo-political. The two countries lacked a common border, but do have common enemies and adversaries.'[32] They also had great commonalties in terms of ideologies, certain types of economic activities, and similar degrees of social and linguistic pluralism.

As with the US–Pakistan relationship, the basis of the relationship was a tentative convergence of Indian and Soviet interests that has involved significant amounts of Soviet aid, and diplomatic support for each other. Between 1955 and 1965 India received Soviet aid to the value of US$ 1.5 billion in credits, while at the end of the 1960s it had received US$ 700 million in military equipment. While lagging far behind US and Western aid in terms of value, Soviet aid was less conditional, and had a high military component. Likewise, the Soviets candidly acknowledged India's influence throughout the NAM and the Third World, and have benefited from the ideological connotations of this support: that the USSR was on the side of poor, ex-colonial nations and committed to their industrial development. As early as 1954, the year in which the Americans undertook to guarantee Pakistani integrity, Khrushchev had addressed the General Assembly in the UN and supported the 'five principles' of *Panscheel* and the NAM.

None the less, Soviet dealings in South Asia have been far less biased than US propaganda maintained. It was relatively even-handed in the pre-1969 period, when it was possible for the Kremlin to mediate over the 1965 Indo-Pak war as an honest broker, and indeed between 1948 and 1969 the Soviets had provided Pakistan with up to US$ 246 million in general aid. The basis of the Indian–Soviet alliance was definitely secured by the growing links between Islamabad and Washington, and furthered by the close Sino-Pak relations in the wake of the Sino-Soviet split. The calculation that, when push came to shove, the Kremlin had more to gain from India than Pakistan, was probably completed by 1970 reflecting the Soviet assessment of India's political stability and future military potential in Asia, compared to Pakistan's, which many expected to disintegrate.[33] The Soviets moreover, apart from initially mistrusting Nehru's Western habits, were deeply suspicious of Pakistan's Islamic dimensions, believing that the state was a theocracy and therefore reactionary.

As with the US–Pakistani relationship, there has always been a tendency to exaggerate the permanence of this accord. India has required Soviet support against China, and against Washington and Pakistan, and has generously received that support both before

1971 and afterwards, but never unconditionally, and always as a process of careful bargaining. Until the onset of the Pakistani civil war, India was reluctant to sign the Soviet friendship treaty – which had been on the drawing board since 1970, but had yet to be given final shape and publicly acknowledged for fear of domestic and foreign criticism over a so-called Moscow 'tilt' in New Delhi's commitment to non-alignment. Yet it was at India's insistence, not Moscow's, that Foreign Minister Gromyko made the trip to New Delhi in August 1971 to conclude the treaty in order to strengthen India's hand within the region, especially against China.[34] Furthermore, in spite of American misperception as to the true nature of the agreement, the treaty was 'more than a non-aggression pact, but much less than an alliance'.[35] It did not even compel the two states to hold joint consultations with each other in the event that one was attacked by a third party

More generally, India's foreign policy has been more complimentary to Moscow than it has been to Washington. India was one of the first countries to recognise the Marxist regime in Afghanistan in 1978. Following Indira Gandhi's election in 1980, India gave diplomatic recognition to the Vietnamese-backed Kampuchian regime following the fall of Pol Pot. Close relations between India and Vietnam – cemented by common concerns over China – complemented Soviet–Vietnamese links. Much the same can be said of India's policy towards Cuba, Iraq and Eygpt prior to the expulsion of the Soviet influence.

The limits to Indo-Soviet co-operation concern the determination of New Delhi to isolate the South Asia region from external influence – even that of the Soviets – unless invited in by the Indians (as in 1971) or unless such action is part of a wider agreement that preserves India's premier position in South Asia and its freedom to act outside the area. It was these reasons that led India to reject Moscow's advice to sign the NPT in 1967, and the offer of an Asian defence pact in 1969 aimed to contain Chinese aggression, and which in 1979–80 led to India's concerns over the Soviet invasion of Afghanistan.

The Afghanistan crisis showed the tensions within Indo-Soviet relations. India had no prior warning about Soviet plans to invade, and appeared genuinely bewildered by the event. Throughout the crisis – potentially embarrassed by its isolation both within the UN and the NAM – India attempted to show solidarity with the Soviet

Union while pressurising the Kremlin in private to withdraw. In the General Assembly debates of January 1980, the Indian ambassador to the UN called for the withdrawal of 'all troops' from Afghanistan and later remarked 'we have no reason to doubt assurances [of a speedy withdrawal], particularly from a friendly country like the Soviet Union with whom we have many important ties'.

While India abstained from condemning Soviet action within the UN, on a state visit to Moscow in 1983 Mrs Gandhi privately raised Indian objections to Soviet policy and remarked during an interview that Soviet troops should be withdrawn.[36] In this respect India failed to alter the Soviet agenda in Afghanistan. When it did change – following the rise of President Gorbachev – it did so for domestic reasons.

By the 1990s, before the actual collapse of the Soviet empire, various structural problems were evident in Indo-Soviet relations. One such problem concerned the growing trade surplus between India and the Soviet Union. During the early 1980s the value of Indo-Soviet trade increased dramatically. In part this reflects increased sales of Soviet oil to India.[37] Until very recently, the degree of technical and industrial co-operation between India and the Soviet Union was far more significant and comprehensive than that between India and the United States. In 1965 India was the Soviet Union's largest non-communist trading partner, and on various occasions Indo-Soviet trade has exceeded Indo-US trade. One explanation for the high level of trade with the Soviets is that India has found the offer of concessional trade and barter agreements – the so-called rouble–rupee agreements – particularly helpful in times of foreign exchange shortages, since both were effectively soft currencies. In 1989 Indian exports to the Soviet Union were estimated at around US$ 3,575 million, while exports to America were US$ 1,883 million.

India's growing dissatisfaction with the quality of Soviet goods and technology, and following the chaotic emergence of the CIS, the prospect of delays and irregularities in deliveries, has been matched by Russian, Ukrainian and Georgian indifference to the quality of Indian exports. Important sections of Indian textiles, handicrafts and manufactured goods relied upon consistent sales to the former Soviet Union and Eastern Europe, and following the subsequent economic restructuring of these economies by 1992, displaced Indian goods have found it more difficult to penetrate into the more affluent, quality-controlled sales of the Organisation for Economic Co-operation and Development (OECD), or indeed to gain access to the EU.

The other cause is the changing perception that the Russian Federation has of India's position in Asia *vis-à-vis* China. Again, this change in perception predates the actual collapse of the Soviet Union. In 1986, following the signing in New Delhi of the joint Indo-Soviet declaration which called for global disarmament and international economic co-operation, Rajiv Gandhi referred to the Soviet Union as an Asian power, firm in his conviction that the Soviets saw India in the same light. Later that year in Vladivostock on 28 July, Gorbachev gave out the Asian version of the earlier European 'common home' speech, and called for a Asian collective security doctrine which, appearing to hinge upon Chinese co-operation and the great future of China, caused some concern in New Delhi.

Subsequent Soviet speeches at Krasnoyarsk (1988) and in Beijing (in 1989) implied that China was not just the subject of a few stray thoughts, but part of a comprehensive re-think of Soviet–Asian policy. Should the Soviets, bolstered by trade agreements and arms reductions, move towards a closer association with Beijing? To what extent would the Russians be willing or able to support India in any future Sino-Indian disagreements? It was widely believed that significant Sino-Soviet improvements on the border question in 1987, especially in the area of the Amur river, pressurised India into seeking its own political breakthrough by dispatching Rajiv Gandhi to Beijing in 1988, although the Chinese repression of the pro-democracy movement in 1989 momentarily stalled this general momentum.[38] None the less, Sino-Indian relations continue to improve, despite the continuing absence of any significant breakthrough on the border question.

By late 1987 it was estimated that the Chinese had demobilised around one million men, a great majority of them stationed along the Soviet border. Paradoxically Indian concerns over the ending of the Cold War in Asia are probably more profound than they would be if the Cold War was in fact to continue. The effects of continuing Sino-Russian *rapprochement* could isolate India in its own private dispute with China and greatly augment China's potential influence throughout Asia. India did not support Gorbachev's call for a Helsinki-style conference on Asia, probably because it echoed earlier Chinese desires for 'Bandung'-like jamborees under the aegis of Beijing and threatened to bypass India's influence – and niche – within the NAM.

The Afghanistan war ended any real basis for normal relations between Pakistan and the Soviet Union, although Pakistan has been consummate in its overtures to Russia, Ukraine and Georgia since 1992. In the wake of the Soviet invasion of Afghanistan, Islamabad had to deal with over three million refugees descending on the sensitive north-western territories, and its support for the *Mujahadeen* alliance in their struggle against the Soviet-backed regime led to numerous violations of Pakistani airspace. On 18 June 1984 Pakistan complained to the Secretary-General of the UN that Soviet MiGs had violated Pakistan airspace on twenty-eight separate occasions since the beginning of the year, and had even carried out bombing raids against refugee camps.[39] Soviet attempts to secure Pakistan's recognition of the Kamal government by assuring Pakistan that the refugees would return as soon as the situation 'normalised' largely failed, despite the acute ethnic pressures (and violence) that the refugee problem was creating. President Zia's personal attachment to the radical Islamic factions within the Mujahadeen was particularly vexing to Moscow, as was their role in the peace summits in Geneva.

In keeping with the general change in diplomatic and foreign policy between South Asia and the international system, recent events hold out the possibility that Pakistan and Russia will come to a fresh set of understandings and accommodations, free of any past bitterness or suspicion. Since 1991, Pakistan has been successful in using its links with the emerging Central Asian Republics as conduits to Russia. In 1993 the Russian foreign minister visited Pakistan to hold free and far-ranging discussions about the situation in Tajikistan and Afghanistan. The Russian delegation were also willing to discuss Kashmir, in so far as it involved the security and integrity of the region as a whole. Proposed security arrangements with the Central Asian Republics, including the construction of infrastructure and the sharing of intelligence, also bring Islamabad closer to Moscow, a point that has not gone unnoticed in New Delhi.[40]

Soviet links to the rest of South Asia were generally perceived through the prism of the 'special relationship' with India. Soviet support for Bhutan, for example, is expressed in the general support for India's security doctrine towards the Himalayan kingdoms, and in Indian economic assistance. As such, the states of Bangladesh and

Sri Lanka have been of little use in deploying Soviet influence and aid as a natural counterweight to Indian influence as the two have tended to be complementary. Soviet–Bangladesh relations reached an all-time low after the 1975 coup, as the Ziaul Rehman regime toyed with Pakistan and then China, but relations have improved during the 1980s, with Bangladesh and Nepal responding favourably to the Vladivostock speech of a common Asian home that would get them out from under the skirts of Mother India. Russian support for a nuclear-free South Asia was well received outside India, and was clearly considered long overdue.

Like most of the small states of South Asia – and unlike India – Bangladesh stands to gain from Sino-Soviet *détente* by increasing its trading links with both. In 1985 the Soviets extended credit facilities to help Bangladesh build a power station, and plans were announced to build a Russian culture centre in Dhaka. Earlier in 1984 Bangladesh secured a five-year trade agreement with China worth US$ 200 million. In 1989 Bangladesh imports from the Soviet Union were worth US$ 69 million, compared to US$ 282.2 million from the United States, and they seem set to improve throughout the 1990s. A Russian trade delegation visited Dhaka in 1993 to explore ways in which Russian trade support could be of mutual advantage to both countries.

For Nepal the proximity of Moscow and New Delhi is still something of a problem, stifling its foreign policy initiatives and reinforcing its perceptions of Indian dominance. Nepal has none the less been the recipient of Soviet aid in the past. By 1966 it had received US$ 14 million and has continued to benefit since. Unlike the United States however, and the global financial institutions that are supported by Western finance, the USSR's contributions in aid have been small.

In comparison to Chinese and American influence, the Soviet Union has commanded a relatively low profile in Sri Lanka, even under the Bandaranaike governments. Relations were obviously soured by the initial anti-communism of the UNP government, and Sir John Kotelawala's virulent outbursts at Bandung. Moreover the Soviet Union repeatedly blocked the membership of Sri Lanka to the UN (twice in 1948 and once in 1949) on the grounds that the island was not an independent sovereign state but a continuing appendage of British imperialism. Soviet objections were only withdrawn when, in 1955, Sri Lanka's inclusion to the UN was based

upon a Western acceptance of Albanian and Mongolian membership.

By 1956, however, following a change in government, the Bandaranaike administration initiated various links with the Soviet
Union and, along with China, was receiving various grants and
loans. Between 1960 and 1964 Sri Lanka's total net receipts in foreign aid from capitalist countries was to the value of Rs 51 million
rupees, while contributions from socialist countries were Rs 67 million.[41]

In total, between 1956 and 1965 and 1970 and 1972, the Soviet
Union contributed Rs 192.8 million to successive SLFP governments in Sri Lanka, compared to the Rs 315 million from the PRC
for the whole period. During the 1970–76 period, Sri Lanka
obtained US$ 436.3 million from the IBRD, and a further Rs 1,748
million in loans from the IMF. Since the late 1980s Sri Lanka has
drawn increasingly from the IMF under various structural adjustment programmes.

Again, as with communist aid generally, while small compared to
Western sources it has the traditional advantage of being at lower
rates of interest and less stringently tied to conditions.[42] Unlike
India, trade links with the Soviet Union remain weak. Sri Lankan
exports to the United States were worth US$ 400 million in 1989,
while exports to the USSR were worth US$ 26. 7 million.[43] By the
mid-1990s, trade with Russia, Georgia and the Ukraine was growing, but remained marginal when compared to trade with the
United States, the EU, and the Australia–Pacific Rim.

Like the Americans, the Soviets have stood to benefit from the
strategic importance of Sri Lanka. The early 1970s were dominated
by rumours that the then socialist government was about to lease
military bases to either the Russians, or indeed the Chinese. In 1971
the Ministry for External Affairs issued a statement denying that
any requests had been made. As would be expected, the Indians
would be as concerned about a Soviet base in Sri Lanka as they
would be with an American one.

South Asia and Central Asia

The emergence of five Central Asian Republics (CARs) on the ruins
of the former Soviet Union created a series of opportunities – and

dangers – for the states of South Asia, in particular for Pakistan. Historically, the Republics of Kazakhstan, Uzbekistan, Turkmenistan, Tajikistan and Kyrgyzstan occupy the cultural interface between several civilisations and, more immediately, provided the landscape in which Russian, British and Chinese imperialism played itself out in the nineteenth century.[44] In terms of culture, all but Tajikistan are associated with Turkic influences and traditions. Tajikistan is characterised by Persian and Iranian influence. By the end of the nineteenth century the area was predominantly Muslim (dominated by various schools of the Sunni sect, again with the exception of Tajikistan), politically characterised by small, localised Khanates superimposed upon tribal societies, and economically poor.[45]

The colonial experience of the CARs under Russian, and then Soviet, administration further emphasises the commonalties with South Asia, especially the north-western zone across Baluchistan, North-West Frontier Province (NWFP), Gilgit, Hunza, Kashmir, Ladakh and north-west China. The rise of civic nationalism, and the creation of existing borders are a direct result of Soviet policy in the mid-1920s. As such, they are as artificial as the borders of present-day Afghanistan, Pakistan and India. They are subject to disputes, in need of clarification and confirmation, and as often as not the borders are porous: cross-cutting ethnic and clan links and creating their own problems of irredentism.

By the 1990s the CARs are all multiethnic states, containing significant minorities conscious of their own cultural identities and anxious to protect them. Issues over language and script are not dissimilar to those experienced in South Asia after independence (see chapter 3), and the political experiences of South Asia in devising ways through which to create, and sustain multiethnic nationalism give both India and Pakistan a particular familiarity with the CARs. Another striking similarity with South Asia, specifically with Pakistan and Bangladesh, is the political link between statehood and religion. All the CARs are technically secular republics, and all the state leaders have tried, to varying degrees and with varying necessity, to set up officially sanctioned Islamic institutions and to make reference to Islam as the need arises. The resulting ambiguity between civil authority (combined with a stress upon personality) and Islam and the Mullahs, is creating tensions over legal, political and economic affairs which are of importance to the region as a whole.

The outbreak of civil war in Tajikistan in 1992, somewhat crudely characterised as a pro-communist north versus a pro-Islamic south, gave rise to anxieties over regional disorder and the fear that the CARs as a whole would collapse into Afghanistan-like end-games of warring factions and widespread violence. Already the noticeable growth in religious sentiments and practices throughout the CARs had given rise in the West to fears of Islamic fundamentalism, based in the Tajikistan case on exaggerated fears of Iranian influence. Concerns that the fighting could easily spill over into neighbouring states led to the intervention of Russia and Uzbekistan in 1992–93, a position supported by both Pakistan and India.

These events had immediate repercussions for Pakistan, determined as it is to avoid any further complications in the NWFP or with troubled Afghanistan. India remains anxious that the CARs enforce their borders and prevent the passage of weapons, drugs and militants down into South Asia. In 1994, New Delhi was increasingly aware of the involvement of Uzbeks and Tajiks within the Kashmir area. Ironically, although the development and setting up of bilateral relations between India, Pakistan and the individual CARs has been competitive, both New Delhi and Islamabad are keen to see the secular and moderate façade of the republics continue. At the same time, Pakistan is keen to offer its own Islamic identity, and its physical proximity, as an advantage over India. Kyrgyzstan, Tajikistan and, Turkmenistan agreed to join the Organisation of Islam Conference (OIC), while Uzbekistan joined the NAM.

Pakistan recognised the CARs in 1991, and quickly set up full ambassadorial links with each one. Moreover, Pakistan was keen to offer economic and security advice from the outset, although it was crowded out by competition from Saudi Arabia, Turkey and – in the case of Tajikistan – Iran. Since 1993, Pakistan has seen the need to work with, and complement, Saudi influence in the area, if it is to have any clout at all. Saudi Arabia has a very important financial input into the area, in terms of economic and infrastructural support, as well as in supporting officially sanctioned cultural and religious institutions and events.[46] Pakistani initiatives, such as agreements to build road and port facilities in Makran, Gwadar as well as to extend facilities at Karachi, have been assisted in part by Saudi money and credits. Yet it has also offered bilateral aid of its own.

India has attempted to make its own links with the CARs,

through financial, trade and defence agreements. In 1994, New Delhi offered US$ 5 million to Tajikistan for economic development, and held conspicuous talks with Prime Minister Abdullajanov on terrorism, religious extremism and border security. Indian and Pakistani leaders have undertaken tours of Central Asia, promising credits to facilitate a growth in bilateral trade, but it is not necessarily clear that such trade can be had. Central Asian and South Asian economies remain asymmetrical, import and export requirements are incompatible, and as regions they compete for loans and grants-in-aid.

The links between the CARs and Russia, and through Russia, the West generally, remain uppermost in the minds of the various Central Asian leaderships. In 1994, the formation of an economic union between Kazakhstan, Kyrgyzstan and Uzbekistan, and the creation of a Central Asian Bank, implies that the scope for economic assistance with South Asia remains limited, at least for the time being.

South Asia and multilateral institutions

Apart from the bilateral relations between the region and the superpowers, South Asia is closely bound up by a whole web of international diplomatic activity that centres on the UN and the NAM. Pakistan, Bangladesh and the Maldives, grouped together through common Islamic ties have participated within various Islamic forums, especially the OIC. The significance of the British Commonwealth – in terms of economic aid and of political support – has declined over the years, but remains symbolically important, and useful for a whole series of bilateral relations. In the early years – before non-alignment became established – the Commonwealth provided India with an important niche within the international system. Since the mid-1980s, especially during the Thatcher governments of 1979–1990, the Commonwealth has suffered from neglect and political controversy in which India – and not Britain – has led a majority of states over various international issues.[47]

Within these forums, India's diplomatic profile is the highest and the most dominant of the South Asian states with the telling exception of the Islamic Conference. In the other forums it has attempted to forge a regional response to specific issues and has been anxious to avoid open displays of regional division and mistrust on the international stage. Many of the South Asian diplomatic initiatives use all three forums simultaneously. The Sri Lankan proposal to make the Indian Ocean a 'zone of peace' was first raised in the Lusaka summit of the NAM in 1970, the Commonwealth Heads of Government meeting, and then introduced into the UN in 1971. India's proposals for disarmament were first brought before the NAM at Cairo in 1964, and then introduced to the UN. Pakistan has brought the matter of Kashmir to the attention of virtually every international organization of which it is a member.

The United Nations and South Asia

Since the Kashmir crisis of 1947–48, India's attitudes towards the UN, and its role within international relations generally, have undergone significant change. Indian foreign policy under Nehru favoured the concept of international equality and the 'rule of law' that was enshrined in the UN Charter. Yet he was the first to appreciate, in the light of the UN debates on Kashmir, the limitations imposed on the organisation by the frustrations and bitterness of the Cold War and a hierarchy of great power states.

Following on from the experiences of Kashmir – and part of the American mistrust of Indian diplomacy – India has favoured UN initiatives with a particularly anti-Western bias, while it has come to disregard or criticise UN intervention in the South Asia region on the grounds that the UN was dominated by external powers and the exclusive interests of the Security Council.

India took an active role in the diplomacy surrounding the Korean war (1950–54), and was a supporter of the PRC's claim to resume its seat in the UN. Throughout the 1980s India was active in the various UN debates against South Africa, and in vigorous calls for global disarmament. While India's commitment to the UN has been ideological it has, like much of India's international diplomacy after the 1950s and the falling out with China, been underscored by political realism.[48] With the ending of the colonial empires (and the West's natural dominance in the UN) India has been clever to use the UN as a forum in which to enhance its prestige by offering mediation and support to the newly emerging states of Africa and Asia, presenting itself as a state opposed to the forces of imperialism and neo-colonialism.[49]

From 1960 onwards India was active on the Special Committee for Decolonisation, while it has been particularly active in the United Nations Conference on Trade and Development (UNCTAD), created in 1964 and which called for global economic reform aimed to assist 'Third World' states undertake economic and social development. The second session of the UNCTAD conference was in fact held in New Delhi in 1982.

As such, India's role within the UN has been controversial. American criticism has centred on India's voting behaviour in the UN which invariably appeared pro-Soviet. On many occasions India has voted in favour of Soviet moves, such as the attempt to secure the UN seat for Kampuchea as opposed to the exiled 'Cambodian' leadership. As already noted, India has abstained in votes that sought to condemn Soviet action, while it has vigorously condemned US policy in Vietnam, Libya and the invasion of Panama in 1989.

Moreover, while critical of the Cold War and the effects this has had on polarising UN diplomacy, India has relied upon the use of the Soviet veto to shield it from international condemnation. During the Bangladesh crisis the Soviet Union vetoed three peace initiatives sponsored by the United States and Britain which, had they been successful, would have hindered India's execution of the war. One element of the Nehruvian legacy is still present, however: India's political elite remain terribly sensitive to UN opinion, especially the risk of being subjected to an adverse UN resolution. Throughout the 1984–87 crisis in Indo-Sri Lankan relations, there was some concern that the Sri Lankan government would refer the matter of Indian assistance to the Tamils to the Security Council and open the matter to 'great power' interference. With the collapse of the Soviet Union, the Indians cannot rely on the Russian veto being used in their favour. New Delhi remains anxious that, without the help of the Soviet veto, India could face censure in the UN over the handling of the Kashmir crisis.

Since the 1960s India has continued its general support for Third World issues, both economically through the various UNCTAD resolutions, and politically through the call for a New International Economic Order (NIEO) made in 1974 at a special session of the UN General Assembly. In 1980, India supported the calling by UNESCO for a New World Information and Communications Order, which many Western states believed was 'overtly political' and well outside UNESCO's charter. Sir Anthony Parsons noted recently that such posturing has led to a malaise within the UN, especially within the UN specialist agencies, a behaviour associated with Indian attempts to draw attention to apartheid in South Africa.

Indian remarks, as part of a general Third World verbal and procedural assault over South Africa, racial discrimination generally and disarmament, have further been construed as attacks against US interests. In a letter to the Director-General of the International Labour Organisation (ILO), Henry Kissinger stated that 'in recent years the International Labour Organisation (ILO) has become increasingly and excessively involved in political issues which are quite beyond the competence and mandate of the organisation'.[50]

In contrast to India's use of the UN for principled statements on foreign and international policy, Pakistan has often appeared to be sidelined. Although active on various UN committees, Islamabad has not taken such a general involvement in global issues. Pakistan's major role in the Geneva talks that brought about the end of the Afghanistan crisis in 1988 were typical of Pakistan's involvement: as a forum to settle matters within the region, rather than to address issues of wider international importance. However, during the collapse of Yugoslavia, and the resulting civil war, Pakistan was active in the UN in articulating Bosnian Muslim interest, and initiated or seconded almost eleven debates in the General Assembly between 1991 and 1995.

Far from using the UN as a window to wider interests, Pakistan has sought to use the General Assembly as a forum in which to condemn India and to frustrate India's regional ambition.[51] Even as recently as 1984, Pakistan provoked Indian condemnation by bringing up the issue of Kashmir in a discussion on the Iran–Iraq war. During the mid-1990s Pakistan still clearly envisaged a role for the UN in finding some lasting solution to the Kashmir dispute, the bilateralism of the Simla Accord notwithstanding. In this, Pakistan has much in common with Nepal, Bangladesh and Bhutan, states that have used voting within the General Assembly as a means to signal disapproval to New Delhi rather than to construct wider-ranging foreign policy initiatives.

Nepal and Bangladesh have voted with China and with the United States on issues aimed to irritate New Delhi. Bangladesh, which became a member of the UN in 1974 has, like Pakistan over Kashmir, attempted to use the UN as a way of isolating India. Sri

Lanka's position towards the UN has been more in line with India, although it has on several occasions voted against the Soviet Union, over the use of force in Eastern Europe and over the Afghanistan invasion.

All of the South Asia states – especially Bhutan, Bangladesh and Nepal – have benefited from the economic and financial institutions of the UN, such as the IMF and the General Agreement on Tariffs and Trade (GATT), as well as the World Bank and its subsidiary institutions, more perhaps than the political and diplomatic dimensions of the UN. On becoming a member of the organisation in 1974, Bhutan was able to move away from its almost total reliance upon India and involved UN expertise within its own development strategies.

In the recently published *A History of the United Nations*, Evan Luard has noted that the decade between 1955 and 1965 was 'the ... period when the United Nations came closest ... to achieving the goals it was set up to accomplish. There has existed no other period in its history when there existed such a widespread willingness to turn to the organisation.'[52]

Between 1979 and 1986 this willingness to co-operate was largely ebbing under increased North–South pressures generated by economic hardships and, following Afghanistan and the onset of the first Reagan presidency, renewed Cold War tensions. Many commentators noted the indifference and indeed contempt expressed towards the UN by the two Reagan Administrations.

During the 1990s, however, the role of the UN has become transformed, even if the extent and nature of UN operations, especially peace-keeping operations, have become more problematic.[53] Following the onset of Soviet reforms in 1985, the situation has been revolutionised. The end of the Cold War has removed, at one stroke, many of the objections that Nehru made of the organisation's activities during the 1950s, by freeing the international agenda of the old Washington–Moscow gridlock. Yet the questions of the future of the UN as an international peace-keeper and – more profoundly – the main forum of a new international order – impinge on the previous discussion of Indian–US relations and India's ability to use the UN without appearing to concur with American dominance. On 15 November 1989, the Soviets and the Americans sponsored a joint resolution (44/21) calling upon all states to support the UN Charter and to take up the 'peace divi-

dends' that were now on offer. Since 1992, US agreement with the
Russian Republic has relied heavily upon the presence of Yeltsin as
President, and the Russian need for soft aid and credits to assist in
its economic restructuring but there are reasons to believe it will
continue even if (and when) Yeltsin is removed. Given the rise of a
US–Russian condominium on key matters of global management,
the role of the UN seems set to increase further, while India's input
may well decline.

India has also been isolated within the UN over matters of environmentalism and cost. India did not sign the Montreal Protocol in
1987 to cut back on the global emissions of the primary ozone
depleting gases (CFCs) on the grounds that it did not recognise the
obligations of the 'developed' world to the industrialising countries.
Interestingly enough, India and China both couched their objections in the language of Third World solidarity, and support the
same position, although unlike China, Indian scientists have not
directly challenged the authenticity of the facts.

India has consistently argued that the industrial nations must bear
much of the costs for cleaning up the environment to the extent of
granting to the less developed countries financial help to switch to
new, cleaner technology. Throughout the 44th session of the UN (in
1989) India insisted that the discussion on the environment be
widened to take into consideration the issue of technological transfers. The United States objected to the demands for the setting up
of a fund of US$ 100 million on the grounds that financial support
was already forthcoming through various other UN agencies, primarily the United Nations Environmental Programme (UNEP) set
up in 1972.[54]

At the November 1990 conference on global warming India was
able to secure some provisions for assistance to the developing
countries, which went some way to removing some of its earlier
objections, but the detailed negotiations over the amount and the
'conditionality' were postponed until February 1991, and the subsequent Earth Summit in Rio, in 1992. Here India successfully
argued for further cash and technological transfers in order to
comply with the phase-out of ozone depleting gases.

Areas of specific disagreement apart, the so-called post-Cold War
era has brought with it the prospect of extensive international co-
operation, and has led to calls to review the structure of the UN,
and to substantially revise the UN's Charter. Indian criticism of the

Security Council is based on the simple fact that, for all practical purposes, the UN Charter enthrones the permanent members above the General Assembly. In particular India believes that Article 12 is too restrictive. Article 12 states that 'while the Security Council is exercising in respect of any dispute or situation the functions assigned to it ... the General Assembly shall not make any recommendations with regard to that dispute or situation unless the Security Council so requests.'[55]

While the General Assembly may return issues back to the Security Council for reconsideration, the Council's decision is final and binding. To India, while the Council consists of fifteen member states, ten elected from the General Assembly, the fact that the permanent members retain the powers of veto is out of line with the emerging realities of the international system. At the moment, the Security Council does not represent the interests of important 'middle powers' such as itself, Brazil, Nigeria or even (arguably) Iraq. The position of the British and the French is also believed to be anomalous, while India has noted that Russia retains its seat as the legatee of the former Soviet Union and not as a state in its own right. Significantly, India is not against the principle of veto in its own right.

There have been various suggestions by India to increase the number of permanent members, with India included, but these have as yet come to nothing. There were persistent rumours in 1994–95 that India would sign the NPT treaty if the Americans supported Indian claims to a revised Security Council. Because of the degree of insecurity within Indo-Pakistan relations, placing India within the Security Council would have serious and immediate repercussions on Pakistan and would not be supported by China. It is possible that the United States would support only if India complies with the NPT and MTCR agreements. The current discussions about the inclusion of Japan and, following unification, Germany, premised upon their international economic influence, has further irritated India, since such a revised Security Council would, once more, approximate to the image of 'great powers' of an essentially prewar order. Ideas and discussions premised on the abolition of the Security Council and carrying out business through majority voting – or through some procedure of standing committees accountable directly to the General Assembly – remain, in the current international context at least, unrealistic.

India's anxiety to break into the charmed circle of the permanent members is tied up with India's image of itself, and especially of its status *vis-à-vis* China. Should India fail to convince international opinion of the need for these changes, its support for the UN will continue, but will probably be more obstructionist, and there will be the growing mistrust within India that the 'international society' of the next century will be as exclusive as the previous one.

The Non-Aligned Movement and South Asia

India has never reserved its international diplomacy solely for use within the UN. Much has been written on the Non-Aligned Movement and the ideological importance of Nehru's involvement in its founding. In much of the Indian literature, Nehru is given the extraordinary status of statesman-philosopher, and the ideological emphasis of much of the writings glosses over Nehru's appreciation of India's access to, and influence over, the emerging states of Africa and Asia. On several occasions, the Indians have used the NAM as an alternative to the UN, as a way of underlying New Delhi's independence, but also to reaffirm the importance of 'Third World' solidarity and India's role in leading it. In 1983, U. S. Bajpal noted that 'while exaggerated notions of India's strength and influence have to be eschewed, we cannot and should not conceive of ourselves as just another developing country'.[56] Nehru's view of India's status and 'calling' were just as candid, although they were disguised by a rather Edwardian style of delivery. The Bandung Conference – held in April 1955 and heralded as the 'first inter-continental conference of the so-called coloured peoples [*sic*]' – confirmed to Nehru the importance of India, and an Indian 'third way' of foreign policy that would steer through the East–West divide.

The NAM is important not just to the international politics of India generally, but to an understanding of its relationship with China. The ideas of non-alignment and Third World solidarity have been one of the main manifestations of Sino-Indian rivalry. The NAM grew out of the Bandung Conference as a smaller, compact body of states who were not members of any military alliance, who had not allowed foreign bases on their territory, and who were committed to both conventional and nuclear disarmament, and to ideas of collective security, for non-nuclear states in particular, but as a global policy generally. In this way at least, the creation of the NAM was complementary to the UN as a forum to avoid war to resolve international tension.

China's views on Third World solidarity differed from India's, especially concerning the role of nuclear weapons and collective security. In 1964 India raised the matter of China's nuclear weapons programme at the Cairo NAM summit on the grounds that it significantly threatened Indian security. China's calls for Afro-Asian summits of the Bandung variety throughout the 1970s were resisted by India who believed that they were merely attempts by China to challenge India within its 'Third World niche' by radical proposals of international revolution and reform. Significantly China has in the past portrayed India's role and influence within the NAM as 'hegemonic' and increasingly counter-revolutionary.

Initiated at Bandung, the Non-Aligned Movement was founded at Belgrade in 1961, and took the 'five principles' – the *Panscheel* – as its rationale. India claims (as to a lesser extent does Sri Lanka) the role of intellectual founder behind the Non-Aligned Movement. The prime function of the NAM was to stabilise the existence of post-colonial states from either US or Soviet interference, and allow them to deal with all their numerous problems of irredentism and 'secession'. It followed that the movement was at its most coherent when the Cold War was at its height.

The institutional structures of the NAM have evolved from the infrequent summits of heads of state, in 1961, 1964 and 1970, from regular meetings at foreign minister level and from the setting up of a co-ordination bureau. The states of India, Sri Lanka and Nepal were all active members in 1961 and have remained committed members since. Bhutan and Bangladesh joined in 1973. The Maldives joined the NAM in 1976 with India's support and encouragement. Pakistan was initially excluded because of its membership to SEATO and CENTO and only applied to join in 1974 following Bhutto's reorientation of his foreign policy and his decision to quit CENTO. Pakistan was finally admitted in 1979 amid serious Indian reservations.

Islamabad's decision to seek readmission was part of a genuine attempt to widen the scope of Pakistan policy towards the Third World, and more significantly towards the moderate Arab states of the Middle East, especially Saudi Arabia. The presence of the Arab League as an observer, as well as the Palestine Liberation Organisation (PLO) at the various NAM summits have allowed Pakistan to pursue its links with the Islamic world on a bilateral basis. While India has been aware of Pakistani overtures in the Gulf and Southwest Asia, it has tended to concentrated on East Asia, using the NAM to extend bilateral relations with Vietnam, and through supporting Vietnam, to reaffirm its commitment to contain China.[57] More generally – as in the fifty-four page political declaration after the 1983 Delhi Conference – India has reaffirmed, at some length, its ideological commitment to the old Nehruvian agenda, even if to Western observers the tone of the declaration seemed particularly antediluvian. In 1989, India called upon the NAM to set up a planet protection fund, to advance the environmental agenda of the developing states.

Forged in the context of global bipolarity, the NAM has tended to respond to changes in the intensity of Cold War hostility, and since the collapse of the Soviet Union in 1991 it has been forced to reassess its rationale for continuing to exist. The 1989 Belgrade Summit was marked by a 'a new sense of realism'. The resulting communiqué was shorter than usual, less rhetorical, and focused on practical matters such as patents and royalties. A meeting of the co-ordination bureau in Bali in 1993 was candid in its call for a detailed self-examination into the purposes of the NAM, and suggested that the organisation must now pursue or support issues in wider forums, and/or turn to economic and ecological issues.

Such a trend would be in keeping with earlier rethinks over Third World priorities. At the eleventh summit of the NAM, held in 1995 in the Caribbean, the organisation called for new ideas on Third World debt and on the restructuring of the UN. This widening of the agenda brings the NAM closer to the UN and its various affiliated institutions, especially UNCTAD, and the United Nations Environmental Programme (UNEP). Whether the NAM can remain as a coherent, meaningful force within the international system, free of the old Cold War agenda, remains to be seen.

The NAM organisation has faced challenges before, and India in particular has been confronted with difficult choices within the organisation itself. In the late 1970s the rise of the so-called 'radical thesis' threatened to destroy it. This thesis, forwarded by Cuba, urged the NAM to move closer toward the USSR as a bulwark against American 'imperialism'. Both America and China protested over Cuba's hosting of the sixth summit in 1979 because of its obvious Soviet links, and their suspicions seemed confirmed following Castro's anti-American speech.

Yet India sided immediately with the 'moderate states' of Yugoslavia and Saudi Arabia in opposing such a move and in retaining the 'no-block' principle. The dispute was complicated by the Soviet invasion of Afghanistan – a member of the NAM – which embarrassed Cuba and India. As with its policy within the UN, India would not openly condemn the move within the NAM – a position that immediately played into the hands of Pakistan and the United States – but merely called for the upholding of the five principles and the withdrawal of all foreign troops from Afghanistan.

There can be no doubt that India's role within the NAM has given it prestige and status. It has also enabled India to take part in various global initiatives. In 1981 it was agreed that India would assist the PLO in an attempt to mediate the Iran–Iraq war, and in late January 1991 India was involved in various attempts within the NAM to try, with Iranian help, to open up a dialogue between Iraq and the US-led Coalition Forces.[58] Although many Western commentators have dismissed the NAM as being a sort of ideological 'critics forum' without weight or real internal consensus, it has provided many South Asian states – particularly the smaller countries – with the scope for extending their bilateral relations outside of the region, in terms of trade and economic assistance.

The Afghanistan crisis occurred during India's presidency of the NAM, as did the Kampuchean/Cambodean issue which was still unresolved in 1995. In 1976, both the ousted Pol Pot regime and the Vietnamese-backed Heng Samrin regime sent delegates to attend the summit. In 1983 India caused some political embarrassment by issuing an invitation to the Heng Samrin government and not to representatives of the exiled Khmer Rouge. Eventually after much discussion India agreed to an 'empty seat' solution. Significantly Sri Lanka has consistently refused to accept the legitimacy of the Heng Samrin government – in both the NAM and at the UN Special Conference on Kampuchea in 1981 – on the grounds that the government had been installed by a foreign power. The foreign ministers' statement claimed that 'to accept the principle of intervention or to give it legitimacy in any form would be to make all small states vulnerable and powerful states belligerent'.[59] Such an argument has obvious parallels to Sri Lanka's relationship to India and was made, in all probability, with such parallels in mind. Sri Lanka rejects the

Indian doctrine that the Heng Samrin government is legitimate
because it has 'effective control' since such a doctrine would legitimate the invasion and control of Sri Lanka.

The increasing divergences within the NAM – and throughout
the various forums of the Third World – reflect the different degrees
of success countries have had in dealing with the problem of nation
building and economic development. As the ideological cohesive-
ness of 'anti-colonialism' has receded, the movement has become
more fragmentary. The language of aggressive anti-imperialism can
still be heard, and often it is still ideologically linked to the 'radical
thesis' that tied the NAM to the Soviet Union. In the 1986 summit
in Harare, Colonel Gadaffi returned to the earlier themes of the
1970s, implying that several NAM members were 'puppets of the
imperialists' and should therefore be expelled. Critical of the
NAM's failure to come to Libya's side during the US bombings,
Gadaffi called for some curious military alliance to declare war
against the 'West'. Such language was seen by India and the other
states of South Asia as being increasingly archaic.

The Commonwealth and South Asia

Alongside the NAM and the UN, the main states of South Asia all
share membership of the British Commonwealth of Nations. Again,
as with the NAM, Pakistan started off as a member following partition, left in 1972 (in protest over the decisions of the United Kingdom, Australia and New Zealand to recognise Bangladesh),
rejoining the organisation in 1989. Indian objections to Pakistani
membership were removed following the election of a civilian government in Islamabad in 1988, this having been one of the key decisions set by New Delhi.

With little constitutional or institutional support the Commonwealth can (and has) been too easily dismissed as an antediluvian
association, a curiously British concept without function or focus.
None the less, the organisation has a well-run secretariat, and con-
venes regularly in summit format for heads of state every two years,
and holds annual meetings of finance and foreign ministers to discuss Commonwealth affairs. The influence of the Commonwealth
has, at times, been seriously compromised by internal disagreement,
in which India has often opposed Britain and British interests.

The 1989 Kuala Lumpur summit ended with a row following British disclaimers to a joint communiqué condemning apartheid in South Africa. Indian criticism about 'British hesitancy' over South African sanctions was prevalent throughout the 1980s, and has only been resolved by the so far successful transition to black majority rule in South Africa under President Mandela. Indian support over the British Falkland expedition in 1982 was also less than categorical. India has also criticised other members of 'the club', including, recently, the Nigerian regime's decision to execute some leading dissidents in 1995. India has not supported New Zealand's initiatives to declare the Pacific Ocean a nuclear free zone.

Undoubtedly, these incidents aside, the strengths of the Commonwealth have been to provide member states with a relatively small and informal arena in which to address international issues. The fact that the Commonwealth contains states such as Canada, Australia and New Zealand also means that it does not duplicate other 'Third World' organisations, and brings South Asian states into contact with other OECD countries.

Of all the states of South Asia, if India's links with the Commonwealth have been the most problematic, they have also been arguably the most important. India's commitment to the Commonwealth after 1947 was crucial to its survival. Had partition not created two states in animosity to each other, and had Nehru not taken such a principled stand on foreign policy against colonialism, it is likely that British ideas over the shape and form of the Commonwealth would have favoured a more centralised, alliance-based structure to uphold Britain's position east of Suez after the end of the war. India and Pakistan's refusal to enter into any common defence or wider 'out of area' security agreement scotched these ideas from the beginning, as did the speed of Britain's decline after 1949.

India's support for the Commonwealth idea opened the way for the African states formed in the late 1950s and early 1960s to seek membership: 'to India belongs the singular credit of opening the Commonwealth door to the Republics'[60] and overcoming the constitutional difficulties of republics associating themselves with a monarchy. Had India withdrawn it is likely that the Commonwealth would have either collapsed or consisted entirely of the former white dominions. India has also favoured the use of the Commonwealth as a forum for inspection or monitoring, on issues such as elections and human rights, but has – as in other international forums – discouraged its activity within South Asia.

India's subsequent support for the Commonwealth, and its generally positive identification with Britain, has tended to follow the ups and downs of Anglo-Indian relations, with New Delhi extremely sensitive to British support towards Pakistan, especially concerning proposed mediation over Kashmir, and sensitive to wider anti-British feelings expressed within the NAM or the UN over issues such as South Africa, the Middle East etc. During the Suez crisis of 1956, Nehru came under direct pressure from within the Congress Party to withdraw in the wider interests of Afro-Asian solidarity. In 1957 India was outraged by British support for a Pakistani resolution calling for the holding of a plebiscite over Kashmir.

Yet – like so much of India's policy – ideological vision has been combined with clear national interest and the Commonwealth, for all its idiosyncrasies, has been particularly useful for India. Like the NAM, the Commonwealth provided India with an area in which to establish close links with African and East Asian countries at a critical time in their struggle for independence, and to participate in various missions and observation teams dealing with Commonwealth issues. India has sent observers to several elections in Africa, Nigeria in 1993, and Uganda in 1996.

By the mid-1960s India was providing technical know-how to thirty countries, the majority of them within the Commonwealth, providing significant levels of aid to the Commonwealth secretariat as well as receiving assistance from it through the Colombo Plan.[61] One analyst has noted significantly that 'India at present [1980] is at once the recipient of the largest quality of foreign aid from the advanced countries, and a donor of massive assistance to other developing countries.'[62] Many of these countries are also members of the Commonwealth. No other South Asian state has used the Commonwealth link so effectively. Moreover, India's links with Britain proved useful in gaining initial access to the European Common Market, and in benefiting under various preferential agreements, such as those of the Lomé convention.

It could be argued that Pakistan failed to take advantage of the Commonwealth links because it allowed the Kashmir issue – and its perception that both the British and the Dominions were pro-Indian – to dominate its foreign policy to the exclusion of almost everything else. At the Commonwealth prime ministers meeting in

London in 1950, Liquat Ali Khan, the Pakistani Prime Minister, threatened to stay away because the Kashmir issue had not found its way on to the agenda. The issue was resolved through 'informal' discussions outside the framework of the main conference. Such incidents tended to improve India's image of moderation and flexibility to the general detriment of Pakistan.

Since 1989 Pakistan has seen the Commonwealth links as a conduit to other states and not simply as an arena in which to criticise and isolate India. Like Islamabad's earlier decision to seek admission to the NAM, the return to the Commonwealth reflects both a restoration of earlier pre-1954 policies and a profound change in outlook about the importance and reliability of the US links that had served to isolate Pakistan considerably. In 1995, the Pakistani government was still in favour of Commonwealth and/or British mediation in the Kashmir dispute, although it still envisaged a central role for the UN.

South Asia and the international politics of the Muslim world

Under Zulfika Al Bhutto, and dictated in part by the need to reconstruct a new state after the loss of East Bengal, Pakistan pursued an active 'Islamic' foreign policy that brought financial and political dividends, especially from Saudi Arabia. By 1974, between 1 and 1.5 million Pakistanis were working in the Arabian peninsular, and between 1975 and 1980 these workers returned US$ 2 billion home in remittances. In 1980, following the invasion of Afghanistan, on a state visit Crown Prince Fahd said that Saudi Arabia and Pakistan were 'now closely associated in terms of security and defence'. Pakistan's support for the *Mujahadeen* opposition in Afghanistan, and President Zia's insistence that a settlement in Afghanistan involved the entire 'Muslim world' also bound Pakistan close to the Islamic community of states within the Middle East. While these links were not new, they have re-emerged at the centre of Pakistan's quest for security and national identity from the 1970s onwards.

After US aid to India in 1962, and as part of the new 'balanced' approach to foreign affairs that opened up close links with China, Ayub Khan began to involve Pakistan within the various Islamic forums, attending an Islamic summit in Jakarta in 1965, and another one held in Rabat in September 1969. These various summit meetings, which drew Muslim countries from the Middle and the Far East, resulted in the founding of the OIC in 1971.[63] The founding of this set of Islamic institutions and specialist bodies coincided with Prime Minister Bhutto's general disillusionment with the US and with the reliability of the West in general. Moreover, following from the establishment (and growing influence) of OPEC, it no longer appeared that the Middle Eastern states were a string of noughts within the global power equation. Pakistan was instrumental in getting the Islamic states to set up the Islamic Development Bank, to which Saudi Arabia and Iran gave substantial collateral, to ensure its viability.

Z. Bhutto pursued active bilateral relations with the Kingdom of Saudi Arabia, the Shah of Iran, and even Gaddafi of Libya, although relations between them were to cool somewhat under pressure from the Shah. This involved taking a high profile in condemning Israeli aggression against the Arab states, and in numerous calls by Pakistan in favour of the setting up of a Palestinian state.[64] In return, Pakistan expected not just material and financial help, but diplomatic support against India over the Kashmir issue, which it has duly received from the OIC on occasion, although in a more muted form than Pakistan might well have hoped for.

In 1991, the Foreign Ministers Conference in Karachi, dominated as it was by the Iraqi invasion of Kuwait, and the outbreak of the Tajikistan civil war, set up a fact-finding mission and proposed that it be sent to Jammu and Kashmir to report on the situation. Following India's refusal to allow the mission into the country, the 1991 summit was more categorical in that it condemned India for violating human rights in the 'occupied' state of Jammu and Kashmir. The OIC also supported Pakistani calls for the formation of a wide and inclusive government in Afghanistan, a necessary precondition for the return of many Pathani refugees still on Pakistani territory. In 1995, the summit in Casablanca received a delegation of Kashmiris from the Hurrayat, a grouping of political parties calling for a plebiscite, although Kashmir did not figure in the final communiqué.

In other matters, the OIC has proved itself useful. Following the demolition of the mosque in Ayodhya, the 1993 meeting of the OIC bureau in Dakar, Senegal, called for the mosque to be re-built without delay and without any attempt to concede Hindu militancy. However, the OIC has not just provided Islamabad with an Islamic forum in which to assert – or confirm – its identity as a Muslim state, it has also provided an alternative set of financial institutions and prospective economic partners.

Pakistan was to acquire a particularly useful relationship with the Saudi military in supplying military expertise and training, an arrangement often facilitated by regular OIC encounters. Saudi Arabia was the first Islamic state to offer Pakistan financial assistance to deal with refugees from Afghanistan: US$ 25 million at the Islamabad meeting in 1980. Pakistan was also to pursue much-needed trade links with Libya and, prior to the 1978 revolution, with Iran. Significantly, Pakistani policy towards the Middle East complemented its earlier links with the United States. Both Saudi Arabia and the Shah were linked to Washington through various defence and economic agreements.

As a secular state, India did not give any particular emphasis to Islam within its foreign policy, despite being the fourth most populous Muslim state in the world. Yet at times – such as the Salman Rushdie affair – the presence of large Muslim minorities has made the state over-sensitive on specific issues and events, controversial throughout the Islamic world. India was the first South Asian state to ban Rushdie's *The Satanic Verses* on the grounds of blasphemy. The status of Kashmir, India's Muslim minorities, and the growing role of Hindu extremism within India's political system generally, make New Delhi currently vulnerable to opinion throughout the Muslim world.

The reasons for Pakistan's anxiety are not hard to find. Within the OIC 'Pakistan did not have to compete with India ... whereas in the third world movement India remained a formidable force'.[65] Pakistan's sensitivity on this matter cannot be over-estimated. In 1969 India had been invited to attend the summit of Islamic states at Rabat but in the face of Pakistan protests, and the threat to withdraw, Saudi Arabia felt sufficiently pressured into cancelling its invitation. India has never been invited to attend any summit since, and there is no evidence that recent Pakistan governments are likely to modify their opinion. Unlike the Indian position on Pakistan rejoining the Commonwealth, the OIC is arguably too important to Pakistan to allow India to join.

Following this diplomatic coup, Pakistan has held various summits and foreign ministers meetings of the Islamic Conference: in Karachi in 1970 just prior to the founding of the Conference, at

Lahore in 1974, and at Islamabad in 1980, and again in Lahore in 1994. Pakistan has played a role within the Islamic Conference almost identical to India's within the NAM. In 1977 Pakistan called for the setting up of nuclear free zones in the Indian Ocean and the Middle East, and in 1980 Pakistan voted in favour of a resolution that called upon Islamic states to deny military facilities to 'foreign powers'. After 1980, Pakistan cut a very high profile within the OIC over the Afghanistan crisis (part of a clear policy of embarrassing New Delhi's support for the Kabul regime), while the Islamic Conference provided the forum for Pakistani diplomatic initiatives such as the mission to try and mediate over the Iran–Iraq war in 1980.

Pakistan's Islamic foreign policy has brought less dividends to its relations with East Asia. Under Ayub Khan, Pakistan moved closer to Malaysia and Indonesia. During the 1965 war with India, Indonesia even offered to provide Pakistan with military help, and to 'seize the Andaman and Nicobar islands' so as to distract India from Kashmir. Pakistan continues to enjoy close relations with Indonesia, although the affinities between these two states have less to do with Islam than with a shared threat perception of India's stratagems in the Indian Ocean and its attempts to 'augment [its] naval power and acquire a power projection capability in the vicinity of the sub-continent'.[66]

The importance of the Islamic world to Pakistan cannot be overestimated. By 1989 there were over twenty-one subsidiary organisations associated with the Islamic Conference, covering areas such as Islamic jurisprudence, economic and technical development, as well as trade and heritage foundations, and Pakistan was actively associated in most of these: in 1989 Pakistan was involved in discussing the importance of the Rushdie affair to the relations between the Muslim world and the West.[67]

Embarrassed by the 1969 fiasco, India has tried to play down its exclusion from the Islamic world by Pakistan, while expressing concern over Pakistan's relationship with Saudi Arabia and, prior to 1978, the Shah. As in the case of China, New Delhi was concerned that arms sales to the Middle East would be diverted into Pakistan, and that technical co-operation and assistance with Middle Eastern states may well assist Pakistan's military rearmament programme after the loss of the east wing. India was particularly concerned that the modernisation of the Shah's army would give Pakistan another powerful, extra-regional ally against India, or even technical help – via the United States – for Pakistan's bomb.

India's attempts to pursue Pakistan into the Middle East, by adopting close bilateral ties with Iraq and Syria have not been very successful since they had tended to support, with the exception of Libya, those Arab states formerly linked with the Soviet Union and opposed to Saudi conservatism. Thus, as with Pakistan, India's support for Egypt, Iraq and Syria mirrored its own bilateral association with the former Soviet Union. Its historical links with Iraq were one of the reasons for India's mute support for the recently concluded Coalition Forces deployed against Hussein, and the controversy over the fuelling of Coalition jets. Such sensitivity has not prevented the recent opening up of diplomatic relations with Israel. Using the peace process within the Middle East as a convenient ruse, India formally recognised Israel in 1993, and up-graded its diplomatic representation to ambassadorial level in 1994. There were mild protests from Pakistan, slower and more cautious in its response to the Middle Eastern peace process, and some demonstrations from domestic parties, but nothing more dramatic. In Bangladesh it was still illegal, in 1996, to trade with Israel.

Against the backdrop of international change and transition since 1989, these sets of relations, Indo-Middle Eastern and Indo-Russia, and Pakistan–Middle Eastern and Pakistan–US have lessened. Moreover Pakistan's ability to pursue both an Islamic and pro-American policy has, like so much of Pakistani diplomacy since the 1980s, been largely coincidental, and there is the growing possibility that Pakistan may well have to choose between them. American–Pakistan relations suffered further, when the United States, conscious of possible terrorist attacks against its personnel situated in Muslim countries, suspected that the Pakistani authorities were either unwilling or unable to help. In a State Department travel warning issued on 14 January 1991, just after the outbreak of the Gulf War, it was stated that 'Non-essential government personnel and all dependants have been ordered to depart Jordan, Mauritania, Sudan, Yemen ... Algeria, Pakistan and Tunisia. American citizens should seriously consider deferring all travel to all of these areas'.[68] More generally, the future scope for Pakistani relations within the Middle East is not necessarily plain sailing, since it depends on the overall degree of consensus within Muslim politics, and, especially within Arab politics in particular, 'through the mid 1980s, the success of Pakistan's Islamic foreign policy is that it has tended to become limited by the divisions within the Islamic world itself'.[69] This is true of the effectiveness of the OIC in general. While Pakistan has been anxious to avoid the internal and factional strife that has so often characterised the relations between conservative and radical Arab States by relying upon Saudi Arabia, it has not always worked, and has often been itself a source of tension.

The Iranian revolution, and the rise of a fundamentalist Shiah regime caused particular concern for Pakistan. Like Saudi Arabia, Pakistan is a predominantly Sunni society, but contains a small Shiite minority. Throughout the early 1980s Iran denounced Pakistan, along with the United States and Saudi Arabia, and Iranian accusations against CIA involvement in the seizure of the Grand Mosque at Mecca in 1979 led to the burning down of the US embassy in Islamabad.[70] The assassination of President Zia in 1988 was linked to possible domestic discontent amongst the Shiite community over the codification of Sharia law, and Iran has made several accusations that Pakistan actively persecutes its Shiites, while Pakistan has been anxious to avoid becoming further embroiled in the factional fighting that is dominating the former state of Afghanistan. Pakistan's contributions to the Gulf War were modest for fear of over-identifying Pakistan with conservative Arab forces.

While Sri Lanka has pursued good relations with the Middle East, it has not given the area any particular priority, although it has a small Muslim minority (about 6 per cent). Mrs Bandaranaike's decision in 1970 to break off diplomatic relations with Israel gave Colombo a favourable press, but – like India – she has pursued Islamic links either bilaterally or through the workings of the NAM. Sri Lanka's exports to the Middle East are generally low, US$ 243.6 million in 1989, compared to US$ 392.6 million with the EC, and remained largely unchanged throughout the 1980s.[71]

While the Himalayan kingdoms of Bhutan and Nepal have virtually no direct links with the Islamic world, and poor bilateral relations with the Middle East – relying upon India's particular diplomacy – both the Maldives and Bangladesh are members of the Islamic Conference. The Maldives have participated in all the Islamic summits, but its main aim has been to use the wider Islamic Conference as an arena in which to develop links with Pakistan and Bangladesh. The Maldives have virtually no trade with the Middle East, and have concentrated on Sri Lanka, Thailand, Singapore and

Hong Kong. Isolated from the sub-continent, the Maldives are characterised more by the maritime Islamic traditions of East Asia, which serve to isolate it from Islam within South Asia and within the Middle East as well.

Like Pakistan, the influence of Islam on Bangladeshi foreign policy has been intimately linked with the long internal search for an Islamic domestic identity that began after 1975. Under Ziaul Rehman and Mohammed Ershad, Bangladesh pursued its links with the Islamic world to even out India's influence, and to bring about a *rapprochement* with Pakistan and assure access to oil.

Initially, several Muslim states withheld recognition of Bangladesh for fear of offending Islamabad. It was two Muslim South-east Asian states – Malaysia and Indonesia – which acknowledged Dhaka first. Yet it was to be within the framework of the Islamic Conference that Pakistan would finally extend its own recognition of Bangladesh, at Lahore in 1974. At the seventh summit of the Islamic Conference, Pakistan called upon other Muslim states to support Bangladesh in its dispute with India over the Ganges river. Yet Islam to Bangladesh has a specific East Asian dimension as well, involving it in close relations with Malaysia and Indonesia. Bangladesh's attempts to use the Islamic Conference to gain access to finance has been largely disappointing, although it has secured good relations with Saudi Arabia, and has had access to the Islamic Development Bank on concessional terms.

In 1988 President Ershad declared Bangladesh to be an Islamic Republic, but although the event was noted in the Middle East, it was directed mainly at a domestic audience. Lacking Pakistan's military expertise and economic size, Bangladesh has none the less succeeded in cutting some profile within international affairs, through the offices of the Islamic Conference. In 1987 Bangladesh hosted the OIC's Foreign Ministers meeting, in a context in which Islam was becoming increasingly important for its internal political structure.

Summary

A regional analysis of superpower relations with India and Pakistan reveals not how India and Pakistan have furthered the strategic aims of the United States or the USSR, but how the superpowers have furthered the strategic interests of New Delhi and Islamabad, both towards each other, and towards the international system generally.

The exact sets of relations which have evolved between the states of South Asia and the superpowers have had more to do with degrees of practical flexibility than ideological interest: in this respect there is no surprise that – for so much of the post-war period – the Soviets supported a democratic regime and the Americans supported an oligarchy. Other forums, such as the UN, the NAM, the Commonwealth and the OIC have been used by Pakistan and India to display the extra-regional dimensions of foreign policy free of superpower involvement, but with an eye to superpower response and accommodation, and with an eye to embarrassing each other in wider global councils. Of the other states, only Sri Lanka has managed to pursue a wider foreign policy free of Indo-Pak rivalries, and has probably been the most genuinely non-aligned of the NAM states.

As this chapter has shown, global events since 1989 are having a profound influence upon the options and flexibility that the states of South Asia have in dealing with each other and with differing parts of the world: but since the cause of the Indo-Pak dispute is regional, wider international events may have little influence on the state of their bilateral relations. These events could well make matters worse. A disengagement of the US–Pakistan relationship could heighten Pakistan's insecurity and weaken its economy, while a disengagement between the former Soviet Union and India could seriously increase India's costs in laying claim to a 'middle power' status. It is not entirely coincidental that, freed from the supporting external priorities (or irrelevancies?) of the Cold War, Indo-Pak relations have so notably deteriorated.

Moreover, within the context of the so-called Pacific Century, the states of South Asia have started to turn increasingly towards East Asia, to the states of Hong Kong, Taiwan, Singapore and South Korea, and Japan. Irritatingly for India, it has come late to the Japanese banquet, discouraged by the strength of the US–Japanese special alliance, and later by the degree of Chinese interest in Japan and Japanese technology. While there has been some degree of technical co-operation between India and Japan, dating back to 1958 (the so-called 'yen loan') Japanese–Indian relations are bedevilled by a series of political misunderstandings, especially over Japanese condemnation of India's position on the NPT, and insistence that further aid be made conditional on India renouncing a nuclear weapons programme. In 1994, Japan denied that it was making further aid to India and Pakistan conditional on their agreement to sign the NPT.

These misunderstandings are found – to a lesser degree – with the other South Asian states generally. India's associations with Japan cooled following its normalisation of relations with China in 1972 through the Zhou–Tanaka communiqué, and following the signing of the Sino-Japanese Friendship Treaty of 1978. Moreover, in 1978, Japan suspended aid to Vietnam, a close ally of India and the Soviet Union, in apparent deference to Chinese sensibilities. Sri Lankan–Japanese relations remain cordial, in part because of some shared Buddhist traditions, and because the Japanese were impressed by Sri Lanka's decision in 1948 to forgo Japanese reparations and to 'confront hatred with love'. Japanese funds to Sri Lanka, to Bangladesh and to the smaller Himalayan Kingdoms and the Maldives are relatively small in an area that does not command much interest within Japanese foreign policy. In 1989 Bangladesh, India, Sri Lanka and Pakistan were respectively fifth, sixth, seventh and eighth in the top ten of Japanese aid receivers, with the first four being all South-east Asian states.

As will be discussed in Chapter 4, there are economic reasons as to why South Asia's share in Japanese bilateral foreign aid remains small: 16.1 per cent (US\$ 1.091 million) in 1989 compared to 32.8 per cent earmarked for South-east Asia. The states of the Association of South East Asian Nations (ASEAN) received 31.5 per cent.[72] India's V. P. Singh government announced in the wake of the 1989 elections that it gave Japan a particular priority in its foreign policy agenda, but it was not clear that this interest was reciprocated. This 'image problem' for Pakistan and India persists when it comes to encouraging foreign investment in high technologies and modern production methods. Despite a series of sectoral deals with Japanese multinational corporations, Japan as a whole remains distracted by Chinese and now Russian overtures, and the policies of the Pacific Rim. These priorities may have to change if recent Indian economic restructuring is to continue and deepen.

Notes

1.   See Ken Booth (ed.), *New Thinking About Strategy and International Security*, Harper Collins, London, 1991.

2.   See Gowher Rizvi's article 'South Asia and the New World Order', in Hans-Henrik Holm and Georg Sorensen (eds), *Whose World Order? Uneven Globalisation and the End of the Cold War*, Westview Press, Boulder, 1995, pp. 69–88.

3.   J. W. Mellor (ed.), *India: A Rising Middle Power?*, Westview Press, Boulder, 1979, p. 359.

4.   See Dennis Kux, *Estranged Democracies. India and the United States 1941–1991*, Sage, New Delhi, 1993.

5.   Nihal Singh, 'Can the US and India Really be Friends?' *Asian Survey*, 23, 1983, p. 1024.

6.   'On Top of the World?' *Economist*, London, 9–15 March 1991, p. 3

7.   Sisir Gupta, 'Great Power Relations, World Order and the Third World', in M. Rajan and S. S. Ganguly (eds), *Selected Essays*, Vikas, New Delhi, 1981.

8.   The Soviets are alleged to have asked why, if India could afford to spend between US$ 18 and 20 million on the Mirage 2000 jet fighter, should they provide her with cheap credit at seventeen years payment at 2.7 per cent interest? See S. N. Singh. 'Why India Goes to Moscow for Arms', *Asian Survey*, 24, 1984, pp. 707–40.

9.   There is some confusion on this matter, since in 1995 it appeared to be the case that the sale was back on again. It is clear however, that India at last realises that Russia cannot provide the shield against US interference, both regionally and within the UN, that the Soviets could.

10.   India – and South Asia as a whole – has tended to be merged into a greater Asian identity dominated by Beijing and South-east Asia. Alan Romberg's review of Washington's priorities in the mid-1980s, entitled 'New Stirrings in Asia', did not even mention India once (*Foreign Affairs*, 64, 1985, pp. 515–38). P. H. Kreisberg's assessment of India following the death of Mrs Gandhi noted the failure of the United States to award India a place in America's strategic thinking: 'India After Indira', *Foreign Affairs*, 63, 1985, pp. 871–91.

11.   See Howard Schaffer, *Chester Bowles: New Dealer in the Cold War*, Harvard University Press, Massachusetts, 1993.

12.   S. P. Varma and K. P. Misra, *The Foreign Policy of South Asia*, Orient Longman, New Delhi, 1969.

13.   R. Thomas, *India's Security Policy*, Princeton University Press, Princeton, 1986.

14.   The Soviet view of India was not particularly favourable until the

mid-1950s. Stalin believed that Nehru and the Indian middle class were essentially the 'running dogs' of US imperialism.

15 Memo cited in A. Jalal, *The State of Martial Rule*, Cambridge University Press, Cambridge, 1992, p. 126.

16 See in particular Ayub Khan's autobiography *Friends, Not Masters: A Political Autobiography*, Oxford University Press, London, 1967.

17 Sultana Afroz 'Pakistan and the Middle East Defence Plan 1951', *Asian Affairs*, 75, 1988, pp. 170–9.

18 See P. I. Cheema, *Pakistan's Foreign Policy*, Oxford University Press, London, 1990, p. 168.

19 Afroz, 'Pakistan and the Middle East', p. 174.

20 Cited in B. N. Goswami, *Pakistan and China: A Study in their Relations*, Progress Publishers, New Delhi, 1971, p. 79.

21 C. Van Hollen, 'The Tilt Policy Revisited', *Asian Survey*, 20, 1980, p. 355.

22 A good read on this subject can be found in Walter Isaacson, *Kissinger: A Biography*, Faber and Faber, London, 1993. See chapter 18.

23 Isaacson, *Kissinger*, p. 373.

24 R. Thomas, 'Security Relations in Southern Asia', *Asian Survey*, 21, 1981, pp. 689–740

25 S. Burke and L. Ziring, *Pakistan's Foreign Policy: An Historical Analysis*, Oxford University Press, Karachi, 1991, p. 417.

26 T. P. Thornton 'Between the Stools: US Policy Towards Pakistan During the Carter Administration', *Asian Survey*, 22, 1982, pp. 959–70.

27 B. Buzan and G. Rizvi, *South Asian Insecurity*, Macmillan, Basingstoke, 1985. See also A. Shahi, *Pakistan's Security and Foreign Policy*, People's Press, Lahore, 1988 and Z. Khalilzad, *Security in South West Asia*, Gower, Aldershot, 1984.

28 G. Quester, *The Politics of Nuclear Proliferation*, Johns Hopkins University Press, Baltimore, 1973.

29 S. Ganguly, 'Avoiding War', *Foreign Affairs*, 69, Winter 1990–91, pp. 57–73.

30 P. Duncan, *The Soviet Union and India*, Routledge, London, 1989, p. 51.

31 W. Anderson, 'The Soviets in the Indian Ocean', *Asian Survey*, 24, 1984, pp. 910–53.

32 Duncan, *The Soviet Union and India*, p. 12.

33 B. Sen Gupta, *Soviet Perspectives on Contemporary Asia*, Sangam, New Delhi, 1982.

34 See R. Sisson and L. Rose, *War and Secession: India, Pakistan, and the Creation of Bangladesh*, Princeton University Press, Princeton, 1989.

35   Duncan, *The Soviet Union and India*, p. 2.

36   Robert Horn, *Soviet–Indian Relations: Issues and Influences*, Praeger, New York, 1982.

37   There are difficulties in comparing Indian and Soviet trade because of the way in which the figures are calculated. Duncan notes that Indian imports often exclude arms sales and thus show a Soviet trade surplus as an Indian one. None the less the trends in trade have become increasingly clear throughout the 1980s, with the Soviets less keen to import poorly manufactured goods, and with India less interested in antiquated technology. These problems persist with current Indian and Russian trade.

38   It has even been suggested that the Indians deliberately contrived the border crisis at Sumdurong Chu to test Soviet, not Chinese, resolve. See Leo Rose, 'India's Foreign Relations', in M. Bouton and P. Oldenburg (eds), *India Briefing 1990*, Westview Press, Boulder, 1990.

39   *UN Year Book*, Geneva, 1984.

40   See *India Today*, New Delhi, 23 May 1993.

41   H. S. S. Nissanka, *Sri Lanka's Foreign Policy: A Study in Non-Alignment*, Vikas, New Delhi, 1984, p. 256.

42   A. J. Wilson, *The Politics of Sri Lanka 1947–1979*, Macmillan, London, 1979, p. 263.

43   *Direction of Trade Statistics*, IMF, Washington, 1990, p. 524.

44   A good introduction to fascinating literature on this subject is Peter Hopkirk, *The Great Game: On Secret Service in High Asia*, John Murray, London, 1990.

45   Recent literature has cautioned, rightly in my view, against the tendency of academics and writers, unfamilar with the CARs, to characterise them as a 'region' and not to distinguish the important differences that exist between the new republics. See the introduction to A. Ehteshami (ed.), *From the Gulf to Central Asia: Players in the New Great Game*, University of Exeter Press, Exeter, 1994.

46   For example, the Saudi's fund the SADUM, or the religious board of Central Asia and Kazakhstan. See M. Olcott 'Islamic Consciousness and Nationalist Ideology in Central Asia', in Ehteshami, *From the Gulf to Central Asia*, pp. 6–24.

47   For a discussion of this see M. Lipton, *The Erosion of a Relationship: India and Britain since 1960*, Chatto and Windus, London, 1975.

48   For an interesting study of the early years of Indian diplomacy on the UN see the Indian Council of World Affairs report on *India and the United Nations*, New York, 1957.

49   For evidence of this see M. Brecher's political study entitled *Nehru: A Political Biography*, Oxford University Press, London, 1959.

50   Douglas Williams, *The Specialised Agencies and the United Nations:*

The System in Crisis, Manchester University Press, Manchester, 1987.

51   See the report prepared by the Pakistan Institute of International Affairs, *Pakistan and the United Nations*, New York, 1957. The report contains a useful discussion of Pakistan's involvement with the UN over Kashmir.

52   Evan Luard, *A History of the United Nations*, Vol. II, *The Age of Decolonisation, 1955–65*, Routledge, London, 1989, p. 514.

53   See the useful contribution by Anthony Parsons, *From Cold War to Hot Peace: UN Interventions 1947–1995*, Penguin, Harmondswoth, 1995.

54   See N. J. Rengger (ed.), *Treaties and Alliances of the World*, 5th Edition, Cartermill, London, 1990, p. 53.

55   *UN Year Book*, Geneva, 1990.

56   U. S. Bajpal, *India's Security: The Politico-Strategic Environment*, Sangam, New Delhi, 1983.

57   M. Ayoob, *India and South East Asia: Indian Perceptions and Policies*, Routledge, London, 1990.

58   *Guardian*, London, 11 February 1991. It is important to note that a great deal of the NAM is simply ignored by the Western media. Just a brief glance at an Indian or Pakistan English daily will reveal not only the fact that global events are reported from different regional angles, but that entirely *different* events are reported altogether.

59   Foreign Ministers' statement to the UN conference. Cited in S. U. Kodikara, *Foreign Policy on Sri Lanka*, Chanakya, New Delhi, 1982, p.155.

60   S. C. Gangal, *India and the Commonwealth*, Vikas, New Delhi, 1970, p. 15.

61   In 1975 India contributed 7 per cent of the Commonwealth Secretariat's funds for multilateral assistance. See D. C. Vohra, *India's Aid Diplomacy and the Third World*, Zed Books, London, 1980.

62   Vohra *India's Aid Diplomacy*, p. 70.

63   For a further discussion of the processes behind the formation of the Islamic Conference, see Hasan Moinuddin, *The Charter of the Islamic Conference*, Clarendon Press, Oxford, 1987.

64   Shirin Tahir-Kheli, 'In Search of an Identity: Islam and Pakistan's Foreign Policy', in A. Dawisha (ed.), *Islam and Foreign Policy*, Cambridge University Press, Cambridge, 1983, pp. 68– 83.

65   Tahir-Kheli, 'In Search of an Identity', p. 72.

66   Ayoob, *India and South East Asia*, p. 42.

67   The slight irony here is that India was the first country on the subcontinent to ban the book, representing a heightened concern over its Muslim minorities, and its vulnerability to criticism within the

Islamic world.

68   State Department text supplied by the US Information Service, Grosvenor Square, London.

69   Burke and Ziring, *Pakistan's Foreign Policy*, p. 463.

70   The Americans took a firm stand on this issue, demanding compensation and guarantees, but modified their position considerably following the Soviet invasion of Afghanistan.

71   *Direction of Trade Statistics*, IMF, Washington, 1990. Within the Middle East, Eygpt is the leading importer of Sri Lankan goods, while Sri Lanka imports a significant amount from Iran: US$ 97.7 million, more than any other Middle Eastern country in 1989.

72   Figures taken from Shafiqul Islam (ed.), *Yen For Development: Japanese Foreign Aid and the Politics of Burden Sharing*, St. Martin's Press, New York, 1991.

3

The domestic politics of South Asia: state–society relations and regional stability

As noted by Jalal in her work *Democracy and Authoritarianism in South Asia*, an overview of the domestic politics of the South Asian states reveals remarkable similarities. With the exception of the Maldives and Bhutan, each state in the region has been characterised by coalition government, in which established parties are in a state of electoral flux, and/or institutional decline. Coalitions contain not just religious parties, but also secular parties ideologically aligned to the left and to the right. In India and in Pakistan, regional parties make up an important element within government coalitions, and indeed the current prime minister of India, Devi Gowda, is a regional leader *par excellence*. He can speak neither Hindi nor English, and indeed was not even a contestant in the recent national elections. As a chief minister of the southern state of Karnataka, he represents to some the 'provincialisation of Indian national politics' – a trend that has been present for some time.

The 1996 general elections in India, held over a period of several weeks in May, confirm the trends established in the late 1980s: the continuing decline in the Congress-I vote, and a clear rise in support for the Hindu chauvinist party, the BJP. Significantly, however, although the BJP increased its share of seats from 116 to 160, emerging as the largest party in parliament, it could not form a government. Many other parties, combined into the so-called 'Third Force' of regional, socialist and communist parties, had emerged as important actors within the political arena, and the Congress still had the largest share of the national vote. On 15 May 1996 Vajpayee, the leader of the BJP's parliamentary party, was invited to form a government amid desperate (and initially unsuccessful) attempts by the opposition to prevent the 'communalists' coming to power. The difficulties were not simply over who would lead an anti-BJP United Front (several people refused, including ex-prime minister V. P. Singh), but over old ideological differences between the left (especially the Communist Party – Marxist (CPM) and the Congress-I). Even in defeat, the Congress remained an important party, with 136 seats.

Short of necessary allies (the Shiv Senn, with sixteen seats, being the only notable exception), the Vajpayee government attempted to placate its critics by reiterating that the party was not communalist, and by appointing a Muslim as External Affairs minister. However, short of the required 273 seats needed to stay in power, Vajpayee resigned on 27 May before facing a formal vote in the Lok Sabha. The Indian president then called the United Front, headed by Gowda, to have a go at forming the government. On 1 June, a fifteen-member cabinet was sworn in by the Indian president, including members from the Janata Dal, and three other regional parties. By the middle of June, the Communist Party of India (CPI) and several other regional parties (themselves grouped into the so-called 'federal front') joined the government. Having cobbled together India's most complex coalition government to date, Devi Gouda's government will be subject to a whole series of internal pressures over social, economic and foreign policy issues. One of the key demands of the federal front was for further political and economic devolution within the Indian federal system.

Pakistani politics presents us with a very similar picture, however different the specifics. 1988 saw the restoration within Pakistan of the principle of party-based elections and civilian rule, after a long period of military control and limited popular participation. The electoral victory of Benazir Bhutto's Pakistan's People's Party (PPP) in 1988 was, however, seriously restricted by the legacies of military rule established by President Zia (1977–88) and the presence of a powerful presidential figure – Mohammed Ishaq Khan. Moreover, since the PPP failed to win an overall majority in the National Assembly it could not amend the constitution and try to further limit the powers of the presidency, or limit the influence of the army. The Benazir government also faced sustained opposition from some of the states, including the Punjab, over issues of national policy. Baluchistan, for example, refused to implement the PPP's National Works Programme, because the PPP had no representation in the Baluchistan assembly.

Amid rumours that the military leadership under General Beg was not reconciled to the full restoration of civilian rule, and constrained by a coalition based upon volatile ethnic and regionally based constituencies,[1] the Bhutto government faced growing domestic criticism over alleged corruption and poor economic performance. In terms of foreign policy the army was also critical of the government's handling of the Kashmir crisis with India, the handling of the Afghanistan resistance to Najibullah (especially in the wake of the so-called Jalalabad fiasco),[2] and Pakistan's policies in the Gulf crisis. Following significant policy disagreements with provincial governments in Sind and Punjab, Bhutto was dismissed in August 1990. Fresh elections were held in November 1990 and resulted in the victory of the Islamic Democratic Alliance under Nawaz Sharif, which won 105 seats out of 207.

The Sharif government was, as much as the Bhutto one it replaced, a coalition government hemmed in by a military and bureaucratic elite, not immediately answerable to civilian control. More seriously, the national government relied upon the support of an essentially regional party – the Mohajir Qaumi Movement (MQM), a party created to advance the interests of the Mohajirs, the Urdu-speaking refugees who had left India at the time of independence. Concentrated in the metropolitan areas of Pakistan, especially Sind, the MQM was in violent confrontation with Sindi speakers over rights to government jobs and benefits. In 1993, the provincial and institutional balance of power sustaining Sharif in power disintegrated.[3] Since Sharif was dependent on the MQM for national support, he could not be seen to move against them in Sind, despite a marked level of ethnic violence in February 1993. Eventually, the military and the president combined to force Sharif to intervene, with the president eventually deciding to dismiss Sharif on the grounds of incompetence and poor government. Not to be cowed, Sharif undertook judicial proceedings against his one-time ally, and sought to frustrate the office of the president. Between April and May, the government of Pakistan effectively came to a standstill. On 25 May 1993, the Supreme Court ruled that Sharif's dismissal was unconstitutional and ordered his government to be reinstated.

However, the 'restored' Sharif government effectively lost control of the government, since Sharif and Ishaq Khan failed subsequently to work together. Behind the president stood powerful anti-Sharif factions situated in the provinces, the army and within his own coalition. A threatened march by provincial parties into Islamabad in July forced the Chief of the Army Staff to intervene. General Waheed secured a curious arrangement wherein both president and prime minister would resign, a caretaker government would be appointed, and fresh elections would be held. In the October 1993 elections, the PPP secured 86 seats out of 202, with Sharif taking 73 seats. The government was again a coalition, dependent upon a complex interplay and balancing of forces, and sensitive to military pressure. The difference, and this may well prove decisive, was that Benazir Bhutto was able to have indirectly elected to the office of the presidency a former PPP member, Leghari. Such an arrangement held out the hope that the arrangements between the office of the prime minister and the president would evolve along a more accountable basis, holding out the hope for the full restoration of civilian rule.

Redefining national security

Why should we be interested in the domestic politics of the South Asian states? What does an understanding of state–society relations have to contribute to an appreciation of international politics? It has been noted above that the realist conception of international relations – which stresses the importance of the state and the interactions of sovereign states within an anarchical environment – directs attention away from the internal structures of states, and the dynamics of state–society relations. Realism refuses to conceptualise the ways in which internal politics, including various historical and cultural attributes, shape and direct a foreign policy agenda, on the grounds that they are irrelevant to any specific outcome. Caroline Thomas has recently noted that: 'the state-centric geopolitical approach to international relations is inadequate for conceptualising the third world security environment'.[4] Buzan has also noted the tendency in the past to treat 'third world national security problems ... as a mere extension of a systemic level dynamic', that is, as a function of superpower or great power rivalry without any reference to the alignment of domestic forces.[5] Given the historical specifics of the post-colonial societies, such negligence is fatal for any real understanding of the genesis of foreign policy.

Some approaches have attempted to overcome the distinction between 'internal' and 'external' policy. What is sometimes referred to as a behaviourist school of international relations stresses the core values and national interest of decision-makers in either sociological or psychological terms. Elite perceptions arise from within a particular type of society and political culture.[6] The advantages of what can be called a behaviourist-inspired approach to the study of South Asian security – compatible as it is with the main characteristics of Buzan's 'security complex' – lie in the fact that it stresses the historical and sociological roots of security within South Asia. Given the degree of social diversity within the region, and the political instability and dissent within all the societies of South Asia, the so-called 'core values' of the realists are neither self-evident, nor more importantly, universally accepted by those subject to the authority of the state in question. 'Core values' that define security and inform some notion of the 'national interest' are produced, reinforced – or discarded – within the domestic political arena by specific elites facing specific challenges.

It follows from this that the view of the state as a 'homogeneous' entity is of limited use for understanding the interactions of *weak* states in which political elites face various levels of domestic dissent, both in terms of cultural and ethnic demands for political decentralisation, or in terms of broad-based secessionist movements. In the recent past, in Pakistan, Bangladesh, Nepal and even Bhutan the institutions of state power have been controlled by small elites with little or no access to wider societal support, and who have faced challenges from broad-based social movements demanding fundamental reform. More complex still, the elites of South Asia – including India and Sri Lanka – face competition from *within* the state structure, from bureaucracies and military personnel over the allocation of resources and the implementation of policies, as well as from broad-based social coalitions demanding access to state power.

Of all the states of South Asia, only India and Sri Lanka can lay claim to being democratic states, in which regular and generally fair political elections take place for national office. In both states, governments have been defeated and removed from power, and have done so with decorum and honour. Yet both states have witnessed delays in elections through constitutional 'states of emergency', in India between 1975 and 1977 at the national level, and quite frequently at the state level. In India as well as Sri Lanka, political parties have been banned, and opposition leaders detained. While, on procedural terms, both the states of India and Sri Lanka can claim to be democratic, this distinction ignores powerful authoritarian elements within the state structure, as well as broader social impediments (illiteracy, malnutrition, intimidation) that restrict the quality of democratic politics. In 1996, the Pakistan press praised the holding of India's general election as a model of impartiality and fairness, while recognising that in specific areas (arguably Kashmir, and specific constituencies over the country), the campaign had been marred by violence.

These high levels of domestic instability not only limit a state's ability to act authoritatively within the international community, they also limit its ability to act upon domestic society with any legitimacy, and to deliver socio-economic packages aimed at bringing about widespread industrialisation.

The politics of development and the crisis of nationalism

One of the most important preconditions of national security in South Asia involves the need for individual states to create continued economic growth and industrial development. Each South Asian state in turn has attempted to carry through an industrial revolution to end poverty, create gainful employment, and recently to increase international trade. The processes of political and economic change – collectively (if not still problematically) referred to as development – keep the positions of elites within the state precariously balanced even as they legitimate their right to rule.

What could be referred to as the wider 'developmentalist' notion of state security has been stated by K. Subrahmanyam: 'anything that comes in the way of development, either *internally or externally* is a threat to India's national security'.[7] Amongst the many criticisms levelled at the political leaderships in India, Pakistan, Nepal and Bangladesh – and which eventually replaced governments in all of them from 1989 to 1990 – was the charge that they had failed to improve economic wealth, significantly reduce poverty, and retain political order. Again, the 1996 Indian elections were less dominated by the themes of secularism and Hindu revivalism, as they were by themes of economic advancement, general prosperity and political corruption.

The interface between electoral politics, economic development and the legitimacy of state action is crucial in that developmental strategies generate internal instability by either failing to meet popular expectations of material advancement, or by failing to distribute the benefits of development equitably. Whatever the specific mix of state and market involvement, even economic strategies deemed to be successful (see chapter 4) increasingly differentiate society and increase perceived and experienced inequalities, however relative these may be. More interesting still, urbanisation and industrialisation lead to the differentiation of social identities, change the nature and extent of various political and social demands, and question and redefine particular cultural values.[8] In Pakistan the economic success of the Ayub Khan years was a major contribution to the military coup that removed him from power. In India, Sikh separatism is closely bound up with the perception that the Punjab was not retaining its wealth, but subsidising poorer, Hindu states throughout the Indian Union. In Jammu and Kashmir, the arguments about political and cultural estrangement from the Indian Union are to a large extent refracted through the belief that Jammu and Kashmir have been economically neglected and marginalised. This is not to reduce everything to an economic explanation, but to recognise that the genesis of many ethnic revivals contains a significant element of economic or material grievance.

Political scientists writing in the 1960s assumed that economic growth would lessen instability, that it would introduce so-called 'modern values' of consensus, initiating a process of cultural convergence in which so-called traditional identities – a euphemism for ethnicity and tribe – would give way to the modern nation. To an extent this was true, but only partially. In South Asia, socio-economic change has helped to construct a Westernised, middle-class elite, yet it has also augmented and exaggerated the more indigenous non-Western elements of social organisation, often redefining them and granting them greater political significance than they previously enjoyed.[9] In some cases, economic development has generated not so much ethnic revivalism so much as ethnic invention. Earlier, somewhat simplistic, theories of modernisation failed to grasp the centrality, and contemporary nature, of ethnic revivalism upon attempts to construct national identities.

Any attempt to separate 'ethnicity' in South Asia from the socio-economic compulsions of nation building is fundamentally flawed, and it follows that the links between ethnic identity and economic development make the issue of ethnicity within post-colonial societies a far more pressing and ubiquitous one than within the developed world itself. In complete contradiction to the earlier belief in convergence and nationalism, in South Asia today:

> The 'national question' [is becoming] the ethnic question, or rather [that] the two issues are appearing simultaneously and partly merging, thus presenting social scientists [sic] with a demanding task, and probably a need to reconsider some conventional wisdoms concerning nation building.[10]

Hettne is one of the many academics who have successfully challenged some of the conventional wisdoms over nation building and ethnicity itself. Empirically, throughout the post-colonial world the tenacity of ethnic identities has questioned the simplistic dichotomy made between 'modern' nationalism, and 'backward' traditional ethnicity by writers in the 1950s. Modernisation has not subsumed or eliminated ethnicity at all: on the contrary, it has spawned differing types of ethnic identities, which in the context of a wider nationalism have challenged the compulsions towards homogeneous social identity.

In recognition of what one author has referred to as the 'ethnic upsurge', or the divergence of identities within the post-colonial state, ethnicity is now rightly perceived in the same way that nationalism was before it – something that is 'acquired', a set of identities that is deeply instrumental and political, an *active* process of identification. Gone is the emphasis on primordiality, the belief that ethnicity was given and timeless. According to Anthony Smith, in his book *National Identity*, ethnicity is now

> a question of attitudes, perceptions and sentiments that are necessarily fleeting and mutable, varying with the particular situation of the subject. As the individual's situation changes, so will (their) group identification ... [Such a view] makes it possible for ethnicity to be used instrumentally to further individual or collective interests.

This new emphasis on ethnicity as a type of 'cultural collectivity', using a variety of devices such as language, 'collective memories', religious practices and customs, or even a specific set of institutions, perceives it as a conscious tool or social strategy to further specific political demands. Such arguments acknowledge the instrumental-ity of ethnicity and recognise that they are not in themselves static: they continue to define and redefine themselves in line with broader political and economic issues. While often an act of imagination as opposed to outright invention, and structured to some extent by what is *historically feasible*,[11] the fluidity of ethnicity is, paradoxically, one of its key characteristics: 'ethnicity has to be a fluid concept, contextual, situational and relational'.[12]

Time and time again within the states of South Asia, ethnic demands have been accommodated in one way, only to re-emerge in differing forms, attached to differing demands. In outline, a given ethnic identity may be couched in terms of what the state structure concedes as 'legitimate' (for example, a linguistic state, political recognition as an economically disadvantaged group). Demands may change however: they may widen or deepen (a state for a religious group or community, special laws for a community exempting them from certain impositions by the state), and the ethnic group itself may change or fracture, with one side announcing that 'they' are the 'real' Assamese, or more 'truly' representative of Kashmiri opinion. Furthermore, ethnic identifiers change and alter in response to state repression or to state accommodation, but they do not disappear.

The ethnic crisis for South Asia is that, within the context of a nation-building project, committed to creating and reinforcing shared cultural experiences, the proliferation of difference has led to a stress upon authoritarian government, even within formal democratic systems such as those of India and Sri Lanka. Such policies have been defended within the international arena through recourse to the out-dated and entirely inappropriate language of sovereignty. Perhaps the greatest challenge that faces the political elites of South Asia is the challenge of recognising the fluidity as well as the tenacity of various ethnic movements, and appreciating that they are a political consequence of state formation itself. Let us now examine each state in turn.

Pakistan and the Islamic state

If India and Pakistan were based upon two separate and competing ideologies, confessional and secular,[13] they were also based upon two quite separate political discourses which would in turn sanction

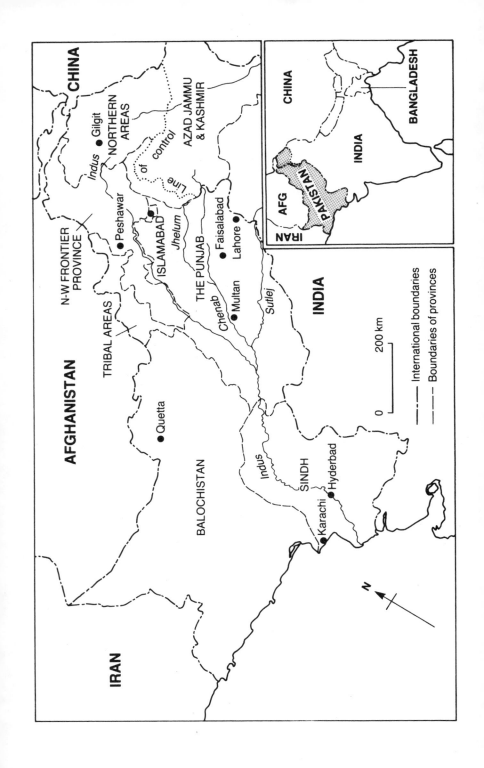

and legitimate different domestic political systems. The languages of secularism and the languages and symbolism of Islam would, in time, provide Indian and Pakistani elites with different nationalism and different institutions, indeed different capacities to rule their respective societies. Yet paradoxically, these different – even competitive – nationalisms would also confront their respective elites with remarkably similar problems of societal management.

In the absence of one, definitive and accepted definition of Islam, and given the lack of any shared cultural perceptions of an Islamic identity between East Bengal and the provinces of Sind, Baluchistan, NWFP and a partitioned Punjab before they formed the state of Pakistan, the question asked almost immediately was: If Pakistan was to be an 'Islamic', theocratic state, then whose definition of Islam will be used to define state–society relations? More problematically still, if Pakistan was *not* to be an Islamic state, but merely a state for 'the Muslims of South Asia', did this not raise serious questions about the logic and indeed the necessity of partition in the first place? Was not the call for a separate state premised entirely upon a mistrust of the secularism of the Congress Party?

While there are well-established, historical lineages of the secular state (even if they are essentially Western in conception), the ideas of an Islamic state remained vague and contradictory in the Muslim League's thinking: was it to be a democratic or authoritarian state, pluralist (and federal) or unitary and hierarchical, civilian or military? Adeed Dawisha asks 'is there really something specifically definable called Islam … a monolith in terms of structure and behaviour?'[14] If so, how could a political party, such as the League, begin to establish such a monolith from the profoundly pluralist societies than ended up being included within the Pakistani state?

Differences of opinion over the political outlines of the Islam state can be traced back to the pre-partition period. Two separate strands of Islamic thinking took shape in the nineteenth century: one based around Aligarh, and another based around Deoband.[15] The Aligarhist strand was revisionist and liberal, committed to reworking the ideas of Islam so as to be relevant to the socio-

Map 4 Pakistan
(*Source*: David Taylor, *World Bibliographical Series*, vol. X, *Pakistan*, Clio Press, Oxford, 1990)

economic and political imperatives of pluralistic societies which contained differing ethnic and cultural identities, and the economic and technological demands of an emerging (predominantly Western) modern world driven by technological innovation and the need to industrialise. The key concept for this, revisionist, strand of Islamic thinking is known as *ijtihad*: critical, disciplined but imaginative interpretation of the Quran and the Sharia in the light of a radically changed global context.

Within this Aligarhist spirit, Islam did not stand in contradiction to the organisational principles of the nation-state or of parliamentary democracy, despite the frequency of this claim by some mullahs and other members of the religious clergy.[16] Jinnah and the founders of the 'Pakistan' movement drew their inspirations, in large part, from this particular tradition of Islamic thinking within South Asia. Just before his death in 1948 Jinnah had outlined his version of a future Pakistan based upon a parliamentary system of government in which 'Hindus, Muslims and Christians could become good citizens of Pakistan'. With such little, explicit reference to Islam within the 1956 constitution, cynical eyebrows were raised both in New Delhi and within Pakistan itself. The dilemma of defending such an Aligarhist position was that it implied a commitment to secularism which other Muslims would come to portray as un-Islamic and thus, in some senses, anti-national.

The second tradition (associated with the seminary at Deoband) concerned itself with what is, in effect, a medieval, hierarchical view of Islam based upon the powers of the clergy (the mullahs) and arguments that saw the Muslim community (or Uhma) as a whole, immune from other divisions and competing loyalties such as the artificial identities and symbols of the nation-state, or even party politics. Of great significance for the Zia-ul-Haq period (1977–88), a Deobandian view upon Islam is openly hostile to the Western discourse of liberalism that stresses elections and a 'numerical' logic of representation.[17] Such a view is not just opposed to individualism, but to an international political order based upon universal human rights.

Initially many of the Deobandian scholars initially rejected the calls for a Pakistan state on the grounds that the ideas of national exclusiveness stood in contradiction to pan-Islamic identity. Maulana Azad, a liberal Muslim who remained within the Indian Congress Party and served in the government of an independent

India, opposed Pakistan on the grounds of his faith. He noted in his biography that 'it is one of the greatest frauds on the people to suggest that religious affinity can unite areas which are geographically, linguistically and culturally different'.[18]

Once confronted with the inevitability of Pakistan, however, the Deobandian tradition came to dominate the Islamic political parties, the Jamaat-i-Islami (JI), the Jamait-ul-Ulema-Islam (JUI), and the Jamait-ul-Ulema-Pakistan (JUP). These organisations, with differing emphasis and slightly differing policies, took up the task of creating and consolidating a real 'Islamic society' based upon the codification of the Sharia, and the sanctioning of religious authority through the teachings and tenets of Sunni orthodoxy with regards to language (the use of Urdu), punishments for adultery, homosexuality and theft, and Islamic ideas on interest, taxes and economic development. Concerning the position of non-Sunni Muslims within Pakistan, and indeed the position of non-Muslims *per se*, the attitudes of the Islamic parties were at best ambiguous, at worst they were openly committed to the construction of an Islamic order that was intolerant of social, cultural and ideological diversity.

What political institutions do these political parties envisage? How should such a state be established, and how would they mediate the links with the wider international political and economic systems of a primarily non-Islamic world? So-called traditionalists, such as the Deobandians, seek to reinstate a pure form of Islam back into societies that have become polluted by un-Islamic thinking and habits. Politics as such would have no place for provincial institutions or federalism, nor a commitment to the holding of regular elections. Within contemporary Pakistan, the JI has consistently rejected talk of party-based politics (although it has continued to participate within national and provincial elections). The party has also rejected the ideologies of capitalism or even socialism as being Western and intrinsically un-Islamic.

Recent writings on the lineages of an Islamic state have stressed the complexity of the Islamic discourses on political authority.[19] Even the Aligarhist and Deobandian schools of thought are cross-cut by differing interpretations between an urban literati which was essentially more moderate, and a basically rural population in which concepts of Islam are either more aligned with the thinking of the mullahs or variants of *Pir* or tribal mysticism, the content of which significantly predates Sunni practice. Mohammad Waseen has recently conveyed the sheer complexity of the so-called 'Islamic tradition' by defining the 'great' and the 'little' traditions, both of which contain elements which are superficially – and to some extent misleadingly – labelled as fundamentalist in the West.[20]

The nature of the Muslim League

The complexities and ambiguities of the debate between what links, if any, should exist between Pakistan and Islam (and if so, what type of Islam) were made infinitely more difficult because it took place within a party and an elite who were so obviously separate from the communities that ended up constituting the territories of Pakistan. The greatest irony of partition must be the simple fact that the electoral verdict for the Muslim League, skilfully deployed after the elections to sanction partition, came from the Muslim minority states that would remain within the Indian Union. As such, the League could not, like the Indian National Congress, orchestrate and manipulate a consensus through a democratic system. Unlike the Indian Congress Party, the Muslim League was a foreign import, staffed by Mohajir – the name given to the Muslim immigrants who had migrated to Pakistan from India – and who were, by the mid-1980s, to constitute a powerful 'ethnic' group, with their own political party, demanding autonomy within Pakistan.

These immigrants, committed to the two-nation theory, displaced local provincial elites in local and national government, especially in East Pakistan. The only local elites able to gain access to the emerging national institutions were an essentially Punjabi one, well represented within the army and the bureaucracy, and later a small Pathani, Pashto element, also established within the army. Apart from a small urban, Urdu-speaking faction from the east, Bengali speakers were excluded from the political structures of the Pakistani state, despite the fact that they constituted over 54 per cent of the population of the two-winged nation.

At the time of its creation, few if any Pakistani leaders openly entertained the idea of an authoritarian, theocratic state. Yet, lacking access to a broad social consensus, and the required prerequisites of party organisation necessary to make party politics successful, many leaders feared that democracy would hand over power to chaotic provincial and district leaders and risk the disintegration of the new state. In a regional environment so deeply hostile to Pakistan's existence, such chaos would surely invite invasion and foreign conquest. What *was* necessary – and this point was conceded by Jinnah – was to create a Pakistani nationalism in which the unifying symbols and language of Islam could be deployed but without handing the state over to the mullahs, without excluding non-Muslims from access to, and protection under, the Pakistani state, and which would align Pakistan with the Muslim world.

Where were these symbols to be had? The answer appeared to be in a reformist, Muslim discourse that, freed of the fear of Hindu domination, could be essentially Muslim in culture and social practice, without being theocratic or monolithic. Yet the use of any such symbolism was fraught with danger: the adoption of Urdu – on the grounds that one national language would speed up the creation of a national identity, and with the added bonus that it was a language associated with Islam – caused immediate provincial violence, especially in Bengal. Only 8 per cent of the Pakistani population spoke Urdu at the time of partition, and subsequent attempts by the state to repress provincial languages (especially Sindhi and Baluchistani) caused deep-seated resentment against the central government. While the government justified its Urdu language policy on the grounds that elevating a minority language to national prominence did not favour any existing language group (i.e. a majority of the new state would have to learn it), many justified the use of Urdu because of its religious, and regional, connotations.

The 1956 constitution

Pakistan's refusal to legitimate regional languages and dialects had a direct impact upon domestic stability, since demands for linguistic autonomy – accommodated in India within a federal system – were seen by Islamabad as essentially secessionist and anti-national.

Centre–provincial friction – of which the agitations over language are just part – have bedevilled Pakistan since its inception. Even before the first military coup in 1958, Pakistan was beset by a desperate search for an internal order sufficiently robust to stand up within the regional and the international environment. It took from 1947 to 1956 to create a constitution that lasted just under two years. Various draft constitutions had been rejected because of the Mohajir–Punjabi prejudice against East Pakistan, and the fear that, as a majority within Pakistan, the Bengalis could possibly align themselves with smaller states within the west (especially Baluchistan and Sind) and put the Punjabis under Bengali control. The 1956 constitution gave no recognition to the provinces as political entities, but merely as administrative units. It did not guarantee them any legislative primacy in areas such as agriculture and education, nor did it assure them that their governments would be free from central interference. Moreover, the 1956 constitution sanctioned the setting up of a unicameral legislature at the centre from which state representation (a common feature in federal states) was completely excluded.

Between 1947 and 1958 seven prime ministers rose and fell in Karachi, brought down through intense intra-elite factional rivalries. Without any general election to link 'national' parties to particular programmes of socio-economic development, horse-trading within the National Assembly made and unmade government majorities, while political parties factionalised along personal lines. Provincial politics was particularly chaotic and increasingly violent. Jinnah's death in 1948 removed Pakistan's leading statesman, while Liquat Ali Khan, a competent prime minister with whom Nehru negotiated over Kashmir, was assassinated in 1951.

Into this vacuum stepped the governor-general. This office – in contrast to the evolution of the office of the president in India – would fail to become a mere adviser to the prime minister but took an active lead within the political process, dismissing the constituent assembly in 1955 because of 'factionalism' and convening another one, and frequently dismissing the prime ministers. In 1955, the governor-general had taken the extraordinary step of dismissing the constituent assembly and had abolished the four 'administrative units' of Sind, Baluchistan, NWFP and Punjab to create the state of 'West' Pakistan (the so-called One Unit policy). Elections for a new assembly were indirect, and carried out in a majority of cases from electoral registers pre-dating the creation of Pakistan itself.

Such instability confirmed the fear of internal disintegration, fears that were underscored by the severity of the regional security environment. In the context of weak (and weakening) party politics, characterised by personalities and factions instead of social programmes or indeed ideological divisions, these fears led to demands to strengthen the bureaucratic and military institutions of the state, and to extend the powers of the government if only to retain order. Rather than stress the Aligarhist links between a reformed Islam and a Pakistan democracy (that was federal and, however paradoxically, secular in outlook), it became critical to rework the emphasis on Islam by either discarding any reference to it at all (which risked causing internal offence within the theocratic and orthodox Sunnis, and the popular sentiments of Mohajirs), or to stress the non-democratic, hierarchical roots of an Islamic discourse. General Ayub Khan, the architect of the second constitution, adopted variants of both strategies: he initially constructed a state structure without an reference to religion, and then used religion as a trapping without granting power to the mullahs.

This sleight of hand was made easier by the risks of internal political chaos that seemed to be overtaking the country. In 1954, the Muslim League had been defeated in the Eastern Wing by a coalition of regional and linguistic forces, demanding political devolution. The new United Front government was committed to a programme of greater autonomy for Bengal, and had ironically used as its election manifesto the Lahore declaration of 1940, which called for an apparently federal Pakistan. Popular demands for decentralisation risked encouraging the smaller provinces in the west to press for more freedoms and jeopardise the very foundations of the state.

The situation was only 'saved' – from an elitist perspective – through the emergency powers of the state governor, authorised by the governor-general, and the dismissal of the newly elected East Pakistan assembly just over three months after it had come to office. From 1956 onwards it became increasingly clear that the interests of the Mohajir–Punjabi alliance would not be furthered within a parliamentary, democratic state. Hence their support for the presidential coup against the last Pakistan prime minister, and their further support for the subsequent coup of Ayub Khan in 1958 and the abolition of the 1956 constitution.

The 1962 constitution

The new Pakistani state, undemocratic and elitist, seemed much better equipped to face the security problems of the region, and secure some consensus within Pakistan's troubled elite. Yet from the outset until its collapse in 1970, the Ayubian state was perceived by a large section of Pakistani society as being domestically illegitimate, an institutional framework without domestic roots or loyalty, and

increasingly incapable of providing the benefits of real independence to anyone other than a small, unrepresentative bureaucratic-
elite.[21] Initially sanctioned by the need for order, Ayub Khan found
himself between a rock and a hard place, unwilling to start any significant internal debates about democracy, or about the role of Islam
within Pakistani society, and yet afraid to stifle debate for fear of further undermining his credibility.

At first – following the declarations of martial law in 1959 – Ayub
Khan approached this dilemma with all the consummate vagueness
of Jinnah. The new constitution was laid out without any explicit
reference to Islam at all. Yet – in the face of a public outcry – Ayub
Khan finally included the term 'Islam' and 'sharia' in the preamble.
Further more, he set up a Council of Islamic Ideology and an Islamic
institute that would attempt to bring the civil code of Pakistan into
line with sharia laws. Both these institutions were without influence
or relevance until the coming of General Zia. The Islamic fig-leaf
aside, the main purpose behind the 1962 constitution was to set up
and sanction a non-democratic political system, which was in effect
secular. Summarising views on the religious nature of the 1962 constitution, Rubya Mehdi notes that: 'Pakistan was neither a theocratic
or a secular state. It was not secular because of all the religious provisions within the constitution, but it was not theocratic either
because government was not carried out by religious agencies'.[22]

General Ayub Khan replaced the 1958 constitution with a novel
political format in which political parties were banned, and in
which the executive office of president was indirectly elected
through a series of tiered councils.[23] Promulgated in 1959, and cod-
ified within Pakistan's second constitution in 1962, basic democracies (BDs) were an elaborate institutional device based upon
indirect election and central nomination. They were devised to
cross-cut provincial identities by conceding powers to the district
and sub-district levels, and to use predominantly rural constituents
to checkmate urban areas. Moreover, the basic democracies provided safe constituencies from which to elect members of the
National Assembly and, in turn, the national presidency.

As such the system deliberately under-represented those 'forces of
political disintegration and conspiracy' (a growing middle class and
a small but articulate working class) on the grounds that they were
difficult to manipulate politically. BDs provided the ideal political
framework within which the Mohajir–Punjabi alliance could press

on with their particular construction of 'a strong Pakistani state', with an economy geared to export-led growth and US investments, and the development of the armed forces.

Because of the BD format, the 1962 constitution made no reference to the provinces or provincial rights for the simple reason that they had been politically emasculated. Ayub Khan's belief in a durable state–society link was that, if circumstances proved favourable (a telling condition), political participation could be encouraged but only along those lines favoured by the centre.[24] Other assumptions made by the elite included the belief that firm central direction would provide a period for the gradual emergence of Pakistan nationalism, cemented through sustained economic growth, without encouraging provincial dissent or opposition. The Islamic rationality behind the state's existence was downgraded altogether within the context of domestic policies. In terms of foreign policy, attention still fell firmly upon Kashmir and the '1,000 year' war with India as a convenient and necessary piece of rhetoric. Few, if any, of these elaborate assumptions were to hold.

The economic performance of Pakistan throughout the 1960s was unprecedented, and is only partially explained by the weakness of the economic and industrial base before 1962. Central rule enabled reorganisations in planning and administration and stability encouraged significant amounts of foreign investments.[25] That the Ayub Khan system had merely ignored (as opposed to accommodated) political dissent was apparent following the failure of *Operation Gibraltar* in 1965. Zulfikar Bhutto – the architect of Pakistan's balanced equation with China and the United States – resigned as Foreign Minister in 1967 because of Ayub Khan's acceptance of the Tashkent agreement with India, which, he believed, was against Pakistan's long-term national interests.

Following this, Zulfikar Bhutto emerged as a bitter opponent to Ayub Khan, and combined an anti-Indian foreign policy with a radical redefinition of the Islamic state through his talk of Islamic socialism. The reintroduction of Islam into the political system – this time from the left – involved a violent urban-based agitation that returned the issues of mass participation to the centre of Pakistani politics and finally brought down the BD system in 1969, in the wake of Ayub Khan's own illness and incapacity. As Omar Noman was to note of the Zia-ul-Haq period, the Ayub Khan interlude is a powerful illustration of the differences between creating a new set of institutions out of necessity on the one hand, and on the other, creating a viable process of institutionalisation that outlives the convenience of any one leader.

The socio-economic basis of the Bhutto regime 1972–1977

The industrialisation of Pakistan had greatly increased the urban-based middle classes, and had thus greatly strengthened the one constituent of Pakistani society that had been deliberately under-represented within the basic democracy format. The period of greatest Mohajir–Punjabi ascendancy had further alienated the Bengalis, who were under-represented in both the army and the bureaucracy. There is considerable economic evidence that suggests that East Pakistan was treated as an 'internal colony', providing raw jute for export, while capital and machine goods were imported to develop the infrastructure of the western wing. It has been estimated that between 1959 and 1960 and 1969 and 1970, the disparities of per capita production between the eastern and the western wing increased from 4 per cent (in favour of the west) to 61 per cent. It has been noted that: 'there is little doubt that these increasing inter-wing disparities which generated growing socio-political tensions were largely the consequence of Pakistan's economic policies and her allocation of resources for development'.[27]

The domestic roots of the 1971 civil war

Ayub Khan was removed from office by another military coup, but unlike the 1958 drama, General Yahya Khan resumed the office of Chief Martial Law Administrator to hand power back to a civilian government. The reasons behind this apparent modesty are crucial to any understanding of contemporary Pakistan: the Mohajir–Punjabi elite, beleaguered by the demands from newly emergent sections of society for popular and democratic politics, especially and most systematically from the East Wing, changed tactics in an attempt to reach some form of accommodation with the local and regional-based elites. Such a strategy opened the way for Pakistan's first – and last – national election. Given the circumstances of 1969–70, it would have been futile to have resisted, head on, popular demands for the return of parliamentary-based politics. At best, the army could attempt to ensure for itself the long-term position as arbiter of the political process.

In December 1969 Yahya Khan announced the holding of a general election, the undoing of the much hated One Unit policy, and subsequent elections within the four provinces. Political parties would be legalised. More importantly, Yahya Khan issued an ordinance known as the Legal Order Framework (LOF), a new constitutional blueprint which set out important preconditions for any future political order: that the National Assembly had to frame a constitution within 120 days, that any agreement would require the consent of the president (i.e. the military) and that it would have to be parliamentary and federal.[28] Significantly, the LOF also made reference to the fact that any subsequent constitution would have to be in keeping with the tenets and keepings of Islam, although it declined from spelling this out in any detail.

The important point – especially in the light of provincial demands and the need to ensure some form of stability – was the mention of federalism. Many commentators have argued that the army still envisaged a role for themselves within the political framework of Pakistan, especially in the likely event of an indecisive outcome and the formation of a weak coalition government of the kind witnessed in the 1950s. The outcome was, unfortunately for the military, to be quite different, and the circumstances so violent that the army itself was to be largely discredited.

Over seventeen national parties campaigned in the winter of 1970. In the West Wing, Bhutto and the PPP received the support of a predominantly urban-based coalition that had been behind Ayub Khan's downfall, attracted by talk of democracy and Islamic socialism. In the East Wing however, the political forces of the Awami League, the basis of which was a middle-class Bengali-speaking elite in a complex coalition with left-wing students and radicals, dominated the political scene. The Awami League campaigned in the 1970 elections on the basis of the so-called 'six points',[29] announced in the mid-1960s, but which, in outline, dated back to the policies of the United Front government of 1954. The implications of the six point programme were ambiguous. To many senior leaders within the Awami League, the points were merely a demand for a truly federal state, bargaining positions from which to negotiate. Yet to many other sections of the League, the six points were a charter for secession. The Awami League did not field any candidates in the West Wing.

The elections revealed that Jinnah's version of Pakistani nationalism had simply failed to appear. In many respects, it could be argued that sub-nationalist identities were more important and more divisive than they had been in 1947. The Awami League won 151 seats out of 300, all of them in the east. The PPP won eighty-one seats, none in the east, with sixty-two from the Punjab alone. The provincial elections – held at the same time – revealed a complex mosaic of competing political identities, with the Awami League clearly established in the east, but with the PPP only in control of two provinces: Sind and Punjab. In reality, the worst fears of the Mohajir–Punjabi elite had been realised: a Bengali-speaking politician had won a national election in Pakistan. The JUI won four seats in the National Assembly, while the JUP won seven.

The polarisation of politics probably took the military by surprise. There is some evidence to believe that Yahya had expected the election to fragment party politics as it had in the 1950s. Moreover, the interaction of provincial and national forces was a new experience for Pakistan. It required significant decentralisation and democratisation of the state's political structures and compromise by its political elites. Yet despite an early announcement by Yahya that he welcomed 'Mujib Rehman as Pakistan's new Prime Minister' there would be no deal over the six-point programme. By March 1971 Bhutto had rejected the logic of sharing power with 'anti-national' forces, insistent that the Awami League was also receiving help from India. Meanwhile, Mujib's attempts to renegotiate the meaning of the six points (always vague) led to the further radicalisation of his own student wing and the possible accusation of compromising with the military.

The calculations of the military in the run up to the 'crack down' in 1971 remain somewhat of a mystery. While Yahya convened several meetings between Bhutto and Mujib, the military were anxious to support Bhutto's rhetoric of betrayal once they had accepted the 'fact' that any settlement with the Awami League would jeopardise national security. The responsibility for the decision to use force against the League and arrest Mujib Rehman in March 1971 lies presumably with Bhutto who was by then *de facto* prime minister, despite a skilful campaign later to blame Yahya and the generals.[30] Bhutto was also anxious to perpetuate the myth – carried on by his daughter – that he was Pakistan's first popularly elected prime minister.

Once force had been used (and, as we shall see, this is a valid point in India and Sri Lanka as much as it is for Pakistan) the option of a political compromise within a particular state structure was ruled out. Had the basic democracies been abolished earlier, or had Pakistan adopted within its first constitution provisions for the use of local languages, or the retention of provincially raised revenues, the situation may well have been different. Had some form of framework existed – had a political language of federalism existed in which the provinces could make demands without implying that they were secessionist – the dialogue between Mujib and Bhutto might well have led to some solutions.

Pakistan under Zulfikar Bhutto 1971–1977

The experience of the Bangladesh war opened up a new phase of state and nation formation within Pakistan. The subsequent humiliation of the army greatly strengthened the possibility that Bhutto and the PPP government would break with the 'martial law state', and as a Sindi, shift state control away from the Mohajir–Punjabi axis. The new state of Pakistan would not be bedevilled by problems of internal 'parity'. It might even be a consolation that, having lost the loyalty of the Bengalis, Pakistan society was better suited to the tasks of nation-building than at any time since independence.

Confronted with an acute national identity crisis in the wake of the Bangladesh war, Bhutto attempted to re-establish democracy and civilian rule based upon a revivalist notion of Islam: looking back to the ideas of Jinnah and the inspiration of Aligarh. Yet Bhutto's attempt to re-work a reformist Islam into a modern state was potentially more radical than Jinnah's. Drawing upon socialist and radical thinking, Bhutto's combination of Islamic socialism was both a commitment to an Islamic Pakistan and one in which rapid socio-economic development would overcome rural poverty and lead to sustained industrial growth.

There was virtually no room for any theocratic, Deobandian elements within Bhutto's early thinking, and thus no obstacles to the participation of the secular left within politics, including many former communists. Initially, Bhutto was willing to reopen the questions that had in part been addressed by Jinnah, but basically ignored by Ayub: 'What aspects of Islamic belief in practice are immutable, and what areas are open to reconstruction and reinterpretation in order to respond to new social and historical conditions?'[31] To the right wing religious parties the term 'Islamic socialism' was both oxymoronic and heretical, contradicting the virulently anti-socialist, anti-communist slant given to Pakistan's domestic and foreign policy during the 1960s.

Bhutto's particular stress upon Islam was the point of departure for a new domestic order. Moreover, Bhutto's encouragement of Arabic within the school curriculum brought immediate benefits to its foreign policy from the Middle East, even at the same time that it engendered a wide debate within Pakistan as to its real national identity. Domestic talk about socialism also helped cement the close ties between Pakistan and China. Both domestic and foreign policy were supported by anti-Indian rhetoric, despite the commitment of the government to uphold the Simla agreement.

High on the domestic agenda, however, was the legacy of the bureaucratic–military framework and the need to institutionalise the new democratic state. Bhutto began to restructure the army, promoting those individuals whom he believed were free of any political motivation, and establishing the principle of civilian authority. At the same time, he sought to appease the high command through increasing the defence budget and stepping up arms procurement. Between 1971 and 1975, defence expenditure rose from 5 per cent to 6.5 per cent of GNP (although its share in the government budget fell). The size of the armed forces increased from 365,000 to 502,000.[32] Bhutto also tried to free the bureaucracy from its predominantly colonial mind-set, through changes in the entrance exams and through a proliferation of differing and state-based services.

The culmination to all these policies was the 1973 constitution. Significantly, however, the opportunity to set the record straight on provincial rights and central obligations was effectively missed.[34] While the constitution recognised the importance of provincial autonomy it did specify those rights, and sought to safeguard them by authorising either the supreme court or the national parliament to oversee the dismissal and removal of provincial governments, ensuring the proper use of executive power. Yet another set of institutions could not, by themselves, mark a significant break with the past. While the Pakistan constitution of 1973 was the only one in Pakistan's history to be drawn up by an elected body, it still attempted to fudge the issues of religious and secular authority.

There were several Islamic elements within the constitution, some in the preamble, some in the so-called principles of policy. Not only did Bhutto attempt to appease both secularists and Islamicists, he attempted to placate both traditionalists and modernists within the Islamic camp itself.[35]

By 1975–76, what gains had been achieved were clouded by Bhutto's own emerging temperament as a leader who took political compromise and accommodation badly, and who increasingly feared the extent to which his control of the political process could be undermined by the left wing within the PPP, theocratic Islamic agitation from the mullahs and the Ulama, and by non-PPP governments in the provinces. By late 1974 Bhutto was turning his back on an earlier belief that provincial ethnicities and identities could meaningfully contribute to nationalist renewal. Having initially endorsed and welcomed the election of a popular non-PPP government in Baluchistan, Bhutto subsequently refused to compromise with the National Awami Party on the grounds that it was secretly embarked upon negotiations for secession (the so-called London plot), and dismissed them from power. Faced with serious provincial violence against non-Baluchis and against the state, Bhutto deployed the army to deal with the Baluchistan crisis and to prevent the province 'doing a Bengal'. For Islamabad, the national security was almost as acute as in 1971, with possible Afghan assistance and almost certain Indian diplomatic encouragement.

Disagreements within the PPP over the handling of this crisis, as well as over the scope and direction of government economic policy, persuaded Bhutto to dismiss various left-wing ministers from his government in 1974. By 1974–75, Bhutto was also bedevilled by various allegations of personal corruption and the political intimidation of the opposition. The growth in urban violence against his regime led him to attempt from 1975 onwards to ditch the social coalition that had brought him to power, away from the urban middle class–students–working class combine, towards a fundamentally rural combination that had, in an earlier and more substantial form, provided the electoral base for the Muslim League in the 1950s.

Bhutto's decision to call a general election in May 1977 took place at a time when the social basis of the Bhutto regime was at its weakest. Part of this weakness was, as it had always been, a failure to establish a deep domestic consensus over the form of legitimate political activity. The election – in which the PPP faced a combined opposition called the Pakistan National Alliance (PNA) – was marred by violence, especially in the cities, and the electoral verdict in favour of Bhutto was put down to vote rigging and widespread corruption.[36]

Bhutto's initial refusal to concede to demands for a fresh poll led to a rapid deterioration in law and order within metropolitan Pakistan. In July 1977 General Zia, a commander picked by Bhutto himself for his apparent commitment to the civilian control of the armed forces, launched a coup, *Operation Fair Play*, for very much the same reasons that Ayub Khan had in 1958. From the viewpoint of the military, political democracy was unpicking the sinews of the nation, destroying earlier hopes for sustained economic development, and making Pakistan 'a laughing stock throughout the world'. Yet his move against a party-based, parliamentary political process took place after Bhutto had conceded to almost all of the opposition's demands and had agreed to hold fresh elections. Significantly, Zia was also a Mohajir, a man of 'plain religious sentiment and conviction'. To defend his 'illegal' move against the constitution (the penalty for this treason was death), Zia invoked a Western-based doctrine known as the doctrine of necessity. When the constitution of a state is imperilled, it is necessary to take unconstitutional moves to ensure the survival of the state.

The 1977 declaration of martial law put Pakistan back almost twenty years, scrapped the 'Islamic socialist' route towards a democratic federal state and backed the political system into a sustained dialogue with the fundamentalist, Deobandian Muslims. Those who came to support and sustain General Zia's 'islamisation of Pakistan' programme, which started in 1979, did so with some apprehension, and some of the Islamic parties (the JUP) were to break with Zia when they believed that he was less committed to Islam than he was to power. Yet Zia's views on Islam were important, and far-reaching, and he was to set in motion a number of social and cultural forces which were to outlive him. Zia's view of the Pakistani state ensured a role for the army within a state sanctioned by Islamic law. Zia tried – like Ayub – to establish a controlled system of participation, without political parties, linked to the two pillars of the old political order – the military and the bureaucracy – but this time much more explicitly sanctioned by religion. Zia carefully turned Pakistan towards an interpretation of Islam that was conservative and hierarchical, in which the symbols of Islam were more emphatically deployed. In sum the system has been referred to as a military theocracy.

While Zia sponsored various debates about the role of Islam, and invited comment from prominent Islamic scholars, he was careful to ensure that dissent from the right (as much as the left) was censored or downplayed. Superficially at least Zia accepted the view that the Islamic community was more than just a sum of individuals: it had a totality and a representative function in its own right, sanctioned by religious traditions that could not be reduced to the numerical arithmetic of elections and political mandates.[37] This was a Deobandian conception of a kind associated with teachers like Maulana Maldudi and JI, and, not surprisingly, received their support.

Zia appeared willing at times to accommodate religious parties and their views to a extraordinary extent. He introduced Islamic banking and finance practices in which the charging of interest was made illegal, despite genuine concern by a Pakistani middle class that this would affect their businesses. Zia introduced the collection of *zakat*, a tax aimed at eliminating poverty and funding social welfare programmes. The Jaamat had long noted that: 'an Islamic economy has to conform to the dictates of the Islamic Shar'ia, in which the clear prohibition of interest is beyond doubt ... Inflation [too] is incompatible with the goals of an Islamic economy, so too are prolonged recession and uemployment'.[38]

Conservative dress codes were encouraged for men and especially for women. Islamic punishments, the basis of the Hudood Ordinances of 1979, were also introduced despite the protests of Pakistani lawyers and various international organisations. Since traditional definitions of crime involved theft, murder, rape, etc. and not fraud, embezzlement and political corruption, the weight of such punishments fell increasingly upon the rural poor. The legal sanctioning of apparent Islamic practices such as the vendetta and the blood feud created serious cases of mob violence and arbitrary justice. Sustained attempts to codify the Sharia led to serious religious violence with Pakistan's small Shiite community. Linked to the wider turmoil within the Islamic world following the Iranian revolution, Zia moved quickly to exempt the Shiite community from any obligations imposed upon them by religious policies they did not accept.

The 'civilianisation' of the regime (heralded after a whole series of local, presidential and national elections and one referendum) was completed in 1985, with the so-called revival of the constitution order. This order reinstated a heavily amended version of the 1973 constitution. The so-called eighth amendment had inverted Bhutto's commitment to a so-called Westminster-style system of government, by asserting the power of the president over the prime minister, allowing the president to appoint the prime minister as well as the cabinet. Without parties, the main basis for prime ministerial power was presidential patronage.

Although the outlines of the four provinces were retained, and the federal system was retained and left in tact, it now operated through the offices and directives of the central government, and indeed the executive. And always – despite the hanging of Bhutto in 1979 and the attempts to isolate and undermine the PPP – there remained the possibility that the language of Islam could well return to a more radical, secular mode. Why did Zia believe that an Islamic state could not sanction political parties? Was this interpretation self-evident from a casual reading of the Koran? Did his views command a widespread support throughout Pakistan, or within the Islamic political parties, with which he frequently consulted? The answer – if it is of any use – is no.

By late 1987 Zia was in disagreement with a whole series of domestic and foreign policy views of Prime Minister Junejo, a man effectively picked by him after the 1985 elections. Even before Zia's assassination, there is enough evidence to suggest that Zia's military theocracy had arrived at the end of another political cul-de-sac. In August 1988 the president dismissed Junejo, dissolved the National Assembly and called for fresh elections. Before these could be held, however, Zia was killed in a mysterious plane crash, along with the American Ambassador. In a curious testimony to the 'special relationship' they had been inspecting a Pakistani military installation equipped with American arms. Portrayed in 1977 as a sort of General Blimp, with a habit of stroking his moustache and saying 'By Jingo', Zia emerged as a formidable leader, with a canny, cynical eye to the logic of power. One is reminded, as so often in the politics of South Asia, of W. H. Auden's epitaph 'The Logic of the Tyrant: What is Possible is Necessary', but not necessarily for the reasons given.

Benazir Bhutto and the restoration of democracy: 1988 to the present

Zia survived longer than many of his critics believed possible. The Soviet invasion of Afghanistan was of profound significance not just for Pakistan's external orientations, but for sustaining the legitimacy of a particular leader. Afghanistan gave Zia an external outlet through which to bolster his domestic regime: both policies were cunningly linked to the shibboleth of the 'pure' Islamic state. His death revealed both the fragility of his regime and the enduring contradictions that have remained within Pakistan since its inception. What of the Pakistan state now, and what of its future? Is it yet secure? Or will it continue to disintegrate and factionalise, coming to resemble a Lebanon, or worst still, an Afghanistan?

Free of the overt personalised emphasis upon Islam that characterised Zia's regime, and weakened by the elections of 1988, 1990 and 1993, the bureaucratic–military framework remains in an uneasy truce with popularly elected governments. In turn, the central government remains a hostage to the stability and durability of provincial politics, especially that of the Punjab. In this respect, the situation is not unlike that experienced between 1971 and 1977. In terms of party politics, and despite the obvious point that elections since 1988 have been on a mass franchise, the multiplicity and instability of party government is reminiscent of the 1950s. Since 1988, three national governments have been hemmed in by powerful military figures such as General Aslam Beg and his successors, and powerful institutions from which popular support is excluded, above all the Inter-Services Intelligence Unit (or ISI). The powers of the president can still in many ways be described as vice-regal, although the recent election of pro-PPP candidates has eased relations with the prime minister. Failure to remove the eighth amendment still leaves in place the institutional framework from which to usurp the prime minister and the principle of popular government.

With Zia's death, the ban on political parties was relaxed in both the 1988, the 1990 and 1993 elections, but until these political parties solidify, weak national coalitions will probably come and go with predictable frequency, brought down in many cases by political violence at the provincial level. Moreover, the hesitancy and ambiguity in central government's role over religious authority and identity make any prime minister vulnerable to partisan religious issues. By 1994, Benazir Bhutto became embroiled in issues such as blasphemy laws and Islamic punishments which distracted the government from wider socio-economic policies. In the mid-1990s, it is fair to say that the whole process of government in Pakistan is unstable and precarious. As such, and however improbable, there remains the excuse for the military to reintervene. Like her father before her, Benazir has yet to provide the necessary institutional dynamism to fully democratise vital institutions of state power and establish clear civilian supremacy over the military.

Yet the more elections that take place, and the more familiar the system becomes both to a new set of political elites and the large mass of Pakistani society, the more likely it is to survive into the next century. After Zia (and Ayub) it is not clear what the legitimate basis would be for a military government to justify the centrality of the state, except the continual reference to provincial instability and the continuing security threat emanating from India. The thought that such centralisation has in fact been a *cause* of provincial instability has rarely occurred to Pakistan's elite. Kemal Faruki stated that: 'The future of Pakistan ... seems almost inescapably linked to the reassertion of the Aligarh spirit and [a] reformist Islamic movement. Pakistan's problems require *ijtihad* of a convincing and wide ranging nature'.[39] This would require a democratisation of the state and an allowance of real participation at the regional level. In an updated version of his book on Pakistan, Noman remarks:

> The Pakistani elite, civil and military needs pressures imposed through accountability ... Elected office at various levels of power, larger allocations to the social sectors to produce a more healthy and educated population, and measures to curb the arbitrary use of powers are necessary conditions for the emergence of a less fractious and fragile nation-state.[40]

Such a mission requires not just a new domestic consensus, free of past mistrust and provincial suspicions, but a new political dialogue in which Islam is not a simple ruse for ignoring (or rigging) a federal system. Pakistan also needs, desperately, a stable regional environment in which the threat perceptions of India recede into the background.

There remains, however, a note of pessimism within Pakistan, that goes back to the lack of a clear nationalist consensus in 1947. The democratisation of the Pakistani state since 1988 has reaffirmed

ethnic and provincial identities as the main identifiers of political
activism within Pakistan, and has led to an outbreak of fresh
demands. The resulting log-jam in exclusive and intolerant ethnic
claims, including the latest demand by the MQM for a separate
province for the Mohajirs, overloads the state's abilities to deal
with citizens defined as citizens of a shared civic space, adhering to
the same aspirations and the same visions of progress and prosperity.

State–society relations in Bangladesh

The dilemmas that Pakistan has faced over the exact relationship
between state and society are also present within Bangladeshi politics. Since its inception, Bangladesh has moved from being a secular
Bengali state to an Islamic state under the auspices of the military.
Since November 1990, the state has returned to a more secularised
view of politics under the Bangladesh National Party, yet the political crisis of 1996 has once more revealed the absence of any real
political consensus over how Bangladeshi institutions are to be run.
The political system remains in flux, and political parties are not
inclined to accept political defeat, or to work with government at
any cost. Party-based elections to the National Assembly held in
February 1996 were boycotted by the main opposition parties, and
forced the incumbent government to call fresh elections in May to
be held under a caretaker government. The subsequent election –
deemed free and fair by a series of international monitors – brought
the Awami League back into power twenty-one years after it was
removed in a military coup.

This apparent duplication of Pakistan's experiences after Bhutto
is extraordinary given the apparent strengths of Mujib Rehman and
a Bengali-speaking vernacular elite in the late 1960s. Of all the
regional states – with the possible exception of the Maldives –
Bangladesh is often cited as the most homogeneous culture, the
nearest thing in South Asia to a 'nation-state'. The break-up of Pakistan had removed the Mohajir–Punjabi elite and undermined their
alliance with the minute percentage of Urdu-speaking Bengalis who
had been committed to the 'two nation' theory. While regional divisions remain in Bangladesh, especially between peoples living in so-
called tribal areas to the east, language has usually been the prime

factor in political mobilisation. Repatriation agreements, between Pakistan and Bangladesh, started in the mid-1970s, have recently opened the way for the return of about 20,000 Bihari speakers to Pakistan. However, 300 of these people arrived in Karachi, in Pakistan, to be greeted by a bomb blast. Mohajirs and Pathanis fear that the Biharis as an ethnic group will take priority in government jobs and benefits.

For Bangladesh, the imperatives of decentralisation raise issues that have less to do with federalism than with local and district representation, and given the relatively low percentage of urban Bengalis, rural representation and the democratisation of village and block administration. Given the apparent simplicity of Bangladesh politics, why has the identity of Bangladesh been so elusive, and the benefits of independence apparently so poor? If the civil war was fought on the grounds that East Pakistan's intrinsic domestic identity and political culture were subject to external domination, why did that identity not emerge in a strong enough form to survive the first five years of independence? To answer these questions, the liberation struggle needs to be located within both a regional and a domestic setting.

For the sake of academic nicety, and at considerable risk of being reductionist, it can be argued that in 1971 there were three main versions of the Bangladesh state–society relationship on offer, with three different sets of political symbolism and language that could be used as the basis to create a modern, independent state. The first version was that of a radical, almost Maoist republic in which a predominantly agrarian-based society would construct a stateless social structure based on communal and local power.[41] Such a programme was articulated by the left of the Bengali movement, predominantly students and intellectuals who combined a tradition of Bengali radicalism with a then-current enthusiasm for Mao Zedong's writings and the successes of the Chinese state. Such ideological enthusiasm existed despite the fact that China would play such a negative role throughout the civil war, and despite Beijing's subsequent attempts to block Bangladesh from joining the UN. The Bengali left were also – significantly – profoundly anti-Indian and contemptuous of Indian bourgeois democracy.

These views were popularised during the civil war itself through the activities and views of the *mukti bahini*, the Bengali militants who fought the Pakistan army, and although aided by and, to an extent, co-ordinated by increasing levels of Indian involvement, never lost their independence. The *mukti bahini* opposed the organisation of a professional army within Bangladesh after independence on the grounds that it would be used as the repressive arm of the state against the people it was alleged to defend. Those militants who were eventually enlisted into a professionalised Bangladeshi army took many of their radical ideas with them. Thus the civil war not only deeply and profoundly politicised Bengali society, it also politicised important sections of the national army.

The second version of Bangladesh was a bourgeois liberal view of the state, in which the institutions of parliamentary democracy would knit together a strong national identity based upon secularism. This was the view most closely identified with Mujib Rehman and the main faction of the Awami League, and the one closest to the Indian position. Mujib, interestingly enough, cited Nehru in his thinkings on nationalism, and not Jinnah. The disagreements between this liberal position of Bangladesh and student radicalism were submerged during the actual war, but emerged into the open once the fighting stopped. Rather like Bhutto, left–liberal divisions would force Mujib Rehman not only to expel left-wing ministers from the cabinet in late 1973, but to eventually close down the parliamentary political system under the rubric of a national emergency.

The third view – totally absent during the civil war itself but emergent later as part of the remains of the Pakistan phase – was what in the context of Pakistan has been referred to above as the Deobandian view of an Islamic state. This vision of an independent Bengal was essentially treasonous to the causes of the civil war. Many who openly proclaimed it, such as members of the Islamic religious parties who had contested the 1970 elections, and members of the Pakistan civil service, were later either charged with collaboration, banned or dismissed from office. Many had their citizenship removed. Yet the pro-Islamic forces regrouped following the repatriation of Bengali officers and soldiers detained in West Pakistan, and the collapse of the Mujib political system in 1975. Many of the soldiers detained in the west were removed from the experiences of the war, deeply distrustful of the left, and sufficiently mistrustful of Indian designs to dislike Mujib's later reliance on New Delhi.

Staunch supporters of the role and value of a professional army, and tinged with Ayub Khan's belief in their domestic value, the 'repatriates' quickly found themselves in ideological disagreement with the 'freedom fighters' whose values and language they believed to be deeply subversive, as well as the civilian leaders of the Awami League. Initially the least popular of the three state–society blueprints, since it was a continuation of the logic of a united Pakistan, it gradually gained ground as the liberal and left-wing versions of Bangladeshi nationalism effectively eliminated each other through purges and systematic bloodlettings. This victorious version of the state was as exclusive and repressive as the Zia-ul-Haq system was to be in Pakistan itself, linked to a controlled political process in which parties would either be controlled or banned.

How do we account for the mutual destruction of a middle-class radical secularism? With the moderate Awami League in exile in India, and Mujib Rehman imprisoned in West Pakistan for the duration of the war, the leadership was cut off from the radicalising effects that the fighting had on the civilian population. Effectively installed by the Indian government, a liberal state could only be constructed once civil society had been depoliticised, put back into the grooves of a passive, 'representative' system based upon parties and elections. Attempts by Mujib Rehman to co-opt the left in such an enterprise, difficult at best, were seriously weakened by the international help and assistance given to the Awami League by India, and by serious disagreements over the type of economic policy, especially with the emerging aid relationship with America and the West.

Part of the pressure upon Mujib Rehman was what New Delhi wanted Bangladesh to look like, or rather more realistically, what it did not want it to look like. The government in New Delhi recognised a potential naxalite movement when it saw one, and was anxious to assist the Mujib government to 'deal with the left'. Radical Maoism in Bangladesh – involving some improbable but not, in the long term, impossible Chinese connection – was to be avoided at all cost. Yet Indian support did not help build a strong, legitimate state. On the contrary, it weakened the state by discrediting the social elite who were trying to construct it as being pro-Indian and therefore anti-national.

The attempts by Mujib Rehman to put the revolutionary genie back into the bottle were further undermined by the acute socio-economic difficulties faced by Bangladesh after the civil war. Like

Bhutto in the west, by 1974, Mujib was bedevilled by charges of political corruption, a situation worsened by economic scarcities and charges of economic mismanagement. The growth in political parties after 1972 quickly reduced the Awami League to a state not dissimilar to the Muslim League in the 1950s: a faction-ridden spoils machine with little ideology, a mere ladder to state power. Coupled with Rehman's policies towards the civil service – again curiously imitative of Bhutto's – the ability of the government to act decisively was seriously weakened. De-professionalised, the civil service was undermined at the same time that it was put in charge of a growing public sector, sanctioned, like Bhutto's policies, through the language of socialism. Moreover, many competent civil servants were further purged because of their association with the previous regime. Aware that the lifetime of the regime might itself be in question, many civil servants fleeced the state for as much as they could get in the time made available to them.

Rampant inflation seriously limited the degree of support a small middle class were willing to give Mujib Rehman, and extend to a parliamentary government. Although the failure of the Rehman government to deal with the agricultural sector was only partially to do with negligence, the possibility of sustained famine destroyed the credibility and legitimacy of his government in the rural areas as well, a serious – indeed a fatal – blow to any government in Bangladesh.

Faced with a series of deep-seated, basically ideological divisions, Rehman attempted to assert the autonomy of the state over all the main sections of the Bangladeshi society, except the members of his own family.[42] Rehman's decision to set up a private paramilitary army in 1974, along with his decision to suspend parliament and create a one-party state in 1975, lost him the support of both the right and the left, both within the civilian parties and within the military. His declaration of a state of emergency, and his sweeping away of the entire political system signalled the decline into personal dictatorship.

The 1975 coups

Much has been written about the drama of Bangladeshi politics since the murder of Mujib Rehman.[43] The most important point to note about the general crisis that overcame the state was that it involved *intra-elite* disputes, taking place without any direct reference to the urgent societal needs such as the elimination of poverty, and without much popular support. The coup that killed Rehman created a vacuum in which the army disintegrated into proto-Islamic and socialist groups and in which the secular, urban middle class were leaderless and dispirited.

There followed an intense period of coups and counter-coups that threatened the very basis of the state itself. The eventual rise of an army officer to power – Ziaur-Rehman as president (assumed 1976, confirmed by referendum in 1977) – was a piece of constitutional innovation inherited from the earlier political discourse of Pakistan. It resorted to a presidential-style system of government in which the prime minister and other members of the cabinet were appointed by loyalty. Superficially, Ziaur-Rehman seemed to represent the rise of the pro-socialist factions, since he had been an active member of the *mukti bahini*. Indeed, ironically, he had been the man who had announced the birth of Bangladesh to the world from the Chittagong military cantonment in 1971. Yet the political trend of his regime was to head back towards Pakistan and Islam in both domestic and foreign policy, and away from India and secularism. Such domestic politics opened the way for the gradual rehabilitation of so-called 'collaborators', as well as the *rapprochement* of Pakistan with Bangladesh within the OIC.

In 1978, Islam was introduced into the preamble of the constitution, while the term 'Bengali' (printed on passports and on permits as proof of citizenship) was replaced by the term 'Bangladeshi'. In foreign policy Ziaur constructed an anti-Indian strategy, and a commitment to regionalism with the founding of SAARC aimed at avoiding India's physical dominance. Paradoxically – but with some success – Ziaur-Rehman was also careful to follow up on Mujib Rehman's commitment to the NAM as well, while also creating powerful links with the United States and with China.

The military leadership of Ziaur-Rehman in Bangladesh faced exactly the same problem that General Zia-ul-Haq faced in Pakistan: how to cement a state–society relationship that preserved the interests of a factionalised elite with reference to Islam, but without losing power to the Islamic political parties. Moreover, how could Ziaur civilianise a military government – and thus retain the integrity of non-military institutions needed for economic development – without encouraging military counter-moves against him

personally? Ziaur-Rehman's first move was to try and profession-
alise the army, a policy that involved the widespread executions of
left wingers within the army command. As with Bhutto, Rehman
ensured that the army budget was maintained in order to keep them
in the cantonments, while officers suspected of radical sentiments
were frequently rotated around command posts to prevent them
establishing regionalised support.

Within the domestic arena, the possible strategy for legitimating
power was either to forge close links with pre-existing political parties, by offering them clear access to state spoils, or by constructing
a party from scratch which would hopefully become the vehicle for
controlled political participation. Ziaur-Rehman adopted the latter
with the Bangladesh National Party (BNP) as an attempt to goad the
other parties (especially the Awami League) into participating
within his president system.

Between 1978 and 1981, various attempts were made to rebuild
the state, but almost all of them failed. Like Pakistan's numerous
'official' versions of the Muslim League under Ayub Khan and Zia,
the BNP failed to free itself from the accusation that it was a mere
creature of the central executive. Foreign policy successes – and
there were several, including Bangladesh's election on to the Security Council of the UN – did not detract attention away from
domestic failings and the weakness of Bangladesh's political institutions.

The assassination of Ziaur-Rehman in 1981 was the result of an
obscure plot by a group of left-wing army officers without support
within the army. In a scene somewhat reminiscent of *Julius Caesar*,
the assassination took place in the vague hope that Ziaur-Rehman's
death would lead to a general rebellion throughout Bangladesh and
within Bengal, and restore the lineaments of the Bangladeshi state
to its pre-1973 radicalism. After a few days of studied silence within
the ranks, and careful manoeuvrings by high command in Dhaka,
some coup leaders were allowed to leave while one of them – General Manzoor – was killed in a shoot-out. The failure of the Ershad
regime to bring the killers of Ziaur to justice remains an important
issue to this day for his wife, who became prime minister in 1991.

For a while the state fell by default into the hands of an interim
civilian administration, with the tacit support of the military under
the leadership of General Mohammed Ershad. The popular election
of President Sattar in November 1981, previously Chief Justice of

the Supreme Court, under the auspices of the BNP was an extraordinary achievement given the circumstances, yet the large number of political parties attempting to contest the subsequent Assembly elections hampered the rule of the civilian leadership and made any attempt to reconvene a constituent assembly impossible. Sattar was unable to establish control of the army, and was finally replaced in a bloodless coup in 1982, when General Ershad assumed control of the state.

Ershad was a repatriated officer and had not experienced the violent and radicalising influences of the civil war. Like General Zia, he was closely associated with Islam, and continued the policies started by Ziaur-Rehman. From 1982 until 1989 Ershad has followed Zia in an attempt to synthesise a Bangladesh nationalism that is Islamic, and in which political participation is controlled by either banning parties or ensuring their registration before election. There were several false starts in which dialogue with the political parties failed, and in which another officially created party in 1983 (the Jatiyo Dal) proved incapable of broadening the support for the regime. His attempt to build a viable political system also involved various local and district government initiatives.

In 1985 Ershad called a referendum in an attempt to bypass the civilian leadership entirely and in order to locate 'Islam' at the centre of both domestic and foreign policy, and to legitimate his claim to personal rule. The referendum asked for general approval for Ershad's attempts to found a new, strong government, and called upon the opposition for 'general support'. The official turn out was 72 per cent, with 94 per cent of the vote in favour. Foreign observers put the turnout as low as 15–20 per cent. Unperturbed, Ershad then called for local elections in 1985 as the next phase in state formation. In 1986 Ershad called parliamentary elections (which a large number of opposition parties boycotted) and presidential elections. Again, the programme is comparable with Zia's ending of martial law in Pakistan, which also took place in 1985.

Yet, like President Zia, while Ershad managed to civilianise his regime he could not establish a political consensus within domestic politics free from army support. In 1987 a decision to extend the appointment of army officers into district and local councils led to sustained opposition by the established political parties. The declaration of an Islamic state in 1988 did not open the way to popular support either, since it ignored the cultural Bengali matrix within which Bangladeshi Islam was set.[44] While it assisted in furthering Bangladesh's links with the Gulf states, it could not sanction a viable internal structure. Nor did Ershad's own political party fare any better as a conduit to link the state with society. In 1988 Ershad held fresh parliamentary elections. The opposition parties boycotted the poll, and called for Ershad's resignation. Amalgamated into two basic coalitions, led by Sheikh Hasina (Mujib Rehman's daughter) and Begum Zia (General Zia's widow) the political parties continued to proliferate and limit areas of potential co-operation between them – except the overall opposition to Ershad and his regime. The ideological content of the parties remains to some extent vague and confused, although the BNP emerged committed to socialist policies and a more revisionist stance on Islam. Both coalitions contained Islamic parties. Disputes over the shape and content of political institutions remain, with Sheikh Hasina wishing to reinstate a prime ministerial system, and with Begum Zia committed to a presidential one. Both the BNP, and the Awami League, while basically secular, are conscious of the position and influence of Islamic parties within their respective coalitions.

The resignation of Ershad in November 1989 was made possible by the army's decision to distance itself from his political fate in the wake of a broad-based student revolt which was quite separate from the parties themselves. The acting president Mr Shahabuddin Ahmed oversaw elections in late February 1991 in which Begum Zia and the BNP won. He was himself replaced by the indirectly elected Abdur Rahman Biswas as president. It would be tempting to conclude that, as if from nowhere, the Bengali secular state has re-emerged, but the socio-economic basis for such a state remains as weak as ever, and religious sentiments remain available for small parties to make short-term political gain. From 1992 onwards, Bangladeshi politics was characterised by a marked rise in violence. The case of Gholam Azam, the leader of the JI party, revealed how the old wounds of the civil war remained. Opposition parties demanded that Azam be placed on trial for 'war crimes' committed during the civil war. Dependent upon the JI in parliament, Begum Zia resisted these demands, despite strikes and violent protests. The incident involving the feminist writer Taslima Nasreen, who was eventually forced to leave the country for blaspheming against Islam, revealed the weakness of a government to stand up against fundamentalist assertions of faith, backed up by force. While the re-election of an Awami League-led government further entrenches elections into the political culture of Bangladesh, it remains to be seen whether Sheikh Hasina can acquire – and retain – the legitimacy a government needs to act decisively.

The state–society relationship in India

The search for political order within the states of Pakistan and Bangladesh has been conducted within a religious idiom, and within an overtly authoritarian framework of government. As such, the resulting institutional structures of the state have been unstable, and the political process deemed illegitimate by a large number of citizens. While Islam has provided useful and purposeful links with outside powers – especially financially – it has not so much defined the national interest as supported the interests of a small, sectional elite.

In many ways, India provides a striking contrast to Pakistan in terms of its stability and the apparent breadth of its political consensus. If scholars of Pakistan have spent a great deal of their time explaining why democracy collapsed, Indian scholars have spent much of their time explaining why it succeeded. It took the Nehru government just a few years (1947–49) to agree upon a constitutional document that is still essentially in existence today.[45] With some notorious exceptions, elections have taken place throughout the political system at regular intervals, and have on the whole been free and fair, monitored by an apolitical Electoral Commission, and regulated by statute and precedents. Yet recent scholarship, most noticeably that of Jalal, has cautioned against the tendency to see India as 'democratic' and Pakistan as 'authoritarian'. Jalal argues that both states, in sharing a common colonial legacy from the British period, have much more in common than this simple dichotomy implies, going as far as to characterise Indian political history as one of 'authoritarian' democracy.

At the time of independence, India's elite consisted of a multiethnic, middle-class elite who were joined together through a multilingualism based upon the English medium, the use of Hindustani (and after independence, the use of Hindi) in conjunction with local vernacular languages. They were further united through their commit-

Map 5 India
(*Source*: John R. Wood (ed.), *Contemporary State Politics in India*,
Westview Press, Boulder, 1987)

ment to a secular ideology and political democracy, despite the fact
that a majority of Indians were Hindus (over 80 per cent). The
Indian National Congress Party ensured that this elite could manage

national politics by relying upon a complex set of patron–client relations that reached right down to the provincial and district level, combining numerous political cultures, including the hierarchical concepts of caste and jati. Thus political participation was controlled by a well-established, regional hierarchy that recognised the rules of the game as set by New Delhi. Moreover, while much evidence suggests that democratic politics was compromised by the hierarchical structures of caste, over time political participation significantly altered caste structures, gradually empowering lower – shudra – castes, and, subject to regional variation, bringing them into government.

The entire basis of India's constitution and laws was to provide a national framework within which the rights of religious communities would be protected, but one in which the language of religion – especially that of the majority Hindus – would not be legitimate, and would be answerable to the same authority of the state and the state laws. The 1950 constitution not only recognised the existence of the provinces (preferring to use the word 'state'), it granted to them important areas of legislation such as agriculture, education, and some limited revenues. Articles 14 and 19 created a charter of individual rights for the 'private' use of religion and political expression, abandoning the previous British practice of separate electorates, which defined communities as religious entities.

Unlike Pakistan, state identities were strengthened – not weakened – by national politics. While claims of political exclusiveness could not be made in terms of religion, language provided a flexible basis for the incorporation of elites into nation-building on the basis of claiming special ethno-linguistic identities.[46] After 1956 the states were increasingly reorganised along linguistic lines and served both to strengthen both national and regional identities in a way quite unthinkable in Pakistan. The language problem in India was resolved relatively easily (although at times, violently), aided by the fact that secularism had no association with any particular language (such as that alleged to exist in Pakistan between Urdu and Islam). India adopted a three-language formula (Hindi, English, and one of the recognised fifteen national languages) and placed them within the constitution. Although it recognised Hindi as the national language, the decision to retain English, and to encourage and support the vernacular languages, was to prove extremely flexible.

Nehru survived long enough as India's first prime minister

(1952–64) to establish the principles of cabinet and parliamentary responsibility, and to prevent the unelected elements within the state structure – the modern governor-generals and viceroys of India, or even the military and the civil service – from usurping popular government. Even though India inherited the same emergency powers as Pakistan, along with a centrally nominated governor acting within each state under the titular authority of the president, to a large extent the governors acted with propriety, deferring to the chief ministers. Nehru's long tenure as an elected prime minister gave Indian democracy an enormous advantage.[47]

By far the most flexible basis for nation-building was paradoxically democracy. Given India's regional diversity, the electoral significance of minorities, and the need to accommodate coalitions of differing minorities became crucial for winning national elections.[48] Key minority groups – especially the Muslims – were courted and grouped together into significant vote banks within the Congress, and retained by patronage and access to state power at differing levels of the federal system. The flexibility within the Congress party was sufficient to accommodate wide regional diversities. In each state, Congress administrations were supported by a bewildering array of differing caste and sectional coalitions.

This flexibility of 'rainbow coalitions' was essential to the success of Indian nationalism and to the success of the Congress party, especially with regard to winning national power. Any system that ignored this – or stressed the exclusiveness of any particular community or a particular ideology – would shatter the nation. Thus unlike Pakistan or Bangladesh, political disagreements within India have not taken place within an authoritarian or religious discourse in which elections have been the exception rather than the rule, or in which provisional autonomy has been mistaken for rebellion. In India the national discourse has being profoundly democratic, even if it initially relied upon a few key political operators situated throughout the federal system to deliver the vote. By the 1960s, electoral politics was generating increasing social and political diversity.

The reasons for Indian strength thus appear obvious: a secular polity within which various identities coexisted with apparent equal legitimacy within the territorial state, a much more clearly defined and institutional federal structure,[49] and a well knit national party that was not uprooted by partition, and was represented within the areas that would remain in India. Throughout the 1950s and the 1960s these institutions continued to respond to rapid social change, and co-opt differing sections of society into an inclusive political elite. Moreover, when non-Congress parties began to form governments in the states after 1967 they were not immediately seen as being anti-national, although the central government was quick to outlaw or restrict those political parties who couched their policies in secessionist terms.

However, by the early 1970s the mediation of mass voting by elites became more problematic. The elites themselves had begun to alter and disintegrate through socio-economic change, and other sections of Indian society were becoming more active and far-ranging in their demands. These new interests, associated with the so-called middle caste identities, often brought non-Congress state governments to power.[50] This decentralisation of the Indian political system and the breaking up of established parties into factions, although part of the success of the experiments with democracy and nation-building, coincided with a complex political centralisation within the Congress party following the 1971 elections and the rise of Mrs Gandhi. These changes made the party less likely to respond to increasing diversities, and less inclined to co-opt these new and more volatile elites, who increasingly turned to their own parties or their own factions.

In a situation in which the number of political parties grew and the strength and distinctiveness of party organisation progressively weakened, the political system became increasingly competitive at the same time that it became disorganised and fragmented. If democratic politics has failed to institutionalise itself in Bangladesh and Pakistan, in India its very success has possibly led to the 'de-institutionalisation' of India's party system.[51] The result is, however paradoxical, the same: sectional and party differences paralyse government and undermine the efficiency of the state. In an article on Bihari politics, Atul Kohli noted in the late 1980s that: 'The government of Bihar has simply stopped functioning. The levels of mobilisation along both caste and class lines are so high that nearly all the groups are fighting each other, often with their own private armies'.[52]

How could political parties win national power within an increasingly diverse – and diverging – political system? How could the Congress centre appeal to what were, in reality, increasingly exclu-

sive interests? Two deceptively simple answers suggested themselves, both based upon the need to find a common denominator.
One was a commitment to socialism, that which characterised the
Indira Gandhi governments after 1967; the other was a commitment to Hinduism. While both strategies were in large part determined by socio-economic changes throughout India that made them
potentially useful, they were articulated by Congress, in the short
term, for reasons of electoral gain. Both strategies rested on a spu-
rious notion of majorities: that a majority of Indians were 'poor',
and that a majority of Indians (somewhere near 80 per cent) were
Hindu, and would respond to a party committed, in some way, to
'Hindu' values.

Much has been written about Indira Gandhi's use of socialism,
and the significance of her 1971 Abolish Poverty campaign.[53] I
would like to concentrate here on the use of Hinduism and the
belief that a covert use of Hindu ideology and symbolism could be
used by a political elite to retain power. The strategy – as it emerged
in Mrs Gandhi's post-emergency administration (1980–84) – was a
high risk one. The use of Hinduism was problematic in that not all
who saw themselves as Hindus subscribed to the same values, in just
the same way that not all the Muslims of South Asia subscribed to
orthodox Sunni values.

The myth of a Hindu majority is borne out by an examination of
caste and jati antagonisms, especially between the sudra (lower
castes) and upper twice-born caste groups, and between twice-born
castes and scheduled castes and tribes over job reservation. Brahmanical Hinduism, which is heavily textual and drawn from the
Vedic and Aryan scripts, is quite alien to lower-caste cults throughout southern and south-eastern India. Many Hindu movements are
in themselves anti-brahmanical, and recent political activities
amongst the scheduled castes and harijans – now known as Dalits –
have sought to remove caste distinctions and reform discriminatory
religious practices,[54] even if they have sought to retain the concept
of caste.

Moreover, even if the use of Hinduism could ensure that a new
coalition of interests could be built to give a national government
security of electoral tenure, what about the non-Hindu minorities?
Any national government, aligned to Hinduism, would surely be on
a collision course with the minorities? Between 1980 and 1984, the
Congress government attempted to deploy the language of minor-

ity rights simultaneously: indeed, even on occasion to create anxiety within the minorities about Hindu domination, in order to ensure their support. The result of these two paradoxical strategies was the same: religion became paramount to a political process that once claimed to be secular.

The rise of the Hindu vote

The rise of political Hinduism is a complex matter, and in large part falls beyond the scope of this book. The political utility of Hindu identity becomes apparent when socio-economic change amongst north Indian Muslims led to a more confident assertion of their religious identity, manifested through a spate of mosque building and the setting up of religious schools and other educational foundations. Linked to a largely unsubstantiated myth that, for reasons of polygamy, the Indian Muslim population was increasing faster than the Hindu, such visible wealth led to growing suspicions by Hindus that the minorities had benefited from secularism disproportionately.

As within Pakistan and the Islamic parties, the political use of Hinduism by the Congress involved some risk that the Hindu parties themselves – of which there were several both before and after independence – would come to prominence on the coat-tails of Congress' Hindu rhetoric. To some extent, this is what has happened since 1989: the covert use of Hinduism ensured that, in moments of crisis, when a collision with the minorities seemed imminent, the Congress would have to prevaricate or indeed retreat. The overt use of Hinduism, as seen by the BJP and its associated parties, gives the impression of conviction and strength. In 1947 various Hindu chauvinist parties called for the creation of a Hindu state on the grounds that the 'majority of Indians are Hindus'. Moreover, linked to the success of specific minorities within a federal India, Hindu parties were from the mid-1960s onwards emphasising the apparent 'belief amongst Hindus in India that since minorities have been better able to deliver blocks of votes, political parties have pandered to their whims against the interest of the majority'.[55]

Since the mid-1980s there has been much more talk of a 'Hindu India' in which minorities, especially Muslims, will become subject to Hindu laws, or at least be compelled to recognise *Indian* culture as 'Hindu' and thus to concede that Hinduism must be given specific recognition within the constitution, if not as a religion, then as a cultural prerequisite.

Political support offered to the Hindu fundamentalist parties (such as the BJP) was, until the late 1980s, reasonably small (less than 10 per cent). In 1989 elections, the BJP's share of the votes increased, and it did surprising well in seats. In some particular localities (such as Bombay and Jaipur) the BJP and aligned Hindu chauvinist parties did well in subsequent state elections, coming to power in Uttar Pradesh, Himachal Pradesh, Rajasthan and Maharashtra. Having formed governments, BJP administrations pursued educational and economic policies hostile to minorities: in the case of Uttar Pradesh, the state government was implicated in the demolition of the Ayodhya Mosque in 1992. Despite electoral set-backs, including a defeat in Uttar Pradesh in 1993, and despite a leadership currently under investigation for corruption, the BJP did remarkably well in the 1996 elections, forcing the Congress-I into second place in the national parliament. The Indian president called A. Vajpayee to form a government, but well short of the necessary number of seats, the provisional government resigned in late May 1996.

Since the mid-1980s, organisations such as the Vishwa Hindu Parishad (VHP), the All India Nationalist Forum, and most extremist of all perhaps, the Shiv Sena of Maharasthra, have gained access to political power, and have sought to reintroduce the symbols of Hinduism within Indian life. This revival involves the public holding of 'punjas' – religious festivals and ceremonial processions, often through Muslim strongholds and past mosques, with the deliberate intention of provoking communal violence. The political policies of these organisations include the abolition of the various constitutional provisions safeguarding minority rights, clear priority to the army and the armed forces within India, and the declaration of India as a Hindu state. Yet, as will be discussed below, as the Ayodhya Mosque incident proved, the relationship between the BJP and other Hindu parties and forums is problematic.

Muslims in India

Since the mid-1980s, the Congress attempts to use both Hindu and Muslim language to ensure political loyalty has merely divided Indian society further. There are two interesting examples of this:

the Shah Bano case, and the demolition of the Ayodhya Mosque itself. The Shah Bano case is, in outline, about 'a fundamental disagreement over how differing communities perceive the concept of justice and a just system of laws'.[56] The Congress' support for the Muslim Marriage Act (which exempted Muslim women from India's civil code and allowed Muslims to undertake their own legislation) enraged Muslim moderates and women's groups, and further offended the Hindus who had themselves accepted a secular code on marriage and divorce in the mid-1950s. Muslim moderates – rather like their Aligarhist cousins in Pakistan – found themselves in the middle of a difficult and dangerous debate since they appeared to sanction adherence to a secularism that was effectively Hindu, or at the very least non-Muslim.

The inability of the Congress leadership to take a decisive stand against communal forces lost it the support of many of the minority vote-banks in the 1989 elections, particularly the Muslims and resulted in a historic national electoral defeat, only its second since 1977. V. P. Singh, an erstwhile cabinet minister of the Congress, had united the opposition and come to power in order to oppose government corruption, and to take a stand in favour of the Muslims and other minorities, but even the new government was forced to confront the realities of a growing 'Hindu' lobby.

The National Front electoral manifesto made specific references to the crisis within Indian nationalism and criticised the Congress for introducing communal themes into politics. They were particularly critical of Rajiv Gandhi's decision to start his campaign at Ayodhya. The election results of 1989 produced almost exactly the same situation as the 1988 elections produced in Pakistan: a minority government containing an extraordinary combination of parties drawing upon radically different support. The Janata Dal party was forced to go into coalition with both the communists and the communalists.

It was within this context that the crisis of the Babari Masjid/Ram Janambhoomi crisis at Ayodhya became so central to the survival of the government and the continuing relevance of secularism to Indian politics. The structure at the centre of dispute was, prior to its destruction, a mosque that many Hindus believe was once a temple and the birthplace of Lord Ram, an important Hindu god. They argued that the mosque was built after the Moghul invasions and that, since the Moghuls have gone (to *their* state of Pakistan) the temple should be restored by the Indian government.

Subsequent demands to demolish the mosque and reinstate the temple had surfaced throughout the British period, and periodically since 1947. From 1987 onwards, Hindu political parties agitated for the demolition of the mosque and the construction of a temple and organised various religious ceremonies in and near the Mosque that significantly raised the communal temperature throughout India. In 1989 the Rajiv Gandhi government dithered between its fear of offending the Hindus and its fear of losing the Muslim vote. The result was a political impasse in which the Hindu parties took the initiative. On 6 December 1992, a group of political activists, associated with but not members of , the BJP, broke through a police cord and tore down the building. The incident sent shock waves throughout the subcontinent: it led to sustained communal rioting throughout India, and the condemnation of the Indian government by Pakistan and Bangladesh. One Pakistani commentator noted that the incident proved beyond doubt that Jinnah's 'two nation theory was correct after all, and that stripped of her pretensions of secularism, India was a Hindu state in which Hindus could act with callous disregard against non-Hindus'.

The Narashima Rao government moved, as it had so often done, to lock the stable door after the horse had bolted. Using article 356 of the constitution, the central government dismissed BJP administration in Uttar Pradesh (in which Ayodhya is located), and other BJP administrations in neighbouring states. Several political organisations were banned, but the Congress-I proved reluctant to ban the BJP itself. Furthermore, in a curious gesture, Advani, the leader, resigned from parliament as a sign of atonement. Yet the damage had been done. The destruction of a mosque had set a serious precedent. Many religious sites in India are shared sites, many mosques are alongside or close to Hindu temples, and both – despite Pakistan – are part of a sub-continental culture. The factual debate about the authenticity of the temple site was irrelevant – as specious as the attempts in Sri Lanka to trace the lineaments of a 'Tamil' kingdom that pre-date the Sinhalese, or vice-versa.

Subsequent attempts by the Rao government to assure both Hindus and Muslims that the 'structure' will be rebuilt as a 'dual place of worship' have been seen as further prevarication to the Muslims, especially in the face of international Muslim opinion to rebuild the mosque. To do so (without any reference to Ram and the

BJP's demands) would risk a serious Hindu backlash: to allow the BJP to build some grandiose structure celebrating the birth of Lord Ram would be massively offensive to Muslim opinion. This impasse remains, despite the eventual success of the Rao government to pass a Religious Sites bill, guaranteeing the safety of all existing religious sites as of 1993. The Nehruvian concept of secularism was not simply that the state would accommodate differing religious demands, but that the language of religion was simply illegitimate within national politics. It had been on this basis that he had so opposed the creation of an Islamic state of Pakistan. The Shah Bano case and the Ayodhya crisis reveal the extent to which secularism has declined.

An alteration in the 'core values' of India from a commitment to secularism towards some notion of cultural Hinduism is not inevitable, but it is a trend that has been encouraged by the weakening of political parties and their ability to resist Hindu pressure. The Muslims are an important and growing minority within India. They number just over 10 per cent of the population. Relatively secure within the framework of a secular state, recent increases in communal violence have not merely exposed their vulnerability, but the inability of the state to defend them. Of particular concern is the failure of the police force to deal with domestic violence: in some cases they have actually joined in or instigated communal rioting. Pakistan has condemned recent incidents in India, such as the outbreaks of violence in Hyderabad and Agra.[57] Despite praise for the success of India's 1996 elections by the Pakistan press, the anxiety remains over religious and cultural intolerance.

Indian nationalism and ethnic revivalism

The crisis of the secular state in India does not only concern the Muslims, however. The assassination of Indira Gandhi in 1984 by her Sikh bodyguard, and the resulting pogrom of Sikhs by Hindus, brought to head a much more curious communal divide between two communities who are directly related and have much in common in terms of religious and social practice.[58] The killing of Hindus by Sikhs sharply redefined the ethnic identity between the Sikh and Hindu communities.

All of the Hindu chauvinist parties define Sikhs as part of the Hindu community, as they do Jainism and Buddhism. Yet the very proximity of the Sikh identity to mainstream Hindu culture, and the degree to which the Punjab has been economically integrated into India, has precipitated a cultural crisis that has threatened to undermine the communities' exclusiveness.[59] In response, sections of Sikh society – and the Sikh political party, the Akali Dal – have demanded greater autonomy within India, while some extreme sections have called for the creation of a separate state altogether.

Moroever, as within Hinduism generally, ethnic identities have been subject to exaggeration by political parties in search of electoral gains. Both 'moderate' Sikhs and 'moderate' Congress officials throughout the 1980s used the threats of terrorists (and even the terrorists themselves) to pursue elections to state or national office. The result has been an escalation of violence and the splintering of Sikh political opinion. In response to the killing of Punjabi-speaking Hindus by Sikh militants, the 'majority' attitude has hardened in support of 'firm action' against all minorities, who are increasingly seen as 'enemies' of the state, funded and abetted by external powers.

Factionalising parties – and the suspension of the normal political process in the Punjab from the early 1980s until 1993–94, led to a sense of crisis and drift, which has in part been used by the Congress to play on the fears of the Hindu majority. In 1990 it was reported that large parts of the Punjab were being run by Sikh separatists, enforcing the use of Punjabi, and enforcing dress codes on the women.[60] By 1994, the Indian state had been able effectively to re-start the political process and was successful in isolating the militants. The durability of any sustained *rapprochement* with the Indian centre will rely on the future of secularism and the ability of the Indian centre to ensure a meaningful degree of devolution to the Punjabi state in social and economic affairs. Yet violence remains. In 1995, a bomb explosion in the state capital of Chandigarh killed the Punjabi state minister and several of his cabinet colleagues.

The most glaring example of an ethnic crisis concerns the disputed state of Jammu and Kashmir.[61] Since 1989, the Indian government has faced a sustained militant threat from a series of groups claiming to represent Kashmiri sentiment in favour of joining Pakistan, or in becoming a separate, sovereign state. This option breaks down further into those groups who wish to declare a secular, independent state, and those who wish to declare an Islamic one. Kashmiri moderates, who stood by the various Indian settlements following the end of the first Indo-Pakistan war in 1948, and participated in elections under the auspices of article 370 (which granted the state special status), were by the late 1980s politically discredited.

Firstly, they had been compromised by central machinations, which involved Indira Gandhi undermining state politics, and messing about with existing constitutional safeguards over Kashmir's autonomy. However, unlike other examples of deteriorating centre–state relations, politics in Jammu and Kashmir has been transformed by a related, but separate, transformation in the way in which Kashmiris, and Kashmiri Muslims in particular, perceive themselves as a religious community, *vis-à-vis* the Kashmiri Pandits (Hindus) and the Buddhists of Ladakh. What was once acclaimed as a common culture, that in part transcended religious identity and was known as the *Kashmiriyat*, began to fragment into confessional constituencies.[62] As in Pakistan, and as discussed in the Preface, ethnicity – now directly associated with inflexible religious identities – emerged as a gridlock over the political process as a whole. Kashmiris whose identities were not defined as Orthodox Sunnis faced an equal persecution from Islamic militants as did Kashmiri Hindus and Buddhists. In the late 1980s for example, tremendous pressure developed on Kashmiri Muslim women to adopt the veil, despite the relative absence of purdah in Kashmir historically.

Political violence has led to the mass migration of the Kashmiri Pandits (Hindus) from the valley area down into the Jammu region, where they have become increasingly susceptible to BJP agitations, who blame Muslim unrest on Congress 'appeasement' and the failure of New Delhi to categorically integrate Jammu and Kashmir into the Indian state. By 1993, there were over 600,000 Indian military and para-military personnel active in the Kashmir area, mainly in the valley districts. They were operating against up to thirty-five differing militant resistance groups, some opposed as much to each other as to the Indians. Although tensions appeared to decline in 1994, and despite several abortive attempts to restart the political process (in August and in December 1995), the holding of elections for the six Jammu and Kashmir Lok Sabha seats in May 1996 was marred by violence and intimidation.[63] While complicated by involvement from Pakistani trained militants, as well as a whole series of other non-state, voluntaristic actors, the dispute is about autonomy and also, again, about secularism. As one ethnic group seeks to assert its rights, other groups react and seek to define and defend their own interests. Kashmir has led to a complex process in which Buddhist-Tibetan ethnic claims are now being voiced by Ladakh, as well as separatist claims by the Hindus of the valley area who are unwilling to return until the Indian centre promises to protect them directly.

Prospects for India

One of the obstacles in the way of a fundamentalist Hindu state is a predominantly urban-based Indian middle class: like Islam in Pakistan, the relevance of Hindu values is stronger within a rural, agrarian setting than it is within the capitalist environment of the cities. Secularism was not just an ideological commitment, it was a route to status and power for a middle-class elite within the party, and through the party, the state. It was also a route to nation-building. Should the government's language and ideological orientation change, the middle class could possible move towards some endorsement of a politicised Hinduism simply as an attempt to guarantee their continued access to power, despite the possibility that long-term contradictions between Hinduism and the material foundations for a capitalist system could endanger the entire future of the middle class.[64]

Of more immediate concern are the problems associated with the idea of the 'Hindu majority' and the existence of minorities within India. Given the size and complexity of India's political structure, the risks of alienating the minorities is a risk of alienating the nation. India has aptly been described as the land of minorities.

Muslims are not the only religious minority, for every religious community, and every linguistic group, faces a minority situation in one or more states of the Indian Union.[65] Sanjib Baruah has noted in the context of Assam that 'the label Assamese can be either inclusive or exclusive, depending upon the exact political use behind the definition'. Moreover, politics constitutes and reconstitutes these categories. An 'ethnic group' is in reality an ethnic coalition potentially divisible into many smaller groups.[66] It is for this reason alone that any attempt to essentialise ethnicity, to make ethnicity fixed and permanent, is doomed to failure.

For if the concept of a 'minority' is relative and fluid, so too is the concept of a majority. Rajendra Singh, political leader of the

Rashtriya Swayamsevak Sangh (RSS) party, a communal organisation with substantial links to the present Bharati Janata Party, noted recently that the goal of the RSS was to create a Hindu nation: 'our society should be homogeneous, let India be a Hindu commonwealth'.[67] The belief that there can exist a 'Hindu nation' is, however, a political fiction, since Hinduism as a religious identity is heavy subsumed by differing languages and local custom. That 82.62 per cent of the Indian population is Hindu is merely academic, as much as the 'two nation theory' that led to the creation of Pakistan is academic. Of the 82.6 per cent of Hindus, less than 40 per cent speak Hindi, and Hindi contains various dialectical differences from region to region. How would a religious state settle the language issue, the legitimacy of the fifteen recognised national languages, if it assumed that spoken Hindi must be given priority within a Hindu state?

The inflexibility of a religious Hindu discourse, even if confused with (or disguised by?) the concept of culture, to deal with the diversity of a democratic, federal India is already self-evident at the state level. If economic issues are considered, then the divisions between dominant and lower castes within Hindu society become even more obvious. In 1990 intra-Hindu violence was sparked off by the announcement that the Indian government would increase the number of job reservations for 'backward classes' – a category that is defined with reference to economic and not ascriptive notions of backwardness. What appeared to be culturally 'homogeneous' (i.e., even Hindu shudra castes) potentially disintegrated under economic pressure. Even if there were subscribed Hindu institutions – laid down within an equivalent of the Koran – a Hindu state will not be a strong state, it will not overcome the problems that have been 'caused' by secularism. It will not give the state access to a ready-made nation. It is not even clear that it could build a state at all.

State–society relations in Sri Lanka

For the pessimists who have written off the 'great Nehruvian' adventure with secularism as a long delusion, a form of Hindu reformism, Sri Lanka is seen as the end-game of a multiethnic society caught within the tensions of the unitary state. A detailed summary of the civil war in Sri Lanka is unnecessary and many issues have now been presented.[68] Rather I will highlight the most salient points of the Sri Lankan crisis in order to make useful comparisons with India, Bangladesh and Pakistan.

Put bluntly, what is at issue is the long felt economic and cultural grievance of a Sinhalese Buddhist 'majority' against an articulate (and indigenous) Tamil minority who, as a minority, have apparently faired far too well both under the British and after independence. As in India, the myths of 'the pampered minority' are the reverse side of the claim that the majority have somehow been suppressed and silenced. What makes this situation more problematic still, is that the Tamil minority makes up an overwhelming majority – 95.6 per cent – of one province, situated on the Jaffna Peninsular, and also constitutes significant minorities in the district of Trincomalee (33 per cent) and a large majority in Batticoloa (70 per cent), situated within the Eastern Province. While the distributions of economic wealth and employment make up much of the grievances felt by both sides, what is also at issue is the role that cultural and religious symbolism plays within Sri Lankan society and within the structures of the state.

The economic development of Sri Lanka has been essentially 'mixed'. Sri Lanka has since independence been committed to a welfare state, and has managed to achieve remarkably high scores on alternative measurement indices, such as the Human Development indices.[69] Government policies on education, food subsidies and basic health care have ensured that 'development in Sri Lanka [has] created conditions that are conducive to continuing public participation in the decision-making process'.[70] This success – which is no small achievement – is none the less part of the process that has sowed the seeds for sustained ethnic conflict within the island.

As with India, Sri Lanka presents a whole series of cross-cutting social cleavages that have, at various times, become openly courted by political parties. The first series of cleavages are linguistic. Sinhala is spoken by the majority of the island (74 per cent) followed by Tamil (about 18 per cent). Members of Sri Lanka's political elite (comprising of initially Westernised Tamils and Sinhala speakers) often speak English as a first or second language. These cleavages are overlaid by a religious one.[71] Sixty-nine per cent of Sri Lanka's population are Buddhist, and an overwhelming majority of these speak Sinhalese, over 15 per cent are Hindus, while 7 per cent are Muslims. A further 6 per cent are Roman Catholics.[72] The Tamil language has tended to unite, until quite recently, Hindus with Muslims, and has incorporated some Christians, although many Christians are Sinhalese speakers. The Muslim community is split between those of Indian, Sri Lankan and Malay origins.

If these socio-linguistic divisions are not enough, they are further broken down by general cultural differences between highland Sinhalese (who provide the backbone of the Buddhist-Sinhalese majority) and lowland Sinhalese, differences that were in part encouraged (and further developed) by the British and British colonial policy. It has already been noted that the Tamil language could not unite the Sri Lanka Tamils with the Tamils of Indian origin, although this situation began to change in the 1970s when, following widespread anti-Tamil violence, Tamil political parties joined into one party, known as the Tamil United Liberation Front.

Ideological issues, rising out of the rapid socio-economic transformations since independence, have also left their mark on various communities, with both Sinhalese and Tamil ethnic extremism being associated in part with left-wing or Marxist and Trotskyist concepts of political action. The language of left-wing extremism is used to further the interests of both the Tamil and the Sinhalese chauvinism. It has radicalised, as opposed to eliminated, ethnic identities. The radical Jathika Vimukthi Peramuna (JVP) movement is both pro-Sinhalese and Marxist, and both ethnic communities have stressed their ideological identities to gain financial support from the communists (either from the former Soviet Union or China). In 1971 the JVP launched an insurgency against a government that was already identified with pro-Sinhalese policies. Many Tamil groups, in attempting to articulate a Tamil identity, conflict with other Tamil groups over ideological orientations.

The genesis of the crisis

In a recent book, Helena Whall has separated the evolution of Tamil demands into three phases:

> (i) a period of responsive cooperation between the English educated middle class of both communities ... until the election of the SLFP. (ii) the emergence of a ... Tamil demand for a federalist state ... (iii) the emergence of political violence and a growing ideology of separatism from 1972 until 1983, culminating in the July riots in Colombo.[73]

In all cases, Tamil demands were articulated in the context of increasingly assertive state policies to make Sinhala, and Buddhism, part of the state. Throughout the 1970s, under SLFP-left coalition of the First Republic (1972–78), the government appeared determined to systematically destroy the Tamil language, to limit Tamil access to the universities (and hence, government jobs), and to enshrine Sinhalese Buddhism as the national religion.

If Sinhalese national identity is problematic based, as in Pakistan, upon an elusive link between language and religion, the concept of an independent Tamil state is even more so. Language has failed to provide the basis for agreement within the Tamils, even though it has provided the basis of opposition against the Sinhalese majority. What has characterised the pattern of communal violence in Sri Lanka's eastern and northern provinces since 1983 has been the killing of differing Tamil groups on the grounds of their ideological orientation, or simply through the escalation of factional competition (much as the Kashmiri militant groups have evolved). Moreover, Tamil-speaking Muslims have complicated the matter by recently demanding significant autonomy for their own community. Under the terms of the 1987 Indo-Sri Lankan Accord, the Indian government adopted and supported a rival group of Tamils, the Eelam Popular Revolutionary Liberation Front (EPRLF) which under Indian support contested provincial elections in 1988. Following the Indian withdrawal, the EPRLF faced the wrath of the Tigers and most of them left with the Indian peace-keeping force.

The Tamil Tigers are just one of many Tamil groups strung between those committed to the creation of an independent Tamil state and those that are still committed to decentralisation and autonomy through some form of federalism. Each successive attempt to deal with the Tamil problem has spawned another set of Tamil parties and interests that have been opposed by other Tamil interests. The real tragedy of Sri Lanka is that, like East Pakistan in 1971, the chance to deal within the framework of the state has probably now passed.

It is necessary to underline several comparative points that link the identity of the Sri Lankan state and the crisis that has beset nation formation with South Asia as a whole. The first point is that the influence of party-based political competition on redefining ethnicity in terms of 'vote banks' and political agendas, as in India, cannot be over-estimated. It was the 'political competition between the Sinhalese political parties, united Sinhalese fronts and Sinhalese Buddhist movements [that] prevented an easy solution to Tamil demands'[74] and it also actually furthered the alienation of Tamils, and shaped the nature of the demands that the Tamils were putting forward themselves.

At the beginning of independence Sri Lanka's political elite was closer to that of India than Pakistan, a multiethnic and multilingual elite united in its use of English and its commitment to Western values. Smaller than its Indian counterpart, the elite was at one remove from the many local and regionalised idioms of the island's politics.

Although communal tensions were certainly not absent during the British period, political elites delivered votes through patronage. Such a system worked indirectly – in spite of the existence of a universal franchise since the 1930s – since between Colombo and the provinces were situated tiers of local interests that did not directly impinge upon national politics. Under the Soulbury constitution that came into effect in 1947, Sri Lanka was secular and parliamentary, with legislation to defend the minorities in the form of section 29 (and the various sub-clauses that defended the freedom of religious practice). Although it has nine provinces and twenty-four districts, these have been administrative as opposed to political units, as in Bangladesh. The British envisaged a unitary state based upon a variant of local governments as practices in Britain, in which political parties were absent, replaced by local and individual issues.

While Sri Lankan Tamil opinion was critical of a relatively centralised state that made no concessions to regional and local districts, Tamils retained their links with national power through the Tamil section of the Westernised political elite. While demands for a federal state were a common part of the Tamil agenda (especially the Sinhalese Tamils) demands for a separate state were made outside the main social elite and did not impinge upon the political language of a unitary state until a crisis of identity set in within the first generation of this Westernised elite itself, and the breakdown in the structure of political mediation.

Here, there are important similarities with India. Political independence after 1950, coupled with broad-based socio-economic change within Sri Lanka, deepened popular participation and brought local and national idioms together for the first time. Part of this resurgence was a demand for a Buddhist, Sinhalese-speaking state. To the first generation of Sri Lanka's elite, such as Don Senanayake (1947–52), Dudley Senanayake (1952–53) and Sir John Kotelawala (1952–56) the importance of Buddhism to Sri Lanka was almost as obscure to them as was the importance of socialism. Yet to other politicians the symbols of language and religion struck a chord, especially since they held out the promise of political power.

The Sri Lankan Freedom Party (SLFP), formed by Solomon W. R. D. Bandaranaike in 1950, was an offshoot from the UNP. It was caused by personal intra-elite differences over party positions, and a disagreement over the role that Buddhism was to play after independence. From 1950 until its first electoral victory in 1956, the SLFP both responded to, and directed, popular agitation in and around the central Kandyan areas to give Buddhism a primary place within independent Sri Lanka. In 1953, the All Ceylon Buddhist Congress had issued a wide-ranging report entitled *The Betrayal of Buddhism*. The report criticised the Western, apparently pro-minority government of the UNP and its rhetoric and values found their way into the SLFP manifesto of 1956.

This commitment, part of a concerted effort to make inroads into the UNP's electoral majority, also involved a commitment to the Sinhalese language. Active in the agitations (focused through the 2,500th anniversary of the birth of the Buddha) was the *bhikku*, the Buddhist clergy who deployed the idiom of a religious community as part of the wider claims in favour of the Sinhalese language and the Sinhalese race. *The Betrayal of Buddhism* had noted that: 'the history of Sri Lanka is the history of the Sinhalese race. Buddhism is the golden thread running through the history of the race and the land.'[75]

In 1956, Mr Bandaranaike passed legislation that made Sinhala the only official language for the island. The result was widespread rioting in the Jaffna peninsular (the heartland of Sri Lankan Tamil identity). Under pressure, Bandaranaike compromised and formed a pact with the Tamil leader of the Tamil Federal Party, S. J. V. Chevanayakam. This pact ensured that the government would legislate for the 'reasonable' use of Tamil through the Tamil Special Provision Act. The result was Bandaranaike's assassination by a Buddhist cleric in 1959 for failing to uphold the interests of the Sinhalese. In 1960, the UNP was returned on a bare minority of seats and in a subsequent election in the same year was defeated by the

SLFP, led by Mr Bandaranaike's widow. Faced with such an electorally successful strategy, the UNP also started to issue statements and policies that would appeal to the Buddhist-Sinhalese majority, recognising the electoral futility of supporting the minority if the result of this was to hand over a Sinhalese majority to the opposition.

As ethnic identities sharpened, the Tamils demanded various constitutional reforms that would preserve their identity especially in the Jaffna Peninsular and in key districts of the Eastern Province. The obvious formula was either a federal state, or some form of local government scheme involving a significant degree of autonomy and access to state funds. By the mid-1960s, with both UNP and the SLFP governments tied to a volatile Sinhalese vote, attempts to meet Tamil demands through political devolution led to increased radicalism on behalf of the Sinhalese Buddhists.

Forced to compromise for fear of losing the 'majority', and driven from behind by a radical Marxist pro-Sinhalese movement, both UNP and SLFP government indecisiveness merely hardened Tamil opinion and Sinhalese demands. The 'turning point' came in 1983. V. Prabhakaran, the leader of the Tamil Tigers instigated a land-mine explosion that killed thirteen Sinhalese soldiers. Throughout the island the Sinhalese retaliated by killing Tamils. Over 60,000 Tamils were displaced from their homes during the subsequent violence, and the violence itself served as a powerful stimulus to reinforcing ethnic divisions through stories of cruelty and betrayal. As in India in 1984 government attempts to secure Tamil lives appeared to some to be half-hearted and even negligent.

Political devolution and reform, 1983–1990

Attempts to satisfy demands from the moderates and extremists within both communities squeezed out the middle ground: in this case the ability of Tamil demands to be settled within a federal constitution and for the Sinhalese majority to accept a significant degree of political devolution. What has made matters worse for Sri Lankan attempts to deal with the Tamils is that Tamil agitation has taken place within a region dominated by India, and the belief that India was both training and funding Tamil terrorists.

Three attempts have now been made to devolve power to the provinces and to restore internal consensus to Sri Lanka. The first attempt, the so-called 'District Development Council' plan of 1982 failed to satisfy Tamil demands because it was based upon district – not provincial – autonomy, and because the principles of direct election were compromised by the principle of nomination by the centre. Rather like Ayub Khan's Basic Democracies, this was partly in order to prevent ethnic solidarity coalescing at the provincial level, but partly in recognition that the ethnic make-up of provinces (especially the key Eastern Province) did not reflect the ethnic make-up of particular districts. Yet the principle of nomination was seen as an attempt by a predominantly Sinhalese centre to 'keep an eye' on Tamil matters. The Tamils also objected to the level of central supervision in the setting up of the councils and the appointment of the district minister.[76]

The second attempt was an integral part of the Indo-Sri Lankan Accord of 1987 which gave significant powers of devolution to the provinces, modelled explicitly along the lines of the Indian constitution. More critically, the accord merged the Northern and the Eastern Province into one, a key demand of the Tamil parties that had not been satisfied by the earlier initiative. This policy was bitterly opposed by radical Sinhalese and the JVP as well as members of the government, including President Premadasa, and most of the principal parties in opposition. For the duration of the Indo-Sri Lankan Accord, the JVP launched campaigns of terror against the Sri Lankan government, appearing to have successfully infiltrated the government's security services, forcing the government on to the defensive in the more prosperous southern areas. Even when the government had apparently crippled the JVP, the sixth constitutional amendment (through which the provinces had been empowered, and through which the Northern and Eastern Provinces had been merged) was bitterly resented, being clearly seen as part of an Indian design. Rather like the first constitution of Bangladesh, the association between the sixth amendment and Indian dominance was too great: it would not survive the physical withdrawal of the Indian presence.

The Indian government was neither capable of negotiating on behalf of the Tamil Tigers nor with them. The Tigers' boycott of the provincial elections within Jaffna undermined their legitimacy and discredited those Tamil groups who were willing to co-operate with the government and the Indian Peace-Keeping Force (IPKF). With the Indian withdrawal, the Premadasa government annulled the

merger of the Northern and Eastern Provinces in preference to Sinhalese sensitivities.

The third attempt followed from the election results of 1994,
which brought to power a government committed to resolving the
ethnic conflict through granting a federal constitution, resolving the
language issue (by making Sihnalese and Tamil joint national languages), and dealing with issues of economic growth and provincial
management. Yet by 1995, the initiative had failed again, with a
growing section of the Sinhalese unwilling to open the way to truly
'federal' Sri Lanka, and sections of the Tamils no longer satisfied
with a mere offer of federalism. As so often in the history of separatism in South Asia, the offer of federalism had come twenty years
too late. The collapse of Jaffna in 1995 has created further, powerful images of Sihalese brutality

Summary

All the states of South Asia are weak, dominated by serious domestic conflict that wastes resources and endangers bilateral relations.
Lawrence Ziring, a well-known commentator on Pakistani affairs,
has recently noted that 'both India and Pakistan have internal problems that they cannot solve and which are likely to intensify with
the passage of time'.[77] Such problems will require joint solutions,
since what is sauce for the goose is also sauce for the gander. The
consequences of this for Indo-Pak relations is important.

Given the degree of domestic instability and flux, and given the
sheer degree of cultural overlap that exists between the states of
South Asia, it is clear that issues and concepts of national security
must be based upon an assessment of domestic politics, and the
nature (and flexibility) of their political systems. There is an old-
fashioned – essentially Western – prejudice that democratic societies
do not go to war with each other. This view has often been
expressed by India about Pakistan. Yet, as has already been noted,
the onset of democracy within Pakistan has narrowed the scope for
any given leadership to address regional issues that risk short-term
unpopularity.

The ability of the various political elites within South Asia to deal
with social tensions is a function of their ideological and institutional strengths. The argument has been in favour of secularism, but

secularism requires a political elite who are committed to it ideo-logically and who benefit from it economically. Even this is not a guarantee that the nation-building project will succeed and that, one fine day, the states of South Asia will reach the fine sunlit uplands of 'modernity', for there are clearly powerful indigenous forces at work within South Asia which question the use – indeed the viability – of secularism as a national ideology, and indeed the viability of the state itself, sandwiched between growing domestic disorder and international pressures. Yet, equally, it would be absurd to set up secularism in India as self-evidently right or correct. Both concepts must be critically re-evaluated, not as part of some fashionable academic undertaking, but as a serious practical endeav-our.

This is the dilemma that India faces towards the end of the mil-lennium. The BJP's argument that the Indian elite's obsession with secularism is part of their colonial baggage, part of their alienness, has been driven home time and time again in recent years. Secular-ism, so the argument goes, makes no sense to the rest of non-urban India – situated between hill and plain – that thinks in some form of pristine Hindu mind-set of *dharamashstra* law and jati affiliation. Such a view is nothing more than a clever bit of Orientalist trickery; it requires belief in the stuff and nonsense of the 'Hindu' mind and timeless 'Hindu' values. It needs to be exposed.

In the context of South Asia, strong states are legitimate states, well integrated within a democratic and economically viable nation-alism. This is a long-term goal for India, Pakistan and Bangladesh as much as it is for the small Himalayan kingdoms of Bhutan and Nepal. Yet the demands (and the disturbances) of development may weaken the state in order to strengthen it.

The degree of internal instability – a key factor of the region's insecurity – cannot be overcome through socio-economic develop-ment *alone* since the pace of transition is contributory to the prob-lem. While growth must be ensured it requires imaginative political management with an elite that is under constant pressure from below. It may even require imaginative and new types of political institutions and ideas of governance.

Notes

1 The PPP government entered into a coalition with the Mohajir Qaumi Movement (MQM) after the elections of 1993. The MQM's social constituency is based in the urban centres of Sind. Serious ethnic violence between the mohijjars (Urdu speakers) and Sindhi speakers has been a characteristic of Karachi and Hyderabad since independence, but the level of ethnic violence reached almost epidemic proportions in the early 1980s and again in the mid-1990s. The MQM has emerged as one of the main opposition parties to the PPP during Benazir's second term.

2 The Pakistani Inter-Services Intelligence Unit (ISI) recommended in January 1989 that the Mujahideen be persuaded to fight an open 'set' battle to take the city of Jalalabad, and move away from its earlier patterns of guerrilla fighting favoured before the Soviet withdrawal. The battle failed and led to attempts by the civilian government to remove the head of the ISI – General Hamid Gul. See S. Burke and L. Ziring, *Pakistan's Foreign Policy: An Historical Analysis*, Oxford University Press, Karachi, 1991, p. 472.

3 Space precludes setting up this crisis in all its glory. Mohammad Waseem has captured it well in his thoughtful book *The 1993 Elections in Pakistan*, Vanguard Press, Lahore, 1994.

4 C. Thomas, 'New Directions in Thinking about Security in the Third World', in Ken Booth (ed.), *New Thinking About Strategy and International Security*, Harper Collins, London, 1991, pp. 267–86; and see P. S. Jayaramu, *India's National Security and Foreign Policy*, Chanakya Press, New Delhi, 1987.

5 B. Buzan 'States, People, Fear', in Edward E. Azar and Chung In-Moon (eds), *National Security in the Third World*, Pinter, London, 1988, pp. 14–43 and see the second edition of B. Buzan's book entitled *People, States and Fear*, Harvester, London, 1991. This contains an elaboration of the security complex idea.

6 Martin Shaw's recent book takes an interesting look at the recent contributions sociological theory has made to international relations. See his *Global Society and International Relations: Sociological Concepts and Political Perspectives*, Polity Press, Cambridge, 1995.

7 S. Subrahmanyam (ed.), *Our National Security*, New Delhi, 1972 cited in Jayaramu, *India's National Security*, emphasis added.

8 The classic text on this is in many senses Ernest Gellner, *Thought and Change*, Weidenfeld and Nicolson, London, 1964. See the chapter entitled 'Living on the Upward Slope'.

9 See for example Lloyde Rudolph, *The Modernity of Tradition: Political Development in India*, Chicago University Press, Chicago, 1967.

10 B. Hettne, 'Ethnicity and Development', *Contemporary South Asia*, 1993. p. 126.

11 The debates between inventors and imaginators seems to have been decisively won by the latter. The difficulty of inventing identities is that it stresses a particular degree of social, and indeed individual, voluntarism which is unsustainable.

12 Hettne, *Contemporary South Asia*.

13 See Sumit Ganguly, *The Origins of War in South Asia*, Westview Press, Boulder, 2nd edition, 1994.

14 A. Dawisha (ed.), *Islam and Foreign Policy*, Cambridge University Press, Cambridge, 1983, p. 4.

15 I. Episoto (ed.), *Islam in Asia*, Oxford University Press, New York, 1986.

16 J. P. Piscatori, *Islam in a World of Nation-States*, Cambridge University Press, Cambridge, 1986.

17 For a further discussion of the ideas of this Islamic community and an explicit Islamic political discourse see the very interesting Farzana Shaikh, *Community and Consensus in Islam: Muslim Representation in Colonial India*, Cambridge University Press, Cambridge, 1988.

18 Cited in Rajmohan Gandhi, *Understanding the Muslim Mind*, Penguin, Harmondsworth, 1987.

19 There is a huge literature on this subject. I found the following works very useful as an introduction: Bryan Turner, *Orientalism, Postmodernism and Globalism*, Routledge, London, 1994. See also Akbar Ahmed, *Postmodernism and Islam: Predicament and Promise*, Routledge, London, 1992.

20 M. Waseem, *Politics and the State in Pakistan*, People's Press, Lahore, 1989. The 'great tradition' is essentially urban, the 'little traditional' is basically agricultural and rural – but Waseem is an excellent and bold introduction to many contemporary debates within Pakistan.

21 See Tariq Ali, *Can Pakistan Survive?* Penguin, Harmondsworth, 1983.

22 Rubya Mehdi, *The Islamization of the Law in Pakistan*, Curzon Press, London, 1994, p. 94.

23 See L. Hayes, *Politics in Pakistan: The Struggle for Legitimacy*, Westview Press, Boulder, 1984, and Omar Noman, *An Economic and Political History of Pakistan*, Kegan Paul International, London, 1990.

24 Ayub Khan's policy has been quite rightly compared to colonial strategies of 'indirect rule' in terms of political representation. And it suffered from the same drawbacks: the construction of 'tame' political forces which lacked credibility because they were seen as being lackeys of a particular regime. See S. Burki, *Pakistan Under Bhutto*,

Macmillan, London, 1989, and the first part of Noman, *History of Pakistan*.

25   See 'The Pakistan Economy Since Independence', *Cambridge Economic History of India*, Cambridge University Press, Cambridge, 1983, vol. II.

26   *Cambridge Economic History*, p. 1022.

27   *Cambridge Economic History*, p. 1023.

28   Noman, *History of Pakistan*, p. 46.

29   One of the main points in the Awami League's programme was the commitment to federalism and provincial power. See L. Rose and R. Sisson, *War and Secession: India, Pakistan and the Creation of Bangladesh*, Princeton University Press, Princeton, 1990.

30   One of the last meetings between Rehman and Bhutto took place in the Governor's Residence in Dhaka, where to the irritation of Bhutto, the Awami League banner was flying in place of the Pakistan flag. Rose and Sisson report that the final conversations took place in a bathroom, because Mujib feared that the main negotiating room had been bugged. See Sisson and Rose, *War and Secession*.

31   See Episoto, *Islam in Asia*, p. 20.

32   Noman, *History of Pakistan*, p. 46

33   See Burki, *Pakistan Under Bhutto*, p. 146 and chapter 7 generally.

34   For an interesting discussion of this period see Stanley Wolpert's biography, *Zulfi Bhutto of Pakistan: His Life and Times*, Oxford University Press, New York, 1993 especially chapters 12–14.

35   See Hayes, *Politics in Pakistan*, pp. 99–103.

36   The evidence for this is far from categorical. Rigging elections in South Asia is much more difficult – even for a competent and elitist bureacracy – than is often assumed. Even in defeat, Bhutto never lost the loyalty of a significant number of Pakistan's working class. Although small, organised labour initially presented a serious threat to the conservative regime of Zia. It was Zia's fear that a free and fair election would in effect restore Zulfikar Bhutto (and lead to his own execution for treason) that led Zia to execute Bhutto in 1979. See Wolpert, *Zulfi Bhutto of Pakistan*.

37   See G. W. Choudhury, *Pakistan: Transition from a Military to a Civilian Government*, Scorpion Books, London, 1989.

38   Ziauddin Ahmed, *Money and Banking in Islam*, Hurriyat Books, Islamabad, 1983, p. 5.

39   See Kemal Faruki, 'Pakistan', in Episoto, *Islam in Asia*, p. 75.

40   Noman, *History of Pakistan*, p. 223.

41   See L. Lifschutz, *Bangladesh: The Unfinished Revolution*, Zed Books, London, 1979, and C. P. Odonnell, *Bangla Desh: Biography of a Muslim Nation*, Westview Press, Boulder, 1984.

42   See the important article by H. Alavi, 'The State in Post-Colonial Societies: Pakistan and Bangladesh', in K. Gough and H. P. Sharma, *Imperialism and Revolution in South Asia*, Monthy Review Press, New York, 1973, pp. 145–73.

43   See Nizam Ahmed, 'Experiments in Local Government Reform in Bangladesh', *Asian Survey*, 28, 1988, pp. 813–29.

44   Zillur R. Khan 'Islam and Bengali Nationalism', *Asian Survey*, 25, 1985, pp. 852–82.

45   This permanence is somewhat misleading since the constitution is easily amended, and has been subjected to massive omnibus reforms in 1975 and in 1979. None the less in terms of 'core values' the constitution has remained at all times politically relevant.

46   Paul Brass has discussed how religious demands could be dressed up as a language issue, as with the Sikh demands for the redivision of bilingual Punjab in 1966. Yet Sikh demands for a Punjabi-speaking state also led to the incorporation of Punjabi-speaking Hindus. See the important book by P. Brass entitled *Language, Religion and Politics in North India*, Cambridge University Press, Cambridge, 1974 and his recent contribution to the New Cambridge History of India, *Politics of India Since Independence*, Cambridge University Press, Cambridge, 1990.

47   See the very useful collection of essays, James Manor (ed.), *From Nehru to the Nineties: The Changing Office of Prime Minister in India*, C. Hurst, London, 1994.

48   This is especially true of India's first-past-the-post electoral system. See D. Butler et al., *Compendium of Indian Elections*, Sterling Books, New Delhi, 1986.

49   It is not my intention to wade into the massive literature that has grown up about Indian federalism; for a useful introduction see L. Rudolph and S. Rudolph, *In Pursuit of Lakshmi: State-Society Relations in India*, Chicago Univesity Press, Chicago, 1987 and earlier Rajni Kothari, *Politics in India*, Sangam, New Delhi, 1970.

50   See C. Baxter (ed.), *Government and Politics in South Asia*, Westview Press, Boulder, 1987 and John Wood (ed.), *Contemporary State Politics in India*, Westview Press, Boulder, 1987.

51   For a review of this debate see Rudolph and Rudolph, *In Pursuit of Lakshmi*.

52   See A. Kohli, 'From Majority to Minority Rule', in M. M. Bouton and P. Oldenburg (eds), *India Briefing 1990*, Westview Press, Boulder, 1990, p. 7.

53   The most useful summary of this period can be found in Rudolph and Rudolph, *In Pursuit of Lakshmi*.

54   This is particularly true of southern India, where sudra castes are

much more frequent. See R. Kothari, *Caste in Indian Politics*, Sangam, New Delhi, 1976.

55 Bal Thackeray, leader of the Bombay Shiv Sena, quoted in Y. Malik and D. K. Vaypeyi 'The Rise of Hindu Militancy', *Asian Survey*, 29, 1989, pp. 311–25.

56 Salman Khurshid, *At Home in India: A Restatement of Indian Muslims*, Sangam, New Delhi, 1986, p. vii.

57 See a special report in *India Today*, 15 January 1991: 'Anatomy of Carnage', pp. 26–9. See also the highly rhetorical M. J. Akbar, *Riot After Riot*, Penguin, Harmondsworth, 1989.

58 See the excellent *Sikhs of the Punjab* by J. S. Grewal, Volume II.3 of the New Cambridge History of India, Cambridge University Press, Cambridge, 1991.

59 It is interesting to note in passing that this is the exact reverse of the economic argument used within East Pakistan to justify the publication of the six-point programme.

60 *The Economist*, London, January 1991.

61 See my *Reclaiming the Past? The Search for Political and Cultural Unity in Contemporary Jammu and Kashmir*, Portland Books, London, 1995.

62 See the very useful article by Balraj Puri called 'Kashmiriyat: The Vitality of Kashmiri Identity', *Contemporary South Asia*, 4, 1, March 1995, pp. 55–64.

63 *Indian Express*, New Delhi edition, 29 May 1996.

64 See the article by Rajni Kothari in the *Illustrated Weekly* of India 7–13 Dec. 1986. See also B. D. Graham, *Hindu Nationalism and Indian Politics: The Origins and Development of the Bharatiya Jana Sangh*, Cambridge University Press, Cambridge, 1990.

65 See Syed Shahabuddin and Theodore Paul Wright, 'India: Muslim Minority Politics and Society', in Episoto, *Islam in Asia*, p. 155.

66 Sanjib Baruah 'Immigration, Ethnic Conflict and Political Turmoil', *Asian Survey*, 26, 1986, pp. 1186–231.

67 Cited in Y. K. Malik and K. Vajpeyi, 'The Rise of Hindu Militancy', *Asian Survey*, 29, 1989, pp. 308–40.

68 See A. J. Wilson, *The Break-Up of Sri Lanka*, C. Hurst, London, 1988. See also J. Manor, 'Sri Lanka: Explaining the Disaster', in *World Today*, November 1983, and David Brown 'Ethnic Revival: Perspectives on State and Society', *Third World Quarterly*, October–December 1989, pp. 1–17.

69 The PQLI index does not measure economic growth. The index, developed by Dudly Seers, measures social welfare and the degree of redistributive social policy. See D. Seers and C. Vaitsos, *Integration and Unequal Development: The Experience of the EEC*, St. Martin's

Press, New York, 1980.

70 James Bjorkman, 'Health Policy and Politics in Sri Lanka: Development of the South Asian Welfare State', *Asian Survey*, 25, 1985, pp. 537–52.

71 See Baxter, *Government and Politics in South Asia*, p. 305. Sri Lankan Moors are sometimes listed as Tamil speakers, although they often speak several languages.

72 Figures taken from A. J. Wilson, *The Politics of Sri Lanka 1947–1979*, Macmillan, London, 1979, p. 8.

73 Helena J. Whall, *The Rights to Self-Determination: The Sri Lankan Tamil National Question*, Tamil Information Centre, London, 1995. pp. 153–4.

74 Wilson, *The Break-Up of Sri Lanka*, p. 39.

75 Wilson, *The Break-Up of Sri Lanka*, p. 72. *The Betrayl of Buddhism* was written as a formal report by the All Ceylonese Buddhist Congress in 1954 and was reissued as a paperback retitled *The Revolt in the Temple*.

76 See B. Mathew 'Sri Lanka's Development Councils', *Asian Survey*, 22, 1982, pp. 1117–35.

77 Burke and Ziring, *Pakistan's Foreign Policy*, p. 467.

4

South Asia and the world economy: transition and the imperatives of reform

The economic problems of nation-building confront all the states of South Asia. Through the complex dynamics of political and social mobilisation, economic management has contributed to the crisis of domestic politics and political order discussed in the previous chapter. To some theorists, it remains the *primary* cause. To all intents and purposes, and regardless of rhetorical asides to the contrary, India, Pakistan and Sri Lanka set out at independence to transform what were rural agrarian societies into urban industrial ones. The social and political effects of economic backwardness compelled Nepal and Bhutan to end their isolation and, under Indian guidance, to undertake policies to industrialise.

More recently, Nepal has been compelled to liberate its economy in line with events in India, and in keeping with the growing necessity of some neo-liberal trade policy. Even for societies like Pakistan, which have witnessed a growing sense of political and cultural estrangement from the West, the material and industrial basis of modernisation remains a primary goal. At the end of the civil war, Bangladesh faced the urgent task of developing its economy after years of neglect and waste and of feeding a rapidly growing population crowded into an environmentally vulnerable area of the subcontinent. It too, is now in the business of attracting foreign investment and handing over to the private sector assets previously owned by the state itself.

At the approach of the twenty-first century, the entire region is still predominantly agricultural with a majority of the population living in the countryside. Even in India, one image of which is that of an emerging industrial giant, agriculture employs on average 60 per cent of the labour force and makes up just over 30 per cent of its gross domestic product. In Pakistan the figures are slightly lower. In Nepal, 95 per cent of the population live in the rural areas and agriculture makes up over 80 per cent of GDP.[1] Have the previous policies failed? And if so will liberalised trading policies have the answer?

The politics of planning

In order to industrialise, the states of South Asia have, at one time or another, followed particular economic strategies of import substitution in an attempt to develop a capital goods sector.[2] Governments have attempted to commercialise and transform their agricultural sectors, mobilise internal capital and savings, and augment their economies through producing for a home market. Significantly, each state has attempted to implement particular economic and social packages with recourse to economic planning. Such plans have aimed to mobilise domestic resources and target priority areas through bureaucratic controls to ensure investments in key areas of the economy: usually capital goods, and industrial manufacturing. Significantly, in all cases – even India – planning has involved inputs of foreign aid.

In each country the institutions of planning have been based upon differing balances between public and private investments, but throughout the region the role of the state has been central. In India, planning created a large state sector that sought to control and contain foreign investment even though it actively co-operated with private Indian capital.[3] From the onset, Indian planning 'included a number of programmes designed to increase directly or indirectly, the welfare of the poorer, underprivileged segments of society ... all [the] programmes involved substantial subsidies to the beneficiaries'.[4] In Pakistan, planning has generally been applied in the interests of private and foreign capital, and did not involve widespread nationalisation until the early 1970s under Zulfikar Bhutto's 'Islamic socialism'. In fact after independence, and particularly during the Ayub Khan period, Pakistan was committed to a particularly virulent neo-classical view of development that stressed the overall importance of growth, but with little direct reference to distribution. Pakistan's approach to development explicitly warned against the possible consequences of premature redistribution of resources to those sections of society with a low propensity to save and invest.[5]

In India much consideration and attention has gone into avoiding the political costs of increasing social differentials caused by rapid growth without redistribution. Indian attitudes towards equity were criticised as premature, compromising subsequent growth rates by diluting capital across pre-existing social divisions, some with very little interest in saving or investing their capital productively.

Sri Lanka has tended to move between these two extremes of planning, depending on which political party is in power. The SLFP has favoured a large state sector, while the UNP has favoured privatisation and has actively encouraged foreign investment. Bangladesh began at the Indian end of the planning spectrum, with state ownership and widespread talk of redistribution, but after 1975 moved increasingly towards the Pakistan variant. Rather like Nepal, the Bangladesh economy in 1994 is dominated by foreign aid and loans, and by debt repayments. In late 1993, the Begum Zia government announced a package aimed at increasing foreign investment, and drafted several technocrats into the cabinet to oversee the privatisation of key industries.

The regional trend towards liberalisation

How can we account for the convergence of economic policy across South Asia since the mid-1980s, and is this convergence a precursor to greater regional co-operation? In India, events since 1991 point towards a sustained rolling back of state ownership in favour of export promotions, the deregulation of the private sector, collaboration with foreign companies, and the active courting of foreign capital investments. Significantly, such trends have been encouraged and sustained by external bodies such as the World Bank and the IMF, mainly through the use of structural adjustment programmes and other condition-driven aid programmes. The liberalisation of the South Asian economies is not without risks, however, both internally and externally. The presence of a large state sector within all of the South Asian economies has contributed much of the material basis for an urban-based middle class. Such a sector lies at the heart of the complex matrix of political patronage that binds political parties to the state and to important sections of society.

In India, the state-led industrialisation has provided a nexus of interests that supported private industrial development and sheltered it from undue competition through subsidies, price support policies and tariffs. As such, the policies of liberalisation have been bedevilled by political and sectional pressures. Those who fear the effects of liberalisation are small-scale producers and small business enterprises that have benefited from various protective measures. In 1980, 353 items of production were reserved for production by small businesses alone.[6] Added to this are around 200 public sector corporations that are run by the civil service and which are generally characterised by low productivity and inefficiency. These interests have suffered from systematic deregulation and were vocal in their protests against the Rajiv Gandhi government's policy throughout 1985–86, and after 1991, against the Congress-I government of Narashima Rao.

Opposed to these interests however, and to the continuation of excessive regulation, are a growing number of large private firms (the classic examples being the Birla and the Tata industrial houses), and a number of joint-stock companies in computer software, services and manufacturing that are currently working in close proximity with the Indian capitalists, who would now benefit from engaging within the world economy, and gaining access to technologies and production processes currently in the hands of multinational corporations.

Indeed, such financial and manufacturing interests within India may well provide the basis for the first Indian transnational corporations themselves. It has recently been argued that the Indian middle class as a whole, keen now to become major consumers in their own right, will gain from an easing up of foreign exchange controls, the eventual abolition of import licenses, and – in the widest meaning of the term – the globalisation of production. Such a class are vocal in their demands for greater consumer choice, and for a political and economic system that is free of corruption.

However, there are interests within the state, separate from societal pressures, that have their own agendas concerning the pace and scope of the ongoing liberalisation process. From 1986 onwards, the Rajiv Gandhi government faced a whole series of allegations over financial 'kick backs' involving arms deals with foreign companies. The 'scarcities' created by planning applications allowed government personnel to extract rents from manufacturers anxious to gain entry to lucrative markets.[7] Under the Indira Gandhi governments of 1970–77 and 1980–84, specific business houses made enormous financial contributions to the Congress' electoral funds on the understanding that this would facilitate complicity with the government on license applications through the bureaucracy, to grant them access to protected markets, in which the consumer had little choice.

Political parties, especially those in power, will find their powers of patronage weakened as economic activity becomes increasingly regulated by market forces. Financial and political corruption, involving party funding and private gains, remain very much at the centre of the Indian political system. In the run-up to the 1996 elections, it led to the call for a complete reform in party funding. Similar problems can also be found in Pakistan and to an extent in Sri Lanka.

Planning vs. liberalisation

Away from the more immediate political considerations of the state ownership/planning versus privatisation/liberalisation debate, the academic literature has focused on issues of efficiency of resource allocation and aggregate growth. The dramatic rise of neo-classical orthodoxy in the late 1970s, tied to the sacred cows of comparative advantage and trade, have tended to obscure the rationale and the gains made by state planning in South Asia, particularly in India. Moreover, the comparison between the states of South Asia and the Pacific Rim economies, especially the so-called 'Four Tigers' of South Korea, Taiwan, Singapore and Hong Kong has questioned the logic behind export pessimism and inward-orientated growth strategies generally.

It could well be argued that such comparisons are in themselves misleading, ideologically informed, and – from the outset – prejudicial to social policy more generally. Planning has had a profound impact upon the economic development of South Asia and has been largely successful in fundamentally reorienting and restructuring *colonial* economies, although this is not to deny that – by the beginning of the 1980s – there was growing evidence that the bureaucratic and regulatory functions of state management had outlived their usefulness.[8]

It cannot be deduced from this last observation, however, that the policies of the last forty years have been wrong. Myron Weiner has referred to the long-standing view, held within the World Bank and the IMF, that 'Western assistance has made it possible for the Indian government to adopt economically unsuccessful policies' and to pass anti-Western economic policies. Many economists, both Western and Indian, pointed out that a regulated, planned economy, with a built-in export pessimism would affect growth and suffer from low levels of investment and returns. Some of their fears came to pass.[9] However, it does not follow that if India had 'liberalised' in the 1950s its growth rates would have been substantially different, or the overall economic picture any better.

The internal constraints: national elites and state power

As will be discussed below, it should be remembered that the economic rationale behind planning in India (and under the SLFP in Sri Lanka as well as in Pakistan under Zulfika Bhutto) was not solely confined to narrowly defined arguments of efficiency: the rationale referred also to job-creation, the need to increase the overall purchasing power of the internal market, and to ensure political stability. The existence of a state sector is also seen by many left-wing groups and political parties as evidence of a real commitment to socialism, and a significant political commitment to the poor and the abolition of poverty. Socialism remains an important word within the political lexicon of South Asia, however tarnished it has become in the West.

In 1985, when addressing the bicentenary of the Indian National Congress in Bombay, Rajiv Gandhi omitted to mention the word socialism in his final statement. There followed an extraordinary outcry – from the opposition and from within the Congress itself – and the statement was reissued with the key word firmly in place. Since then, Congress has been able, under the control of Narashima Rao, to move quietly away from socialism and to press ahead with economic reforms, but the government has remained sensitive to the issues of IMF (i.e. 'foreign') involvement, and vulnerable to the argument about being anti-poor.

In 1995, following a whole series of political defeats at the state level, Congress-I's Finance Minister, Manmohan Singh set out in the autumn budget a whole series of policies aimed at eliminating poverty. Such policies included increases in education and rural development schemes. Opposition parties, most notably the BJP, had since 1992 successfully drawn attention to issues of poverty and increasing inequalities through the use of anti-Western, anti-free trade rhetoric. Following India's ratification of the GATT Uruguay Round agreements, formally concluded in 1993, the BJP led several mass demonstrations against the government for abandoning the poor. Yet Congress-I attempts to square populism with conditionality remain problematic, as they do for the current National Front government of Devi Gowda. In 1995 the Reserve Bank of India warned the government to avoid 'throw away' policies in the run-up to the Lok Sabha elections, and the World Bank cautioned against fiscal laxity.

While these counter-claims are more important within the Indian context (where planning and socialism have long been combined in opposition to foreign capital and an intellectual dislike of unfettered capitalism) they can also be found within Pakistan and within Sri Lanka. Because of their shared colonial heritage, much of South Asia's elite remain ambivalent in their attitudes towards international capital, if only because of its association with the West, and more distantly, the images of Western dominance. The fact that none of these states has any real voice within the global financial institutions such as the IMF and the World Bank reinforces this sense of falling under foreign dominion.

In Bangladesh the radical left's opposition to capitalism that surfaced after the civil war has been effectively neutralised, but the present government of Begum Zia contains several political groups who oppose external interference within the economy, or are opposed to a further role for the World Bank in the restructuring of Bangladesh's economy. Many of these parties combined socialist and nationalist objections to conditionality with an emphasis upon Islam.

In Pakistan the possible anti-capitalist, anti-commercial tendencies of an Islamic political system (apparently so vital to the internal legitimacy of the regime) could cause problems for Western investment, especially concerning the payment of interest on capital funds. Since 1989 the predominantly anti-US attitudes of the government has affected future US corporate investment. Even under the UNP, Sri Lanka has been criticised by international financial agencies because of a failure to cut back on 'non-developmental' expenditure – a curious euphemism for welfare policies and food subsidies. In 1994, the outgoing UNP government faced serious labour unrest following the decision to sign up to an enhanced structural adjustment programme which required further cuts in welfare, and a further retrenchment on public sector pay.

Furthermore, even given the current vogue of liberalisation, there are many arguments that still favour some form of planning exercise, albeit more along the lines usually associated with the newly industrialising countries (NICs) of East Asia. The argument that an investigation of the NICs reveals an absence of planning, as opposed to a different type of planning activity, is impossible to sustain.[10] Planning for a 'free market' is as complex, and as necessary, for planning within the state sector.

It is often one of the conditions of the IMF that states seeking financial help and 'restructuring' submit economic plans for consideration, plans which are encouraged to formulate long-term strategies aimed at promoting exports, encouraging investment, and developing an 'entrepreneurial culture'. In 1995, for example, the World Bank extended a US$ 700 million loan to assist the Indians in providing the necessary information and expertise needed to privatise public sector banking, and to co-ordinate private banking practice with the actions of the Reserve Bank itself. As India (and Pakistan) move into the game of liberalising public utilities, the state will have to provide regulatory functions to maintain standards and to protect the rights of consumers.

The international imperatives: world trade and global production

It has been argued above that one of the main motivating forces behind the move towards liberalisation came from within the states of South Asia themselves. One way of accounting for the degree (and sustainability) of this move is to recognise the conjunction of events that place domestic events into a changing international context. The crisis of public finance in the states of South Asia, although generated in each case by differing circumstances, coincided with the collapse of state planning in the USSR and Eastern Europe. Attempts at liberalisation had been made within India before 1989–91 in 1975–77, and then briefly in 1985–86, but they had petered out with little effect. Between 1985 and 1990 deregulation appeared sufficiently permanent to encourage a number of US–Indian joint ventures, but India showed a reluctance to reform various anti-monopolies legislation to facilitate private corporate expansion, or indeed to reform legal requirements that compelled equity shares in any foreign collaborations.

The reforms after 1991 seemed to most commentators to be more sustained if only because the domestic – and international – circumstances were so acute. In 1990, for example, the World Bank noted that: 'Perhaps the abandonment of central planning and increased reliance on the market in eastern Europe will powerfully affect basic approaches to economic development in the coming decades in both Africa and Asia'.[11] In 1994, the World Bank praised the Indian government for their deepening commitment to economic reform, which the Bank firmly believed was the necessary condition for the successful elimination of poverty. In 1995 the World Bank and the IMF remained convinced that only if India continues the push towards liberalisation, will it be able to fully benefit from changes taking place within global production. The possibility that there remains a contradiction (or at least an asymmetry) between Indian liberalisation and the dynamics of the world economy is not considered a serious possibility.

None the less, in the middle of the 1990s there are some reasons to doubt that the growth in world trade will be able to support further industrialised economies attempting to compete for shares in value-added export markets. Firstly, regardless of how effective the economies of South Asia are in attracting foreign investment in the long term, in the short term, liberalisation and restructuring required the continual access to concessional and 'soft' loans, either through the international financial institutions associated with the Bretton Woods Agreement, or through other agencies such as the Asian Development Bank, the Islamic Development Bank, and the Colombo Plan, founded in 1951.[12]

With the sudden emergence of many weak states from under the aegis of the USSR, South Asia's share in concessional loans has declined. The so-called 'transitional' economies of Eastern and Central Europe are in many respects more immediately attractive than South Asia. *The Far Eastern Economic Review* noted in 1990 that IMF and World Bank support to Asia – and particularly the smaller states such as Sri Lanka, Bangladesh and Nepal – has fallen relative to Latin America and Africa. This trend has continued throughout the 1990s. In 1994, the World Bank-led aid consortium for India pledged US$ 2,100 million, down on the previous year (US$2,150 mn) and less than requested as essential. Bilateral donations from other sources came to US$ 3,200 million, also down from the previous year. The same picture is evident for Sri Lanka, Pakistan and Bangladesh.

While India and Pakistan have access to regional financial institutions, it is not clear that they can on their own provide the necessary credits needed to sustain economic restructuring. Paradoxically, both India and Pakistan have been victims of their success. In the mid-1980s, for example, the United States raised objections to further IMF financial assistance to India, on the grounds that it no longer required 'concessional loans' since it was to all intents and purposes a substantial economy. As such, conditions for future loans ought to be in keeping with commercial considerations applicable to developed states.[13] Elsewhere, the United States has also shown a marked reluctance to make any exceptions for Indian policies on trade and development generally.

In 1989 the US Trade Department invoked the 'super 301' clause of the omnibus Trade Act against Brazil, Japan and India for 'unfair' trade practices and a failure to reciprocate trade liberalisations, especially within insurance markets, again indicative that they were going to treat India as a 'developed' state. US action, in 1989 and again in 1993, is evidence that, if India is to prove successful at penetrating US markets it must do so on the basis of strict reciprocity as specified in the GATT agreements. Should India attempt to argue for concessions based on its 'developing status' there is every possibility that the United States would accuse it, as it has accused Japan, of 'unfair' trading practices and habits, and seek some form of redress involving trade restrictions.

Like US complaints against Japan, accusations of protectionism are often aimed at so-called informal practices and distribution outlets, and the use of non-tariff barriers.[14] America has complained about India's patent protection acts, which offer limited protection to the 'intellectual property' of US multinationals. Significantly the United States remains India's largest source of direct foreign investment, one of the few Asian countries in which it has not been replaced by the Japanese. Indian attempts to encourage further US investments were a clear part of India's overall foreign policy towards the United States in the late 1980s, initiated under the Rajiv Gandhi administration. India's response to the '301' incident was remarkably constrained, and quite different from previous incidents, such as the rupee devaluation in 1966 which, widely believed to have been a result of American pressure, embarrassed the government and soured Indo-US relations for some time. Yet pressures to reform domestic trade and industrial policies within South Asia are also coming from Japan and from the EU. New Delhi's recent attempts to encourage Japanese investment led to criticisms about Indian business management procedures, low levels of productivity and problems of quality control.

While Japan is involved in development projects in the Maldives, Bhutan and Sri Lanka, it has not found the various incentives to invest very encouraging. Japan has co-operated with India's indigenous car manufacturer Maruti, but the Suzuki Corporation has complained about Indian government restrictions and internal bottlenecks affecting what is a potentially large middle-class market. India has in turn complained about the transfer of designs and royalty payments, and the repatriation of profits to Japan and to the East Asian NICs. In recent years, and in spite of communal unrest, Sri Lanka has benefited from the relocation of textile and manufacturing industries from South Korea and Taiwan, which have been attracted by its skilled workforce.

An increased need to find foreign markets for South Asian manufactured and processed goods comes at a time when Western markets (particularly the United States) are succumbing to domestic pressure to protect their own industries, especially in areas most important for South Asia: textiles and intermediate goods. Even if India could get access to advanced technology to modernise its industrial and manufacturing base, there is no guarantee that it would have access to foreign markets in which it can sell back non-primary, value-added goods.

Trade tensions between the United States and Japan have highlighted the sensitivity of the industrialised world to allowing technological co-operation to undermine their own industrial production and technological advancement. The possibility of extensive Third World manufactured goods penetrating the developed market economies is a state of affairs that the United States and many OECD countries would find difficult to tolerate. Not only would it lead to calls for further protectionism within the industrialised countries, it would also further demands that Third World states should also reduce their tariff barriers, a situation that would almost certainly complicate attempts by the states of South Asia to create an indigenous manufacturing base.[15]

Protectionism and tariff barriers

Non-tariff barriers (NTBs) proliferated throughout the international economy from the mid-1970s as an indirect form of protectionism because the presence of the GATT agreements outlawed tariff structures. It has been calculated that by 1987 NTBs in automobiles, textile production and the steel and iron industries constituted a _de facto_ external tariff of approximately 25 per cent of all LDC imports to the OECD countries.[16]

While the successful conclusion of the GATT Uruguay Round extended a liberal trading regime into areas previously excluded from GATT rounds (such as agriculture, intellectual property rights and entertainments), the NAM countries expressed their concerns in 1994 and 1995 that GATT gave the OECD countries an unfair advantage over the developing world. The NAM were particularly concerned about the call for the removal of agricultural subsidies (despite concessions over lead in times). The NAM countries also expressed anxieties over regionalism.

The fear of establishing regional trading blocs based upon the European Union, the North American Free Trade Association and the Pacific Rim feeds a general South Asian anxiety that, as a region, it will remain marginal to the world. South Asia does not automatically belong to the US, the European, and the Japanese–Pacific areas. More seriously, it is not clear that it, in itself, constitutes an economic region. It follows that if such bloc rivalries are established, South Asia would find it difficult to attract and compete with foreign capital and trade, which would tend to gravitate towards the much more lucrative markets of the United States and the EU.

While the eventual form that European tariffs will take is still unknown, it is very likely that they will further discriminate against South Asian goods. The probable extension of special trading preferences to Eastern European states may well fill import quotas currently at the disposal of Third World states. Pressure from GATT to remove barriers on manufactured imports could well have a damaging effect upon European manufacturing industries: taking up to 10 or 15 per cent of the domestic market.[17]

> Trade will count for more in the 1990s than it has for many years. Eastern Europe cannot embrace capitalism successfully without unimpeded access to Western markets. Debt burdened developing countries cannot grow their way back to creditworthiness without trade, and Europe will reap the benefits of 1992 only if its producers face global competition.[18]

But as domestic pressure to retain living standards grows with the OECD countries, and mitigates against policies aimed at improving the international competitiveness of their industry, protectionism makes short-term, electoral sense in many of the Western market economies.[19]

European amalgamation, for example, is creating one of the largest markets in the world: combining the states of Western Europe into a single economic unit of 320 million people with a combined GDP of US$ 6 trillion. Even if South Asia could successfully combine itself into a regional common market, consisting of one-fifth of the entire planetary population, it is still likely that it would not command a significant economic profile. In 1977 the regional GDP was US$ 120 billion. In 1989 it was estimated at just over US$ 341 billion, and in 1995 just over US$ 400 billion. India has long expressed concerns that one of the possible consequences of European integration will be to further regional trade between and within the developed world at the expense of Third World economic prosperity, a view that India expressed throughout the Uruguay Round, and more recently at various NAM meetings.

This is not just India's concern. Even after thirty years of the 'special relationship' between Washington and Islamabad, the percentage of US direct investment in Pakistan is a very small percentage of US global investment. Despite encouragement from both Zia and Benazir Bhutto, US corporations remain unwilling to invest in industrial production preferring to invest in the growing service sector. In spite of the efforts made by Zia, Pakistan has not been very successful in persuading the Japanese to undertake industrial joint ventures in the telecommunications and tourist industries: two noticeable growth areas in India, for example. Furthermore, and following on directly from the issues discussed in Chapter 3, internal dissent and violence, be it in Bombay, Karachi or Colombo, discourages foreign investment, while coalition governments imply to many foreign observers short-term expedience and political instability and stop-go macro-economic policies.

In 1992, the World Bank noted that the problems of so-called trade diversion, caused by changes in regional and inter-regional trade might overcome any general benefits to the developing world of a growth of world trade, but by 1994–95, the Bank was more robust in its views about the benefits. The 1994 World Bank report notes that the amount of world trade occurring within regions as a percentage of world GDP increased from 7 per cent in 1948 to just over 17 per cent in 1990, but increases in inter-regional trade have remained fairly stable, at about 16–17 per cent. Moreover, the WTO remains committed to ensuring that regionally integrated areas (RIAs) cannot create barriers for the entry of third party members.

There is optimism too concerning economic activity generally. Growth in world trade remained sluggish in the early 1990s, if mainly because of continual recession in Europe. However, the Bank believed that the implementation of the market access provisions negotiated during the Uruguay Round would add between US$ 200–300 billion to world trade by the year 2005. According to the GATT secretariat, complete implementation of Uruguay will increase merchandise trade by up to 12 per cent by the end of the next decade, probably more, if services are included.[20]

Where the GATT has been able to reconcile the agenda of developing countries with the priorities of the OECD, is with reference to the Multi-Fibre Agreement (MFA). The MFA has been a particular cause of irritation for states with buoyant textile and clothing industries, because it prevented countries with low unit costs benefiting from comparative advantage. Cheap labour, and often poor and inadequate health and safety standards, give countries such as India, Pakistan and Bangladesh a huge advantage over domestic textile production within the OECD, and have long been a target for NTBs.

The MFA came into force in 1974. Wolf has remarked that the object of the agreement was: 'to expand trade through the progressive liberalisation of the world trade in textile products, ensuring the orderly and equitable development and avoiding [its] disruptive effects in both the importing and the exporting countries'.[21] Such a statement reads as a rather long euphemism for protectionism when and if market penetration disrupts domestic textile production.

Even worse, there has been a tendency since its inception to extend the scope of the original agreement. India, Pakistan, Sri Lanka and Bangladesh have long protested that the MFA is against the spirit of GATT, and that it ought to be progressively phased out.

Bangladesh provides an interesting example of how pernicious the MFA has been. In response to World Bank pressure to increase and diversify exports, Bangladesh attracted foreign investment from South Korean joint ventures and set up several small-scale manufacturing units. By the mid-1980s, the exports of textiles to Canada, the United States, the United Kingdom and France produced US$ 100 million of much needed hard currency, with the United States making up about 80 per cent of the market.

Under domestic pressure, however, by 1987 the United States had invoked the MFA and issued thirteen separate quotas that restricted Bangladeshi imports, despite the fact that they constituted a mere 0.5 per cent of America's total textile imports. India and Pakistan have been denied access to lucrative markets on the implicit basis of 'unfair' trading. All the states of South Asia were agreed, throughout the Uruguay Round, to press for the removal of the MFA and were successful in getting the MFA to be progressively phased out over a period of ten years.

The formation of SAARC: is regionalism the answer?

If South Asia fears exclusion from the *de facto* regionalism of world trade, would not formation of a robust and integrated South Asian trading bloc be the answer, in providing economies of scale in terms of both markets and expertise? Unusually, until the mid-1980s, South Asia lacked any regional organisation within which the separate states could come together to discuss or act upon common problems. Since 1985, despite obvious gains, economic co-operation has been bedevilled by political mistrust and suspicion.

The initiative leading to the formation of the South Asian Association for Regional Co-operation (SAARC) came from the Ziaur-Rehman regime in Bangladesh. Between 1977 and 1980 President Ziaur-Rehman undertook various attempts to initiate a summit of the seven South Asian states, and in 1980 he issued a working paper on the likely form and scope of a regional organisation. Anxious to encourage Indian participation, the paper stressed economic and cultural factors over political and bilateral issues. Indian coolness to the proposal, based upon a traditional fear of being isolated within the region by a Pakistan-led coalition, was tempered by a wish to avoid being accused of wrecking the initiative altogether. In August 1983, the proposal for SAARC was drawn up, and then ratified at New Delhi in 1985.[22]

Between these two dates, a series of meetings took place at foreign minister and secretary of state level to establish the principles of the organisation. It was agreed that the association would be established on the principles of the 'equality' of each member, a significant concession from India, although India reiterated its demand that bilateral issues could not, in themselves, be taken up by SAARC. SAARC evolved the practice of rotating the presidency of the organisation between the member states, a practical application of the principle of the equality of each state. Such a move ensures that states such as Nepal and the Maldives attain a significant profile within the region that will be of immediate benefit to them.

It was further agreed that a Common Action Programme (CAP), first discussed in 1983, would prioritise specific areas and delegate them to specific countries. The CAP established separate committees on agriculture, rural development, telecommunications, meteorological forecasting, and on health and population control. Yet both India and Pakistan reiterated their belief at the outset that SAARC would not discuss political issues, and would not even supersede bilateral discussions on trade.

SAARC was, not surprisingly, enthusiastically received by Nepal, Bhutan and Sri Lanka. Yet the curious point about SAARC is that it is still neither an economic nor a political organisation in the sense of organisations like the EU or ASEAN, and more importantly, it lacks any common security perceptions that act as an incentive for collective action. Disagreements between India and Pakistan over Soviet, Chinese and American policies (and throughout the late 1980s, arguments between India and Sri Lanka), impinged upon the degree of co-operation that was possible even in matters such as trade and technical co-operation. Sri Lanka complained in 1989 at the SAARC foreign ministers meeting in Islamabad about India's refusal to withdraw the IPKF. Nepalese sympathy for Sri Lanka's position – surfacing at the same meeting – became part of the general deterioration in Indo-Nepalese relations. In 1993, following the eventual meeting of heads of state in Dhaka, both Bangladesh and Pakistan did not waste the opportunity to embarrass India. As such, although it has outlined several areas for discussion, the actual aims of the organisation have yet to be realised.

None the less, the tenacity of the idea of multilateralism and SAARC is truly amazing. Despite the large degree of dislike and irritation, the states of South Asia have been able to press ahead with suggestions and ideas for the future, if only in the hope that one day the regional circumstances will provide a more fruitful arena in which to implement policy. For example, the 1993 summit managed to discuss the logic of creating a regional development bank, and to discuss in greater detail arrangements for regional preferential trading. In 1995, the eighth summit of SAARC, held in New Delhi, identified twenty-two items of trade that would benefit from the creation of a common market. Yet the paucity of regional trade remains.

If partly to keep the momentum behind SAARC alive, and to avoid dealing with the current realities of the degree of South Asian co-operation, there has been a tendency to add to SAARC's agenda, as opposed to consolidating specific areas. In 1986 a permanent headquarters was set up to house the organisation in Dhaka. In 1990 SAARC also set up a post of secretary-general to help with overall co-ordination of policies. The institutionalisation of SAARC has been uneven however. The 1991 agreement on a common fund, an issue on which other initiatives depend, had still to be implemented in 1995. The 1987 agreement, concerned with the setting up of special bureaux dealing with narcotics trafficking, the role of women in development, and terrorism, are poorly managed and suffer from a lack of co-operation with the intelligence wings of the various member countries. Significantly – given the level of irredentism within South Asia – the 1987 meeting failed to come to any agreed definition over terrorism, or to issue a strongly worded condemnation of terrorism throughout the region. In 1993 the best SAARC could do was to agree, in principle, against funding militant organisations and undermining neighbouring states.

As Indo-Pakistan relations deteriorated throughout the early 1990s, SAARC provided one of the few forums in which the two states could meet in an atmosphere free of suspicion and anger. While an emphasis upon the frequency of meetings at various levels of government has tended to exaggerate the importance of the organisation, it has without doubt provided a useful forum for important 'informal' bilateral discussions within the region. In 1990 for example, the November summit held at Male, capital of the Maldives, allowed India's then recently elected prime minister Chandhra Senkhar to meet his Pakistan counterpart Nawaz Sharif. Both discussed the situation in Kashmir and the rise of militancy generally. In 1995, Narashima Rao and Benazir Bhutto took time off to talk in private about the Kashmir situation and issues relating to the NPT.

More broadly, however, the potential for SAARC becoming a collective security arrangement is remote. Until this takes place it is fair to assume that the real benefits of economic co-operation will be denied. In 1989 Pakistan suggested that, like ASEAN, SAARC should take on issues of regional security in order to facilitate wider economic and regional issues. India cautioned against 'premature moves' and also warned that SAARC had no jurisdiction to represent the region in any external body such as the UN, the Commonwealth or the NAM. Yet it is possible that SAARC could provide the region with a framework in which to establish confidence-building measures between New Delhi and Islamabad.

For the present, the benefits of economic integration for South Asia are elusive. If attempted, it would firstly have to work hard to improve intra-regional trade links. Trade within South Asia is very small: about 4 per cent of South Asia's US$ 54 billion trade total in 1993. In 1995, SAARC made up a mere 3 per cent of India's total foreign trade by value. Attempts to use SAARC as a platform from which to launch joint industrial or manufacturing ventures threaten the smaller states with further integration into India, while India remains reluctant to allow access to what is still an essentially protected domestic market. Pakistan has continued to restrict Indian trade because of strategic considerations, especially involving investments by private Indian firms, which might displace Pakistani firms from lucrative markets, or more problematically, from emergent third markets in Central Asia.

The economies of the South Asian states are not compatible. SAARC does open the way for various commodity agreements (such as on tea and on coffee) and in some cases combined overseas marketing. Yet with the practical exceptions of Nepal and Bhutan, the remaining states are all attempting to diversify their trade away from primary commodity goods. While regional integration may be complementary to wider trade liberalisation, it is not an alternative to wider links with the global economy, since it will not automatically provide the required economies of scale for the types of goods that these economies now wish to trade in, especially India.

In a symposium on SAARC held in 1985, Mohammed Ayoob noted that 'we therefore have a situation in South Asia that is conducive neither to regional co-operation nor regional polarisation'. SAARC will only work when these tensions have been resolved. Yet whether it will help resolve these tensions remains questionable. Let us now examine the economic policies and dynamics of each country in turn.

The Himalayan kingdoms of Nepal and Bhutan

Nepal, Bhutan and the former kingdom of Sikkim are amongst the poorest areas in the world. All three states are characterised by a low domestic savings ratio, poor 'basic' educational and health facilities, and a high degree of rural unemployment and landlessness. In terms of trade, these areas remain dominated by India. Sixty per cent of Nepalese trade was with India in 1994. Bhutan's share was even higher: just over 85 per cent.

In 1987 Nepal's trade deficit with India was US\$ 144.06 million, increasing to just over US\$ 230 million in 1994. Trading relations with Pakistan are minimal, and while Bangladesh and China's contributions (both as suppliers of material and markets) have grown throughout the 1980s, India's remains paramount. To some critics this is the deliberate outcome of a long period of Indian influence: the economic side of the defence agreement. In many respects, however, it is the inevitable outcome of Nepal's geo-political location.

Under Indian influence Nepal adopted formal planning in the 1950s, and in the 1956–75 period launched five separate five-year plans. The planning strategy aimed initially at developing basic infrastructure, and secondly at increasing agricultural output and improving educational facilities. Under the terms of an internationally supported 'adjustment programme' announced in 1985 more direct basic needs were adopted aimed at eradicating rural poverty, through a rural works programme and a mass literacy drive.[23] From 1990 onwards, Nepal has also moved towards a commitment to liberalisation, despite frequent changes in government.

The success of planning in Nepal has been mixed, partly because of the degree of extreme economic backwardness prior to 1951, and partly as a failure of the economic priorities within the plans themselves. The first two plans were not decisive enough in tackling agricultural production and were too 'urban biased' in their outlays. Over-influenced, perhaps, by Indian thinking on industrial self-reliance, the plans sought to stimulate agricultural output and transfer resources towards industrial development. Although Indian experts correctly conceptualised Nepal as suffering from a classic low income equilibrium trap, where investments were low because of the low level of domestic resources, they over-estimated the general health of the agricultural sector to stand up to a sustained squeeze on revenues, or to respond to so-called market incentives to produce more in areas of ecological vulnerability.

The reasons for the poor state of Nepalese agriculture are not hard to find: it has long suffered from a period of neglect under the pre-colonial period. Cultivation practices varied from district to district, as did tenurial rights and agreements. Legal complications over land ownership affected the efficiency of modern cultivation, while attempts at land reforms ran into serious political opposition and were difficult to reinforce. The difficulties of undertaking land reforms were part of the political crisis that overcame Nepal's first multiparty constitution in the early 1960s, and which led to the abolition of party politics.

The physical environment of Nepal is hostile to increasing food production through increasing the area under cultivation. Apart from the flat fertile Terai area that makes up 17 per cent of Nepal's area, food crops are grown in hill areas that are vulnerable to rapid soil erosion. This is one of the reasons why, along with a failure to disseminate modern technologies and increase irrigation, yields actually decreased between 1966 and 1973. As productivity fell behind the annual population growth rate, export earnings declined as food was used for internal consumption. Between 1974 and 1975 and 1984 and 1985 Nepal moved from being net exporter of food to a main importer.[24]

Since Nepal's entire development strategy was based upon increased per capita incomes through agriculture, the failure to increase agricultural output meant the foreign sources quickly came to dominate plan outlays, initially from India and other multilateral aid consortia. Yet concessional loans and grants failed to jolt the economy into a pattern of steady growth. In 1987 there appeared little return from an investment of about Rs 30,378 million since 1951. Some engineering projects have been a success in that they have started to utilise Nepal's energy potentials. By 1989 US\$ 29.2 million had been invested into two small hydro-electric generators. Yet such capital projects must be part of a comprehensive strategy to deal with industrial and urban development which, in turn, had to address the issues of political decentralisation and participation within the development processes by the population as a whole.

Popular demands for a greater say have long been at the root of both Nepalese and Butanese political unrest, and by the late 1980s, they were greatly influenced by political events within the Soviet Union and Eastern Europe. Following the decision in 1990 to move towards a multiparty system, there is now a possibility that greater public participation will improve the scope and effectiveness of the plan outlines, yet the most urgent matter to tackle remains rural poverty, agricultural productivity and a programme of population control to avoid further pressure on scarce resources. Party-based political competition has been somewhat unstable and testing, and by 1994–95 there appeared little evidence that party-based politics would provide the stimuli needed to break from Nepal's traditional pattern of growth. In some respects, party government may well have compounded the problems of economic management.

Between 1951 and 1956 there were four changes in the government along with two periods of direct control from the monarchy. The 1960 royal coup led to a series of institutional reforms that over-centralised economic policy formulation. The entire basis of the panchayat schema within Nepal was, in part, to neutralise a national opposition, somewhat along the lines of the BDs. Although it sanctioned the setting up of a National Assembly, the powers of patronage and appointment remained firmly in the hands of the king and his advisers. Unlike the Indian versions of local and district councils, they had no development functions at all and were not involved in the drawing up of growth targets. By the late 1980s, Nepal's leading economist – Dr Devendra Pandey – called upon international donors to withhold all future sources of funding until Nepal was committed to democracy, on the grounds that previous funds have been wasted.[25] He, and other leading members of the Nepalese Congress, reiterated this demand during 1990.

Attempts to diversify economic activity away from agriculture towards the encouragement of small-scale industrial projects had largely failed because of high rates of illiteracy, inefficient government support for local and district initiatives, and low levels of domestic demand. At the end of the fifth plan (1975–80) the Nepalese government noted that: 'if the nation fails to make a concrete improvements in the existing economic conditions during the course of the next five to ten years, the social and economic consequences for Nepal could well be serious'.[26]

On coming to power in 1991, the Nepalese Congress party adopted an economic strategy aimed at liberalisation, which involved a basic needs strategy aimed at agricultural investment and price support. These two strategies remained potentially contradictory, since Nepalese agriculture remains dependent upon a series of subsidies and state assistance in order to be productive.

The 1991 publication of the eighth Nepalese Five-Year Plan revealed the extent to which nationalist thinking on socio-economic development had converged with World Bank and IMF thinking. In terms of industrial ownership, by 1994 some fifty-one state industries had been ear-marked for privatisation, and by 1995, seven had been successfully sold off. The brief interregnum of communist government did not by itself interrupt the momentum of Nepalese policy, with far-reaching changes in the exchange rates, liberalising trade policy, and an attempt to encourage foreign investment.

As in India, the widespread commitment to liberalisation should not disguise the extent to which the process generates popular misgiving and resentment. The 1991–94 government oversaw a general rise in prices. In the wake of the previous difficulties with the Indian embargo, which many people associated with the panchayat system itself, the inability of an elected government to satisfy high expectations led to a collapse of political support. Such a change in public opinion led the way for the election of Nepal's first communist government. Constrained by the logic of coalition, the United Communist government attempted to pass a populist bill (public and social welfare, a mass literacy drive) without upsetting Nepal's international commitments and their donors. The policy has failed, and has resulted in a new government (this time made up by the Congress party) to form Nepal's third government since 1991.[27]

Bhutan

Sharing similar environmental conditions with Nepal, Bhutan seems to offer little prospects for agricultural development through extensive cropping.[28] Only about 5 per cent of the landscape is suitable for cultivation. Increased production can only come through the rationalisation of small peasant holdings and improved irrigation and water control. As a remote kingdom, Bhutan had no infrastructure at all prior to its first five-year plan in 1961. Prior to 1974 the economy was not even fully monetarised, with taxes often being collected in kind, and with the Indian rupee circulating along with the official currency, the Ngultrum.

Yet Bhutan has several advantages over Nepal: a low, relatively static population, a resource-rich environment, especially in timber and minerals, and a high percentage of concessional loans that, given the overall size of the economy, have had a significant impact upon economic performance. Bhutan has had, until very recently, little scope for private and foreign trade and investment. Virtually all trade is carried on through the public sector, such as the Bhutanese Food Corporation, set up by Indian public finance. The Royal Monetary Authority is itself regulated by the Reserve Bank of India. Planning in Bhutan has moved away from developing essential infrastructure towards developing various resource-based projects such as logging and pulp production. The Mitsui Corporation of Japan have recently completed a telecommunications centre, and have installed direct dialling facilities to India.

Recent schemes have also involved joint ventures being set up with Indian private companies, especially in chemical processing, and the Sankosh multipurpose hydro-electric project opened in 1993. In 1989 the Bhutanese Development Financial Corporation (BDFC) decided to try and encourage a dramatic increase in private and foreign investment. Following similar developments in the Maldives, it has recently been recognised that tourism could well provide sound economic prospects for the future, but there are still sources of domestic opposition. It is still feared that any foreign input – be it in the form of investment or tourism – could prove destabilising to so-called traditional society.[29] Attempts to encourage industrialisation without 'detribalising' society must also attempt to ensure sound environmental management in order to avoid the sort of damage witnessed in Nepal (and parts of India's north west states, such as Himachal Pradesh and the infamous Sanjay Gandhi hydro-electric project on the Sutlej river). Some attempts are already being made. Private fellings and loggings are banned, and extractive industries are carefully licensed through the state. The UNEP recognises Bhutan as a unique ecological site.

Bhutanese planning is, like Nepal's, an offshoot of India's own development experience. Since the early 1970s Bhutan has gradually created its own economic institutions of planning. In 1971 Bhutan set up its own Planning Commission after joining the UN, while in 1988 the government regrouped the pre-existing Bhutanese zonal councils (the so-called *Dzongkhags*) to facilitate decentralisation within decision-making in order to stimulate growth. As with Nepal, this was partly in response to demands for greater participation by a monarchical regime facing social unrest, and partly under parental guidance of India. Yet in 1996 political parties are still banned, although the regime utilises a universal franchise. 1990 saw the formation of the Bhutanese civil service, although a large number of entrants are educated within India through variously sponsored Indian placements. India still provides a large part of Bhutan's plans' outlays – over 52 per cent between 1983 and 1987, down to just under 40 per cent in 1993. The World Bank has provided various funds for specific projects, such as US$ 5.4 million for a forestry development project.

The rest of Bhutan's much needed foreign resources come from the UN and the work of the specialist agencies. The Food and Agriculture Organisation (FAO) have helped to finance a project aimed at developing food buffer stocks. In terms of trade agreements, Bhutan signed a bilateral treaty with Bangladesh in 1989, while attempting to encourage some expansion in trade and assistance from China. The recently opened 336 MW Chukha hydro-electric power station was constructed by Indian expertise, and was funded by a mixture of Indian grants and loans. The station will export 85 per cent of its power to India. Indian technical expertise also helped construct a radio station at Thimphu.

The apparent successes of Bhutan have still to be judged, yet they appear to be more successful than Nepal. The example of the Chukha project – although relatively small – holds out an example for Indian policy towards Nepal and the Himalayan region as a whole, with less grandiose schemes such as increasing primary education and basic health care also to be pursued. The pace of economic change must be dramatically increased, while at the same time both Bhutan and Nepal must evolve the political institutions through which to manage such change, and deal with the political and economic conflicts such developments will almost inevitably entail.

Bangladesh

In 1993, the monetary and fiscal basis of the Bangladesh economy was showing marked signs of improvement. Inflation was dropping, and public savings were increasing. Yet the economy remained desperately poor. In 1987 Bangladesh per capita income was US$ 160; by 1994 it was just under US$ 180. Thirty per cent of the Bangladesh population are classified as landless labourers, and the government has consistently failed to achieve planning targets for rural employment programmes. Bangladesh has a serious problem of indebtedness despite a high level of concessional loans. In 1988 Bangladesh received grants of US$ 214 million for food aid, US$ 580 million for commodities, and US$ 1.2 million of project aid. Despite some successes in increasing paddy production throughout the 1980s, food output was slow to recover from the terrible flooding of 1988. Moreover, the political instability which followed in the wake of the restoration of party-based government was complicating the matter of long-term economic management.

In common with the two Himalayan kingdoms, Bangladesh has since independence laboured under a large external debt, and has been characterised by a low domestic savings ratio. Since 1975 Bangladesh has been relatively successful in attracting foreign funds and support from a whole range of international agencies and countries, especially the Middle East, although it was not always clear that these funds had been properly utilised. Like Pakistan, the trends in favour of privatisation have been much greater, if only because the traditions of an established public sector are so much weaker, and the basis of the modern economy so much smaller. Even under the Awami League government, planning institutions were weak and generally advisory,[30] and the mismanagement of public enterprises led to the inefficient allocation of resources and a mistrust over the government's ability to deal with the economic well-being of the country and not just the interests of a narrow, self-serving elite made up of military officials and landowners.

The commitment to far-reaching public sector ownership in Bangladesh ended in 1975 with the assassination of Mujib Rehman. After the ending of India's influence, Bangladesh's planning apparatus has attempted to encourage foreign and private investment along lines similar to Pakistan under Ayub Khan, but Bangladesh's requirements are excessive. In the 1990s Bangladesh development will require more than just the panacea of economic liberalisation, and there remains a limit to how far small-scale NGO initiatives, such as the Gramaan Bank, can in themselves provide locally based economic growth,[31] combined with job opportunities premised on self-help.

What Kissinger allegedly named the 'international basket case' has been criticised by the World Bank for increased budget allocations into what the Bank rather curiously calls 'non-development' expenditure, i.e. relief programmes, government health schemes, subsidising food prices for farmers, as well as setting fair prices in the urban areas in order to retain political legitimacy. Vast amounts of money have been required to deal with the profound consequences of environmental disasters, most notably flooding, and a large majority of this has come from overseas or has been administered within Bangladesh by NGOs. Structural adjustment deals, signed between elected government and the IMF have led to sustained cuts in poverty elimination programmes and a rise in urban unrest. Begum Zia, while committed to the logic of liberalisation through conditional lending, had none the less been cautious to balance donor pressures against domestic pressures, utilising both as scapegoats in order to retain power in the run-up to the 1996 elections.

As with Nepal and Bhutan, the staple food crop of Bangladesh is paddy, yet the conditions of production could not be more different. The delta lands of Bangladesh – regularly inundated with silt – are amongst the most fertile in the world. Yet continual population pressure has led to a form of agricultural involution in which, given constraints on increasing the area of production, each plot of land has been more and more intensively worked. An added problem is that, under Muslim property law, the redivision of land amongst the sons leads to the continual fragmentation of landholdings, despite government attempts to consolidate ownership. As with Nepal, political mistrust of district politics followed by a certain degree of institutional neglect has discouraged local initiatives and encouraged an inefficient reliance upon the central government. Population pressure has continued to force people to live in close proximity to the Ganges flood delta, and on many of the lowlying islands and spits that are constantly emerging – and submerging – in the mouths of the Ganges.

As Bangladesh approaches the next century, it will continue to require a vast amount of financial aid to assist in agricultural development, in attempts to improve schooling and the general health of the population, and to develop its manufacturing base. Ensuring continued support will be difficult, especially because levels of efficiency within Bangladesh are often criticised by international aid agencies, and because the amount of aid to Bangladesh is conditioned by demands from other areas such as the Middle East and Africa.

As Just Faaland and J. R. Parkinson have noted: 'it is not easy to see how donor countries can be persuaded to maintain an effort on the scale needed [to ensure development]. Bangladesh is not a country of strategic importance to any but its immediate neighbours',[32] especially if it is directed at illegitimate regimes supported by the military. These circumstances have changed since November 1989, but the recent typhoon and floods of May 1991 and 1995–96 merely emphasise how reliant Bangladesh is on the so-called international community, regardless of the type of regime. More seriously, it remains to be seen whether a democratic regime (recognised in the West and by international donors) is any more legitimate than a military one.

The fourth Five-Year Plan (1990–95), disrupted as it has been by the restoration of a civilian regime, was premised on the need to provide further tax incentives to attract further foreign investments: although like Nepal, a fundamental lack of a skilled labour force is one of the greatest obstacles to foreign investment, as is the continuing lack of any real political stability. Moreover, increment aid aimed at solving short-term appeals for assistance has not made an appreciable impact upon the Bangladesh economy, especially since one of the main problems remains that of population growth. In 1987–88, Bangladesh's export earnings paid for a mere 40 per cent of the import bill. In the same year, its had loaned US$ 10 bn from multilateral aid sources, 52 per cent of its GDP.[33] This ratio has remained fairly consistent throughout the 1990s. The entire agenda of Bangladesh's foreign policy must address its need for foreign assistance. One Bangladeshi scholar recently noted: 'the door must be kept open to all possible sources of economic aid, as a development strategy, the policy of non-alignment is quite a powerful weapon because it draws the best from both blocks'.[34]Bangladesh has yet to reassess the implications of 1989 for such a strategy. Perhaps like Nepal and Bhutan, the artificiality of the Bangladesh state stands to benefit only when it is drawn into a 'common market' premised largely on Indian industrialisation and growth, a logic that defies the tenacity of Bangladeshi nationalism. It is difficult to see how these two positions can be reconciled.

The Sri Lankan economy

Throughout the 1950s and early 1960s Sri Lanka's economy seemed as promising as its democratic record.[35] Since the 1970s Sri Lanka has failed to maintain its outstanding position amongst LDCs, and has only made a partial transition from a predominantly agrarian economy to an industrial one. As with all the other states of South Asia (with the exception of Nepal and the Maldives) the service sector makes up the largest share of GDP, with industry making up on average 31 per cent of its GDP in 1994. Until 1972 much of Sri Lanka's plantation economy remained under foreign ownership, while most of its exports remained essentially 'traditional' primary products. Coexisting alongside this enclave economy was a peasant-based system of cultivation, growing and marketing some cash crops, such as rubber and coffee.

Under the Bandaranaike SLFP–Left-Wing coalition governments, and under the first Republican constitution (1972–78), Sri Lanka extended its public sector through nationalisation and set up a rigid planning framework as part of a general commitment to socialism. In an attempt to absorb growing unemployment amongst a well-educated workforce, public sector employment soared during the mid-1970s. In 1976 the state was the largest employer in the country. As part of its socialist programme, the government also extended food subsidies and general welfare policies that increased government spending at a time when revenues from traditional exports were falling rapidly. The result was an extended balance of payments crisis, deficit financing, and high levels of domestic inflation. The change in government and constitution in 1977 took place against a growing budget deficit, diminishing foreign investment and increasing long-term indebtedness.

As one would expect, the World Bank has been critical of Sri Lanka's welfare expenditure, which in 1994 was calculated to consist of 4 per cent of Sri Lanka's GDP, down from previous regimes, but still considered too high. Such programmes, including the infamous free rice scheme, date back to the 1950s and are unique within the South Asian region. While recognising that a specifically targeted scheme would bring great benefits to the poorest sections of society, the Bank believe that the Sri Lankan scheme is too inclusive and wastes important scarce financial assets. Since the 1990s, the Bank has moderated its views on food subsidies, but remains critical of what it considers populist measures. The World Bank of the 1990s is more likely to assist in the cost of liberalisation than it was in the 1980s, especially with regard to increased food costs and displaced labour.

Under the SLFP, World Bank criticisms of Sri Lanka consisted of the standard complaint that extensive state involvement tended to encourage inefficiencies and adversely affect productivity. Since 1978, the UNP has turned further towards international institutions such as the IMF, the World Bank and the Asian Development Bank for both short- and long-term economic assistance. Unlike the SLFP, the UNP was willing to act upon the World Bank's critique of a large public sector and a high degree of subsidies, and open the way for a significant degree of privatisation. The Jayewardene government started to deregulate the economy soon after coming to power, limiting the role of the state and encouraging private enterprise. The new industrial strategy was an attempt to encourage Sri Lankan exports and further its participation within the global economy, not just in traditional exports, but in manufactured goods, and in some finished machine parts.

Certainly by the mid-1980s these policies appeared to be working: the unemployment rate was dropping while a strong growth rate of 4–5 per cent ensured a healthy balance of payments. Yet the growing effects of the civil war, along with a failure to diversify and promote exports meant that the momentum could not be maintained. Since 1987 Sri Lanka has witnessed increasing inflation and a return to rising unemployment, with an increasing resource gap between revenues and expenditure. The election of the SLFP–Left

Front government in 1994 implied to many a return to socialist policies, but Prime Minister (and subsequently President) Kumuratunga has, like the communist regime in Nepal, proceeded with the cautious liberalisation of the economy, and the courting of foreign investment.

Sri Lanka's trade profile is unique within South Asia. A larger share of Sri Lanka's goods goes to the developed world market than India: 62 per cent in 1989, compared to India's 43.8 per cent, up to 70 per cent by 1993. Traditionally, there has been a much greater amount of foreign investment within the Sri Lankan economy as a percentage share of GDP than is the case with India; direct foreign investment makes up nearly 3 per cent of Sri Lanka's GDP. Since the late 1970s Sri Lanka has also attempted to encourage foreign investment from Japan and the East Asian NICs, especially into its manufacturing and capital goods industry. While Sri Lanka has shown some interest in joining ASEAN, this is primarily for security reasons aimed at avoiding Indian regional dominance.

As with the other South Asian economies, the role of the international financial agencies is subject to domestic political infighting. The present government blames current economic hardships on the previous UNP governments, and their habit of 'imprudently' borrowing from private commercial sources to meet current spending requirements: in short, 'of selling the island to the West'. Like other South Asian states, Sri Lanka must increasingly compete for significant concessional loans against East European states, and must seek to fulfil the requirements of efficiency and performance laid down by donor countries. In both countries such conditionality can – and has – fuelled resentment.

As with India, economic criticisms of Sri Lanka's welfare policies miss their *political* rationality. As with the provision of government jobs, many economic policies are aimed at dealing with a deeply politicised society. They are part of an attempt to 'buy back' sections of the population into mainstream politics. For Sri Lanka the consequence of high unemployment is not simply an idle workforce, it is a radicalised workforce that could (and has) fallen prey to the many political factions currently engaged in domestic violence. Since 1990, unemployment has been rising in Sri Lanka, especially amongst the urban youth, who are then prone to join military organisations.

Until recently, high budget deficits have led to soaring domestic interest rates and have discouraged investment because local firms and businesses are unable to borrow the large sums of money needed to start new projects. Moreover, the failure of the UNP government to bring peace to the island has also had an effect upon the economy. Multinational corporations are unlikely to invest in areas where conditions are bordering upon civil war, although it is often argued that since terrorism is confined to the north and the northeast, its effects upon the economy are marginalised.

Calculating the effects of the civil war on Sri Lanka's economy is notoriously difficult, since it is hard to attribute trends within the economy to one or two variables, especially in an economy that is as open as Sri Lanka's.[37] The number of dead between 1987 and 1991 has been calculated to be somewhere in the region of 60,000.[38] Since 1989–90, the level of violence in and around Jaffna has continued unabated, with heavy fighting reported throughout August 1990 as the Sri Lankan security forces attempted to relieve troops cut off in Jaffna fort. In early 1991 the National Security Minister was assassinated in Colombo. Sadly, by early 1995 the ceasefire between the Liberation Tigers of Tamil Eelam (LTTE) and the new government had collapsed, and by late October the town of Jaffna was once more under siege by the Sri Lankan security forces. The bombing of Colombo's financial district by Tamil Tigers in the spring of 1996 was a deliberate attempt to undermine investor confidence in the Sri Lankan economy.

The level and intensity of ethnic violence since 1983 has set an atmosphere of doubt and suspicion over the government's ability and willingness to deal with the situation.[39] The number of joint ventures declined rapidly between 1983 and 1985, from 56 a year to less than 30. The effect of violence on tourism has also been serious, with the Sri Lankan tourist board reporting losses of Rs 2,285 billion for 1985 alone. It has been calculated that civil disturbances since 1983 have cut as much as 1 per cent off the annual growth rate in both 1984 and 1985.[40] The 1994 budget contained a 3.4 per cent surcharge for reasons of defence, dashing hopes of any significant peace dividends.

Many Tamil organisations have threatened multinational corporations with violence unless they withdraw. In 1987 there was a threat by the Eelam Revolutionary Organisation of Students (EROS) to poison exports of Sri Lankan tea to the United States and British markets. One effect of indiscriminate public terror by both Tamil and Sinhalese groups has been to increase public transport costs and the time of journeys. Rose and Samaranayake note that a six-hour train journey from Colombo to Jaffna now takes about thirty-six hours. There is also little confidence in public bus companies since these have often been the target of attack. In early 1996, the island is still contained within a unitary state, but the price of retaining it has been incredibly high. The bomb attack in Colombo in early 1996 was explicitly aimed at scaring away foreign investors.

The effects of terrorism are not just confined to Sri Lanka, they are also found throughout the states of South Asia. The level of political terrorism in the Punjab, prior to 1994, has had an incalculable effect upon the prosperity of one of India's wealthiest regions. Civil unrest throughout metropolitan Pakistan in the 1989–90 period, especially in and around Karachi, undermined confidence in the economy as a whole. Since the mid-1980s a great many businesses have moved away from Karachi to safer – but significantly less developed areas – in the north-west, yet the sheer level of violence in Sri Lanka, and the scale of the government's response, is unfortunately unique in South Asia, and discourages foreign investment in what is otherwise a potentially lucrative economy with a skilled workforce, good infrastructure, and good knowledge of markets and production.

Sri Lanka requires a continual aid commitment over the next decade in order to manage its economy and pursue its industrial development plans. In the mid-1980s the Jayawardene government set up a series of commissions to increase the efficiency of the remaining state-run industries and to continue to encourage foreign investment through the setting up of special export zones, exempt from income and local taxes, and other trading restrictions. While India too has increased its bilateral contributions (US$ 80 million in credits were offered under the auspices of the Indo-Sri Lankan Accord) political factors rule out any closer economic co-operation for the time being. While the present government is committed to targeting donor aid towards industrial projects it must do so in a context of growing social division and the ubiquitous presence of competing ethnic identities. Recent evidence shows that income inequalities have worsened within rural areas and between rural and urban areas, and this has become part of the Tamil–Sinhalese agitation.[41]

Finally, it is worth attempting to calculate the likely economic costs of partition for Sri Lanka, and what the prospects would be for a sovereign state of Eelam. The territorial dimensions of the state are disputed by differing Tamil groups, especially with regard to the exact proportion of the eastern and southern provinces claimed. However, maps produced by the LTTE, and used in their propaganda in Jaffna make Eelam smaller than Bhutan, just slightly larger than Wales. The terrain is low lying, relatively dry land with some irrigation facilities but little immediate prospects for economic growth. It has been suggested that the prime exports of a Tamil state would consist of onions, dried fish and mineral exports extracted from seaweed.

Such a state would make little sense, either in terms of the national and social consensus it could construct, or with regard to its degree of economic independence. This is not to dismiss the Tamil experiences of suffering and exclusion, but to question whether the creation of another state is the appropriate response to Tamil needs. Given the current divisions within the Tamil groups fighting for a state of Eelam, such a territorial state would be subject to massive socio-political instability, and the instant animosity of the Sri Lankan state. Because of internal divisions within the Tamil majority, the prospects of such a state falling under southern Indian control is extremely likely, even if it was against the better political judgements of a federal government in New Delhi.

The Indian economy: transition amidst political uncertainty?

India's commitment to planning was much more intellectually consistent and sustained than that of any of its neighbours, and much more systematically executed. From the time of the Industrial Policy Resolution (1948) onwards,[42] India has adopted a highly bureaucratic approach to economic management that emphasised the internal resources of the country and downplayed the importance of external trade. Unlike Pakistan, and covered under the general rubric of socialism, India did not follow an export-led growth strategy nor encourage foreign investment within its economy. In this respect India had an unusually small profile within the world economy after 1947, and its share of world trade actually declined throughout the 1970s.

In 1973–74, India's share of world exports was little more than 0.5 per cent.[43] In 1973 India imported a mere 9.5 per cent of all manufactured goods, while its ratio of imports to GNP was 6 per cent – one of the lowest figures in the world.[44] Its imports were likewise skewed away from manufactured goods: in 1989 only 9.1 per cent of India's world imports consisted of manufactured goods, compared to 51.1 per cent for Pakistan, 48.3 per cent for Sri Lanka and 76.5 per cent for Bangladesh.[45] By 1993, these figures were beginning to change. Indian imports in manufacturing were closer to 20 per cent for 1993–94.

In the 1960s, the economists Bhagwati and Desai remarked that India's policies on trade and production 'could be summed up cynically but realistically: that India should produce whatever it can, and that India should export whatever it produces'. While India could export some of its manufactured goods to the communist bloc states and parts of the Third World, because of controlled prices or even barter agreements, India did not actively promote exports. As noted above, Indian planners expressed export pessimism, a conviction of the ills of large (and indeed foreign) companies, and a belief in the need to ensure redistributive policies.

Strict anti-monopoly laws and emphasis upon equity shares have discouraged multinational operations and joint ventures between Indian capital and foreign companies. Somewhat paradoxically, however, India has always needed foreign aid to fund its plan outlays, because of its failure to mobilise domestic resources efficiently. By the end of 1964, India was receiving bilateral foreign aid from twenty-one countries, and through three multilateral agreements. In fact until 1966, the United States remained India's largest single aid giver. In the second and third Five-Year Plans, foreign assistance contributed between 18 and 25 per cent of plan outlays.[46] The legacies of planning have been impressive. John Mellor noted as long ago as 1979 that: The building of post-colonial India has moved on three inter-related fronts: the political system has been broadened, and the administrative structure and the industrial base have been extended'.[47] Yet compared to Pakistan, India's overall growth rate has tended to be disappointing: 4.5 per cent as opposed to 3.5 per cent on average throughout the 1970s, although recently the growth rate has tended to pick up. Provisional figures put the GNP growth rate for 1995–96 at near 6 per cent. Yet the record for Indian agricultural development, following the application of the Green Revolution technology from the mid-1960s on, has led to a dramatic breakthrough in food production. Between 1960–1980,

Indian agriculture grew on average 30 per cent faster than China, and 23 per cent faster than Pakistan. The momentum was sustained throughout the 1980s, with India well provisioned with food supplies and with some talk of being a net wheat exporter by the end of the century.

In a recent book on India, one commentator noted that the late 1980s were characterised as a period of high growth, based upon dramatic increases in agricultural production, buoyant industrial output and increasing exports.[48] Increasing exports has involved India in both Western and Eastern markets, and much of the post-colonial world. The move towards reform appears to have confirmed these earlier trends – but can they be sustained?

Optimism about the overall dynamics of the Indian economy was qualified in the late 1980s by several areas of doubt: the persistence of poverty, especially in the urban areas, the failure to innovate and invest in productive outlets, a growing amount of international indebtedness, and a poor export profile. Political instability, both before and after the 1996 election campaign, underlined India's vulnerability to the nerves of foreign investors.

Calculations over levels of poverty are difficult and controversial, but evidence points to persistent areas of poverty within India, especially within the countryside. It has been calculated that in the mid-1980s, there were over 320 million Indians living below the poverty line.[49] The definition of what constitutes the poverty line is a profoundly political concept to arrive at, as indeed are attempts to calculate how many individuals fall below the poverty line. The Indian Planning Commission defines it as those people living on Rs 20 per month at 1961 prices. The belief that India's poor are worse off now than at any time since independence, and that they have missed out entirely because of the particular bias of Indian planning, is not borne out by the evidence. Between 1970 and 1988 'the percentage of persons living in poverty have decreased in all periods and the total number living in ultra-poverty has also decreased'.[50] Yet since the mid-1970s the poor in India have become increasingly concentrated in specific areas and thus require specific, district or provincial-based anti-poverty programmes. Raising average annual growth rates is only one condition for the elimination of poverty, the key issues are still distribution and gainful employment, especially in the countryside. None the less, the poor remain a powerful and increasingly vocal section of India's political system. No government can choose to ignore them, or to give them the impression that its policies are not attempting to improve their condition. One explanation for the BJP's vote in 1996 was to do with its stress upon poverty and rural development. Electorally at least, India remains a country of villages.

Detailed analysis of the Indian economy over the 1980s shows an increasing shortfall between government revenue and government expenditure, on both the current and the capital accounts.[51] There are several key causes for this increasing gap in resources. One is a large and antiquated tax structure that is inefficient and unrealistic in its demands. High direct taxation has usually encouraged widespread evasion, while indirect surcharges have often shifted the burden of taxes on to the poor. During V. P. Singh's period as finance minister, a much needed reform of the tax system took place, but the government was reluctant to allow the ministry to raid business premises to ensure that revenues were collected, and that political corruption was adequately dealt with. It was Rajiv Gandhi's failure to support V. P. Singh, both as finance minister and at the Defence Ministry, that led to his dismissal from office and from the party, and his eventual formation of the Janata Dal Party.

By 1986 it was noted that domestic revenue merely balanced current spending, while borrowed money was used to finance planned development.[52] Even with a domestic savings rate of 23 per cent (the highest within South Asia, and high even by OECD standards) India has consistently failed to utilise the required level of funds to fill its growing development expenditures. From 1975 to 1985 the amount of current government spending has increased dramatically. One significant area has been that on defence, especially the increase in the financial year 1989–90. Other costs concern an increase in government subsidies to various pressure groups within India such as the rural poor, and support to farmers to ensure cheap fertiliser and diesel. In 1985 the budget estimates for an anti-poverty programme (outside of the plan outlay) was in the region of Rs 18.5 billion. Attempts to cut back on these programmes led to wide-spread political resistance against Rajiv Gandhi, and did much to rejuvenate the opposition parties.

In 1989 India's public and private debt was over US$ 44 billion. V. P. Singh came to power in 1989 to accuse the former Congress-I administration of having handed the new government an empty treasury. By 1991 increased borrowings had depleted Indian reserves and led to a series of emergency meetings with the IMF to gain access to credit. In February 1991 the Indian economy was in a state of free fall, with the budget estimates for 1991–92 being suspended for a period of four months following the fall of the Chandra Senkhar government, and a major crisis in foreign reserves.[53] It was reported that India had just US$ 42.5 million in its foreign currency reserves, the equivalent of about two weeks of imports.[54] The V. P. Singh government, and the interim Chandra Senkhar administration, had little choice but to negotiate the first of a whole series of stand-by agreements, the largest loans India had ever agreed to over US$ 4 billion.

The decision to suspend the budget (bitterly opposed by the finance ministry) did not seriously undermine the Indian government's ability to subsequently restore confidence in the public finance, but it illustrated the centrality that economic reform has within the Indian political system. With the (then) minority Congress-I government committed to liberalisation, compromise and negotiation became essential for both government survival and the fulfilment of structural adjustment. Despite the complexities of Indian politics free of Congress dominance, the emergence of Manmohan Singh as a competent and reformist finance minister meant that Indian economic reform moved swiftly. By 1993–94, the budget pushed ahead with the full convertibility of the rupee, the restructuring of the tax system, tariffs, state ownership and the regulation of capital, bond and stock markets. Yet dissent emerged as to the extent and logic of the changes, by some factions within the Congress, but most notably the BJP.

Part of the anti-liberalisation argument of the BJP is that an open Indian economy will not only increase poverty and inequality, but that it will lead to the destruction of those benefits that have derived from a planned economy, especially its much vaunted independence and self-reliance. There is also, of course, the wider xenophobic strand of thinking that liberalisation equates with Westernisation, and Western culture will destroy self-evident 'traditional' Indian values. As the medium-term forecasts for India stress macro-economic instability and poor growth prospects, it is possible that the current political instability within India could produce a government that may attempt to return to a more isolationist policy. John Adams noted in the early 1990s that:

In many ways the National Front [of V. P. Singh was] more attuned to the continuities of Indian economic policy than was Rajiv's Congress ... in that it was more in keeping with the talk of self-reliance and socialism than were the free marketeers associated with the Congress.[55]

The Narashima Rao government of 1991–96 proved how far the Congressite free-marketeers would go when placed into government, but were probably insensitive to issues of poverty and to the accusation that they have sold out the country to foreign interests. Yet, as with the other states in South Asia, one is struck by the degree of political consensus about the necessity of liberalisation. None of the constituent parts of the current United Front government under Prime Minister Devi Gowder wish to return India to the heyday of planning. It is unlikely that, if in power, even the BJP would contemplate such a thing. What parties (and more seriously, governments) are attempting to do is to implement structural adjustment without seriously undermining their electoral support, and the rhetoric of national independence. This is a complex balancing act, in which domestic and international forces act like pincers on the autonomy of government and the power of the state itself.

The economic prospects for Pakistan

At times, like India, Pakistan has favoured import substitution, as during the first five-year plan announced in 1955. While economic policy has been more open than in India, it has none the less been sporadic, tied up with the fate and interests of particular regimes. Moreover, even under Zulfikar Bhutto economic regulation has never reached the elephantine excesses of New Delhi's bureaucracy and has usually been confined to the public sector only. In this respect Pakistan's economic history is in many ways the exact opposite of India's. Pakistan's growth rates have been generally higher and had a higher share in world trade. Between 1950 and 1980 income per capita more than doubled, and between 1977 and 1988, per capita incomes grew on average at 3.8 per cent per annum. The World Bank reports Pakistan as a 'middle-income' bracket, which puts it in the company of countries like Turkey, Brazil and Mexico. The Ayub Khan period was without doubt the heyday of the 'liberal' economy, as much as it was the heyday of Pakistan–US co-operation. Pakistan benefited from export promotion and diversification, which laid the foundations for later industrial gains in such sectors as steel, petrochemicals and some services. The momentum failed during the political crisis that overtook Pakistan in the late 1960s, in which Pakistan lost access to the (declining) foreign revenues of the East Wing, and fell victim to the inflationary effects of the war and the subsequent US embargo. Zulfikar Bhutto moved economic policy and management towards a specific version of India, with a large socialist sector and active state management. The commanding heights of the economy were brought into the hands of the state bureaucracy at the very time that this was being de-professionalised and opened up to less qualified entrants.[56]

These policies, as much out of favour with the IMF as the socialist policies of the SLFP in Sri Lanka, were reversed by Zia. As with his fellow officer Ayub Khan, Pakistan under the military appeared more inclined to fulfil the requirements of IMF conditionality than a civilian regime. None the less the economic successes made by Pakistan in the 1980s were very real, even if the distributional aspects have arguably left something to be desired. In a classic study of Pakistan, Griffin and Khan noted that 'experience shows that faster growth does not inevitably lead to greater prosperity. In some cases it can actually lead to a decline in the standards of living for the rural and urban poor'.[57] During the 1960s it was frequently alleged that most of Pakistan's industrial and financial wealth was owned by a mere twenty-one families.[58] It has already been noted that the economic disparities between East and West Pakistan contributed significantly to the political alienation of the Bengalis. Despite the reversal of Zulfkar Bhutto's nationalisation, many of Pakistan's remaining public sector corporations are run bureaucratically, and with an eye to internal political gains. Unlike India, there have not been any moves as yet to deinvest public sector undertakings through private flotations.[59] Yet, interestingly enough, Pakistan's record on poverty is as good as, if not slightly better than, India's.[60]

As with India, future development plans must rely increasingly on foreign resources and deregulation. Pakistan has a low domestic savings ratio, and its record of mobilising domestic funds through tax and revenue has consequently been poor. Growth rates in agriculture have generally lagged behind those of India, especially in the

Punjab. While India favoured a decentralised scheme of spreading and supporting Green Revolution technology, Pakistan favoured a highly mechanical approach based upon extending irrigation works through a centralised bureaucratic system. Evidence suggests that agricultural investment and productivity also suffered from large-scale imports of cheap grains from the United States from the late 1960s onwards. India's agricultural growth has generally been more sustained than Pakistan's.[61]

Until the recent crisis in India, Pakistan's indebtedness was amongst the worst – about 25 per cent of GDP – of the South Asian economies. High domestic interest rates have created conditions unfavourable for sustained domestic investment, and have led to an increased search for loans and grants from abroad. While Pakistan has continued to received a regular inflow of remittances from the Gulf states, and from other bilateral and multilateral aid consortia, these have been declining in recent years. It has been estimated that between 1979 and 1987 Pakistan's total aid commitment from all sources totalled US$ 10 billion, an average of US$ 1.45 billion per annum.[62] One of the growing difficulties for Pakistan, and indeed for other South Asian economies, has been the growth of a large 'informal' or black economy whose resources technically elude the state. In Pakistan, the growth in the black economy is linked to the heroin trade. Exact measurements are hard to come by, but following the Soviet invasion of Afghanistan, the 'parallel' economy has expanded in border states such as Baluchistan and NWFP. It has recently been calculated that as much as 40 per cent of Pakistan's actual GDP goes unrecorded, because it is illegal and hence unrecognised.

Since 1989 Pakistan's trade deficit has increased, and its indebtedness has continued to grow steadily. Since 1988, the civilian governments of Benazir Bhutto and Nawaz Sharif have remained committed to an open economy while stressing a 'basic needs' strategy to eliminate rural poverty. In 1989 the Bhutto government announced a medium-term adjustment programme in which public spending would be targeted at basic education and public hygiene, while at the same time, like its counterparts in India, Nepal and Bangladesh, the government recognised the need to undertake economic reform under the aegis of the Bretton Woods institutions. Sharif's period in office did not break the momentum of reform, while the economic policies of the caretaker government under

Moeen Qureshi were far-reaching and complementary to those started under Benazir's first administration.

Yet as with India (and Sri Lanka) such increases in welfare spending and 'anti-poverty' programmes, while generally favoured by the World Bank, will be increasingly scrutinised to ensure that they do not violate existing agreements on conditionality and structural readjustment.

Finally, it is necessary to note that all of the South Asian economies remain vulnerable to increasing energy costs. Following Iraq's invasion of Kuwait, oil prices doubled between August 1990 and January 1991, even though these prices were not as severe as was feared. These increases had serious economic repercussions for the states of South Asia. While India, Pakistan and Bangladesh all have limited access to some domestic fossil fuel reserves (coal, oil and gas), they remain dependent upon Middle Eastern supplies. The war dramatically curtailed workers in the Gulf States from sending back remittances. Bangladesh has over 100,000 people working in Kuwait and Iraq, and throughout the 1980s they have provided the Bangladeshi economy with an average of US$ 100 million per annum. This is also the case with Pakistan.

India has over 200,000 people working in the Gulf states, and these are drawn disproportionately from the states of Kerala and Gujarat. Given India's federal system, these two provinces faced serious revenue losses in excess of 1 per cent gross state product.[63] Sri Lanka has been seriously affected by the price increases and in February 1991 sought US$ 450 million to deal with a foreign exchange crisis caused by increased oil bills. While the individual Gulf states, along with Japan, the EU and the United States have created a common fund to help developing countries, only Bangladesh and Pakistan have been mentioned in the South Asia region. Significantly both of these states committed troops to the services of the US-led coalition, while India did not.

Finally, both India and Pakistan are potentially large energy users, and also potentially large global polluters. India in particular has been sensitive to recent global initiatives to outlaw CFCs, thereby increasing the costs of specific coolants and lubricants necessary for modern industry. While India has been successful in getting some multilateral help to cover these costs – mainly through the UNEP – it is critical, along with China, of environmental criteria adding another layer of 'conditionality' to India's economic development.

Summary

An overview of economic development throughout the 1980s reveals that the economies of South Asia are divided into two distinct sets: those of India, Pakistan and Sri Lanka that contain a manufacturing/services sector, and which have witnessed periods of sustained growth and relative macro-economic stability comparative to Latin American and some of the more prosperous African countries. The states of Nepal, Bhutan and Bangladesh, on the other hand, still face significant difficulties in terms of infrastructural development and economic diversification.

The Maldives fall between the two: as a micro-state it has a relatively environmentally limited economy which is dependent upon tourism, and some fish food processing aimed primarily at the Japanese market. As yet it lacks a significant industrial and manufacturing base, and much of the social or territorial prerequisite needed to support them. Like Bangladesh, the Maldives remain vulnerable to environmental change and escalating costs of ensuring adequate protection against rises in sea levels, being on average a mere 10 metres above sea level. In 1978, the Maldives joined the Asian Development Bank, the World Bank and the IMF in order to gain access to international aid so as to begin the construction of expensive sea defences.

It is often asked, in comparison to the economies of the so-called Asian Tigers, why has India's and Pakistan's development been so disappointing to many. The comparison is obviously unfavourable, given the regional dimensions of India and Pakistan to what are in a majority of cases 'enclave' economies. Yet the comparison is often made in the developmental literature to support a counterfactual argument against planning and 'inward orientated' growth.[64] There are serious methodological problems behind such comparisons.

Certainly both India and Pakistan are facing the social and political difficulties of opening up their economies, and they suffer from the additional anxiety of doing so at a time when a global liberal trade regime is itself in transformation. In stark contrast to the military notions of strength discussed earlier, the economic problems of South Asia – cause and consequence of the enormous social strains discussed in Chapter 3 – make it marginal to the world economy and the perceptions of other states outside the region. This is particularly true of India.

In contrast to its emergent military profile, India's economic muscle is minute. In 1989, Indian imports from the region are about 1 per cent, while regional exports make up a mere 28 per cent.[65] Of all the states of South Asia, India can only be said to really dominate Nepal and Bhutan in an economic sense: and it has done that in such a way as to cause resentment and misunderstanding. The Maldives, for example, is dominated by Far Eastern trade, and bilateral aid from Japan. Srikant Dutt has noted how many of India's foreign joint ventures with other developing countries were either moribund or sustained for purely political reasons. At the beginning of the 1990s, for an economy of its size and territorial dimension, the size of trade was remarkably undeveloped. How do these economic weaknesses affect India's political and military claims throughout the region, and indeed throughout the world?

The implications are – and they are discussed in the final chapter – that they substantially diminish the nature of its claims. The importance of economics was well understood by Nehru, and it gave Indian foreign policy under Nehru an essential consistency. In a seminar on India's military deployment, held in the late 1980s, a Soviet academic asked the telling question of whether or not India's military and strategic plans outstripped the country's economic strengths to sustain them, an ironic question in retrospect, given the impending collapse of the USSR. What use is a blue-water navy, deployed to extend some non-existent or under-utilised 'extended economic zone' across the Indian Ocean when the costs of maintaining it constitute a serious economic liability? For an economy with little or no external trade, what is there to defend apart from the immediate land borders to the east and the west? It is because of its lack of economic strength that Indian claims to 'great power' status strike many commentators as absurd. India must continue to reform and liberalise, without compromising on matters of poverty elimination and redistributive policies. India will never be a economic tiger, but there is no reason why it cannot be a swift-footed elephant.

Notes

1   *World Development Report*, World Bank, Washington, 1990 and *Economic Trends in the Developing Economies*, World Bank, Wash-

ington, 1989. By 1995, these figures have not changed significantly.

2 Keith Griffin, *Alternative Strategies for Economic Development*, London, 1989.

3 This is a complex affair. In 1950 Indian government expenditure accounted for barely 8 per cent of aggregate national expenditure, and by 1967 this had more than doubled. Yet private capital had also grown dramatically. See S. Clarkson, *The Soviet Theory of Development: India and the Third World in Marxist–Leninist Scholarship*, Macmillan, London, 1978.

4 *The Cambridge Economic History of India*, vol. II, Cambridge University Press, Cambridge, 1982, p. 958.

5 A good overview of the thinking behind Pakistan's first two decades of 'development economics' can be gleaned from reading W. W. Rostow, *The Stages of Economic Growth*, Chicago University Press, Chicago, 1971.

6 Stanley Kockanek, 'Brief Case Politics in India', *Asian Survey*, 27, 1987, pp. 1278–301.

7 For an excellent discussion on the Rajiv Gandhi government and the corruption scandals over Bofors, see Nick Nugent, *Rajiv Gandhi: Son of a Dynasty*, BBC, London, 1990.

8 There is of course a massively involved debate as to whether planning was ever useful: J. N. Bhagwati and S. Desai, *Planning For Industrialisation. Industrialisation and Trade Policy since 1951*, Oxford University Press, London, 1971. See also I. Little, *et al.*, *Industry and Trade in Some Developing Countries*, Oxford University Press, London, 1970 and Ian Little, *Project Appraisal and Planning for Developing Countries*, Heinemann Educational, London, 1974.

9 See Jagdish Bhagwati, *India in Transition: Freeing the Economy*, Clarendon Press, Oxford, 1993.

10 See Robert Wade, *Governing the Market: Economic Theory and the Role of Government in East Asian Industrialisation*, Princeton University Press, Princeton, 1990.

11 *World Development Report*, Washington, 1990, p. 24.

12 The Colombo Plan – an abbreviation for the Co-operative Economic Development in South and South-East Asia – was founded in 1951. Arising from a Commonwealth initiative it was finally extended to involve six non-regional states, including the United States and Japan. It is made up of twenty-six countries.

13 Sarbjit Johal, 'India's Search For Capital Abroad', *Asian Survey*, 29, 1989, pp. 971–1002.

14 See Raju Thomas, 'US Transfers of Dual-Use Technologies to India', *Asian Survey*, 30, 1989, pp. 560–631.

15 Under the present GATT regime, Third World states are allowed to

set up tariffs for 'developmental' purposes to protect infant industries etc. Once these industries have been established the tariff barriers were to be gradually withdrawn.

16 *World Development Report*, Washington, 1990.

17 All figures here are taken from the *World Development Report*, 1990.

18 Editorial, *The Economist*, London, 1–7 December, 1990, p. 2.

19 This is one of the arguments that has been put forward by Robert Gilpin, *The Political Economy of International Relations*, Princeton University Press, Princeton, 1987.

20 *World Development Report*, Washington, 1994.

21 M. Wolf, *Indian Exports*, World Bank, Washington, 1982.

22 See Craig Baxter *et al.* (eds), *Government and Politics in South Asia*, Westview Press, Boulder, 1987, p. 305.

23 See P. Blakie *et al.*, *The Struggle for Basic Needs in Nepal*, Clarendon Press, Oxford, 1980, and L. Rose and J. Scholz, *Nepal: Profile of a Himalayan Kingdom*, Westview Press, Boulder, 1980. See also L. S. Baral, *Political Development in Nepal*, Vikas, New Delhi, 1983.

24 Narayn Khadka, 'Nepal's 7th Five Year Plan', *Asian Survey*, 28, 1988 pp. 555–68. See also A. Schloss, 'Making Planning Relevant. The Nepal Experience 1968–1976, *Asian Survey*, 20, 1980, pp. 1008–20.

25 *Far Eastern Economic Review*, Hong Kong, November 1989, p. 32.

26 Shanker Sharma 'Nepal's Economy: Growth and Development', *Asian Survey*, 1986, 26, pp. 897–905.

27 I am indebted to Siddhant Pandey for discussing his MSc thesis with me, submitted at the University of Bristol in 1995, entitled 'Economic Liberalisation in Nepal: Dimensions of the Transformation Process'.

28 See Leo Rose, *The Politics of Bhutan*, Oxford University Press, London, 1977, and the excellent Imaeda Yoshira and Imaeda Pommeret, *Bhutan: A Kingdom of the Eastern Himalayas*, Portland Books, London, 1984.

29 For a general economic and political assessment of the impact of tourism within South Asia see Linda K. Richter, *The Politics of Tourism in Asia*, University of Hawaii, Honolulu, 1989.

30 See N. Islam, *Development Planning in Bangladesh: A Study in Political Economy*, C. Hurst, London, 1977.

31 The Gramaan bank is one of the most successful micro-credit schemes, aimed specifically at rural women, in the world. See Najmul Abdedin, 'The Gramaan Approach to Development in Bangladesh: An Overview', *Contemporary South Asia*, 5, 2, July 1996, pp. 207–14.

32 Just Faaland and J. R. Parkinson, *Bangladesh: The Test Case of Development*, C. Hurst, London, 1976.

33 *Economic Trends*, World Bank, Washington, 1989.

34 Cited in E. Ahamed (ed.), *The Foreign Policy of Bangladesh: Imperatives of a Small State*, People's Press, Dhaka, 1984, p. 24.

35 D. R. Snodgrass, *Ceylon: An Export Led Economy in Transition*, Homewood, Irwin, 1966. See also A. J. Wilson, *The Politics of Sri Lanka 1947–1979*, Macmillan, London, 1979.

36 *Direction of Trade Statistics*, IMF, Washington, 1990.

37 Sri Lanka's growth rate has been on average 4 per cent between 1965 and 1980, and 4.9 per cent between 1980 and 1986. It has been above India's but below Pakistan's, which averaged nearly 7 per cent between 1980 and 1986. See *World Development Report*, 1988, This slowed in 1989–90, and after 1994.

38 European Parliamentary Report, cited in *Keesings Contemporary Archive*, 1990.

39 The unwillingness of the government to deal with district administration is one of the themes in A. J. Wilson's book *The Break-Up of Sri Lanka*, C. Hurst, London, 1988. See also M. R. Singer 'New Realities of Sri Lankan Power', *Asian Survey*, 30, 1990, pp. 409–28.

40 Leo Ross and Tilak Samaranayake, 'Economic Impact of the Recent Disturbances', *Asian Survey*, 26, 1986, pp. 1240–85.

41 *Economic Trends*, World Bank, Washington, 1989.

42 See V. N. Balasubramanyam, *The Indian Economy*, Weidenfeld and Nicolson, London, 1984 and S. K. Ray, *The Indian Economy*, Oxford University Press, New Delhi, 1987.

43 M. Weiner, 'Assessing the Political Impact of Foreign Assistance' in J. Mellor (ed.), *India: A Rising Middle Power?*, Westview Press, Boulder, 1979.

44 Only the Soviet Union was below India. See Wolf, *Indian Exports*.

45 *Far Eastern Economic Review Year Book*, Hong Kong, 1990.

46 Clarkson, *The Soviet Theory of Development*.

47 Mellor, *India: A Rising Middle Power?*, p. 6.

48 John Adams, 'Breaking Away: India's Economy Vaults into the 1990s', *India Briefing 1990*, p. 76.

49 See Alan Heston, 'Poverty in India: Some Recent Policies', *India Briefing 1990*, p. 103. For a general discussion on this see Iqbal Khan, *Fresh Perspectives on India and Pakistan*, Bougainvillea, Oxford, 1985.

50 Heston, 'Poverty in India', *India Briefing 1990*, p. 107.

51 Some have no such doubt, however. See 'A Survey of India', *The Economist*, London, 4 May 1991.

52 Cited in A. Benard, 'A Maturation Crisis in India', *Asian Survey*, 27, 1987, pp. 408–18.

53 *Financial Times*, London, 11 February 1991.

54 *Financial Times*, London, 21 February 1991.
55 Adams, 'Breaking Away', *India Briefing 1990*, p. 97.
56 See S. J. Burki, *Pakistan Under Bhutto*, Macmillan, London, 1989. The result was to increase corruption and the misuse of state funds.
57 Keith Griffin and Azizur Rahman Khan, *Growth and Inequality in Pakistan*, Macmillan, London, 1971.
58 See Tariq Ali, *Can Pakistan Survive?* Penguin, Harmondsworth, 1983.
59 See R. LaPorte and M. B. Ahmed, *Public Enterprises in Pakistan: The Hidden Crisis in Economic Development*, Westview Press, Boulder, 1989 and S. J. Burki and R. LaPorte, *Pakistan's Development Priorities*, Westview Press, Boulder, 1984. See also William James and Subroto Roy (eds), *Foundations of Pakistan's Political Economy: Towards an Agenda for the 1990s*, Sage, New Delhi, 1993.
60 *Economic Trends*, 1989. See also the *World Development Report*, 1990 that deals in some depth with the measurements of poverty and assesses how policies have tried to eliminate it.
61 H. Sims, 'The State and Agricultural Productivity', *Asian Survey*, 26, 1986, pp. 483–500.
62 See LaPorte and Ahmed, *Public Enterprises*.
63 See ODI Briefing Paper, *The Impact of the Gulf Crisis on Developing Countries*, London, March 1991.
64 See for example the excellent book by Griffin, *Alternative Strategies for Economic Development*.
65 *Far Eastern Economic Review Asian Yearbook*, Hong Kong, 1990.

5

Future prospects for regional stability and disarmament in South Asia

Having fleshed out the region's domestic and international linkages in some detail, it is necessary by way of conclusion to return to Indo-Pak relations. Much reference has been made to Indian claims to regional pre-eminence, and always, the hint of global ambition. This has often been presented by Indian's political elite as a claim to either 'great power' or 'regional power' status. Yet what do these terms mean? How are Indian claims perceived throughout the region and throughout the world generally? P. N. Haksar's statements are typical of the nature of India's claims: 'The events of 1971 in our sub-continent sent a message across the chanceries [sic] of the world – that Indira Gandhi's India, with its triumph over Bangladesh, was emerging as a power in its own right'.[1] Such essentially Edwardian language is common to many official and elite statements about India's capabilities after the Bangladesh war, although they have been recently tempered by New Delhi's experience during the Sri Lankan fiasco. India has certainly seen its international reference points as being, not Pakistan or Sri Lanka, but China, the former Soviet Union and to a lesser extent the United States. In a famous broadcast to the nation Nehru once referred to India's manifest destiny to become the 'third or fourth' most powerful nation in the world.

Perhaps not surprisingly, nowhere in official statements and publications is the word 'power' quantified or discussed. One may forgive politicians and elder statesman a degree of rhetorical excess, but even in India's large (and growing) security/foreign policy literature, the terms 'great' and 'regional' are used without precision as if they are interchangeable.[2] As noted in the previous chapter, more often than not the term power is equated in India with a particular martial logic and military success without any resulting economic dimensions.[3]

Great powers and middle powers: global vs. regional capabilities

Berridge and Young have argued that a great power is a state with hegemonic powers working in defence of 'special interests' involving the management of the world system.[4] This global managerial function is a crucial aspect of the definition: it denotes a state at or near the top of an international hierarchy of states, capable of setting the international agenda and maintaining systemic order either alone, or through collective action with other great powers. Although the term 'great power' has subsequently become confused with the expression 'superpower',[5] great powers must have a capacity to act globally. A state's capacity to act globally also has a clear economic dimension to it. Within much of the literature on international political economy, emphasis is placed upon the role powerful states play in underwriting economic regimes, and ensuring that lesser states comply with norm-bound economic behaviour.

Furthermore, global reach cannot be defined in terms that simply limit power to military capability, or to military 'power projection'. Even in its particular nineteenth-century usage, 'great powers' were invariably states with global economic, commercial and indeed cultural hegemony. Military strength alone is not enough to ensure 'great power status'. As we have seen in the case of the Soviet Union, an attempt to sustain a global military reach without a dynamic and growing economy can lead to political collapse and global disengagement.[6]

What then of non-great powers? Within an international system as a whole, great powers act upon lesser powers as subjects. Baldur Nayar has referred to subject powers as the mere 'objects' of great power policy: without leverage to influence the shape of the international system.[7] Yet it follows that if the international state system consists of a hierarchy, not all the subject states are themselves equal, but are further differentiated in terms of power and their overall ability to resist and influence great powers. It is at this juncture that the term 'middle power' is introduced into the literature.

A middle power is essentially a regional power, unable to sustain a global role, but dominant within a particular regional context.

Nayar defines 'middle power' as a state that has enough capability 'to foreign policy autonomy within a specific region, an ability to lay claim to regional primacy, and 'the rights to police and uphold a particular regional order which may at times significantly diverge from great power interests.' To some commentators the term 'region' has presented some difficulties; does it, for example, refer to a geographical, cultural or a political subsystem? Is such regional identity self-evident, self-elected, or does it to an extent remain arbitrary? Nayar, following Wight,[8] defines a region as being a 'geographically restricted area culturally united but often politically divided', an idea that is closely related to the Buzan and Rizvi concept of 'security complex'. I propose to combine the two terms and apply them to help explain events throughout South Asia.

India as a middle power?

Thus defined, India appears to have good grounds to claim 'middle' power status but not yet 'great power' capability, i.e. its position of regional supremacy is not yet matched by real global influence in terms of military reach and also in terms of economic importance. New Delhi may well aspire to global influence, but has yet to claim it. Much of the literature on 'middle powers' (such as Brazil, for example) stresses that such states may seek to graduate further up the hierarchy of states. At the end of the 1970s, Mellor noted that 'middle powers' refer to a series of 'rising political, economic and military' states that because of their 'large aggregate size' indicate that they 'will eventually play a global role'. To do so, states must augment their power capabilities[9] and must (a) accept the basic principles and values that underpin the current world system and (b) be tacitly accepted as bona fide great powers by those states currently enjoying great power status. Bull has referred to the dangers of adjustment that follow from the 'promotion' of states to great power status – leading to possible resistance: 'the security dilemma within the international system is such that [existing] great powers may well resist the emergence of others', or equally as serious, 'subject' states may fail to recognise a specific state's claims to great power status.

If this terminology is used to address the concrete examples of South Asia, we appear to be on familiar ground. Yet arguably there are still difficulties in allotting the term 'middle power' automatically and uncritically to explain India's regional policy since 1971. The definition of a middle power is still a multi-dimensional one, which combines economic and political strength with military capability. It follows from the discussions on India's political and economic difficulties that, on close examination, even its claims to regional supremacy can be summed up as being one-dimensional: based upon military projection alone. Moreover, military commitments (modelled on Bangladesh, and badly applied to Sri Lanka in 1987) are not so much part of an attempt to positively restructure external relations, but are generally reactive and poorly thought through. Invariably India has been compelled to act through domestic weakness, and an extension of domestic concerns. This was indeed true of the 1971 Bangladesh war, however skilfully India acted on Pakistan's weakness. Moreover, as already discussed, the collapse of the Indo-Sri Lankan Accord raises serious questions about the ability – and indeed the legitimacy – of Indian actions within the region.

Moreover, within India's elite there is a marked divergence between the rhetoric of power and the realities of that power. Rajiv Gandhi initiated the Indo-Sri Lankan Accord with the remarks that 'the agreement is a major landmark in the four decades of India's freedom. It is an agreement that does not have a parallel anywhere in the world'. Yet just four months into the accord it became clear that India's real abilities were much limited.

The Indo-Sri Lankan fiasco is indicative of one major drawback to India's regional policy. In *The Anarchical Society*, Bull argued that great power status relied upon the acceptance of that status by other great powers, and by lesser states subject to great power management. It is possible to extend this caveat to the term 'middle power': a middle power must be recognised by other states within the region as a paramount power, otherwise the claim is based upon coercion and diplomatic intimidation. Throughout the previous chapters it has been shown that India's 'large aggregate size' has not automatically advanced its claims to regional pre-eminence, and that many of the smaller states have submitted to India's claims with great reluctance, and often with the accusation that they have been bullied. At the first opportunity, they have appealed to extra-regional actors for help.

Given Pakistan's size and history, Pakistan's attitude to India is not in itself surprising. Of all the states of South Asia, it has been Pakistan's consistent refusal to succumb to India's dominance that has most irritated New Delhi, and has cast Pakistan in the capacity of 'spoiler'. Pakistan has refused to concede to New Delhi on the grounds of national security, alleging that India has never yet reconciled itself to the creation of a Pakistani state, and has never once wavered from a single-minded obsession with undoing partition.

The entire basis of the Indo-Sri Lankan Accord was that of implied threat and unattainable objectives. Although the Maldives turned to India to ask for help in November 1988, they had first turned towards the Sri Lankan government for help.[10] As soon as the Indians had dispatched over 1,000 paratroopers the Gayoom government was reported to be 'grateful but alarmed' and urged them to be returned as soon as possible. In 1989 following the trial of the coup leaders, Gayoom called for a 'collective security' doctrine based upon the UN and the Security Council, despite clear Indian offers to come to a comprehensive security arrangement. These sentiments are found elsewhere within the region, even within sections of the Bhutanese court. The net effect of such regional mistrust makes the prospects for a collective security arrangement centred upon Indian primacy impossible, and yet India will not accept anything else.

If India's claims to middle power status are questionable in terms of their regional legitimacy, and sustainability, it follows that India's claims to nascent great power status must also be re-examined. Nayar noted in 1978 that 'India is a middle power with great power ambition since given its size, population, strategic location and historical past, India cannot *but* aspire to great power status'.[11]

Yet such ambitions fall foul of India's ambivalent position within the world, with one face staring forward into the future where its potential will have been realised, the other looking back into domestic poverty and regional instability. It is only at this point that the full dilemma of India's position in the closing years of the twentieth century becomes clear. With the ending of the Cold War, and with the transformation of US–Russian global relations, many of India's previous policies are redundant. Yet attempts to derive a new consensus over domestic, regional and foreign policy issues occurring at a time when, in terms of domestic politics, India's elite consensus over core nationalist values has almost disintegrated, and its institutional processes of government are clogged by ethnic and regional tensions. The growth of Hindu chauvinism within India is having direct repercussions on regional politics. It is not even necessary for a Hindu party to come to power to ensure that certain aspects of their programme are taken up by weak coalitional governments, anxious to retain their electoral support. In early 1996 for example, the Rao government turned down an offer from the Benazir Bhutto government for 'full and frank' discussions on Kashmir. This was despite having stated earlier that India would respond to any unconditional Pakistani overtures. The reasons for the Indian decision lay in the timing of the offer from Islamabad: Rao and the Congress were in the run-up to a general election, in which national security was emerging as a key issue. The Indian government was anxious not to appear as if it was offering concessions to Pakistan.

Finally, the termination of the old Cold War linkages between South Asia and the wider international system may well *downgrade* the region's significance compared to other regions, such as the Middle East, the so-called Pacific Basin, or even Europe. Such disengagement make it less likely that foreign powers could influence South Asian affairs should some form of emergency or crisis occur between India and Pakistan. In 1965, and to a limited extent in 1971, the United States and the USSR were able to bring some pressure to bear upon India and Pakistan. It is not clear whether in 1997 or 1998, such pressure would have much effect. A 1996 publication by the Rand Corporation noted the probable failure of the international community to decisively intervene in any future Indo-Pak conflict.[12]

Indo-Pak nuclear ambitions and nuclear strategy

The tendency to equate 'power' with military capability alone has profound consequences for the future stability of the region, especially given Pakistan's refusal to concede to Indian primacy. India and Pakistan stand at the centre of a conventional arms race that, since 1974, has threatened to go nuclear with the deployment of a nuclear device followed by the continual proliferation of more and more nuclear weapon systems. Between 1980 and 1990, Indian defence expenditure increased by 250 per cent. In 1993 India remained one of the largest importers of weapons in the world, despite strict economic conditionality. Yet as a proportion of its

GNP, and in terms of its per capita spending, Pakistan continues to have the highest defence budget in the region.

Throughout most of its history, Pakistan's level of expenditure has been supported by a combination of military (or military-backed) governments, and concessional aid and 'soft loans' from the United States. Given the uncertainties over the future of US–Pakistan relations, the fear that India will move into a position of overwhelming conventional superiority has suggested to some strategists that what Pakistan needs – and needs urgently – is an atomic bomb, to level India's obvious size.

Since the early 1970s, sections of the Pakistan military have stressed both the counter-value and the counter-force utility of nuclear weapons: that is, as weapons of fear against large and vulnerable civilian targets in India, and for battlefield use against a conventionally superior foe. Moreover, Stephen Cohen has argued that the Pakistani doctrine of 'offensive defence' – seen in the context of conventional wars with India – could easily accommodate a strategic doctrine of first or pre-emptive nuclear strikes against Indian nuclear facilities or rather large massings of mechanised Indian infantry on the Pakistan border.[13]

There are also clear signs that sections of India's military (and their political masters) want to acquire atomic weapons, and in anticipation of deployment, have already developed aspects of a pre-emptive nuclear strategy. Throughout the 1996 campaign, the BJP made several statements related to defence and the need for India to develop and to deploy nuclear weapons. This desire is in spite of having the conventional edge on Pakistan. It should not be surprising that in both India and Pakistan strategic planners assume that an opponent would use a nuclear weapon to underscore a sudden pre-emptive, conventional attack on either Kashmir or Azad Kashmir.[14] The discussion of actual nuclear doctrine has been remarkably absent within both India and Pakistan. Apart from the official options school (discussed below) the Indian debate reveals two other clearly identified camps: the 'great power minimum deterrence' group and the 'war fighting group'. It seems reasonable to assume that such groups also exist within Pakistan.

The first group – the minimum deterrence school – believe that there would be little relationship between nuclear deterrence in South Asia and Western literature on vertical proliferation. That is, it would not be necessary for India to become involved in increasingly complex and sophisticated systems such as assured second-strike capabilities, hardened silos and increasingly expensive C3 (Command, Control and Communication) equipment. Recently one commentator pointed out that: 'the strategic doctrines of nuclear war that are applicable to the developed world are not quite relevant here [in India]. Concepts like massive retaliation, assured second strike, graduated response do not apply to third world scenarios'.[15] It is believed that a few deployments – either on a strategic wing of the airforce or on an adapted liquid fuel missile – will be enough to underscore India's defence commitments without risks of further escalation.[16] The logic of the minimum deterrence school is that the use of a bomb lies as much in its political symbolism than in its actual credibility to be used. Following actual deployment, there is very little need to work out any particular strategy, since actual deployment is premised on the belief that the weapon will never be used. Its mere existence will deter any attack.

The war fighting school, however, believe that India should deploy immediately (and should have deployed after India's first test in 1974), and that once deployment has taken place, India must accept the logic of deterrence and press on to add expensive additions to stockpiles, and continually update the strategies of when and how nuclear force will be used in response to Pakistani deployment, and the evolution of Pakistani strategic thinking. Interestingly enough, the war fighting school assume that Pakistan (or, from the Pakistan side, India) already has the bomb. The minimum deterrence school are criticised for failing to appreciate the link between deployment, strategic doctrine and credibility. Moreover it is argued that given India's security environment *vis-à-vis* Pakistan and China it is extremely unlikely that a relatively small weapons system would suffice to compel deterrence.

It is argued that the sophistication of conventional weapons means that the minimum deterrence school make assumptions that are far too naive. The complexities of Indian and Pakistani air defences would make a nuclear airstrike difficult, while simple missile technology would have to be carefully placed to ensure maximum deterrence – and this would raise issues for both countries. For India to cover both Pakistan and China would mean deploying intermediate range ballistic missiles (IRBM) in some of its most politically unstable areas (the north-east), while because of Pakistan's territorial depth, the only locations that would be safe from possible attack would put missile sites up against the Afghan–Iranian border.

Even before the 1974 peace nuclear explosion (PNE), the Indo-Pak nuclear game of 'yes we have, no we don't' was curiously asymmetrical, despite common security doctrines. Pakistan desired an atomic device in order to finally contain the Indian military modernisation programme. Sections of India's political elite wanted the bomb, not necessarily to intimidate Pakistan (although this would have been an added bonus), but to point at China, and – more crucially – to symbolically underscore its aspirations to be a great power. This asymmetry in Indian and Pakistan calculations remains. Obviously if Pakistan was to deploy first, India would react immediately, but Pakistan's nuclear goals are only part of the complex motive that propels India's nuclear ambitions. One clear motive is the belief that great powers are also nuclear powers, and that nuclear powers – enthroned in the Security Council of the UN – have 'special interests' in the management of global affairs. Such sentiments are expressed by many self-proclaimed 'Third World' writers. Ali Mazrui believes that to insist that non-nuclear states should renounce access to nuclear weapons is to deny these states access to the essential symbols of an apparent modernity.[17]

Based upon the dubious authenticity of Nixon's remark about China, some Indian policy makers believe that although the United States can ignore over 900 million Indians at the onset of the New World Order, it would be difficult to ignore over 900 million Indians with nuclear weapons. Are nuclear weapons a short cut to global influence? And if so, does India have the technological capability to develop and deploy them? What would it cost, economically and diplomatically, to possess them? Would a nuclear weapons programme detract further from the wider priorities of industrial and economic development? And what would be the effects of a nuclear India on China and Pakistan, and the wider international community?

The response of the smaller South Asian states to a nuclear arms race within the region would be to increase their support for a nuclear free zone, and to articulate their opposition within the international forums of the UN, NAM and the Commonwealth. Nepal has tried since the mid-1970s to sell its idea of a 'peace zone' and would strongly resist the deployment of nuclear weapons, as would Bhutan. Sri Lanka would be particularly concerned about an Indian bomb, because of the consequences of its own minority problem, and because of its implications for the Indian Ocean. Such states, including Bangladesh, would have no immediate benefits from any mutual defence agreements with India: a nuclear India would increase all of their fears and would probably involve general appeals to the wider international community for security guarantees. The wider political reverberations would be endless because of the NPT. While India is determined to stand by its earlier decision not to sign the NPT, New Delhi is clearly reluctant to flaunt international opinion and actually deploy a weapons system. In 1983 Sen Gupta concluded that: 'In sum a nuclear India will have to face at least for some time, a hostile West, a frigid USSR, a perturbed China, an angry Pakistan, and a cluster of fearful smaller states.'[18]

In early 1996, rumours that the Indian government were preparing a second atomic test at the Pakoram site in Rajasthan were firmly denied by the government. Despite Indian claims that it was 'cleaning its facilities', some analysts believed that the activities at the test site were an elaborate attempt to test international reaction to any test in the future.

Pakistan: the weak link?

Given the fact that some Indian strategists believe in the political status of the bomb, and that since 1974 India has generally pursued a diplomatic strategy of preserving its options, it could be argued that India poses the most immediate threat to the non-nuclear status of South Asia. Yet – paradoxically – the key weakness in the chain of nuclear proliferation for South Asia is Pakistan, because of the severity of its security complex against India's conventional military profile. The only way out of this conundrum is either for Pakistan to receive a watertight nuclear guarantee from a nuclear power (the United States, or possibly China), or to persuade India to mutually forgo the nuclear option altogether *as well* as to open the way for conventional arms limitation talks. Such proposals, that tie New Delhi to Islamabad but do not require any response from Beijing, are not what the Indians wish to hear. Evidence for this comes from India's responses to the numerous Pakistani proposals aimed at opening up regional nuclear installations for inspection, outlawing pre-emptive strikes against each other's nuclear installations, forgoing the use of a nuclear first-strike strategy, and ultimately planning to declare the entire zone of South Asia a nuclear free zone. India will co-operate with anything short of giving up the option to deploy, and yet it is that very option itself that threatens Pakistan. New Delhi's official doctrine under the Rajiv Gandhi, V. P. Singh, and the 1991–96 Rao administrations, is to reserve the options to deploy nuclear weapons conditional on Pakistan moves, but not to forgo the nuclear option just to satisfy Islamabad. Under the Rao government, the Indians have moved to deploy the missile systems such as the Prithvi, and to continue the development of the intermediate Agni system, in contravention of the US-led attempts, via the MTCR, to prevent the proliferation of such technology. Any future BJP government would be very robust in this regard, and is politically committed to developing and deploying nuclear weapons. In response to these developments, Pakistan falls between the devil and the deep blue sea: it cannot get New Delhi to categorically reject the bomb, it cannot get the United States to underwrite its security, and it is condemned by United States administrations for buying foreign missile systems, such as the recent M-11 systems from China. In the early 1980s, Stephen Cohen rather candidly mused that: 'it is an open question whether the new mutual dependencies that will be created between the United States and Pakistan will in the long run enhance or weaken Pakistan's security'.[19] The answer, that has been emerging since the signing of the Geneva Accords in 1988–89, and the collapse of Afghanistan into a series of warring factions, is that it has weakened Pakistan's security, because US support was premised upon a special set of circumstances that went against the trend of a declining US–Pakistan relationship throughout the 1970s.

South Asia and the NPT

The key to eliminating nuclear weapons from the South Asian equation is a security regime that satisfies both India and Pakistan. This would seem, to all intents and purposes, impossible. From the onset of the nuclear age, there existed a general consensus amongst the nuclear powers (with the exception of China after 1964) that the horizontal proliferation of weapons into the hands of more and more states would greatly add to global instability.[20] Thus the United States, Britain, France and the Soviet Union agreed to draw up an international treaty aimed at preventing the testing and developing of nuclear weapons by non-nuclear powers. The treaty, adopted by the UN General Assembly in 1968, sanctioned the use of nuclear technology for civilian purposes under the international supervision of the International Atomic Energy Association (IAEA). Yet the agreement outlawed attempts by non-nuclear states to 'divert' nuclear materials and information towards a weapons programme. A non-nuclear state was defined as those states that had not 'manufactured and exploded' a nuclear device prior to January 1967. Elaborate institutions were set up to ensure that no more states would cross the nuclear threshold.

India objected to the treaty because it 'froze in' the permanent nuclear powers and restricted the sovereign rights of other states to defend their national security. The treaty of 1968 made no specified provisions for collective security against non-nuclear states threatened by states already in possession of nuclear weapons. In this respect India was once again conscious of China's nuclear explosion in 1964 and the threats that a nuclear China posed. To assume that, in the event of another border clash with China, the international community would come to the rescue of India would to be highly irresponsible, and contradicted India's fundamental principle of foreign policy, namely self-reliance.

India also objected to the NPT on the grounds that it did not differentiate between horizontal proliferation, the graduation of more and more states to nuclear weapons, and vertical proliferation, the acquisition by the already existing nuclear powers of more and more nuclear weapons systems. This difference is a critical one given the perception of India's foreign policy elite that the NPT was not just an arms control agreement but an arms reduction agreement.[21] Yet the finished document nowhere compelled the nuclear powers into making arms reductions at all.

Prior to the NPT, India had supported and initiated various calls within the NAM to limit and *remove* all nuclear weapons.[22] India's policy approach, outlined at the eighteenth National Disarmament Conference in 1962–63, was that any treaty that dealt with nuclear weapons must do so comprehensively, it must eliminate them within a specified time subject to satisfactory guarantees, and must not merely reflect the strategic concerns of the great powers. Sen Gupta has summarised India's refusal to sign the treaty on three grounds: 'the imbalance of obligations between nuclear and non-nuclear powers, inadequate security guarantees [for the non-nuclear powers] and discrimination for the use of peace nuclear explosions (PNE)'.[23] These views were reiterated at New York in 1995 at length. India's policy towards the NPT not only ensured that Pakistan would not sign, but led to international speculation that there was some ulterior motive: the desire to join the 'nuclear club' of the five permanent members, or to acquire the symbolism of great power status as a short-cut to international ambition.

India's decision to conduct a PNE in 1974 – the first nuclear test by a previously non-nuclear state since China – reinforced this speculation and led to international condemnation. India's insistence that it was a 'peaceful' device was seen as being particularly duplicitous since it did not jeopardise any extant agreements India had signed with foreign countries to assist it with its civilian nuclear power programme.[24]

Like so much of India's posturing on global issues, it would be absurd to pretend that an ideological objection to nuclear weapons was not also part of a realistic policy aimed at reserving India's *option* to deploy such weapons. In 1986, the *enfant terrible* of India's security analysts K. Subrahmanyam argued that

> nations that are not signatories of the NPT have reserved their options ... and have as much ethical, legal and strategic justification to have nuclear weapons as [the] signatories ... Proliferating nations preaching non-proliferation create distrust as to their intentions in practising coercive diplomacy and dominance over the rest of the world.[25]

India's position on the NPT implies that New Delhi is in favour of other states advancing similar arguments. Does this mean that India, like China in the 1960s, supports nuclear proliferation? Many commentators believe that this is not the case. The late Hedely Bull noted with reference to France, China and India that

> while they have sometimes justified proliferation with arguments that apply to others as well as themselves, they have at no time argued in favour of general and complete nuclear proliferation. [They] have been principally concerned to remove the obstacles to their own inclusion into the nuclear weapon's club.[26]

India's objections to the NPT are based simply upon power: the desire to have the right to be a nuclear state if it wishes, or if circumstances dictate.

It is possible that, if granted the status of a nuclear power India could be brought into the 'fire break' and co-opted into preventing further violations of the NPT regime. This – with various other conditions – would be the price that New Delhi would try to exact for forgoing the deployment of nuclear weapons. In 1974 George H. Quester noted that 'if we [the US] concede that India has made it safely into the ranks of the nuclear explosives nations (sic) New Delhi may still not wish to allow many other nations into these ranks'[27] because, like all the other great powers, it may well begin to resist the dilution of its influence through having to share it with other, subsequent, nuclear states.[28] Yet Pakistan, technically a threshold state, although it has never acknowledged a nuclear test, would not tolerate the sanctioning of an Indian bomb, however theoretical it was, regardless of the security arrangements offered by the United States.[29] Its response would be to move rapidly to develop and deploy its own device, which would force India to respond in kind regardless of any previous understandings with the wider international community. The dilemma facing anyone anxious to prevent nuclear deployment in South Asia, and to prevent subsequent nuclear escalation and proliferation of nuclear weapons systems, is that the security complex of the region is extremely tense, and profoundly asymmetrical. As noted by one scholar: 'Fundamental asymmetry pushes India and Pakistan to define their national security in fundamentally different ways and makes the tasks of establishing common security needs particularly difficult'.[30]

The costs of the nuclear option

Let me assume, for the moment, that the international community would sanction some form of selective proliferation within South Asia, or would probably – after some months of high rhetoric – accept the deployment of weapons by India and Pakistan. Could India and Pakistan afford such a deployment, and what effect would this have upon their current developmental policies? The 'guns versus grains' argument about defence expenditure is inconclusive, and often uncritically assumes that the relationship between defence expenditure and development is automatically inverse.[31] The World Bank noted with obvious displeasure that 'military expenditure has increased more than twice as fast as per capita incomes in the developing world since 1960': but is such expenditure obviously non-productive?

That military spending has distorted economic growth and redirected scarce resources away from productive investment appears, superficially, to be truer for Pakistan than for India, especially for the first decade after independence, yet even then the evidence is speculative and counterfactual. Indian defence expenditure may well have grown, but recent figures suggest that government spending on defence has declined as a proportion of government expenditure from 31 per cent in 1964 to an average of 20 per cent throughout the 1970s. In 1988 it stood at 19.3 per cent. This compares favourably to the Pakistan figures of 39.9 per cent (1972) and 29.5 per cent (1988), and Sri Lanka's figures of 9.6 per cent in 1988.[32] Recent increases, especially in India and Pakistan from 1994 onwards, have bucked the trend, with the Rao government attempting to cut defence expenditure in 1995–96.

These resources might well have been invested into export-based industries and have resulted in real gains in foreign exchange, or subsequent foreign exchange used to purchase expensive Western arms might well have been freed for capital goods imports, but it could just as well have ended up in the public sector being invested in under-utilised and inefficient stock. Moreover, while a considerable literature has grown up that identifies military expenditure as inflationary because of pricing and demand rigidities, there is little correlation within India whose domestic inflation has been traditionally quite low.

Increased defence spending can have potentially beneficial connotations for an economy, providing jobs within the public sector, and if sufficiently co-ordinated alongside domestic production, providing backward and forward linkages with other public companies. In India, Hindustan Aeronautics has benefited substantially from defence contracts, and has gained access to foreign technologies that would have been costly to develop. And India seems set to begin an arms export drive to help fund the increasing costs of its defence requirements.[33]

That poor states cannot and should not commit themselves to a sophisticated military establishment, including ones that subscribe to the manufacture and deployment of nuclear weapons, is hotly debated. K. Subrahmanyam has dismissed the entire debate as a 'foreign fabrication, a piece of neo-colonial brainwashing',[34] since in the past India's economic growth has been capable of supporting 'necessary increases' in defence outlays as the need arose. Certainly defence spending throughout South Asia has not been excessively out of line with overall economic performance (as has been the case, arguably, in the former Soviet Union or indeed in Israel), but it is also equally misleading to see the contributions of arms expenditure to development in the same way as increases in primary health care, or basic schooling. Moreover there is growing evidence that current military expenditure, coinciding with a period of general economic transition and increased regional insecurity, could well provide growing pressures on scarce investment resources and have distorting effects on overall economic growth, especially under conditionality. There can be no doubt that the extent and degree of Soviet aid towards India's modernisation significantly disguised the real cost of its rearmament and that in current circumstances it may well face increased costs. Likewise, India's desire to move away from Russian procurement will complicate command and operational protocols, and put pressure on future currency reserves. There can be little doubt that arms deals for Jaguar and Mirage fighter-bombers helped contribute to the seriousness of India's balance of payments by the late 1980s.

The same can be said for the degree of concessional US aid to Pakistan, especially during the 1970s. With the present US–Pakistan disengagement over Pakistan's nuclear weapons programme, costs will increase and Pakistan has found its access to American technology severely limited. Both India and Pakistan are now under strict IMF conditionality as to the type and scale of government expenditure. Since India's defence industry still relies upon expensive imports of foreign technology, restrictions on imports and the encouragement of currency devaluations will seriously restrict planned modernisation. In the absence of a sustained drive to sell Indian weapons abroad in which profits are ploughed back into weapons production and research, there can be little doubt that recent increases in defence expenditure would have had more immediate returns if spent on primary health care or education.

Amit Gupta has noted that while India has proved largely incapable of competing with advanced technologies like aircrafts and tanks, it has developed an almost entirely indigenous missile programme. The success of the Prithva (SRBM) and the Agni (IRBM) tests at the end of the 1980s are therefore of immediate significance in circumstances where India's dependence on complex foreign conventional technology elsewhere is increasing. The declining cost of the bomb relative to 'smart' technologies will further tempt both states to deploy it. Quester has noted in a recent article on threshold states that: 'for decades the general worry about global nuclear proliferation has not been that nuclear weapons would prove to be too expensive, but rather that they would be too cheap'.[35]

It has been calculated that a modest weapons programme for India could be funded for around US$ 700 million, which is not out of line with conventional spending, and would probably prove less over time.[36] In the early 1980s Sen Gupta calculated that the costs of developing a fairly sophisticated nuclear weapons system would add an additional 5 per cent of GNP to defence expenditure (increasing it to about 9 per cent GNP).[37] Given Pakistan's lower defence costs in absolute terms, the price estimates for Pakistan would be slightly higher, which might increase defence expenditure towards 10–12 per cent of GNP.

Even if we accept this assumption there are great difficulties in arriving at a cost-benefit analysis of a nuclear weapons programme for either India or Pakistan, since the debate is largely hypothetical and based upon comparisons with conventional expenditure. There is sufficient evidence to support the argument that in the *short term* the option is cheaper. Yet this calculation is premised on the assumption that nuclear deployment in South Asia will be a relatively simple affair, and that it will not involve an arms race, driven by a rapid and sustained vertical proliferation of more accurate and precise weaponry, an assumption made by the minimum deterrence school.

This assumption is highly dubious, since the experience of the conventional arms race shows that a balance of power on the basis of mutual security has been elusive; thus the assumption of a stable nuclear balance (and hence the assumption of cheapness) must be examined further. While there are obvious differences between conventional and nuclear weapons, and care must be taken in extrapolating the dynamics of conventional strategy into the nuclear domain, the assumption of continued nuclear stability following actual deployment is highly unlikely, especially when examined in the light of the region's political history since 1947. It is much more likely that the two states will be locked into a nuclear arms race. At every stage of Pakistan's rearmament after 1979 India protested that the types of weapon being supplied were far in excess of Islamabad's requirements. India has attempted tirelessly to match specific weapons systems and to fill in perceived conventional weaknesses. India's search for a deep-strike aircraft, which led to the expensive Western arms deals with Britain and France, was based upon the fears of Pakistan's American-supplied F-16s. A nuclear arms race in South Asia would then, on the face of it, involve vertical proliferation and would dramatically destabilise the region, having knock-on effects in China and the Middle East, *if* the states were themselves able to sustain it.

Nuclear deployment and international sanctions

Let us now turn to the possibility that the international community will continue to aggressively police the NPT, and will continue to use sanctions to prevent any more states crossing the nuclear threshold. How successful can they be? In the absence of any collective security arrangement between India and Pakistan, is there anything the wider international community can do to prevent a sustained nuclear arms race within the sub-continent? The intriguing factor about South Asia is that although the psychological and military conditions are now favourable to supporting the deployment of nuclear weapons, there is still some doubt as to whether India and Pakistan could sustain a nuclear arms race in the face of international sanctions authorised by the NPT, and historically supported by both Soviet and American domestic policy. The Achilles' heel for both states would be that sustained vertical proliferation would involve access to sophisticated Western technology that would not be forthcoming unless both states guaranteed their non-nuclear status.

The commitment of the United States and the Soviet Union to the NPT hardened appreciably after the mid-1980s, especially with regard to 'threshold' states. China has also been attending the various review conferences on the treaty as an observer since 1985. At both the 1985 and the 1990 conferences, it has been noted that 'a great number of countries throughout the world genuinely welcome a barrier to further nuclear proliferation' even in circumstances in which horizontal proliferation is not linked to the controversy of vertical proliferation. Again, at the 1995 conference, it was clear that there was a general consensus over the need to limit the number of states with access to nuclear weapons, especially between Washington and Moscow.

There is an essential irony in the current Pakistani position over the nuclear dilemma that escapes most commentators: Pakistan's determined resolve to get the bomb has led to the current US arms embargo, which has in turn exacerbated Pakistan's sense of insecurity. By undermining Pakistan's external supply of weapons and aid, the current US sanctions policy has merely furthered the determination of previous regimes to get hold of an atomic device. The most obvious move for any US administration would be to resume sufficient arms sales to reassure, as in 1954, that it is committed to Pakistan's territorial integrity. Unlike 1954, it will have to do so with sufficient conviction for Pakistan to believe it, and to make the situation more difficult still, US aid would take place in a domestic arena in which Islamic groups express anti-Western sentiments.

Such a policy would lead to further outrage and consternation from New Delhi. The initial US response to the PNE in 1974 was remarkably tame, much less than the British reaction. While India has been the subject of US technical embargoes, these have often had less to do with the threat of their 'deflection' from industrial to military use, than the fear that they would find themselves in the hands of the Soviets. Pakistan's nuclear industry has proved much more vulnerable to sanctions than India's. In 1971 India had signed a trilateral agreement between the United States and the IAEA to safeguard its civilian programmes, but a significant part of its programme established by Dr Bhabha and the Atomic Energy Commission, involving co-operation with the Canadians, was unsafeguarded and almost certainly provided the plutonium used for the 1974 test. Thus even if the United States was capable of buying Pakistan's support, India would attempt to exact a much higher price. New Delhi would probably demand not just US weapons at rates identical to Pakistan, but also greater access to industrial technology, and even probably some higher profile within the UN. Yet until the root of the insecurity between India and Pakistan is removed, such policies will only further the conventional arms race (even if with sufficient alacrity to prevent the desire for nuclear weapons), and more seriously, there remains the possibility of either state acquiring some device behind the back of any US administration, or the powers of the U.N.

The effectiveness of safeguards

The problems about how effective safeguards are in preventing states going nuclear were discussed at the time of the NPT. Most IAEA safeguards apply to nuclear fuel reprocessing and not enrichment, since it is extremely difficult to 'divert' plutonium from spent fuel rods into a weapons programme, while enrichment presents profound technological difficulties.[38] Despite continual allegations that plutonium has been removed from the KANUPP plant in Pakistan, there is little concrete evidence to prove this.[39] In 1980 it was reported that 'Pakistan was still unable to design and build its own nuclear power plants, although she has demonstrated its ability to restart, fuel and operate KANUPP'.[40] Indigenous production of heavy water and fuel rods have all been voluntarily placed under IAEA safeguards.

Earlier, under the regime of Benazir's father, the Americans were successful in pressurising the French to withdraw from a deal to construct a nuclear reprocessing plant signed in 1973, the CHASMA plant near Karachi. The French withdrew in 1979 but only after most of the blueprints had been delivered to the Pakistani scientists. It is alleged that CHASMA has a small-scale 'experimental' enrichment process that could provide material for a fusion bomb. Pakistan has an operational reprocessing plant and CANDU power station (KANUPP) near Karachi. The station burns 'natural' uranium (U 235) and the fuel is safeguarded. Pakistan also has further research facilities at PINSTECH, near Nilore, which are now believed to be capable of fuel enrichment.

Various scare stories about damaged cameras and poor monitoring equipment at KANUPP significantly underestimate the stringency of IAEA procedures. What safeguards cannot automatically prevent (at least as they were conceived within the NPT) is the determined efforts of a regime to assemble expertise and equipment from a variety of foreign sources to provide the basis for an indigenous bomb programme. Although the 'London Club' organisation was formed in 1976 to ensure that nuclear suppliers could monitor the sales of nuclear-related technologies to non-nuclear states this is not as clear-cut a process as is often suggested, since much of the technology involved is so-called 'dual-use'. More seriously, as discussed above, the logic of international agreement is that states are clearly defined entities accountable to each other. Pakistan is a complex state–society amalgam, in which several decision-making processes parallel each other, some of which are unaccountable and indeed probably unidentifiable.

Pakistani ingenuity appears to have laid hold of some very sophisticated technology – mainly through industrial espionage or simple theft – such as gas centrifugal capabilities.[41] As recently as 1990 a Pakistani national was arrested in the United States for attempting to purchase high-temperature furnaces from the US company Consarc. Corp. New Jersey.[42] This followed an announcement in 1988 by the infamous Dr Khan that Pakistan now has the technology to enrich natural uranium to about 90 per cent of weapons grade material.

The recent US embargo against Pakistan was carried out because of apparent evidence that Pakistan was clandestinely acquiring nuclear technology inspite of American support (i.e. from about 1973 onwards, before the Indian test), and for consistently refusing to open up its nuclear research facilities to international inspection. Even following the waivering of the Symington Amendment, the Americans continued to call on Pakistan to renounce its ambitions. Although such statements were dismissed by the Indians as a careful ploy to disguise actual US–Pakistan co-operation, there is no evidence to prove that Pakistan was a special candidate for 'selective' proliferation, or that the Americans were themselves insincere about their policies.

Official denials by Benazir Bhutto before a joint sitting of Congress that 'Pakistan did not have a bomb and had no intention of building one',[43] were ignored by the Bush presidency, and contradicted later by a statement issued by the then deposed prime minister, Nawaz Sharif in 1993. The Benazir Bhutto government sought to assure the United States that Pakistan's nuclear programme was entirely civilian, aimed at coping with its increasing energy demands and its developmental needs. As early as 1989 a report prepared by the US Foreign Affairs and National Defence Division noted that:

> Under President Zia, Pakistan has moved apparently to the brink of a capability to build nuclear weapons, or possibly even to deploy a small number of nuclear weapons. The nuclear weapons option enjoys broad support within policy making circles and among the public at large.[44]

Of the two routes that a state can take towards acquiring nuclear weapons – reprocessing and enrichment – Pakistan is believed to have taken the latter one, a process that India has apparently yet to master.[45] It is believed that international sanctions, led by the United States, have proved crucial for directing Pakistan's research efforts in favour of enrichment, and hence towards clandestine methods of procurement. It was widely believed that illegal plutonium transfers, intercepted in Russia in the early 1990s, were intended for Pakistani buyers.

Certainly Z. Bhutto was determined to undermine the NPT by utilising Western technological support, Middle Eastern finance, and co-opting skills from China. Ashok Kapor speculates that following his death in 1979, General Zia merely continued the project, and decided to pursue the scheme without an actual test. Sen Gupta has argued that without a series of testings it is almost impossible to effectively weaponise a system. Up to fifty tests may be carried out to conclude the designs for one warhead. Other specialists argue that there is no need to test a weapons system before its actual use. George Quester notes that the bomb that was dropped on Hiroshima had not been previously tested. While it is possible that the Pakistanis have asked the Chinese (or, as some Indians suggest, the Americans) to test a device, it remains unlikely.

Much of the work on the Pakistani bomb is pure speculation, and the assumption that it exists (or worse, that it is already being stockpiled) is greatly exaggerated. Yet by the middle of the 1990s, Pakistan is widely believed to have a 'bomb in the basement', wherein it has 'produced but not detonated a nuclear weapon and has made a practice of keeping the warheads disassembled … perhaps requiring only a few turns of the screwdriver to complete assembly.'[46] However, there is little chance that such speculation can be verified. Recent speculation has concerned the existence of a nuclear stockpile. A report in the British press in March 1996 stated that US intelligence now believes that Pakistan could be preparing for its first nuclear test in Baluchistan.

If 'many of the hypothetical scenarios concerning the development of an Islamic bomb are totally misleading and unrealistic in their conceptualisation, their basic arguments, and in their conclusion',[47] the same argument can be used about Pakistani speculation over the Indian bomb, in spite of the 1974 PNE. The Sarabhai Profile[48] of 1970–80 was a ten-year integrated programme of developing nuclear civilian research and remote sensing/satellite technologies for India, the key element of which was a 'peaceful' explosion. While this was successful, and was to many analysts a 'disguised weapons programme' it cannot be automatically assumed that India has been able to press on with the development of a nuclear weapons arsenal – although it often is. To many commentators since then, the test was premature,[49] since India suffered under international embargoes on sophisticated technological equipment which postponed further tests and design refinements. Such vulnerability remains, as revealed by India's sensitivity to Russia's initial decision, in 1993, to cancel sales of cryogenic rockets to the Indian space agency.

Sanctions affect not just any potential weapons programme, but also India's civilian power programme. Although India's nuclear expertise is more broad-based than Pakistan's, and has led to the domestic construction of several plutonium reactors (the R-5 stations), and an experimental fast breeder programme, much of the programme is suffering from slippage and delays in the completion and commissioning of plants. India has one unsafeguarded output of Pu-239 from the CIRUS reactor.[50] India is supplied with enriched uranium for the CIRUS reactor from the United States, but has continually complained about the delays in delivery. An agreement with France to replace US supplies has recently been superseded by an agreement with China. Since 1988 India's heavy water projects have also fallen behind schedule. Currently India plans to create a civilian power capacity of 1,200 MW by the beginning of the next century, yet of the five nuclear power stations announced in 1985, only three have been commissioned and are reported to be functioning well under capacity.

These technical bottlenecks will have created some difficulty in the amount of the production of Pu-239 to be used for fissile weapons. It has already been noted that India appears to suffer from all the difficulties of enrichment associated with developing a fusion bomb (U-235). While associated technology such as delivery and guidance systems in both India and Pakistan had reached high levels of sophistication, the availability of nuclear materials for warhead development, and the designs and the development of the warheads themselves are a major constraint on an actual weapons deployment programme, especially one in which the pressure would be to undertake rapid vertical proliferation. There is, then, some evidence that the effectiveness of international sanctions has had some effect in slowing down Indian and Pakistan research on fissile, and in particular, fusion weapons.

None the less, whatever the uncertainty, it seems reasonable to argue that the international community's approach to South Asia as a non-nuclear region is no longer valid. The prospects for some form of meaningful dialogue between India and Pakistan, and between the states of South Asia and the rest of the international community, would be greatly improved if it was accepted that both states are, in effect, nuclear states. The realities of the South African bomb are testimony to the ability of states to acquire technology if they are so determined (although the South African decision to sign the NPT and renounce the bomb is an interesting case study to which I shall return later). Such a decision would clear the way towards thinking what for many people has remained the unthinkable: how can we contain the control of nuclear weapons between India and Pakistan, how can we stop them being used, how can we restore the status quo ante? The beast is out. It is already a question of arms control.[51]

Creating a collective security framework for South Asia

Could US (and international) sanctions, combined with adequate security guarantees, compel a move towards arms control in South Asia, and eventually, a non-nuclear South Asia? Only if the states of South Asia themselves accept the legitimacy of such an arrangement, and complement it with their own policies of confidence-building measures. This, not surprisingly, is the main problem. Many of the arguments presented in this book are premised on the fact that, throughout the coming decade, South Asia will be subject to a whole series of contradictory pressures, some emanating from the international environment, some from purely regional trends, and others from domestic political changes. Much has been made of how the economic interactions at these various levels will create both tensions and opportunities towards further growth and development, although the tone has been one that is predominantly cautious and even at times gloomy. Concerning specific matters of defence and security, the picture is more ambivalent, and requires both Indian and Pakistani elites to 'come clean' about the extent of their nuclear ambitions and to end a period of 'non-weaponised' deterrence by stating their intentions. Confidence-building measures require, more than anything else, transparency.

While the domestic and regional pressures are set to reinforce Indo-Pak misconceptions and maintain high levels of defence expenditure, and while the pressures are themselves capable of maintaining an arms race, the type and scale of this race is still critically dependent upon foreign involvement and support. This is particularly true of a nuclear arms race. External support for both India and Pakistan have fuelled a conventional arms race far in excess of what these two states were capable of producing – the fact that India's reliance was on foreign collaboration in production and not on arms imports merely served to disguise India's dependence.[52] While the dynamics of regional instability would tend to lead to vertical proliferation of nuclear weapons systems, it is unlikely that either state would be able to produce and innovate the technological know-how unless it was based upon further foreign help.

What has happened since 1989 is a process of disengagement in which international 'Cold War' issues have gradually been unwound, in which US and Soviet, now Russian, interests have been redefined both with respect to themselves, and to their so-called client states throughout the world. Although it is possible to exaggerate the areas of international consensus at the end of the Cold War, the NPT review conference illustrated the priority still given to restraining the horizontal proliferation of nuclear weapons. It follows from this that there is a unique opportunity to address the problems of nuclear proliferation in South Asia at the international level, and to rethink and readdress some of the long-standing criticisms that have been made about the NPT by the Non-Aligned Movement, and by India in particular. This rethinking is essential for ensuring that regional attempts to foreclose deployment (based upon a bilateral arrangement between India and Pakistan) can be agreed upon in the very near future.

Of the many criticisms India has of the NPT, three are crucial: that it did not prevent vertical proliferation within the already existing nuclear powers, that it did not open the way towards the eventual total elimination of nuclear weapons, and that – for the duration of the interim period necessary to totally disarm – the security guarantees to defend non-nuclear powers from nuclear powers were inadequate.

Even with the ending of the Cold War, it seems unlikely that the second condition will ever be fulfilled. The Gorbachev era has seen successful arms reduction talks in the European and the Asian theatres, and some weapons systems have been eliminated under the 1987 Intermediate Nuclear Force (INF) treaty, but the commitment to some form of nuclear arsenal remains, and China remains to many (even within India) a pariah state with which it is impossible to come to any real agreement. Even if the status of nuclear weapons as a realistic, useful weapons system is now at an all-time low (reinforced by the experiences of the Gulf war), the world is a long way from actually outlawing them, or so reducing them in status that no state has the desire to obtain them.

On the other hand the ability to place *limits* on vertical proliferation is a real one. Since the first edition of this book, the possibility of states renouncing nuclear capabilities has been demonstrated by South Africa, Ukraine and Khazakstan. Although the ratification of the START talks has proved a slow business, it is clear that genuine attempts to eliminate nuclear arsenals are being made. There is a possibility that the international community could now provide one of the necessary conditions for India to actually sign up with the NPT: the gradual removal of all weapons, but this raises questions for other states about the necessity of retaining nuclear weapons.

One problem remains in the way of India's acceptance of a reworked NPT commitment that would make the elimination of nuclear weapons a distinct possibility: and that is the time frame. In the immediate term, India would need a collective security arrangement that would rely upon the use of extra-regional support – primarily a UN force, ostensibly an American one.[53] While this would be acceptable to Pakistan (and almost every other state within the South Asia region) it remains impossible for India to concede because of its claims to 'middle power/great power status'. It is at this point that the argument returns to the problems of 'one dimensionality' discussed above: the symbolic significance that the atomic bomb has for India's political elite, and the importance of an independent foreign policy that is seen to be free from manipulation and pressure. In some respects this is the most intractable problem. India's criticism of the 1996 proposed Comprehensive Test Ban Treaty once more focused on the absence of any timetable for the total disarmament of already existing nuclear powers.

To renounce the bomb is, for the Indian elite, to renounce any global ambitions. To accept external mediation in times of regional crisis or conflict would be to lose claims to be the regional security manager which, again, is part of the psychological claim India has to being a middle power with global aspirations. While many of these claims have been shown to be unrealistic, they are politically important to India, more so now than at any other time, and to accept a collective security doctrine, either at the level of the UN or under a mutually supportive US defence agreement between India and Pakistan, remains unacceptable, unless it could be attached to a greater role for India within the UN. In other words, it is not that the NPT fails to guarantee the security of the non-nuclear states, it is simply that it prevents them from doing it themselves.

The greatest difficulty here, like so much of India's current thinking on international relations, is to try and change India's conceptualisation of power and influence, away from a military, overtly geo-strategic logic, towards one of economic influence and commerce. Such attempts to do so, however, come up against the economic difficulties that India has been facing since the mid-1970s, and the apparent failure of its economic policies within the region to date. The greatest challenge to Chinese hegemony, if such a challenge has to be made, would lie not in a nuclearised India, but in a dynamic and expansive Indian economy able to influence the economies of the Near East and the Pacific Basin, and to which China would be attracted for reasons of its own modernisation programmes, and its own economic development.

In an interesting paper published in 1987, C. Subrahmanyam noted that India would only ever renounce the nuclear weapon option when there had been a shift in the general global attitudes against nuclear weapons themselves and their supposed influence. He argued that some form of treaty – less along the lines of the NPT and more along those of the 1925 Geneva Protocol outlawing chemical weapons – could 'strip nuclear weapons of their legitimacy, their mystique, and their use as the currency of international power'.[54] While such a transformation in attitudes towards weapons of mass destruction appears to be taking place within international opinion, it is not taking place within India or Pakistan. Both sets of elites still believe 'arguably – that nuclear weapons enhance national security in their external and internal spheres'.[55]

To 'opt' for a non-nuclear status would have to rest upon a domestic consensus within India and Pakistan. This of course returns the entire discussion to the internal political systems of the two main states and the changes that have been taking place within India and Pakistan since the mid-1980s. The 'one-dimensionality' of Indian claims to regional and global influence – an influence based upon military capability and power – is a curious inversion of the Nehruvian view inherited at independence, that influence was to be conveyed through diplomacy and high morals. This change reflects the sad fact that the imagery and symbolism of Nehruvian foreign policy have almost gone. In a much welcomed contribution to the literature on India's foreign policy since 1971, Bradnock noted that:

> throughout the 40 years of independence, India's foreign policy has retained a fundamental consistency of strategic outline which has survived both changes in personal leadership and changes in government – Nehru's Panscheel – are still held up today as the basis of New Delhi's foreign policy today.[56]

Yet undue emphasis upon this continuity draws attention away from the very profound changes that have taken place within India's outlook on the world, and within the world itself. Until this changes, no level of international reassurance can guarantee the security requirements of both India and Pakistan.

Conclusions

The middle class and the ideology that supported Nehru's commitment to 'internationalism' have been undergoing radical changes since the mid-1970s. While there remains an ideological affinity to the aspirations of the UN, there is little belief that as an organisation it is capable of accommodating India's needs. Since the 1971 war, these needs have become increasingly defined in terms of military power and special Indian security interests. Present international changes may revive the Nehruvian language of co-operation and mutual respect, but this language has little value within India, let alone within the emerging discourse of India's political elite. Devi Gowda's emergence as prime minister is interesting in this regard, evidence of the rise of regionalism into a nationalist arena once dominated by a Westernised, anglophile elite. Gowda does not speak Hindi or English, and he is an untouchable in caste terms.

The terrible truth is that the unravelling of India's political system might not only collapse an internal order based upon secularism, parliamentarianism and redistributive economic policies, it could also distance India's ability to share in what Hedley Bull referred to as international society: a series of commonly held cultural values which – if incorporated into a state system – could provide added cohesion, unity and security. State systems have rarely rested upon shared values other than those of threat or coercion. The expansion of international society[57] was ostensibly Western in origin, based upon a legal and diplomatic definition of state behaviour, which in turn was seen as being part of the language of being 'modern'. Bull puts it much more elegantly:

> If contemporary international society does have any cultural basis, this is not any genuinely global culture, but it is rather the culture of so-called modernity ... if we ask what is modernity in culture it is not clear how we can answer this except by saying that it is the culture of the dominant Western powers.[58]

There can be no doubt that Nehru and his generation (as much as Jinnah and Senanayake) were committed to the material benefits of so-called modernity, even to the point of encouraging cultural reforms and changes. This generation has passed on, and although it has been replaced in part by a Western educated middle class, it has also been replaced by something else, something more stridently 'indigenous' and culturally chauvinistic and, apparently, authentic.

If should not be surprising that in Pakistan, fundamentalist religious parties reject not just a capitalist, urban-based economy, but the 'core values' of individualism and consumerism that sustain it. To conceptualise such obscurantism as a new medievalism may seem deeply offensive (or even uninformed) but it seems to many to adequately describe what is happening within some Islamic thinking. How long such thinking will remain out of government remains a moot point.

A 'Hindu India' would suffer from many of the problems and drawbacks encountered by an Islamic Pakistan – a state exclusiveness that affects economic integration by affecting policies, an obscurantism that affects the use and development of scientific knowledge and research, and which fuels the sort of endemic provincial violence that has done so much to undermine the very real gains India and Pakistan have made since independence. It has often been noted that the images and themes of India are to do with 'peace' and inner harmony, in which the country has become – to the Western mind at least – a sort of massive ashram. Such an image disguises one of the most violent societies in the world. As early as 1951 the noted historian and diplomat P. N. Panikkar remarked:

> our vision [of Indian interests] has been obscured by an un-Indian wave of pacifism ... Apart from the Buddhist and Jain heresies [sic] which the good sense of the Hindus rejected long ago, it is not known what religious basis there is in Hinduism for the form of pacificism which has come ... to be associated with the Hindu.[59]

This is not to dismiss indigenous Hinduism as violent, or inferior, but to question the institutional forms in which culture is used by politicians, and how the language and symbols of such a culture can be adapted to deal with India's developmental needs. The tragedy of Pakistan is not that it is Islamic, but that Islam has become the cover for every political fudge and compromise by a discredited and illegitimate elite. An explicit and chauvinistic Hinduism will limit the social and intellectual interchange that has taken place between South Asia and the Western world since the onset of world history, to the mutual benefit of each, and to the gradual development of international society. It will also further the crisis of nation forma-tion and the overwhelming economic rationality and interdepen-dence that must sustain it.

The disintegration of India has been a favourite prediction from many academics and journalists over the years. Such pessimism has usually overlooked the extraordinary dynamism and resilience within India, and the strength of its political elite, and the success of its development programmes. As the 1990s unfold, these predic-tions will be readdressed and reissued to deal with the rise of ethnic-linguistic exclusiveness. The real threat for India is not that the state will disintegrate and 'balkanise' but that the ability of the state to interfere in and organise civil society will falter, and that the state will fail to protect its citizens and to ensure them the material advancements they need.

Notes

1   P. N. Haksar, *India's Foreign Policies and Its Problems*, Orient Long-man, New Delhi, 1989, p. 53.

2   See P. Singh, *India and the Future of Asia*, Progress Publishers, New Delhi, 1966, J. N. Chaudhuri, *India's Problems of National Security in the 1970s*, Vikas, New Delhi, 1973, and D. Kennedy, *The Security of Southern Asia*, Chatto and Windus, London, 1965. See also the interesting Yu T. George, *Intra-Asian International Relations*, Westview Press, Boulder, 1989.

3   In a recent conference paper submitted to the ECPR conference in 1990, a student from the University of Oslo has referred to 'Great Regional Powers' – evidence of the sort of confusing terminology that is rife within this particular area of study.

4   G. Berridge and J. Young, 'What is a Great Power?', *Political Studies*, 36, June 1988, pp. 224–34.

5   This term was first used by W. R. T. Fox in his book *The Superpowers*, London, 1944.

6   Japan is an interesting example of a state that has increasing managerial responsibilities within the world economy, but as yet no military apparatus (or even global foreign policy) through which to undertake those responsibilities. See Kazuo Chiba 'Japan and the New World Order', *The Pacific Review*, 4, 1991, pp. 1–4.

7   See B. R. Nayar, 'A World Role: The Dialectics of Purpose and Power', in J. W. Mellor (ed.), *India: A Rising Middle Power?*, Westview Press, Boulder, 1979.

8   M. Wight, *Power Politics*, University of Leicester, Leicester, 1978.

9   J. S. Nye and R. O. Keohane, *Transnational Relations and World Politics*, Cambridge University Press, Cambridge, 1971.

10 *Far Eastern Economic Review Asia Year Book*, Hong Kong, 1989.

11 Nayar, 'A World Role', in Mellor, *India*, p. 122, emphasis added.

12 Zalmay Khalilzad (ed.), *Strategic Appraisal 1996*, A Report Prepared for the United States Airforce, Rand Corporation, California, 1996.

13 S. Cohen, *The Pakistan Army*, University of California Press, Berkeley, 1984.

14 Rather like the two Berlins after World War Two, Kashmir provides the setting for much of Pakistan and Indian war-gaming. See A. Bannerjee, *The Indian Defence Review*, New Delhi, 1989.

15 Bannerjee, *The Indian Defence Review*.

16 See R. Ram, 'India's Nuclear Defence Policy' *Indian Defence and Strategic Analysis Journal*, 14, 1982.

17 Noted in Caroline Thomas, *In Search of Security*, Wheatsheaf, Brighton, 1987. Thomas refers to Ali Mazrui's belief that all states should have the right to acquire nuclear weapons as symbols of 'statehood'. See Mazrui's essay entitled 'Africa Entrapped: Between the Protestant Ethic and the Legacy of Westphalia', in H. Bull and A. Watson (eds), *The Expansion of International Society*, Clarendon

Press, London, 1987, pp. 289–308.

18   B. Sen Gupta, *Nuclear Options for India?*, Vikas, New Delhi, 1983, p. 23.

19   Cohen, *The Pakistan Army*, p. 152.

20   See B. Buzan (ed.), *The International Politics of Nuclear Deterrence*, Pinter, London, 1987.

21   Again, see Thomas, *In Search of Security*.

22   See A. K. Chopra, *India's Policy on Disarmament*, Chanayka, New Delhi, 1984.

23   Gupta, *Nuclear Options for India?*, p. 2.

24   Interestingly enough, America's initial reaction was quite lame. The State Department redrafted the official US response after vigorous British protests and then under pressure from the non-proliferation lobby. See J. S. Nye, 'Non-Proliferation: A Long Term Strategy', *Foreign Affairs*, 56, 1978, pp. 601–23.

25   Cited in Buzan, *International Politics of Nuclear Deterrence*, p. 100.

26   H. Bull, *The Anarchical Society*, Macmillan, London, 1977, p. 243.

27   George Quester, 'Can Proliferation be Stopped?', *Foreign Affairs*, 53, 1974, pp. 77–97.

28   See the very useful overview of the proliferation debate in Peter Lavoy, 'Strategic Consequences of Nuclear Proliferation', *Security Studies*, 4, 4, 1995, pp. 695–753.

29   It is possible that a Pakistani device has been tested in China under the protocol of an agreement signed in 1986. China continues to deny this.

30   Praful Bidwai and Achin Vanaik, 'India and Pakistan', in Regina Karp (ed.), *Security With Nuclear Weapons? Differing Perspectives on Non-Nuclear Security*, Oxford University Press/SIPRI, London, 1992, p. 269.

31   See P. Terhal, 'Guns vs Grains: Macroeconomic Costs of Indian Defence 1960–70', *Economic and Political Weekly*, Calcutta, 5 December 1981, pp. 1998–2014. More generally see E. Benoit *Defence and Economic Growth in Less Developed Countries*, Lexington, 1973.

32   *World Bank Report 1990*, Table 11: Central Government Expenditure. See also Raju Thomas, *India's Security Policy*, Princeton, 1986. J. Benard has argued that India has reclassified various aspects of its defence budget under different headings (especially pensions and salaries) to disguise the increase in the defence spending. See A. Benard, 'A Maturation Crisis in India', *Asian Survey*, 27, 1987, pp. 408–18.

33   *Keesings Contemporary Archives*, Longman, 35, 1989, p. 37006.

34   K. Subrahmanyam, 'Indian Nuclear Forces in the 1980s', *Indian*

Defence and Strategic Analysis Journal, 5, 4, 1972, New Delhi.
35 G. H. Quester, 'Conceptions of Nuclear Threshold Status', in Karp, *Security Without Nuclear Weapons?*, p. 214.
36 See M. V. Bratersky and S. I. Lunyov, 'The Costs of India's Nuclear Weapons Programme', *Asian Survey*, 30, 1990, pp. 927–42.
37 See Gupta, *Nuclear Options for India?*
38 Sen Gupta notes that the basis of IAEA safeguards is to place the burden of proof on the directors of specific nuclear installations to establish that fissile material has *not* been diverted into a weapons programme.
39 Not surprisingly KANUPP has been the subject of a series of speculations. It has been alleged that the authorities have deliberately carried out 'slow burns' on fuel rods (to increase the amount of Pu-239) for subsequent extraction. This still involves a complex recovery process since Pu-240 is also produced, an isotope that is poisonous to fissile reactions and has to be removed.
40 A. Sreedhar and K. C. Subrahamanyam, *Pakistan's Bomb: A Documentary Study*, Vikas, New Delhi, 1986.
41 The classic case is the 'Khan Affair', wherein between 1972 and 1975 Dr A. Q. Khan is alleged to have obtained specifications for gas centrifugal equipment from a Dutch research institute essential for fuel enrichment. See Sreedhar and Subrahamanyam, *Pakistan's Bomb*, which reproduces the entire report from the subsequent Dutch investigation.
42 See 'No Nukes, Please', *Newsweek*, Washington, November 1990, pp. 38–9.
43 *Keesings Contemporary Archives*, Longman, 35, 1989, p. 36736.
44 R. P. Cronin, *Pakistan After Zia: Implications for Pakistan and US Interests*, US Foreign Affairs and National Defence Division, Congress, 25 January 1989.
45 Thorium can provide access to U–233 which can provide the trigger for a nuclear fusion device.
46 Quester, 'Conceptions of Nuclear Threshold Status', in Karp, *Security Without Nuclear Weapons?*, p. 212.
47 B. Rasul, 'Pakistan's Nuclear Power Programme', *Asian Survey*, 25, 1985, p. 11. The author is particularly critical of D. K. Palit and P. K. S. Namboodri, *Pakistan's Islamic Bomb*, Mohan, New Delhi, 1982.
48 Sen Gupta, *Nuclear Options for India?*, See also Anita Bhatia, 'India's Space Programme: Causes For Concern', *Asian Survey*, 25, 1985, pp. 1013–54.
49 See for example the discussions in N. Ram, 'India's Nuclear Policy', and K. Kant, 'Should India Go Nuclear?' *Indian Defence and Strategic Analysis*, 14, 1982.

50   The Madras Atomic Power Plant produces poor weapons' grade plutonium because it is contaminated with Pu-240, which is poisonous to a chain reaction.

51   In a recent paper presented in America, Peter Lavoy argues that the Indian defence community confuse arms reduction with arms control. See his draft paper entitled *South Asia's Nuclear Revolution: Has it Occurred Yet?*, Paper presented with ISA, 1996.

52   See Andrew L. Ross, 'Arms Acquisition and National Security: The Irony of Military Strength', in E. E. Azar and C. In-Moon (eds), *National Security in the Third World*, Pinter, London, 1988, pp. 152–87.

53   This is because India still sees the UN as being very much an extension of United States diplomacy, either because it is manipulated by the US and her allies, or because the organisation is incapable of standing up to Washington in circumstances where they disagree. This links up with Indian criticisms for changes to be carried out within the UN to make it more representative.

54   K. Subrahmanyam cited in Buzan, *International Politics of Nuclear Deterrence* p. 112.

55   Sreedhar, A. and K. C. Subrahmanyam, *The Pakistani Bomb*, Vilak, New Delhi, 1980, p. iv.

56   R. W. Bradnock, *Indian Foreign Policy Since 1971*, Pinter, London, 1990, p. 17.

57   See the excellent series of essays produced in Bull and Watson, *The Expansion of International Society*.

58   Bull *The Anarchical Society*, p. 39.

59   K. M. Panikkar, *India and the Indian Ocean*, Weidenfeld and Nicolson, London, 1951, p. 12.

Bibliography

Abdedin, N. 'The Gramaan Approach to Development in Bangladesh: An Overview', *Contemporary South Asia*, 5, 2, July 1996, pp. 207–14.

Afroz, S. 'Pakistan and the Middle East Defence Plan 1951', *Asian Affairs*, 75, 1988, pp. 170–9.

Ahamed, E. (ed.), *The Foreign Policy of Bangladesh: Imperatives of a Small State*, People's Press, Dhaka, 1984.

Ahmed, A. *Postmodernism and Islam: Predicament and Promise*, Routledge, London, 1992.

Ahmed, N. 'Experiments in Local Government Reform in Bangladesh', *Asian Survey*, 28, 1988, pp. 813–29.

Ahmed, Z. *Money and Banking in Islam*, Hurriyat Books, Islamabad, 1983.

Akbar, M. J. *Riot After Riot*, Penguin, Harmondsworth, 1989.

Ali, T. *Can Pakistan Survive?* Penguin, Harmondsworth, 1983.

Alavi, H. and Harriss, J. (eds), *The Sociology of Developing States: South Asia*, Macmillan, Basingstoke, 1987.

Anderson, W. 'The Soviets in the Indian Ocean', *Asian Survey*, 24, 1984, pp. 910–53.

Ayoob, M. *India, Pakistan and Bangladesh*, Sangam Books, New Delhi, 1975.

Ayoob, M. *India and South East Asia: Indian Perceptions and Policies*, Routledge, London, 1990.

Azar, E. E. and In-Moon, C. (eds), *National Security in the Third World*, Pinter, London, 1988.

Bajpal, U. S. *India's Security: The Politico-Strategic Environment*, Sangam, New Delhi, 1983.

Balasubramanyam, V. N. *The Indian Economy*, Weidenfeld and Nicolson, London, 1984.

Bannerjee, A. *The Indian Defence Review*, New Delhi, 1989.

Baral, L. S. *Political Development in Nepal*, Vikas, New Delhi, 1983.

Baruah, S. 'Immigration, Ethnic Conflict and Political Turmoil', *Asian*

Survey, 26, 1986, pp. 1186–1231.

Bauman, Z. *Postmodern Ethics*, Blackwell, Oxford, 1993.

Baxter, C. *et al.* (eds), *Government and Politics in South Asia*, Westview Press, Boulder, 1987.

Benard, A. 'A Maturation Crisis in India', *Asian Survey*, 27, 1987, pp. 408–18.

Benoit, E. *Defence and Economic Growth in Less Developed Countries*, Lexington, 1973.

Berridge, G. and Young, J. 'What is a Great Power?', *Political Studies*, 36, June 1988, pp. 224–34.

Bhaduri, S. and Karim, A. *The Sri Lankan Crisis*, Popular Press, New Delhi, 1989.

Bhagwati, J. *India in Transition: Freeing the Economy*, Clarendon Press, Oxford, 1993.

Bhagwati, J. N. and Desai, S. *Planning For Industrialisation. Industrialisation and Trade Policy since 1951*, London, Oxford University Press, 1971.

Bhatia, A. 'India's Space Programme: Causes For Concern', *Asian Survey*, 25, 1985, pp. 1013–54.

Bidwai, P. and Vanaik, A. 'India and Pakistan', in Regina Karp (ed.), *Security Without Nuclear Weapons*.

Bjorkman, J. 'Health Policy and Politics in Sri Lanka: Development of the South Asian Welfare State', *Asian Survey*, 25, 1985, pp. 537–52.

Blakie, P. *et al.*, *The Struggle for Basic Needs in Nepal*, Clarendon Press, Oxford, 1980.

Booth, K. (ed.), *New Thinking About Strategy and International Security*, Harper Collins, London, 1991.

Bouton, M. and Oldenburg, P. (eds), *India Briefing 1990*, Westview Press, Boulder, 1990.

Bradnock, R. W. *Indian Foreign Policy Since 1971*, Pinter, London, 1990.

Brass, P. *Politics of India Since Independence*, Cambridge University Press, Cambridge, 1990.

Brass,. P. *Language, Religion and Politics in North India*, Cambridge University Press, Cambridge, 1974.

Brassey, *The Strategic Survey*, IISS, Oxford, 1994–95.

Bratersky, M. V. and Lunyov, S. I. 'The Costs of India's Nuclear Weapons Programme', *Asian Survey*, 30, 1990, pp 927–42.

Brecher, M. *Nehru: A Political Biography*, Oxford University Press, London, 1959.

Brown, D. 'Ethnic Revival: Perspectives on State and Society', *Third World Quarterly*, October–December, 1989, pp. 1–17.

Bull, H. *The Anarchical Society: A Study of Order in World Politics*, Macmillan, London, 1977.

Bull, H. and Watson, A. (eds), *The Expansion of International Society*, Clarendon Press, Oxford, 1987.

Burke, S. and Ziring, L. *Pakistan's Foreign Policy: An Historical Analysis*, Oxford University Press, Karachi, 1991.

Burki, S. J. *Pakistan Under Bhutto*, Macmillan, London, 1989.

Burki, S. J. and LaPorte, R. *Pakistan's Development Priorities*, Westview Press, Boulder, 1984.

Butler, D. *et al.*, *Compendium of Indian Elections*, Sterling Books, New Delhi, 1986.

Buzan, B. *People, States and Fear*, Havester, London, 1991.

Buzan, B. (ed.), *The International Politics of Nuclear Deterrence*, Pinter, London, 1987.

Buzan, B. and Rizvi, G. *South Asian Insecurity and the Great Powers*, Macmillan, Basingstoke, 1985.

Chaudhuri, J. N. *India's Problems of National Security in the 1970s*, Vikas, New Delhi, 1973.

Cheema, P. I. *Pakistan's Foreign Policy*, Oxford University Press, London, 1990.

Chiba, K. 'Japan and the New World Order', *The Pacific Review*, 4, 1991, pp. 1–4.

Chopra, A. K. *India's Policy on Disarmament*, Chanayka, New Delhi, 1984.

Choudhury, G. W. *Pakistan: Transition from a Military to a Civilian Government*, Scorpion Books, London, 1989.

Clarkson, S. *The Soviet Theory of Development: India and the Third World in Marxist-Leninist Scholarship*, Macmillan, London, 1978.

Cohen, S. *The Pakistan Army*, University of California Press, Berkeley, 1984.

Cronin, R. P. *Pakistan After Zia: Implications for Pakistan and US Interests*, US Foreign Affairs and National Defence Division, Congress, 25 January 1989.

Dalton, D. and Wilson, A. J. (eds) *The States of South Asia: The Problems of Natural Integration*, C. Hurst, London, 1982.

Dawisha, A. (ed.) *Islam and Foreign Policy*, Cambridge University Press, Cambridge, 1983.

de Silva, K. M. *Regional Powers and Small State Security*, Johns Hopkins University Press, London, 1995.

Dharamdasari, M. D. *India's Diplomacy in Nepal*, Keynotes, Jaipur, 1976.

Duncan, P. *The Soviet Union and India*, Routledge, London, 1989.

Dutt, V. P. *India's Foreign Policy*, Sangam Books, New Delhi, 1984.

Ehteshami, A. (ed.) *From the Gulf to Central Asia: Players in the New Great Game*, University of Exeter Press, Exeter, 1994.

Episoto, I. (ed.) *Islam in Asia*, Oxford University Press, New York, 1986.

Evens, H. 'Bangladesh: South Asia's Unknown Quantity', *Asian Affairs*, 75, 1988, pp. 306–16.

Faaland, J. and Parkinson, J. R. *Bangladesh: The Test Case of Development*, C. Hurst, London, 1976.

Farmer, B. H. *An Introduction to South Asia*, Methuen, London, 1983.

Gandhi, R. *Understanding the Muslim Mind*, Penguin, Harmondsworth, 1987.

Gangal. S. C. *India and the Commonwealth*, Vikas, New Delhi, 1970.

Ganguly, S. *The Origins of War in South Asia*, Westview Press, Boulder, 2nd edition, 1994.

Ganguly, S. 'Avoiding War', *Foreign Affairs*, 69, Winter 1990–91, pp. 57–73.

Gellner, E. *Thought and Change*, Weidenfeld and Nicolson, London, 1964.

George, Yu T. *Intra-Asian International Relations*, Westview Press, Boulder, 1989.

Gilpin, R. *The Political Economy of International Relations*, Princeton University Press, Princeton, 1987,

Goswami, B. N. *Pakistan and China: A Study in their Relations*, Progress Publishers, New Dehli, 1971.

Gough, K. and Sharma, H. P. *Imperialism and Revolution in South Asia*, Monthly Review Press, New York, 1973.

Graham, B. D. *Hindu Nationalism and Indian Politics: The Origins and Development of the Bharatiya Jana Sangh*, Cambridge University Press, Cambridge, 1990.

Grewal, J. S. *Sikhs of the Punjab*, Cambridge University Press, Cambridge, 1991.

Griffin, K. *Alternative Strategies for Economic Development*, Macmillan, London, 1989.

Griffin, K. and Khan. A. R. *Growth and Inequality in Pakistan*, Macmillan, London, 1971.

Gupta, A. 'The Indian Arms Industry', *Asian Survey*, 29, 1989, pp. 846–61.

Gupta, B. S. *The Fulcrum of Asia: Relations Amongst China, India, Pakistan and the USSR*, Vikas, New Delhi, 1970.

Gupta, B. S. *Soviet Perspectives on Contemporary Asia*, Sangam, New Delhi, 1982.

Gupta, B. S. *Nuclear Options for India?*, Vikas, New Delhi, 1983.

Haksar, P. N. *India's Foreign Policies and Its Problems*, Orient Longman, New Delhi, 1989.

Hayes, D. E. *Rhetoric and Ritual in Colonial India*, University of California, Berkeley, 1991.

Hayes, L. *Politics in Pakistan: The Struggle for Legitimacy*, Westview Press, Boulder, 1984.

Hettne, B. 'Ethnicity and Development', *Contemporary South Asia*, Vol. II,

2, 1993, p. 123–50.

Hewitt, V. *Reclaiming the Past? The Search for Political and Cultural Unity in Contemporary Jammu and Kashmir*, Portland Books, London, 1995.

Hobson, H. V. *The Great Divide: Great Britain, India and Pakistan*, Oxford University Press, Karachi, 1985.

Holm, H. and Sorensen, G. (eds) *Whose World Order? Uneven Globalisation and the End of the Cold War*, Westview Press, Boulder, 1995.

Hopkirk, P. *The Great Game: On Secret Service in High Asia*, John Murray, London, 1990.

Horn, R. *Soviet–Indian Relations: Issues and Influences*, Praeger, New York, 1982.

Husain, I. *The Strategic Dimensions of Pakistan's Foreign Policy*, Vanguard Books, Lahore, 1989.

Hyder, S. *Reflections of an Ambassador*, Vanguard, Lahore, 1988.

Isaacson, W. *Kissinger: A Biography*, Faber and Faber, London, 1993.

Islam, N. *Development Planning in Bangladesh: A Study in Political Economy*, C. Hurst, London, 1977.

Islam, S. (ed.) *Yen For Development: Japanese Foreign Aid and the Politics of Burden Sharing*, St. Martin's Press, New York, 1991.

Ispanhani, M. Z. *Roads and Rivals: The Politics of Access in the Borderlands of Asia*, Tauris Books, London, 1991.

Jackson, R. H. *Quasi-States: Sovereignty, International Relations, and the Third World*, Cambridge University Press, Cambridge, 1990,

Jalal, A. *Jinnah: The Muslim League and the Demand for Pakistan*, Cambridge University Press, Cambridge, 1985.

Jalal, A. *The State of Martial Rule: The Origins of Pakistan's Political Economy of Defence*, Cambridge University Press, Cambridge, 1992.

Jalal, A. *Democracy and Authoritarianism in South Asia: A Comparative and Historical Perspective*, Cambridge University Press, Cambridge, 1995.

James, W. and Roy, S. (eds) *Foundations of Pakistan's Political Economy: Towards an Agenda for the 1990s*, Sage, New Delhi, 1993.

Jayaramu, P. S. *India's National Security and Foreign Policy*, Chanakya Press, New Delhi, 1987.

Johal, S. 'India's Search For Capital Abroad', *Asian Survey*, 29, 1989, pp. 971–1002

Kabir M. G. and Hassan, S. *Issues and Challenges Facing Bangladesh Foreign Policy*, People's Press, Dhaka, 1983. p.xi

Kant, K. 'Should India go Nuclear?' *Indian Defence and Strategic Analysis*, 14, 1982.

Kapur, A. 'India's Foreign Policy: Perspectives and Present Predicaments', *Round Table*, 295, 1985, pp. 230–9.

Kapur, H. *India's Foreign Policy, 1947–92: Shadows and Substance*, Sage Publications, New Delhi, 1994.

Karp, R. C. (ed.) *Security Without Nuclear Weapons? Differing Perspectives on Non-nuclear Security*, Oxford University Press/SIPRI, London, 1992.

Kennedy, D. *The Security of Southern Asia*, Chatto and Windus, London, 1965.

Khadka, N. 'Nepal's 7th Five Year Plan', *Asian Survey*, 28, 1988, pp. 555–68.

Khalilzad, Z. *Security in South West Asia*, Gower, Aldershot, 1984.

Khalilzad, Z. (ed.) *Strategic Appraisal 1996*. A Report Prepared for the United States Airforce, Rand Corporation, California, 1996.

Khan, A. *Friends, Not Masters: A Political Autobiography*, Oxford University Press, London, 1967.

Khan, I. *Fresh Perspectives on India and Pakistan*, Bougainvillea, Oxford, 1985.

Khan, Z. A. *Pakistan's Security*, People's Publishing House, Lahore, 1990.

Khan, Z. R. 'Islam and Bengali Nationalism', *Asian Survey*, 25, 1985, pp. 852–82.

Khurshid, S. *At Home in India: A Restatement of Indian Muslims*, Sangam, New Delhi, 1986.

Kockanek, S. 'Brief Case Politics in India', *Asian Survey*, 27, 1987, pp. 1278–1301.

Kodikara, S. U. *Foreign Policy of Sri Lanka*, Chanakya, New Delhi, 1982.

Kothari, R. *Politics in India*, Sangam, New Delhi, 1970.

Kothari, R. *Caste in Indian Politics*, Sangam, New Delhi, 1976.

Kux, D. *Estranged Democracies. India and the United States 1941–1991*, Sage, New Delhi, 1993.

Lamb, A. *Kashmir: A Disputed Legacy, 1846–1990*, Roxford Press, Herefordshire, 1991.

LaPorte, R. and Ahmed, M. B. *Public Enterprises in Pakistan: The Hidden Crisis in Economic Development*, Westview Press, Boulder, 1989.

Latter, R. *Strengthening Security in South Asia*, Wilton Park Paper 108, HMSO, London, 1995.

Lavoy, P. 'Strategic Consequences of Nuclear Proliferation', *Security Studies*, 4, 4, 1995, pp. 695–753.

Lavoy, P. *India as a Great Power: Assimilating the Pressures of Political Culture and International Competition*, ISA paper, April 1996.

Lavoy, P. *South Asia's Nuclear Revolution: Has it Occurred Yet?* Paper presented with ISA, 1996.

Lifschutz, L. *Bangladesh: The Unfinished Revolution*, Zed Books, London, 1979.

Lipton, M. *The Erosion of a Relationship: India and Britain since 1960*, Chatto and Windus, London, 1975.

Little, I. *Project Appraisal and Planning for Developing Countries*, Heinemann Educational, London, 1974.

Little, I. *et al. Industry and Trade in Some Developing Countries*, Oxford University Press, London, 1970.

Luard, E. *A History of the United Nations*, Vol. II, *The Age of Decolonisation*, 1955–65, Routledge, London, 1989.

Madan, T. N. *Non-Renunciation: Themes and Interpretations of Hindu Culture*, Oxford University Press, New Delhi, 1987.

Malik, Y. and Vaypeyi, D. K. 'The Rise of Hindu Militancy', *Asian Survey*, 29, 1989. p. 311

Manor, J. (ed.) *From Nehru to the Nineties: The Changing Office of Prime Minister in India*, C. Hurst, London, 1994.

Marwah, O. and Pollack, J. *Asia's Major Powers*, Westview Press, Boulder, 1978.

Mathew, B. 'Sri Lanka's Development Councils', *Asian Survey*, 22, 1982, pp. 1117–35.

Maxwell, N. *India's China War*, Penguin, Harmondsworth, 1962.

Mehdi, R. *The Islamization of the Law in Pakistan*, Curzon Press, London, 1994.

Mellor, J. W. (ed.) *India: A Rising Middle Power?*, Westview Press, Boulder, 1979.

Mitra, S. (ed.) *Sub-Nationalism in South Asia*, Westview Press, Boulder, 1996.

Moinuddin, H. *The Charter of the Islamic Conference*, Clarendon Press, Oxford, 1987.

Moore, B. *The Social Origins of Dictatorship and Democracy*, Penguin, Harmondsworth, 1966.

Moore, R. J. *Making the New Commonwealth*, Clarendon Press, Oxford, 1987.

Nayar, K. *Distant Neighbours*, Vikas, New Delhi, 1972.

Nehru, J. *Letters to the Chief Ministers*, 5 vols, Oxford University Press, New Delhi, 1988–93.

Nissanka, H. S. S. *Sri Lanka's Foreign Policy: A Study in Non-Alignment*, Vikas, New Delhi, 1984.

Noman, O. *An Economic and Political History of Pakistan*, Kegan Paul International, London, 1990.

Nugent, N. *Rajiv Gandhi: Son of a Dynasty*, BBC, London, 1990.

Nye, J. S. 'Non-Proliferation: A Long Term Strategy', *Foreign Affairs*, 56, 1978, pp. 601–23.

Nye, J. S. and Keohane, R. O. *Transnational Relations and World Politics*, Cambridge University Press, Cambridge, 1971.

Odonnell, C. P. *Bangla Desh: Biography of a Muslim Nation*, Westview Press, Boulder, 1984.

Oldenberg, V. *The Making of Colonial Lucknow*, Princeton, Guildford, 1984.

Palit, D. K. and Namboodri, P. K. S. *Pakistan;'s Islamic Bomb*, Mohan, New Delhi, 1982.

Panikkar. K. M. *India and the Indian Ocean*, Weidenfeld and Nicolson, London, 1951.

Parsons, A. *From Cold War to Hot Peace: UN Interventions 1947–1995*, Penguin, Harmondsworth, 1995.

Piscatori, J. P. *Islam in a World of Nation-States*, Cambridge University Press, Cambridge, 1986.

Puri, B. 'Kashmiriyat: The Vitality of Kashmiri Identity', *Contemporary South Asia*, 4, 1, March 1995, pp. 55–64.

Quester, G. *The Politics of Nuclear Proliferation*, Johns Hopkins University Press, Baltimore, 1973.

Quester, G. 'Can Proliferation be Stopped?' *Foreign Affairs*, 53, 1974, pp. 77–97.

Rajan, M. and Ganguly, S. S. (eds) *Selected Essays*, Vikas, New Delhi, 1981.

Ram, N. 'India's Nuclear Policy', *Indian Defence and Strategic Analysis*, 14, 1982.

Ramakant, A. *Nepal, China and Indian Relations*, Vikas, New Delhi, 1976.

Rao, R. *Sikkim: The Story of its Integration with India*, Chanakya, New Delhi, 1978.

Rasul, B. 'Pakistan's Nuclear Power Programme', *Asian Survey*, 25, 1985.

Ray, D. *Smash and Grab: The Annexation of Sikkim*, Vikas, New Delhi, 1984.

Ray, S. K. *The Indian Economy*, Oxford University Press, New Delhi, 1987.

Rengger, N. J. (ed.) *Treaties and Alliances of the World*, 5th Edition, Carter-mill, London, 1990, p. 53.

Richter, L. K. *The Politics of Tourism in Asia*, University of Hawaii, Honolulu, 1989.

Rose, L. *The Politics of Bhutan*, Oxford University Press, London, 1977.

Rose, L. and Scholz, J. *Nepal: Profile of a Himalayan Kingdom*, Westview Press, Boulder, 1980.

Rose, L. and Sisson, R. *War and Secession: India, Pakistan and the Creation of Bangladesh*, Princeton University Press, Princeton, 1990.

Ross, L. 'Arms Acquisition and National Security: The Irony of Military Strength', in Azar and Moon, *National Security in the Third World*.

Ross, L. and Samaranayake, T. 'Economic Impact of the Recent Disturbances', *Asian Survey*, 26, 1986, pp. 1240–85.

Rostow, W. W. *The Stages of Economic Growth*, Chicago University Press, Chicago, 1971

Rudolph, L. *The Modernity of Tradition: Political Development in India*, Chicago University Press, Chicago, 1967.

Rudolph, L. and Rudolph, S. *In Pursuit of Lakshmi: State–Society Relations in India*, Chicago University Press, Chicago, 1987.

Said, E. *Orientalism*, Penguin, Harmondsworth, 1995.

Samad, Y. *A Nation in Turmoil: Nationalism and Ethnicity in Pakistan 1937–1958*, Sage, London, 1995.

Saravanamuttu, P. and Thomas. C. *Conflict and Consensus in South–North Security*, Pinter, London, 1989.

Schaffer, H. *Chester Bowles: New Dealer in the Cold War*, Harvard University Press, Massachusetts, 1993.

Schloss, A. 'Making Planning Relevant. The Nepal Experience 1968–1976', *Asian Survey*, 20, 1980, pp. 1008–20.

Schofield, V. *Kashmir: In the Crossfire*, Tauris Books, London, 1996.

Seers, D. and Vaitsos, C. *Integration and Unequal Development: The Experience of the EEC*, St. Martin's Press, New York, 1980.

Segal, G. (ed.) *Arms Control in Asia*, Macmillan, Basingstoke, 1987.

Shaha, R. *Nepali Politics*, Sangam Books, New Delhi, 1978.

Shahi, A. *Pakistan's Security and Foreign Policy*, People's Press, Lahore, 1988.

Shaikh, F. *Community and Consensus in Islam: Muslim Representation in Colonial India*, Cambridge University Press, Cambridge, 1988.

Sharma, S. 'Nepal's Economy: Growth and Development', *Asian Survey*, 26, 1986, pp. 897–905.

Shaw, M. *Global Society and International Relations: Sociological Concepts and Political Perspectives*, Polity Press, Cambridge, 1995.

Sims, H. 'The State and Agricultural Productivity', *Asian Survey*, 26, 1986, pp. 483–500.

Singer, M. R. 'New Realities of Sri Lankan Power', *Asian Survey*, 30, 1990, pp. 409–28.

Singh, J. 'Indian Security: A Framework for National Strategy', *Stategic Analysis*, 11, 1987, pp. 898–917.

Singh, N. 'Can the US and India Really be Friends?' *Asian Survey*, 23, 1983, pp. 1024–38.

Singh, P. *India and the Future of Asia*, Progress Publishers, New Delhi, 1966.

Singh, S. N. 'Why India goes to Moscow for Arms', *Asian Survey*, 24, 1984, pp. 707–40.

Sisson, R. and Rose, L. *War and Secession: India, Pakistan, and the Creation of Bangladesh*, Princeton University Press, Princeton, 1989.

Smith , A. *National Identity*, Penguin Books, Harmondsworth, 1991.

Smith, C. *India's Ad Hoc Arsenal*, Oxford University Press/SIPRI, London, 1994.

Snodgrass, D. R. *Ceylon: An Exported Economy in Transition*, Homewood, Irwin, 1966.

Squires, J. (ed.) *Principled Positions: Postmodernism and the Rediscovery of Value*, Lawrence and Wishart, London, 1993.

Sreedhar, A. and Subrahamanyam, K. C. *Pakistan's Bomb: A Documentary Study*, Vikas, New Delhi, 1986.

Stubbs, R. and Underhill, G. *Political Economy and the Changing Global Order*, Macmillan, Basingstoke, 1994.

Subrahmanyam, K. C. 'Indian Nuclear Forces in the 1980s', *Indian Defence and Strategic Analysis Journal*, 5, 4, 1972, New Delhi.

Terhal, P. 'Guns vs Grains: Macroeconomic Costs of Indian Defence 1960–1970', *Economic and Political Weekly*, Calcutta, 5 December 1981, pp. 1998–2014.

Thakur, R. 'Normalising Sino-Indian Relations', *Pacific Review*, 4, 1991, pp. 5–18.

Thomas, C. *In Search of Security*, Wheatsheaf, Brighton, 1987.

Thomas, R. *The Defence of India: A Budgetary Perspective of Strategy and Politics*, Lexington, 1978.

Thomas, R. *India's Security Policy*, Princeton University Press, Princeton, 1986.

Thomas, R. 'The Armed Services and India's Defence Budget', *Asian Survey*, 20, 1980, pp. 280–97.

Thomas, R 'Security Relations in Southern Asia', *Asian Survey*, 21, 1981 pp. 689–740.

Thomas, R. 'US Transfers of Dual-Use Technologies to India', *Asian Survey*, 30, 1989, pp. 560–631 and pp. 825–45.

Thornton, T. P. 'Between the Stools: US Policy Towards Pakistan During the Carter Administration', *Asian Survey*, 22, 1982, pp. 959–70.

Turner, B. *Orientalism, Postmodernism and Globalism*, Routledge, London, 1994.

Tinker, H. *South Asia: A Short History*, Macmillan, Basingstoke, 1990.

Van Hollen, C. 'The Tilt Policy Revisited', *Asian Survey*, 20, 1980.

Varma, S. P. and Misra, K. P. *The Foreign Policy of South Asia*, Orient Longman, New Delhi, 1969.

Vohra, D. C. *India's Aid Diplomacy and the Third World*, Zed Books, London, 1980.

Wade, R. *Governing the Market: Economic Theory and the Role of Government in East Asian Industrialisation*, Princeton University Press, Princeton, 1990.

Wang, Hong Wei, 'Sino-Nepali Relations in the 1980s', *Asian Survey*, 25, 1985, pp. 512–34.

Waseem, M. *Pakistan Under Martial Law 1977–1985*, People's Publishing House, Lahore, 1987.

Waseem, M. *Politics and the State in Pakistan*, People's Press, Lahore, 1989.

Waseem, M. *The 1993 Elections in Pakistan*, Vanguard Press, Lahore, 1994.

Whall, H. J. *The Rights to Self-Determination: The Sri Lankan Tamil National Question*, Tamil Information Centre, London, 1995.

Wight, M. *Power Politics*, University of Leicester, Leicester, 1978.

Williams, D. *The Specialised Agencies and the United Nations: The System in Crisis*, Manchester University Press, Manchester, 1987.

Wilson. A. J. *The Politics of Sri Lanka 1947–1979*, Macmillan, London, 1979.

Wilson, A. J. *The Break-Up of Sri Lanka*, C. Hurst, London, 1988.

Wolf. M. *Indian Exports*, World Bank, Washington, 1982.

Wolpert, S. *Zulfi Bhutto of Pakistan: His Life and Times*, Oxford University Press, New York, 1993.

Wood, J. (ed.) *Contemporary State Politics in India*, Westview Press, Boulder, 1987.

Yoshira, I. and Pommeret, I. *Bhutan: A Kingdom of the Eastern Himalayas*, Portland Books, London, 1984.

Zillur, Z. and Khan, R. 'Islam and Bengali Nationalism', *Asian Survey 25*, 1985, pp. 852–82.

Index